W9-BGR-833

Margaret Mering
Elna Saxton
Editors

Roaring into Our 20's: NASIG 2005

Roaring into Our 20's: NASIG 2005 has been co-published simultaneously as *The Serials Librarian*, Volume 50, Numbers 1/2 and 3/4 2006.

Pre-publication REVIEWS, COMMENTARIES, EVALUATIONS . . .

ROARING INTO OUR 20's: NASIG 2005

Proceedings of the NORTH AMERICAN SERIALS INTEREST GROUP, Inc.

20th Annual Conference
May 19-22, 2005
Minneapolis, Minnesota

Roaring into Our 20's: NASIG 2005 has been co-published simultaneously as *The Serials Librarian*, Volume 50, Numbers 1/2 and 3/4 2006.

Monographic Separates from *The Serials Librarian*

For additional information on these and other Haworth Press titles, including descriptions, tables of contents, reviews, and prices, use the QuickSearch catalog at http://www.HaworthPress.com.

Electronic Journal Management Systems: Experiences from the Field, edited by Gary Ives, MLS (Vol. 47, No. 4, 2005). *"A valuable addition to the professional development collection of every academic library. Solutions to the challenges of 'back office' management of electronic subscriptions, as well as solutions for facilitating and streamlining access for library patrons are described." (Anne Prestamo, EdD, MLIS, BM, Associate Dean for Collection and Technology Services, Oklahoma State University Libraries)*

E-Serials Cataloging: Access to Continuing and Integrating Resources via the Catalog and the Web, edited by Jim Cole, MA, and Wayne Jones, MA, MLS (Vol. 41, No. 3/4, 2002). *"A very timely and useful reference tool for librarians. The best . . . on various aspects of e-serials: from standards to education and training, from policies and procedures to national and local projects and future trends. As a technical services librarian, I found the sections on policies and procedures and national projects and local applications very valuable and informative." (Vinh-The Lam, MLS, Head, Cataloging Department, University of Saskatchewan Library, Canada)*

Women's Studies Serials: A Quarter-Century of Development, edited by Kristin H. Gerhard, MLS (Vol. 35, No. 1/2, 1998). *"Candidly explores and analyzes issues which must be addressed to ensure the continued growth and vitality of women's studies. . . . It commands the attention of librarians, scholars, and publishers." (Joan Ariel, MLS, MA, Women's Studies Librarian and Lecturer, University of California at Irvine)*

E-Serials: Publishers, Libraries, Users, and Standards, edited by Wayne Jones, MA, MLS (Vol. 33, No. 1/2/3/4, 1998). *"Libraries and publishers will find this book helpful in developing strategies, policies, and procedures." (Nancy Brodie, National Library of Canada, Ottawa, Ontario)*

Serials Cataloging at the Turn of the Century, edited by Jeanne M. K. Boydston, MSLIS, James W. Williams, MSLS, and Jim Cole, MLS (Vol. 32, No. 1/2, 1997). *Focuses on the currently evolving trends in serials cataloging in order to predict and explore the possibilities for the field in the new millennium.*

Serials Management in the Electronic Era: Papers in Honor of Peter Gellatly, Founding Editor of The Serials Librarian, edited by Jim Cole, MA, and James W. Williams, MLS (Vol. 29, No. 3/4, 1996). *Assesses progress and technical changes in the field of serials management and anticipates future directions and challenges for librarians.*

Special Format Serials and Issues: Annual Review of . . . , Advances in . . . , Symposia on . . . , Methods in . . . , by Tony Stankus, MLS (Vol. 27, No. 2/3, 1996). *A thorough and lively introduction to the nature of these publications' types.*

Serials Canada: Aspects of Serials Work in Canadian Libraries, edited by Wayne Jones, MLS (Vol. 26, No. 3/4, 1996). *"An excellent addition to the library literature and is recommended for all library school libraries, scholars, and students of comparative/international librarianship." (Library Times International)*

Serials Cataloging: Modern Perspectives and International Developments, edited by Jim E. Cole, MA, and James W. Williams, MSLS (Vol. 22, No. 1/2/3/4, 1993). *"A significant contribution to understanding the 'big picture' of serials control. . . . A solid presentation of serious issues in a crucial area on librarianship." (Bimonthly Review of Law Books)*

Making Sense of Journals in the Life Sciences: From Specialty Origins to Contemporary Assortment, by Tony Stankus (Supp. #08, 1992, 1996). *"An excellent introduction to scientific periodical literature and the disciplines it serves." (College & Research Libraries News)*

Making Sense of Journals in the Physical Sciences: From Specialty Origins to Contemporary Assortment, by Tony Stankus, MLS (Supp. #07, 1992, 1996). *"A tour de force . . . It will immeasurably help science serials librarians to select journal titles on a rational and defensible basis, and the methodology used can be extended over time and to other fields and other journals." (International Journal of Information and Library Research)*

The Good Serials Department, edited by Peter Gellatly (Vol. 19, No. 1/2, 1991). *"This is recommended for library educators, students, and serials specialists. It should be useful both to novices and veterans." (Journal of Academic Librarianship)*

The North American Serials Interest Group (NASIG) Series

Roaring into Our 20's: NASIG 2005, edited by Margaret Mering and Elna Saxton (Vol. 50, No. 1/2/3/4, 2006). *A compilation of visionary papers from the North American Serials Interest Group's twentieth annual conference held May 2005 in Minneapolis, Minnesota.*

Growth, Creativity, and Collaboration: Great Visions on a Great Lake, edited by Patricia Sheldahl French and Margaret Mering (Vol. 48, No. 1/2/3/4, 2005). *"If any serials librarian wants one place to go to find the latest and greatest on serials issues, these proceedings are the first place to go. . . . A wide range of contributors from the who's who of the serials world." (Dan Tonkery, Vice President and Director of Business Development, EBSCO Information Services)*

Serials in the Park, edited by Patricia Sheldahl French and Richard Worthing (Vol. 46, No. 1/2/3/4, 2004). *Proceedings of the 18th. Annual NASIG conference (2003, Portland, Oregon), focusing on the most significant trends and innovations for serials.*

Transforming Serials: The Revolution Continues, edited by Susan L. Scheiberg and Shelley Neville (Vol. 44, No. 1/2/3/4, 2003). *"A valuable and thought-provoking resource for all library workers involved with serials." (Mary Curran, MLS, MA, Head of Cataloguing Services, University of Ottawa, Ontario, Canada)*

NASIG 2001: A Serials Odyssey, edited by Susan L. Scheiberg and Shelley Neville (Vol. 42, No. 1/2/3/4, 2002). *From XML to ONIX and UCITA, here's cutting-edge information from leading serials librarians from the 16th NASIG conference.*

Making Waves: New Serials Landscapes in a Sea of Change, edited by Joseph C. Harmon and P. Michelle Fiander (Vol. 40, No. 1/2/3/4, 2001). *These proceedings include discussions of the Digital Millennium Copyright Act, and reports on specific test projects such as BioOne, the Open Archives Project, and PubMed Central.*

From Carnegie to Internet 2: Forging the Serials Future, edited by P. Michelle Fiander, Joseph C. Harmon, and Jonathan David Makepeace (Vol. 38, No. 1/2/3/4, 2000). *Current information and practical insight to help you improve your technical skills and prepare you and your library for the 21st century.*

Head in the Clouds, Feet on the Ground: Serials Vision and Common Sense, edited by Jeffrey S. Bullington, Beatrice L. Caraway, and Beverley Geer (Vol. 36, No. 1/2/3/4, 1999). *"Practical, common sense advice, and visionary solutions to serials issues afoot in every library department and in every type of library today. . . . An essential reference guide for libraries embracing electronic resource access." (Mary Curran, MA, MLS, Coordinator, Bibliographic Standards, Morisset Library, University of Ottawa, Ontario, Canada)*

Experimentation and Collaboration: Creating Serials for a New Millennium, Charlene N. Simser and Michael A. Somers (Vol. 34, No. 1/2/3/4, 1998). *Gives valuable ideas and practical advice that you can apply or incorporate into your own area of expertise.*

Pioneering New Serials Frontiers: From Petroglyphs to Cyberserials, edited by Christine Christiansen and Cecilia Leathem (Vol. 30, No. 3/4, and Vol. 31, No. 1/2, 1997). *Gives you insight, ideas, and practical skills for dealing with the changing world of serials management.*

Serials to the Tenth Power: Traditions, Technology, and Transformation, edited by Mary Ann Sheble, MLS, and Beth Holley, MLS (Vol. 28, No. 1/2/3/4, 1996). *Provides readers with practical ideas on managing the challenges of the electronic information environment.*

A Kaleidoscope of Choices: Reshaping Roles and Opportunities for Serialists, edited by Beth Holley, MLS, and Mary Ann Sheble, MLS (Vol. 25, No. 3/4, 1995). *"Highly recommended as an excellent source material for all librarians interested in learning more about the Internet, technology and its effect on library organization and operations, and the virtual library." (Library Acquisitions: Practice & Theory)*

New Scholarship: New Serials: Proceedings of the North American Serials Interest Group, Inc., edited by Gail McMillan and Marilyn Norstedt (Vol. 24, No. 3/4, 1994). *"An excellent representation of the ever-changing, complicated, and exciting world of serials." (Library Acquisitions Practice & Theory)*

Roaring into Our 20's: NASIG 2005 has been co-published simultaneously as *The Serials Librarian*, Volume 50, Numbers 1/2 and 3/4 2006.

The development, preparation, and publication of this work has been undertaken with great care. However, the publisher, employees, editors, and agents of The Haworth Press and all imprints of The Haworth Press, Inc., including The Haworth Medical Press® and Pharmaceutical Products Press®, are not responsible for any errors contained herein or for consequences that may ensue from use of materials or information contained in this work.

The Haworth Press is committed to the dissemination of ideas and information according to the highest standards of intellectual freedom and the free exchange of ideas. Statements made and opinions expressed in this publication do not necessarily reflect the views of the Publisher, Directors, management, or staff of The Haworth Press, Inc., or an endorsement by them.

Cover logo by Michael Garzel

Cover design director: Thomas J. Mayshock Jr.

Library of Congress Cataloging-in-Publication Data

North American Serials Interest Group. Conference (20th : 2005 : Minneapolis, Minn.)
Roaring into our 20's : NASIG 2005 : proceedings of the North American Serials Interest Group, Inc. 20th Annual Conference, May 19-22, 2005, Minneapolis, Minnesota / Margaret Mering, Elna Saxton, editors.
p. cm.
"Co-published simultaneously as The serials librarian, volume 50, numbers 1/2 and 3/4 2006."
Includes bibliographical references and index.
ISBN-13: 978-0-7890-3287-4 (alk. paper)
ISBN-10: 0-7890-3287-2 (alk. paper)
ISBN-13: 978-0-7890-3288-1 (pbk. : alk. paper)
ISBN-10: 0-7890-3288-0 (pbk. : alk. paper)
1. Serials librarianship–North America–Congresses. I. Mering, Margaret. II. Saxton, Elna. III. Serials librarian. IV. Title.
Z692.S5N67 2005
025.17'32–dc22

2006000943

In Memoriam
Marla Joan Schwartz
(1949-2005)

These proceedings are dedicated to the memory of Marla Schwartz who died from complications of ovarian cancer on August 8, 2005. At the time of her death, Marla was Head of Acquisitions and Technical Systems Department at the Pence Law Library, Washington College of Law, American University in Washington, DC. Marla was a charter member of NASIG and served the organization on several committees and task forces. She also was active in the American Association of Law Libraries and was a past chair of the Serials Section of the Association for Library Collections and Technical Services, American Library Association. More importantly, she was a fine colleague, a generous mentor, and a warm, gracious, faithful friend. NASIG dedicates these proceedings to honor Marla and to recognize her tireless commitment to the serials profession.

ROARING INTO OUR 20's:
NASIG 2005

Proceedings of the
NORTH AMERICAN SERIALS
INTEREST GROUP, Inc.

20th Annual Conference
May 19-22, 2005
Minneapolis, Minnesota

Margaret Mering
Elna Saxton
Editors

The Haworth Information Press
An Imprint of
The Haworth Press, Inc.
New York • London • Oxford

Indexing, Abstracting & Website/Internet Coverage

This section provides you with a list of major indexing & abstracting services and other tools for bibliographic access. That is to say, each service began covering this periodical during the year noted in the right column. Most Websites which are listed below have indicated that they will either post, disseminate, compile, archive, cite or alert their own Website users with research-based content from this work. (This list is as current as the copyright date of this publication.)

Abstracting, Website/Indexing Coverage . . . . Year When Coverage Began

- *Academic Abstracts/CD-ROM* **1993**
- *Academic Search: Database of 2,000 selected academic serials, updated monthly: EBSCO Publishing* **1993**
- *Academic Search Elite (EBSCO)* **1993**
- *Business Source Corporate: coverage of nearly 3,350 quality magazines and journals; designed to meet the diverse information needs of corporations; EBSCO Publishing <http://www.epnet.com/corporate/bsourcecorp.asp>* **1993**
- *CareData: the database supporting social care management and practice <htp://www.elsc.org.uk/caredata/caredata.htm>* . . . **2003**
- *Chemical Abstracts Service–monitors, indexes & abstracts the world's chemical literature, updates this information daily, and makes it accessible through state-of-the-art information services <http://www.cas.org>* **1982**
- *CINAHL (Cumulative Index to Nursing & Allied Health Literature), in print, EBSCO, and SilverPlatter, DataStar, and PaperChase. (Support materials include Subject Heading List, Database Search Guide, and instructional video.) <http://www.cinahl.com>* **1985**
- *Computer and Information Systems Abstracts <http://www.csa.com>* **2004**

(continued)

- *Current Cites [Digital Libraries] [Electronic Publishing]*
  [Multimedia & Hypermedia] [Networks & Networking]
  [General] <http://sunsite.berkeley.edu/CurrentCites/> 2000
- *EBSCOhost Electronic Journals Service (EJS)*
  <http://ejournals.ebsco.com> 2001
- *Elsevier Scopus <http://www.info.scopus.com>* 2002
- *Foods Adlibra* .... *
- *FRANCIS.INIST/CNRS <http://www.inist.fr>* 1992
- *Google <http://www.google.com>* 2004
- *Google Scholar <http://scholar.google.com>* 2004
- *Handbook of Latin American Studies* 1992
- *Haworth Document Delivery Center*
  <http://www.HaworthPress.com/journals/dds.asp> 2004
- *Hein's Legal Periodical Checklist: Index to Periodical Articles*
  Pertaining to Law <http://www.wshein.com>. 1989
- *IBZ International Bibliography of Periodical Literature*
  <http://www.saur.de> 1993
- *Index Guide to College Journals (core list compiled by integrating*
  48 indexes frequently used to support undergraduate
  programs in small to medium sized libraries) 1999
- *Index to Periodical Articles Related to Law*
  <http://www.law.utexas.edu> 1990
- *Information Reports & Bibliographies* 1992
- *Information Science & Technology Abstracts: indexes journal articles*
  from more than 450 publications as well as books, research reports,
  and conference proceedings; EBSCO Publishing
  <http://www.epnet.com> 1970
- *Informed Librarian, The*
  <http://www.informedlibrarian.com> 1993
- *INSPEC is the leading English-language bibliographic information*
  service providing access to the world's scientific and technical
  literature in physics, electrical eng., electronics, communications,
  control eng., computers and computing, and information tech.
  <http://www.iee.org.uk/publish/>. 2002
- *Internationale Bibliographie der geistes- und*
  sozialwissenschaftlichen Zeitschriftenliteratur ... See IBZ
  <http://www.saur.de> 1993
- *Journal of Academic Librarianship: Guide to Professional*
  Literature, The 1992

(continued)

- *Konyvtari Figyelo (Library Review)* **1995**

- *Library & Information Science Abstracts (LISA) <http://www.csa.com>* **1990**

- *Library and Information Science Annual (LISCA)*
  <http://www.lu.com> **1997**

- *Library Literature & Information Science*
  <http://www.hwwilson.com> **1989**

- *Linguistics & Language Behavior Abstracts*
  (LLBA) <http://www.csa.com> **1996**

- *Links@Ovid (via CrossRef targeted DOI links)*
  <http://www.ovid.com> **2005**

- *Magazines for Libraries (Katz) ... (see 2003 edition)* **2003**

- *Masterfile: Updated Database from EBSCO Publishing* **1993**

- *Ovid Linksolver (OpenURL link resolver via CrossRef targeted*
  DOI links) <http://www.linksolver.com> **2005**

- *PASCAL, c/o Institut de l'Information Scientifique*
  et Technique. Cross-disciplinary electronic database covering
  the fields of science, technology and medicine. Also available on
  CD-ROM, and can generate customized retrospective searches
  <http://www.inist.fr> **1992**

- *Referativnyi Zhurnal (Abstracts Journal of the All-Russian*
  Institute of Scientific and Technical Information-in Russian)
  <http://www.viniti.ru> **1986**

- *RESEARCH ALERT/ISI Alerting Services <http://www.isinet.com>* **2000**

- *ScienceDirect Navigator (Elsevier)*
  <http://www.info.sciencedirect.com> **2002**

- *Scopus (Elsevier) <http://www.info.scopus.com>* **2002**

- *SwetsWise <http://www.swets.com>* **2001**

- *WilsonWeb <http://vnweb.hwwilsonweb.com/hww/Journals>* **2005**

- *Worldwide Political Science Abstracts (formerly: Political Science &*
  Government Abstracts) <http://www.csa.com> **1996**

Special Bibliographic Notes related to special journal issues (separates) and indexing/abstracting:

- indexing/abstracting services in this list will also cover material in any "separate" that is co-published simultaneously with Haworth's special thematic journal issue or DocuSerial. Indexing/abstracting usually covers material at the article/chapter level.
- monographic co-editions are intended for either non-subscribers or libraries which intend to purchase a second copy for their circulating collections.
- monographic co-editions are reported to all jobbers/wholesalers/approval plans. The source journal is listed as the "series" to assist the prevention of duplicate purchasing in the same manner utilized for books-in-series.
- to facilitate user/access services all indexing/abstracting services are encouraged to utilize the co-indexing entry note indicated at the bottom of the first page of each article/chapter/contribution.
- this is intended to assist a library user of any reference tool (whether print, electronic, online, or CD-ROM) to locate the monographic version if the library has purchased this version but not a subscription to the source journal.
- individual articles/chapters in any Haworth publication are also available through the Haworth Document Delivery Service (HDDS).

NASIG Officers and Executive Board

2004/2005

Officers:

Steve Savage, President, San Diego State University
Mary Page, Vice President/President Elect, Rutgers University
Elizabeth Parang, Secretary, Pepperdine University
Denise Novak, Treasurer, Carnegie Mellon University
Anne McKee, Past President, Greater Western Library Alliance

Executive Board:

Jill Emery, University of Houston
Beverley Geer, YBP Library Services (Oct.-May)
Judy Luther, Informed Strategies
Carol MacAdam, JSTOR (June-Oct.)
Kevin Randall, Northwestern University
Stephanie Schmitt, Yale Law School
Joyce Tenney, University of Maryland, Baltimore County

Ex-Officio:

Charlene Simser, *Newsletter* Editor, Kansas State University

2005 Program Planning Committee

Co-Chairs:

Marilyn Geller, Independent Consultant

Emily McElroy, New York University

Committee Members:

Norene Allen, Swets Information Services

Michael Arthur, Old Dominion University

Sarah George, Illinois Wesleyan University

Tonia Graves, Old Dominion University

Joe Harmon, Indiana University Purdue University, Indianapolis

Kittie Henderson, EBSCO Information Services

Lee Krieger, University of Miami

Pat Loghry, University of Notre Dame

Paul Moeller, University of Colorado at Boulder

Bonnie Parks, Oregon State University

Erika Ripley, Southern Methodist University

Rose Robischon, United States Military Academy Library

Allison Sleeman, University of Virginia

Virginia Taffurelli, New York Public Library

Dana Walker, University of Georgia

Board Liaison:

Mary Page, Rutgers University

Fritz Schwartz Serials Education Scholarship

Sarah M. Vital, San Jose University

NASIG Conference Student Grant Award Recipients

Jenny Benevento, University of Illinois at Urbana-Champaign
Martha Cannon, Drexel University
Rebecca Davies, University of Maryland
Christine Freeman, Texas Woman's College
Andrea N. Schorr, Drexel University
Tammy Steinle, University of Missouri-Columbia

Mexico Student Conference Grant

Claudia Haydee Barba Valdes, School of Library Science, Faculty of Philosophy and Arts, National University of Mexico

NASIG Champion Award

Tina Feick, Swets Information Services, Inc., North America

ABOUT THE EDITORS

Margaret Mering is Principal Serials Cataloger and Metadata Librarian at the University of Nebraska-Lincoln. She holds a BA in History from Whittier College and an MLS from the University of Arizona. She has been a frequent trainer for the Serials Cataloging Cooperative Training Program and co-authored its *Advanced Serials Cataloging Workshop Manual*. She is an active member of NASIG. She served two terms as secretary of NASIG and co-chaired its Continuing Education Committee. She co-edited NASIG's 2004 proceedings.

Elna Saxton is Head of the Serials and Electronic Resources Department at the University of Cincinnati, University Libraries. She holds a BA in Business Administration from Indiana University of Pennsylvania, an MLS from University of Missouri-Columbia, and an MA in Labor and Employment Relations from the University of Cincinnati. She has been a contributor to three editions of *Magazines for Libraries*, as well as *The Serials Librarian* and *Serials Review*. She is an active member of NASIG, with service on the Database and Directory Committee and author of several reports for proceedings and newsletters.

Roaring into Our 20's: NASIG 2005

CONTENTS

Introduction 1
    Margaret Mering
    Elna Saxton

PRECONFERENCE PROGRAMS

Serials Holdings Workshop 7
    Catherine Nelson, Julie Su, Presenters
    Lisa Hanson O'Hara, Recorder

Serials Esperanto: Helping Librarians, Vendors and Publishers
  Understand Each Other 11
    Adam Chesler, Phil Greene, Kim Maxwell, Presenters
    Stephen Headley, Recorder

How to Avoid Death by Meeting: Strategies for Better Meetings 21
    Betty J. Kjellberg, Presenter
    Elna L. Saxton, Recorder

VISION SESSIONS

Chaotic Transitions: How Today's Trends Will Affect
  Tomorrow's Libraries 29
    Marshall Keys, Presenter
    Buddy Pennington, Recorder

Painting America Purple: Media Democracy and the Red/
  Blue Divide 37
    Leif Utne, Presenter
    Paul Moeller, Recorder

STRATEGY SESSIONS

Access to Scholarly Literature: Publishing for an Extended
   Readership   49
   John Cox, Presenter

Identifiers in Libraries: ISSN Revision Unique   69
   Regina Romano Reynolds, Presenter

FRBR and Serials: An Overview and Analysis   83
   Steve Shadle, Presenter

Negotiation for the Rest of Us   105
   Joan E. Conger, Presenter

CROSSREF: From Linking to Cross-Provider Search   119
   Amy Brand, Presenter

Cross-Provider Search: New Standards for Metasearch   125
   Jenny Walker, Presenter

Serials Industry: Truth or Dare   137
   Dena Schoen, Julia Gammon, Zac Rolnik,
   Bob Schatz, Panelists
   Elizabeth Lowe, Donna Packer, Recorders

Ensuring Consistent Usage Statistics, Part 1:
   Project COUNTER   147
   Oliver Pesch, Presenter

Ensuring Consistent Usage Statistics, Part 2: Working
   with Use Data for Electronic Journals   163
   Alfred Kraemer, Presenter

Talk About: E-Resources Librarian to the Rescue?
   Creating the Über Librarian: Turning Model Job
   Descriptions into Practical Positions   173
   Katy Ginanni, Presenter
   Susan Davis, Michael A. Arthur, Recorders

"We Own It": Dealing with "Perpetual Access" in Big Deals   179
    Andrew Waller, Gwen Bird, Presenters

If We Build It, *Will* They Come (Eventually)?
    Scholarly Communication and Institutional Repositories   197
    Carol Hixson, Presenter

TACTICS SESSIONS

Using Customer-Service Software to Manage Serials
    Online Access Issues   213
    Carol Ann Borchert, Presenter
    Tonia Graves, Recorder

Metadata Management Design   217
    Nathan Rupp, Presenter
    Elizabeth L. Bogdanski, Recorder

Beyond Article Linking: Using OpenURL in Creative Ways   221
    Morag Boyd, Sandy Roe, Presenters
    Sarah E. George, Recorder

Binding Journals in Tight Times: Mind the Budget   227
    Lucy Duhon, Jeanne Langendorfer, Presenters
    Sandhya D. Srivastava, Recorder

A Collaborative Checklist for E-Journal Access   235
    Rocki Strader, Alison Roth, Bob Boissy, Presenters
    Wendy Robertson, Recorder

Issues in Scholarly Communications: Creating
    a Campus-Wide Dialog   243
    Jennifer Duncan, William Walsh, Tim Daniels, Presenters
    Joe Becker, Recorder

Adding Value to the Catalog in an Open Access World   249
    Anna Hood, Presenter
    Mykie Howard, Recorder

Collection Development in Public Libraries   253
   Tina Herman Buck, Stephen Headley,
   Abby Schor, Presenters
   Susan M. Banoun, Recorder

Challenges of Off-Site Library Storage Facilities:
   Cataloging, Access and Management of Off-Site Serials   259
   Susan Currie, Sarah Corvene,
   Zoe Stewart-Marshall, Presenters
   Sarah John, Recorder

The Big E-Package Deals: Smoothing the Way
   Through Subscription Agents   267
   Tina Feick, Gary Ives, Presenters
   Jo McClamroch, Recorder

Subscription Cancellation Projects: How to Quiet
   Some of the Roar   271
   Clint Chamberlain, Beatrice Caraway, Presenters
   Susan Andrews, Recorder

Examining Workflows and Redefining Roles:
   Auburn University and The College of New Jersey   279
   Jia Mi, Paula Sullenger, Presenters
   Pat Loghry, Recorder

AACR3 Is Coming–What Is It?   285
   Paul J. Weiss, Presenter
   Molly R. T. Larkin, Recorder

Tracking Usage of E-Government Publications   295
   Susan L. Kendall, Celia Bakke, Presenters
   Lisa McDaniels, Recorder

Do You See RSS in Your Future?   305
   Paoshan Yue, Araby Greene, Presenters
   Lisa S. Blackwell, Recorder

Analyzing How Much Publisher Packages Are Worth?   311
    Nancy Macomber, Presenter
    Julie C. Harwell, Recorder

Presentations That Keep Your Audience Interested and Awake   315
    Beth Bernhardt, Presenter
    Karen S. Fischer, Recorder

The RFP Process at the University of Memphis:
    A Work in Progress   319
    Elizabeth McDonald, Presenter
    Jerry R. Brown, Recorder

POSTER SESSIONS   325

20th ANNUAL NASIG CONFERENCE REGISTRANTS

NASIG Conference 2005–Registrants by Last Name   331

NASIG Conference 2005–Registrants by Affiliation   345

Index   359
    Kathryn Wesley

Introduction

The North American Serials Interest Group convened in Minneapolis, Minnesota, for its twentieth anniversary conference, May 19-22, 2005. Minneapolis and its twin city, St. Paul, mark the beginning of the roaring Upper Mississippi River, which inspired the conference's theme, "Roaring into Our 20's." This setting proved to be the perfect setting to celebrate an organizational milestone, to reflect on years gone by, and to dream about the future.

This year's conference began with three preconferences. Julie Su and Catherine Nelson presented the Serials Cataloging Cooperative Training Program's Serials Holding Workshop, which reviewed the MARC 21 format for Holdings Data standards. The second preconference introduced the concept Serials Esperanto, "a common language for communication among publishers, vendors, and librarians." The presenters demonstrated that confusion can be dramatically reduced if all parties have a common understanding of each others' roles and responsibilities. A dozen or so librarians attended Betty Kjellberg's preconference to learn techniques that can improve meeting effectiveness.

Each morning, conference attendees started their day by attending a no-conflict vision session designed to stimulate broad thinking about the larger context of serials work and libraries. Marshall Keys' entertaining presentation was an inspiring and thought-provoking review of today's technological trends and how they will impact libraries down the road. Four previous NASIG presidents and a former award winner who is a current Board member made up the panel for the Anniversary

[Haworth co-indexing entry note]: "Introduction." Mering, Margaret, and Elna Saxton. Co-published simultaneously in *The Serials Librarian* (The Haworth Information Press, an imprint of The Haworth Press, Inc.) Vol. 50, No. 1/2, 2006, pp. 1-4; and: *Roaring into Our 20's: NASIG 2005* (ed: Margaret Mering, and Elna Saxton) The Haworth Information Press, an imprint of The Haworth Press, Inc., 2006, pp. 1-4. Single or multiple copies of this article are available for a fee from The Haworth Document Delivery Service [1-800-HAWORTH, 9:00 a.m. - 5:00 p.m. (EST). E-mail address: getinfo@haworthpress.com].

Available online at http://www.haworthpress.com/web/SER
doi:10.1300/J123v50n01_01

Special Program. Dan Tonkery, Susan Davis, Tina Feick, Connie Foster, and Jill Emery presented a history of the serial industry and NASIG during the last twenty years. During the final vision session, Lief Utne, the associate editor of Minneapolis's own *Utne Magazine*, addressed the poisonous tone of the United States' political debate, what media is doing to exacerbate the problem, and what media can do to foster civil dialogue.

Three of the strategy sessions focused on issues relating to scholarly journal publishing. John Cox's session explored current and future trends in providing access to scholarly publishing, including open access, and the interrelationships that characterize the publishing industry. For the session called "Serials Industry: Truth or Dare," a panel comprising an academic librarian, a publisher, and two vendors discussed the challenges facing each member of the scholarly communication chain. Carol Hixson looked at the problems and opportunities institutional repositories offer at the University of Oregon and around the world and the effect such repositories will have on the changing nature of serials and scholarly communication.

The remaining strategy sessions covered a wide range of topics. One session considered how FRBR (Functional Requirements for Bibliographic Records) might apply to serial publications. Several sessions covered different aspects of electronic resources. Regina Romano Reynolds discussed the function ISSN and other unique identifiers have in libraries, particularly in the current environment where precision is crucial to identification and electronic linking of resources. Amy Brand and Jenny Walker teamed up to present the efforts underway to facilitate simultaneous searching across information resources. The session "'We Own It': Dealing with 'Perpetual Access' in Big Deals" presented the results of a survey of Canadian university libraries that investigated whether libraries have been able to stay informed of the many changes that affect their access to electronic content. Alfred Kraemer and Oliver Pesch provided both theoretical and practical perspectives on usage statistics for online resources. Katy Ginanni led a "talk about" discussion session which assessed the need for separate electronic resource librarians and attempted to identify where managing e-resources fits into organizational structures. A final strategy session explored how to create sustainable relationships between librarians and vendors through cost- and benefit-based negotiation.

This year's conference had eighteen tactic sessions. The predominant topic was managing access to e-resources, a universal challenge for which widely varying solutions and workflows are in place. Analysis of e-workflow, usage statistics, OpenURL, and the Big Deal are some perennial topics in the e-management arena. Fresh topics and tools such as utilizing customer service software, RSS to push out subject blogs or new book lists, and metadata repositories introduced practical tools and new technology to conference goers.

The work of managing e-resources is not the only unifying topic for Serialists–presentations on cancellation projects, journal binding, developing RFPs, collection development, and ramifications of off-site storage provided further insight into the complexities of serials in today's library environment. Managing the balance of print versus online formats and the increasing pressure on collection budget makes communication skills essential. Presentation skills and scholarly communication were tactic sessions that built on the pre-conference and strategy sessions of conducting effective meetings and strengthening negotiation skills.

Serials cataloging tactic sessions included the imminent reconstruction of AACR2. "AACR3 Is Coming: What Is It?" provides an extensive look at the AACR3 development process and anticipated implementation timeframe for this work of the Joint Steering Committee for the Revision of AACR.

NASIG is well known as an organization of active volunteers who give their time to foster professional development for themselves and their colleagues. This year, more than 550 people attended the annual conference, representing institutions in the United States, Canada, Mexico, Europe, the West Indies, and elsewhere. Over 125 of the attendees also had a role in creating the conference itself, whether planning, hosting, presenting, writing, troubleshooting or taking care of some other aspect of behind-the-scenes work. Each one of them deserves recognition for the part they played. Special thanks go to the Conference Planning Committee and the Program Planning Committee. The editors give a personal thanks to the speakers and recorders whose work is represented in the published proceedings. Without them, there would be no written record of the information shared at the conference. Thanks also go to our Executive Board liaison, Kevin Randall, for his wise counsel and steady support. And, lastly, thank you to the staff at Haworth Press, especially our editor, Nancy Deisroth.

Margaret Mering
Elna Saxton
Editors

NOTE

The editors note the omission in this volume of Ted Koppel's paper for the strategy session entitled "Unique Identifiers in Libraries: What Works; What Doesn't Work; and What's in (or Should Be in) the Works." A paper was not prepared for the vision session entitled "20th Anniversary Special Program."

PRECONFERENCE PROGRAMS

Serials Holdings Workshop

Catherine Nelson
Julie Su

Presenters

Lisa Hanson O'Hara

Recorder

SUMMARY. The Serials Cooperative Cataloging Training Program's Serials Holdings Workshop was developed in 2001 with the attempt to introduce and provide training for the new MARC 21 format for Holdings Data (2000) standards and format and to promote its implementation in libraries and local systems. The course material has gone through major revision with the publication of the second edition in 2002 and the latest revision in 2004 to include sample implementations of various local library systems. The course includes background information and a brief history of the development of the standards. The instructions and exercises focus on creating MARC holdings and publication patterns. The MARC coding instructions are system-neutral yet the course includes samples of local system implementation and includes time for discussion of local implementation and workflow issues. *[Article copies available for a fee from The Haworth Document Delivery Service: 1-800-HAWORTH. E-mail address: <docdelivery@haworthpress.com> Website: <http://www.HaworthPress.com>]*

[Haworth co-indexing entry note]: "Serials Holdings Workshop." O'Hara, Lisa Hanson. Co-published simultaneously in *The Serials Librarian* (The Haworth Information Press, an imprint of The Haworth Press, Inc.) Vol. 50, No. 1/2, 2006, pp. 7-10; and: *Roaring into Our 20's: NASIG 2005* (ed: Margaret Mering, and Elna Saxton) The Haworth Information Press, an imprint of The Haworth Press, Inc., 2006, pp. 7-10. Single or multiple copies of this article are available for a fee from The Haworth Document Delivery Service [1-800-HAWORTH, 9:00 a.m. - 5:00 p.m. (EST). E-mail address: getinfo@haworthpress.com].

Available online at http://www.haworthpress.com/web/SER
doi:10.1300/J123v50n01_02

The Serials Holdings Workshop was developed by Frieda Rosenberg of the University of North Carolina at Chapel Hill and Thom Saudargas of the College Center for Library Automation as the second course for the Serials Cataloging Cooperative Training Program (SCCTP). The workshop was delivered at the 2005 NASIG conference as a pre-conference by Julie Su and Catherine Nelson. Participants in the workshop received a trainee manual which included PowerPoint slides, exercises and their answers, and a number of appendixes.

The workshop began with the presenters and attendees introducing themselves and identifying the ILS systems that their libraries use. Interestingly, more than half of those present were Innovative users. Su gave an introduction to the workshop and its goals. She explained that many library functions are served by serials holding standards and remarked that studies have shown that forty percent of reference transactions deal with serials holdings. Standards benefit both the individual libraries and the library community by providing consistency and promoting cooperation and resource sharing. The history of holdings standards creation was reviewed including the holdings display standard (ANSI Z39 Committee) and the holdings communication standard MARC Format for Holdings (MFHD). MFHD, initially developed by a group of research libraries in the southeast United States, can be used for both display and communication.

In the next session of the workshop, Nelson discussed MARC fields 001 to 852 of the holdings record. Most of this session was straightforward for catalogers who are used to working with MARC. However, workshop participants did discuss field 008/16 which gives an estimate of how much of the serial is held by the institution. They were unclear as to whether a cataloger should code for completeness based on what is owned by the library or what is available (the entire run of the serial). The instructors agreed to refer the question to CONSER. The consensus was that cataloguers should be consistent in how they code and remember what they did.

Su talked about how to record holdings in the fourth session of the workshop. She explained that holdings are recorded in paired fields, one field which includes the captions and publication pattern (MARC fields 85Xs) and one which includes the actual enumeration and chronology (MARC fields 86Xs). Holdings can be coded at the issue level, the physical volume level and the "range" or summary level. All levels have different uses and functions. Different fields are used for basic units (853/863), supplements (854/864) and indexes (855/865). Caption data in 85X fields can be either an enumeration caption (e.g., Vol., no.,

Bd.) or a chronology caption (e.g., a division of the year). Chronology captions are recorded in parentheses because although the chronology itself is displayed as recorded in 86X fields, they do not need a caption such as "Month" or "Year." On the other hand, enumeration does need a caption such as "Vol." or "Bd." Abbreviations in the captions are from *Anglo American Cataloguing Rules, Second edition, 2002 revision*, Appendix B or ISO 832. The structure for 85X and 86X fields was explained including how the paired fields are connected through subfield $8. How to code enumeration, gaps and changes in captions and other special problems were discussed.

The fourth session continued with a discussion of compression and expansion of holdings statements as found in the coding of the first indicator in the 85X fields and the second indicator in the 86X fields. This area was one of the most complex covered in the workshop. Examples were given for each of the possible values. Su explained that compression or expansion is often dependent on whether publication patterns are recorded in 85X fields. The other indicators, including the 86X fields' first indicators, level of specificity, were also discussed in this session. Most holdings records are coded as "4" for detailed holdings.

Nelson began the fifth session with an explanation of how publication patterns are recorded in fields 853, 854, 855 in subfields $u to $x. She noted that many systems have predictive check-in but not all. Serial holdings records allow you to record publication patterns by coding the number of bibliographic units per next higher level (subfield $u), the numbering continuity (subfield $v), the frequency (subfield $w), the calendar change (subfield $x) and the regularity pattern (subfield $y). Examples of each of these subfields and how it would be coded were covered in the workshop.

Holdings can also be recorded in textual holdings and item fields as Su explained in the workshop's next session. Textual holdings fields combine captions with enumeration and chronology data and are for display only. This information recorded in the 866 (basic bibliographic items), 867 (supplements) and 868 (indexes) fields. The instructors talked about how textual holdings are often used for retrospective holdings when the library simply wants to display what it owns. These fields also link with subfield $8 and can display between coded holdings, replace the display of coded holdings with the same link number, or display as the only holdings.

An entire session was devoted to special problems, with possible solutions discussed. Nelson covered cases where problems arise because systems do not fully work with the MFHD. In other cases, problems arise because the MFHD is not sufficiently robust. Further work between vendors, librarians, standards experts and system designers is necessary to handle some situations that arise with serials.

Trends and issues in MARC 21 Holdings were discussed in the eighth session. Su described the CONSER experiment which began June 1, 2000, which allows libraries to replace records in OCLC and to add pairs of 891 fields containing caption and pattern information and enumeration and chronology data for the first issue in that pattern. The data are available in the MARC records for cutting and pasting or otherwise importing into local systems. The audience was encouraged to participate in this program.

Finally, the workshop participants and instructors discussed workflow and implementation issues with MARC 21 holdings records. Because of the way different library systems are designed, work is often completed in different areas of the library that should logically be done in one area. Conversely, expertise in creating holdings records may reside in one particular area of the library which can also affect the logical workflow as dictated by the ILS. Su finished the pre-conference workshop with some screen shots of how holdings records function in some systems.

CONTRIBUTORS' NOTES

Catherine Nelson is Head of the Serials Department at the University of California, Santa Barbara. Julie Su is Head of the Serials Unit and Digital Resources at San Diego State University. Lisa Hanson O'Hara is Electronic Resources Cataloger at the University of Manitoba Libraries.

Serials Esperanto:
Helping Librarians, Vendors and Publishers Understand Each Other

Adam Chesler
Phil Greene
Kim Maxwell

Presenters

Stephen Headley

Recorder

SUMMARY. As defined at http://www.esperanto.net, "Esperanto's purpose is not to replace any other language, but to supplement them: Esperanto would be used as a neutral language when speaking with someone who doesn't know one's own language." The theme of this pre-conference was the concept of people who speak different languages communicating on an equal footing. Publishers, vendors, and librarians are often at odds with each other for a variety of reasons. The presenters of this program seek a common ground on which the three sides can communicate more effectively and better understand one another. *[Article copies available for a fee from The Haworth Document Delivery Service: 1-800-HAWORTH. E-mail address: <docdelivery@haworthpress.com> Website: <http://www.HaworthPress.com>]*

[Haworth co-indexing entry note]: "Serials Esperanto: Helping Librarians, Vendors and Publishers Understand Each Other." Headley, Stephen. Co-published simultaneously in *The Serials Librarian* (The Haworth Information Press, an imprint of The Haworth Press, Inc.) Vol. 50, No. 1/2, 2006, pp. 11-19; and: *Roaring into Our 20's: NASIG 2005* (ed: Margaret Mering, and Elna Saxton) The Haworth Information Press, an imprint of The Haworth Press, Inc., 2006, pp. 11-19. Single or multiple copies of this article are available for a fee from The Haworth Document Delivery Service [1-800-HAWORTH, 9:00 a.m. - 5:00 p.m. (EST). E-mail address: getinfo@haworthpress.com].

Available online at http://www.haworthpress.com/web/SER
doi:10.1300/J123v50n01_03

Adam Chesler, Phil Greene, and Kim Maxwell presented this pre-conference. Chesler was the publisher representative. He is the Assistant Director for Sales and Library Relations for the American Chemical Society (ACS). Greene was the vendor representative. He is co-founder of Greene Consulting LLC and was formerly Vice President at EBSCO. Maxwell was the librarian representative. She is the Serials Acquisitions Librarian for MIT Libraries.

Maxwell opened the pre-conference by briefly explaining its title. She presented some definitions of Esperanto. At http://www.esperanto.org/angle, it is defined as, "A language created for people who speak different native languages. It is neutral, international and easy to learn." She explained that a Serials Esperanto would, therefore, be "a common language for communication among publishers, vendors, and librarians." She said that when the three presenters decided to propose this program, they thought they knew what the others did. They had all worked together before in various capacities. However, they then began to ask each other questions about their respective jobs and realized that they did not know as much as they thought they did The result was a handout listing questions for librarians, publishers, and vendors asked by the three presenters to each other. This list was to be used to facilitate questions during the pre-conference should the need have arisen.

Maxwell presented the program's goals as seeking to provide participants:

> an understanding (though not exhaustive) of the history of publishers and vendors, an understanding of the different roles librarians play in the purchasing arena, a common understanding of language and terms we all use, and a discussion of and answers to some questions about why publishers, vendors, and libraries do things the way they do them.

As a way of understanding their audience, Maxwell asked for a show of hands of participants who were publisher or vendor representatives. The audience had only four publisher representatives and eight representing vendors. The vast majority of the audience was from libraries.

Greene presented the "evolution and revolution of the subscription agency," based in part on his many years of working for EBSCO. Moore-Cottrell was the first U.S. subscription agency, beginning in 1869. Frederick Wadsworth Faxon came on the scene in the early 1900s and served as a subscription agent for the Boston Public Library. Outside the United States during this time, local bookstores and state-controlled outlets provided this service, with companies such as Harrrassowitz in Europe and Dawson and Hanson and Bennett in Canada filling the role of subscription agents. Later, in the 1930s in the United States, the magazine subscription business took the form of door-to-door selling and also being sold in department stores. A real entrepreneurial spirit was taking over. During World War II, the founder of EBSCO came up with the idea to tap into the military bases' recreational funds and to sell magazine subscriptions to the bases for their day rooms.

Soon after this time, subscription agents began focusing on libraries because they provided publishers with a larger readership reaching a wider demographic group. This focus was also beneficial to libraries, Greene said, because subscription agents saved them time and money. During the early years of the Cold War in the 1950s, the library business exploded as libraries were beneficiaries of huge amounts of funding that was being provided for research. By the early 1960s, there were many more subscription agencies in the U.S. and more outside the U.S. As libraries became more important clients, library conferences became more important to subscription agencies. At the end of the 1960s, the Audit Bureau of Circulation (ABC) listed 153 subscription agencies, with about a dozen of them serving academic libraries. At the top of these agencies was Faxon with estimated sales of $40 million.

In the 1970s, some big changes started to take place. The competition among subscription agencies heated up, especially as European agencies began to seek business in the United States. Mergers and acquisitions of agencies began to affect the landscape. The first major acquisition was when EBSCO acquired Franklin Square. During this time, economics were also having an impact as the dollar was losing value and inflation was causing periodical prices to rise. Publishers were reacting by insisting on non-cancellable titles and instituting two-tier pricing. It included not only the different costs of individual subscriptions and institutional subscriptions, but also United Kingdom and European titles were higher for United States institutions than they were for United Kingdom and European institutions.

In the late 1960s, subscription agencies faced challenges as they had to charge less for their services due to increased competition, but were expected to provide more or better service. They were affected by early automated library systems. These systems generated more claims faster than what they were used to. This challenge led to cooperation between subscription agencies, publishers and library automation vendors to establish automated claiming standards and awareness so that claims would be more accurate.

In the 1980s, Greene explained that library budgets increased as did inflation. Actual buying power was less than it had been before. Economically, the dollar gained strength, but that only masked the increasing prices of United Kingdom and European scientific, technical, and medical (STM) titles. The two-tier pricing of these titles became a significant issue in the 1980s. One study revealed that "584 titles in 1984 were 66% higher in cost in the U.S. compared to the U.K." As a result, United States subscription agencies and libraries worked together to break the two-tier pricing. Also, in the 1980s, corporate libraries received more funds to be spent to support research, especially in aerospace, information technology (IT), and biomedical areas. Some of this increased funding went to universities as research grants. "Pressure was put on libraries to increase STM periodical purchases at the expense of liberal arts and monographs," Greene explained. United States subscription agencies started to expand into international markets and also actively pursued orders for STM titles, which had previously been purchased by libraries either directly from the publishers or from international agencies.

In the 1990s, libraries' budgets were reduced, which led to reductions in book budgets to maintain periodicals collections. The dollar, once again, weakened adding "10-18% to the cost of European journals." The relationships between publishers and libraries became more confrontational. Librarians became activists, to a certain degree, as they threatened legal action to stop the mergers of publishers. They began to cancel duplicates and non-English language titles. They used subscription agency collection development reports for title analysis which led to more cancellations. The publishers, in return, "made veiled threats to bring anti-trust litigation for group cancellation projects." Subscription agencies began to embrace new business models as they produced aggregated periodical databases and e-journal access programs and got involved in the book selling business. These new models led to larger sales staffs, including professional librarians. This expansion by the agencies narrowed profit margins as the services they provided grew and became more expensive. They were expected by libraries to continue to provide these new services in a more competitive marketplace.

In the late 1990s, some subscription agencies began to experience financial problems. Libraries and publishers had growing concerns over the future of various agencies. This perceived instability in the serials world was also evident in the large number of acquisitions and mergers among the major publishers, subscription agencies, and library ILS vendors. Financial pressure on subscription agencies was increased by the costs of research and development that was necessary to maintain and produce technological advances.

The twenty-first century ushered in the "most significant changes in the history of agencies," according to Greene. Agencies offered a "full slate of delivery options for libraries" and also partnered with publishers. For libraries, subscription agencies provided "classic service of consolidation of orders and payments" and access to e-journals, and also provided negotiation services with publishers. For publishers, subscription agencies developed electronic versions of publishers' print journals and negotiated "with libraries and consortia for package deal pricing and delivery options."

Despite this new relationship with subscription agencies, many STM publishers began to compete with these agencies as they initially required libraries to order directly through them for some e-journal subscriptions and most packages and Big Deals. These publishers were attempting to establish more control. They also had concern with the instability of the subscription agencies. At first, libraries did not object to this change. Subscription agencies were greatly affected by the "lost hard copy revenue, reduced profit levels, and increased service and order entry cost." Libraries were affected in that they now had "multiple customer service and payment points," and faced difficulties "establishing accurate holding/order records for working with publishers to convert to e-journal format, in receiving invoices that mesh with ILS and budget records, and maintaining order records reflecting title changes." Publishers were also affected, in ways both expected and unexpected. They faced increases in "sales and service staffs, overhead cost, and collection costs." Publishers also received negative publicity and had to deal with a great amount of "back office" expense.

Greene summarized the subscription agency business as it presently exists. He said that the agencies have "refined all 'back office' procedures." Libraries and consortia have come back to subscription agencies as they have realized the costs involved with direct orders to publishers. Consequently, "some major academic and research libraries have required STM publishers to work through agencies." Most of these publishers have "relaxed" their insistence on direct orders.

Looking to the future, Greene made the following predictions: "E-journals are here to stay, hard copy will remain but continue to be a smaller part of the budget, aggregators will continue to grow, (it's) not likely that the number of agencies will grow, (and) there will be greatly increased cooperation between agencies, libraries, and publishers."

Some lessons learned from this examination of the history of subscriptions agencies revealed that changes can be cyclical. "Revolutions" in the industry are simply part of its evolution. Cooperation between the various players in the industry "has always come out of confrontation," Greene stated, but has been greatly beneficial.

Chesler spoke on the publisher's role in the serials industry. He gave a brief history of the publishing industry from the time of the Chinese inventing paper to the twentieth century's electronic publishing. Today, several different types of publishers have emerged including STM or scholarly publishers who publish journals, and trade publishers who publish magazines. While the scholarly publishers are focused on the number of subscriptions to their journals, trade publishers focus more on the amount of advertising revenue. As mentioned by Greene, the advent of the Cold War inspired an increase in spending on science and research. Commercial publishers attracted researchers by not imposing page charges like society publishers or other major academic journals. As library budgets have leveled off or decreased, the amount of publishable material has nevertheless continued to increase dramatically, which along with increased infrastructure (including labor and technology) costs has resulted in higher prices.

Chesler outlined the various departments that exist within a publisher's operations. These different departments included publishing and acquisitions, manufacturing, marketing and public relations, sales, fulfillment, customer service, accounting and finance, and IT and communications. The fulfillment department is responsible for print delivery and storage. Customer service is a much newer concept with publishers than with others in the serials industry. However, the biggest change for publishers came in the IT department. Not only does research and development for new technologies cost a great deal, but IT staff were needed in abundance for this work as well as for updating current technology. These professionals were not cheap. At ACS, their IT staff increased from seven in 1998 to seventy-five in 2005.

Chesler explained the process of developing content for journals. He said that the number of new researchers each year equaled the number of new people publishing, emphasizing the great amount of content presented to publishers each year. Each publisher has a manuscript submission and review process. Content is chosen through research and networking with authors, professionals, and faculty in academic institutions. This process is also the way new journals are developed. New journals generally take up to seven years before they begin to make money. Until that time, the publisher is essentially subsidizing these new journals and incurring considerable expenses with their production.

The commercial issues a publisher faces are, first and foremost, the cost of its infrastructure and background costs, such as staff. As mentioned earlier, the cost of technology is significant as well. The costs include technical upgrades and also the employing of a growing number of IT staff needed to maintain the technology. Content development is also a considerable commercial issue. These issues are not only relevant for commercial publishers, but also apply to "non-profit" publishers, such as society publishers and university publishers.

Chesler described how the Internet has affected publishers and their products. The Internet has provided a new way of developing and writing materials. Scholars and researchers are now accustomed to reading more online and conducting research online. He used an analogy from *The Wizard of Oz* to demonstrate another way that the Internet has affected publishers. In the print world, publishers listened to issues, concerns, or requests much like the man at the Emerald Palace treated Dorothy and her friends. They would politely open the top part of door to listen, shut the door to "consult" with senior management (the Wizard), and then come back saying "thanks but no thanks" and quickly shut the door. With the arrival of e-journals the door has been thrown wide open by the publishers, who are inviting and welcoming open communication, negotiation, compromise, and change. This electronic playing field has presented new opportunities for the publishers, but has also introduced new players, such as independently published e-journals, institutional repositories, and aggregators.

The key issues that remain for publishers were identified by Chesler. The pricing of journals will continue to be important. While publishers have faced considerable criticism over this issue, Chesler pointed out that information does not "yearn to be free." Other issues include archiving and digital preservation and the question of ownership versus access, which deals with licensing agreements and negotiations. The distribution of information and how people are notified of its availability is another important issue. Copyright or fair use laws versus licensing agreements continue to be an important issue for publishers. The basic motivation to publish, by either commercial or "non-profit" publishers, is another issue. Finally SPARC-like initiatives, where library collaborators are working with publishers, will also be important.

Maxwell presented the librarian's role in this triangle of information. Two types of librarians interact with publishers and vendors: one who is concerned with selections and one who is concerned with acquisitions. Although their responsibilities are becoming blurred in the world of on-line access, these two types of librarians have very distinct responsibilities. To demonstrate this confusion, Maxwell listed a number of job titles, one list for those involved in selections and one list for those involved in acquisitions. She asked participants for any other titles that they knew of that were not listed. All of these different job titles emphasized the point that the job titles are not indicative of job responsibilities to publishers and vendors. Even more confusing is when a number of institutions may have a person with the same job title, such as Electronic Resources Coordinator. However, in each of those institutions, the person with that job title has different responsibilities, such as negotiating licenses, setting up the technical work for access, making the selection and acquisition decisions, or any other combination of these and other duties. Publishers and vendors are left guessing as to whom they should be contacting. When libraries are working with publishers and vendors, they should involve other library staff that have a stake in the outcome of an acquisition. Subject librarians, catalogers, and anyone else who may have some work to do that involves the acquisition process. By bringing all the interested parties together from the beginning, you ensure that everyone's needs are met and everyone has a better understanding.

Maxwell referred to the handout "Definitions of Common Terms Used by Publishers, Vendors, and Librarians: A Step Toward Serials Esperanto." This handout of definitions, from "abstract" to "warranty," was compiled by the three presenters independently from each other, each offering definitions for the terms they thought most important to understanding each other. Insight can be gained by noting the similarities and/or differences in how each term is defined by each person. It also serves to point out how important it is for communication to be clear between publishers, vendors, and librarians.

In dealing with publishers and vendors, Maxwell discussed some common issues. Access problems for online access were identified as a major issue. Terminology should be standardized between publishers, vendors, and libraries. Sometimes, publishers and vendors need a piece of information, but they may all have different names for that piece of information. For example, one might call it an "account number," another might call it a "customer code," and a third might call it a "subscription number."

Electronic products certainly have changed the dynamics of the "serials triangle." In discussing problems libraries experienced with vendors, Greene stated that a library must clearly define what it wants from that vendor. In some instances, a vendor has legal limitations in dealing with institutions and publishers. He went on to say that vendors, on the other hand, should clearly define what they can and cannot do. He emphasized that communication is vital and that libraries should never give up in seeking answers to their questions.

A question-and-answer period followed the presentation. One question was if articles rejected by publishers were always self-published. Chesler responded to this question by saying that because there are so many publishing outlets that if one publisher rejects an article, it likely will be accepted by another publisher. In some cases, the article may be rejected by a publisher for its major publication, but it might be accepted in one of its minor or more specialized publications. When asked what effect Google Scholar will have on publishing, the presenters did not have much reaction. Chesler believed that it would force publishers to re-think how their content is displayed and produced. Another question asked why e-journals were more expensive than print when they are cheaper to produce. Chesler replied that he wanted to dispel the myth that e-journals are cheaper to produce than print. He explained that e-journals require more IT staff to not only maintain them but also provide and develop innovations in displaying and delivering, as well as for finding, that content. As mentioned before, not only are salaries for IT staff expensive, but so are the costs associated with technological upgrades. He stated that he believed the prices for print journals and e-journals would only come down if the production of print journals were dramatically reduced.

After the "question-and-answer" time, each presenter gave some closing observations. Greene predicted that e-journals will eventually be available individually and that the Big Deal will no longer be an issue. Chesler speculated that, aggregator databases will be more attractive for access, rather than libraries having to make decisions on access to individual titles. Maxwell left the audience with two questions to ponder: What have you learned from the different representatives of the "serials triangle"? What can you do to establish a Serials Esperanto?

CONTRIBUTORS' NOTES

Adam Chesler is the Assistant Director of Sales and Library Relations at the American Chemical Society. Phil Greene is a co-founder of Greene Consulting and was formerly Vice President of EBSCO Information Society. Kim Maxwell is the Serials Acquisitions Librarian at MIT. Stephen Headley is the manager of the Magazines and Newspapers Department at the Public Library of Cincinnati and Hamilton County.

How to Avoid Death by Meeting: Strategies for Better Meetings

Betty J. Kjellberg

Presenter

Elna L. Saxton

Recorder

SUMMARY. Meetings can be great opportunities to create the synergy that leads to better productivity and a more satisfying work experience. Leaders can create a "POP–Purpose, Outcome, and Plan" to uncover specific goals and identify the best methods to achieve them. Agendas should be carefully formatted with the desirable result in mind. Adding time specifications, assigning names to topics, and providing a layout conducive to resulting action assists both leaders and meeting participants. Facilitation techniques assure active participation by everyone and help move the discussion toward a productive outcome. *[Article copies available for a fee from The Haworth Document Delivery Service: 1-800-HAWORTH. E-mail address: <docdelivery@haworthpress.com> Website: <http://www.HaworthPress.com>]*

A dozen or so busy librarians took time out of their schedule to attend this pre-conference to learn techniques that can be used to improve meeting effectiveness. Common themes immediately came to light as

[Haworth co-indexing entry note]: "How to Avoid Death by Meeting: Strategies for Better Meetings." Saxton, Elna L. Co-published simultaneously in *The Serials Librarian* (The Haworth Information Press, an imprint of The Haworth Press, Inc.) Vol. 50, No. 1/2, 2006, pp. 21-26; and: *Roaring into Our 20's: NASIG 2005* (ed: Margaret Mering, and Elna Saxton) The Haworth Information Press, an imprint of The Haworth Press, Inc., 2006, pp. 21-26. Single or multiple copies of this article are available for a fee from The Haworth Document Delivery Service [1-800-HAWORTH, 9:00 a.m. - 5:00 p.m. (EST). E-mail address: getinfo@haworthpress.com].

Available online at http://www.haworthpress.com/web/SER
doi:10.1300/J123v50n01_04

participants listed the problems they regularly encounter during meetings: inefficient use of time, lack of engagement, staying on track, and no clear outcomes at meeting's end. These common themes were further depicted in a role-play scenario. Five individuals accepted standard meeting roles and conducted a brief meeting. From this experience, the observers were able to identify a multitude of typical problems.

Kjellberg emphasized that the work of the meeting should begin well in advance of the actual meeting time. Meeting planning is necessary–creating a "POP," Purpose, Outcomes, and Plan–to ensure the proposed meeting will achieve desired goals. Questions such as "what is the purpose of the meeting?", "what are the desired outcomes?", and "what is the meeting plan?" are needed to uncover specific goals. The meeting participants also impact meeting effectiveness. The inclusion of appropriate stakeholders and an awareness of individual politics and agendas will help foster a successful meeting. Being selective and clear regarding potential invitees will more effectively garner the critical input needed for decision-making. At times, a meeting may not be the best method to achieve the outcome, a one-on-one discussion or e-mail communication might be just as useful, and a more effective use of time. Holding meetings to facilitate team bonding can be a legitimate reason to meet. However, this purpose should be acknowledged from the outset.

AGENDA DEVELOPMENT

The agenda is a useful tool if carefully formatted for results. The layout can delineate the action that is needed, for example discussion versus decision-making. Establishing an allotted time for agenda items can control the flow of the meeting. When the allotted time has expired, the group must decide how to move forward (e.g., with a vote, assigning a task force, or by tabling the discussion for another meeting). Establishing the lead for agenda topics can also be useful and is readily accomplished by assigning people to topics on the prepared agenda. To get buy-in from meeting participants, participation in agenda building is highly desirable. Individuals and groups can identify priority issues and areas in which administrative or team support is needed.

MEETING PROTOCOL

Meeting protocol can be established and maintained in many creative ways. A common problem is a culture that permits a late start to meetings. This practice is typically an unwritten rule that should be aired with the group so that a ground rule on meeting time can be established. Once the group is aware that starting on time has become the rule, always start on time. Do not put habitual latecomers first on the agenda. The goal is not to embarrass individuals, nor is it to hinder the progress of the meeting.

SCRIBE

Protocol for regularly established groups should include determination of a meeting recorder. The chair of the meeting should not take this role, as facilitating the meeting is a weighty task in itself. A good practice is to rotate recording responsibilities according to a set schedule. By establishing a form for the minutes of the meeting, such as topic/issue/action, the written outcome of the meeting will naturally include summaries of decisions and specific action items. When homework from the meeting is clearly listed by action, name, and date, the Chair can readily follow-up with a phone call to offer support and maintain individual and group accountability for tasks. Three examples of forms that can be utilized by the meeting scribe follow.

Example #1				
AGENDA TOPIC	Summary of issue	Action	Name	Date

Example #2		
ISSUE	PRO	CON

Example #3	
DISCUSSION TOPIC	Questions and Issues:

FLOW

The merging of action and awareness that occurs in effective meetings leads to "flow" in groups. Flow is a term used to describe total concentration on the task at hand, when a loss of self-consciousness is achieved, and participants lose track of time. This profound level of concentration is most likely to occur when a meeting has clear goals and timely feedback for participants. Asking the group to describe their level of effectiveness during a meeting can lead to greater awareness of individual responsibility for group success.

FACILITATION STRATEGIES

Often, facilitation is conducted by an unbiased third party, but the techniques that are used can be applied by any team or committee leader. Facilitation can be used to analyze root causes, generate ideas, set priorities, and identify issues. A fishbone diagram can be used to identify the roots of a problem. Looking like a fish skeleton, the problem under review is placed at the head, and factors contributing to the problem are drawn as 'ribs' in the skeleton. Another way to search for root causes is the "five whys"–first choosing the symptom to explore, then asking "why," recording the responses, and repeating this process five times. Phrasing questions sensitively can assist moving the discussion forward, for example "help me understand" or "I'm trying to figure this out." Brainstorming is a popular way to generate ideas. Kjellberg uses a method of individual brainstorming by having the individuals develop their own list, then breaking into small groups to share those ideas. Affinity diagrams also generate ideas. Participants work in small groups, identifying eight to ten ideas, placing each on a single piece of paper with three to five words that describe the idea. The large group exercise involves clustering the ideas to distill the larger categories of issues. A technique of force field analysis can be compared to a "pro/con" list, with the issue at the top of the flip chart. In two columns, participants describe forces driving for change versus restraining change.

After generating ideas, groups can become mired in discussion on topics that may not be a priority. Dot-voting quickly pinpoints the level of group interest or enthusiasm for any particular item listed for potential discussion. Rules for voting are needed. For example, the group might determine that an individual may place only one vote on any single issue. A decision grid also facilitates moving toward priority activities–the criteria related to listed options are calculated numerically to arrive at a mathematical conclusion. A less scientific approach is to take the temperature of the room using a stoplight metaphor. Each participant is given three index cards (green, yellow, and red). Green indicates the group is ready to move forward, yellow shows strong agreement with some additional discussion needed, and red alerts the group to stop and voice concerns.

Another frequent problem with meetings is control of the discussion. Setting ground rules in advance will assist in keeping the meeting focused, and provide the leader with a tool to return the focus to the issues in a non-judgmental manner. Side issues can be relegated to a "parking lot," a listing of items that are important, but tangential to the immediate discussion. The group leader can appoint roles to share meeting ownership–such as co-facilitating, scribe, or timekeeper, among others. Getting the group started with informal conversation or round-robin sharing can set the tone for an active and fully engaged meeting.

RESOURCES

Alice Collier Cochran, *Roberta's Rules of Order: A guide for nonprofits and other teams* (San Francisco, CA: Jossey-Bass, 2004).

Michael Doyle and David Straus, *How to make meetings work!* (New York: Berkley Books, 1993).

Patrick Lencioni, *Death by meeting* (San Francisco, CA: Jossey-Bass, 2004).

Roger K. Mosvick and Robert B. Nelson, *We've got to start meeting like this!* (Indianapolis, IN: Park Avenue, 1996, Rev. ed.).

Eva Schindler-Rainman et al. *Taking your meetings out of the doldrums* (San Diego, University Associates, 1988, Rev. ed.).

John E. Tropman, *Making meetings work: Achieving high quality group decisions* (Thousand Oaks, CA: Sage, 2003, 2nd ed.).

Alvin Zander, *Making Groups Effective* (San Francisco CA: Jossey-Bass, 1994, 2nd ed.).

WEB SITES

EffectiveMeetings.com: Your Meeting Resource Center. "Teams" http://www.effectivemeetings.com/teams/teamwork/creighton.asp

The CEO Refresher. "More effective meetings" http://www.refresher.com/archives33.html

The Banff Centre. "Leadership Compass" (issues often include an article by the "Meeting Doctor.") http://www.banffcentre.ca/departments/leadership/leadership_compass/past_issues/six.asp

CONTRIBUTORS' NOTES

Betty J. Kjellberg is with Association Solutions, LLC. Elna L. Saxton is Head of the Serials and Electronic Resources Department at the University of Cincinnati.

VISION SESSIONS

Chaotic Transitions:
How Today's Trends Will Affect Tomorrow's Libraries

Marshall Keys

Presenter

Buddy Pennington

Recorder

SUMMARY. Marshall Keys' entertaining presentation serves as an inspiring and thought-provoking stroll down today's technological trends and how they will impact libraries down the road. His examination of chaotic transitions within users, information technology and information seeking provides tremendous insights into the changes libraries will need to undertake in order to successfully serve the next generation of library users. Only by transforming ourselves to handle the needs of emerging users will we be successful in the future. These emerging users value community over privacy, want to be able to personalize the technology they use, and carry more technology in their pockets than libraries provided users just a few years ago. *[Article copies available for a fee from The Haworth Document Delivery Service: 1-800-HAWORTH. E-mail address: <docdelivery@haworthpress.com> Website: <http://www.HaworthPress. com>]*

[Haworth co-indexing entry note]: "Chaotic Transitions: How Today's Trends Will Affect Tomorrow's Libraries." Pennington, Buddy. Co-published simultaneously in *The Serials Librarian* (The Haworth Information Press, an imprint of The Haworth Press, Inc.) Vol. 50, No. 1/2, 2006, pp. 29-36; and: *Roaring into Our 20's: NASIG 2005* (ed: Margaret Mering, and Elna Saxton) The Haworth Information Press, an imprint of The Haworth Press, Inc., 2006, pp. 29-36. Single or multiple copies of this article are available for a fee from The Haworth Document Delivery Service [1-800-HAWORTH, 9:00 a.m. - 5:00 p.m. (EST). E-mail address: getinfo@haworthpress.com].

Available online at http://www.haworthpress.com/web/SER
doi:10.1300/J123v50n01_05

INTRODUCTION

This is your twentieth anniversary, and I want to talk about the things that have been the big issues at each of the five years since you began. In 1985, the hot technology was the fax machine and the big concern for librarians was the OPAC. The large libraries had them, but many smaller ones did not. We were asking ourselves how our workflows and processes were going to fit into the OPAC environment. In 1990, the issue was the Internet. As incredible as it sounds today, the big question at the time was, "How are we going to get people to use it?" By 1995, we were on the World Wide Web and many were switching from MOSAIC to the Netscape browser. The answer to the big question of Internet use was giving people a graphical user interface. By 2000, we had seen the rise of Google and the collapse of the dot-com bubble. We had learned the lesson that the old lessons still apply. The failure of many dot-coms proved that new technology alone would not fuel the new economy. My presentation today will look at what is critical for 2005 and the next ten years.

I will start out with the assumption that the future of libraries, good or bad, depends on their ability to meet the *emerging* needs of users. Not last year's needs or the needs of ten years ago but the future needs of users. Who will these users be and what will these emerging needs look like? How will library operations change to meet these emerging needs? In other words, how can libraries respond to the changing needs of users?

The unifying theory for today's presentation is that of chaotic transitions. Everyone understands the basic growth curve. One of the ideas of a fascinating book by Theodore Modis[1] is that for every growth curve there are competing alternate growth curves. If you take a look at the growth of personal computing, for example, the first growth curve would be the early computers developed by Apple. The alternate growth curve would be those computers with Windows-based operating systems, which started later and has surpassed the growth seen in the earlier Apple curve. And for each growth curve, there can be many competing growth curves that overlap.

The period of time where these different curves are competing with each other is the period of the chaotic transition. There are never neat and easy transitions between one curve and another. A good example of chaotic transitions is the variety of formats for recorded music. Currently, one can see cassettes, CDs, DVDs, and digital formats such as MP3s, competing for the attention of music listeners.

Chaotic transitions exist for libraries. There is currently no dominant technological model. More specifically, we do not know what tools people will be using in ten years to access information. Secondly, there is no dominant business model for the distribution of information content. Finally, there is no dominant conceptual model for what the library should look like ten years from now. When we were children and were told to envision what a library looked like, we all had a very similar picture in our minds. That is not true today. What is the library of 2005 and what will it be in 2015? In the areas of technology, business models and even intellectual concepts, libraries are experiencing a series of chaotic transitions.

CHANGES IN USERS

The next generation of library users is quite different from what we are used to. This really came home to me one day on the subway when I overheard a young woman–someone who looked like a college senior–ask, "What is a cassette?" It was then that I realized that there was another world out there that I did not know much about. And so I began to explore this world to better understand what young people are doing.

One thing I discovered pretty quickly was Buzznet.[2] Buzznet is one of the earliest photoblogs. People with camera phones take pictures and post them on Buzznet for others to comment on. This whole blog concept was completely new to me.

And what have I discovered about the blogger mentality? The first thing is that what I, the blogger, think is important. The second thing is that what I, the blogger, think is important to other people so I am going to publish it. The third thing is that things are important because I, the blogger, think they are important. The philosophers in the room may recognize the Latin phrase "esse est percipi" or "to be is to be perceived." I know I exist, because you are listening to me and reacting to what I am saying. Teens overcome their sense of powerlessness through blogs. They exist and feel validated when others respond to what they are saying. Fifty-one percent of bloggers are between thirteen and nineteen; ninety percent are under thirty. Critical for libraries to understand is that privacy is not valued by bloggers. It is all about communities. And bloggers are our users, future users, and the next generation of library staff. Negative reactions to the blogosphere from library leaders, such as Michael Gorman and Blaise Cronin, are not encouraging. They are smart individuals, but from a different generation and are missing the point.

When we look at emerging users, we see three dominant themes: community, personalization, and portable, ubiquitous technology. Web sites such as Friendster[3] foster communities among Internet users. Customizing one's cell phone is an example of the growing trend to both personalize and to carry our technology. We, as librarians, have a tradition of providing technology for our users, but users are now carrying around more technology in their pocket than we provided on our desktops ten years ago.

CHANGES IN TECHNOLOGY

The cell phone is no longer a phone but an information appliance. Through the cell phone you can send and receive e-mail, send notes to friends through text messaging, surf the Web and more. The marketing message here is that you are no longer tied to old stuff like computers. Messages depicting the library as a place with computers as well as books are behind the curve. You can use your phone as a modem. You can take pictures with your phone and send them to your friends. Nowhere in the advertisements does it mention using the phone to actually speak to people. It's not a phone anymore, but something else. We are increasingly living in a world of ubiquitous, multi-media communication.

The old slogan "everything is on the Internet" is quickly becoming "everything is on the phone." In the United Kingdom, there exists a reference service called AQA–Any Question Answered.[4] Cell phone users can text message a question and get an answer back within ten minutes at the cost of one pound. This phenomenon is quite interesting in both completely bypassing the library and establishing the value of a reference question.

What does this mean to libraries? We are seeing an emerging generation of users for whom the phone is a major information appliance, if not *the* major one. Libraries will need phone-based interfaces to local catalogs and other information resources. There will be more reference services provided through text messaging. Libraries may also be utilizing camera phones for interlibrary loan. Instead of pulling an item off a shelf and taking it to a copy machine or scanner, the library staff person will simply take a picture of the page and send it on. We have users who are willing to pay for information. They are willing to pay as long as it is delivered the way they want it. And this growing use of portable technology to access networked information is resulting in major bandwidth and graphical interface issues that need to be dealt with.

Besides the phone, a lot of other transitions are taking place in the area of information technology. Wireless networks are here, and ubiquitous computing is the next step. The coming generation does not see much difference between television and the Internet as they watch their favorite shows on their laptops. They are accustomed to the idea of watching or listening to anything on any device that is nearby.

Making predictions is always a risky business, but I'm going to make some anyway. The failure of Apple's Newton was simply because it was an idea ahead of its time. We are now in the era of portable computing. OVID databases and library catalogs, such as Innovative's Airpac, are available through wireless Personal Digital Assistants (PDAs). The tyranny of the unified computing model is being increasingly undermined by distributed computing. You are all familiar with the foldable keyboards that you can use with your PDA. Siemens has a virtual keyboard product which projects an infrared keyboard onto your desk. Distributed storage is being made available through flash drives and iPods. And the iPod is more than just a storage device. Accessories make it possible to capture sound, for example. Distributed processing can be seen as Linux becomes available in portable devices like watches and iPods. The increasing miniaturization of portal computing devices raises output issues, but digital glasses, projecting displays on walls, and paper-thin screens are some options to address that.

CHANGES IN INTELLECTUAL PROPERTY

The information industry is quite concerned about keeping their intellectual property intact. In Japan, bookstores complain about digital shoplifting, wherein someone with a camera phone, instead of buying a magazine, snaps pictures of the magazine's pages and e-mails them out to friends. With a camera phone, anything you see can be captured and shared with others. We've seen the lawsuits by the Recording Industry Association of America, and we've seen the hackers shut down the RIAA Web site. The courts have consistently sided against the RIAA. The issue is coming to a head with the United States Supreme Court and it will be interesting to see what the Supreme Court judges have to say. Will they get it?

But it doesn't really matter what the courts decide. Earth Station 5[5] is a peer-to-peer Internet site that lets people swap files with each other. And it has one very important competitive advantage. It is located in the Jenin refugee camp in the Palestinian West Bank. Filing a lawsuit against Earth Station 5 would be an exercise in futility. Today's technology allows thieves of intellectual property to move just about anywhere. How about Vanuatu, an island in the South Pacific, whose business laws make it very easy for individuals to remain anonymous and untouchable? The next generation does not care about intellectual property, and all the lawsuits in the world are not going to stop them.

CHANGES IN CONTENT PROVIDERS

We are seeing chaotic transitions in the content business. The fluctuation in Elsevier's share values over the past five years is an indication of this chaos. Business models are changing. Elsevier's Big Deal unraveled in 2004. Elsevier recovered by changing it. We've seen consolidation in the publishing industry, such as Taylor & Francis purchasing Marcel Dekker for 138 million dollars. A big unknown will be the impact of the Google Print[6] project, wherein Google is digitizing books and making them accessible to the world. It is not an era of stability for publishers and information providers. We've seen numerous companies go bankrupt. Others are merging or being purchased by venture capital firms. Obviously these venture capital firms intend to make a profit on their investment. And who else besides libraries will be providing these profits?

More service work is going offsite. At a McDonald's in Cape Girardeau, Missouri, when you place your order through the drive-thru you are actually speaking to someone in Colorado Springs.[7] The technician in Colorado Springs takes your order and sends it back to the McDonald's along with a picture of you so the staff at McDonald's knows who to give the order to. The argument here is that the work can be done more effectively by people who are not distracted by the hustle and bustle behind the McDonald's counter. Consumers are going offshore. Knowledge work is going offshore. The movement of information technology jobs to India is old news. How will this trend affect libraries? It will be fairly easy to move technical services, technology services, and reference services offshore in much the same way as moving them from one building on campus to another.

CHANGES IN INFORMATION SEEKING

The information gathering model is also changing. The previous model was that of the individual studying in the library, using formal resources "authorized" by the library through the selection process. It was a solitary activity. Today's studying is a group activity utilizing peer-to-peer networks. Learning takes place through social networks, and everyone is in touch all the time through virtual study groups.

There are new ways of finding information. Portals are becoming increasingly personalizable. RSS feeds enable people to get the information they want without having to go anywhere to get it. Amazon[8] is an example of the increasing value of the community experience. Amazon users can easily see how others have rated specific titles. We are not seeing this in libraries because of privacy concerns. What would the American Library Association say about this? Emerging users value these community interactions over their own privacy. We have personalized search engines, search engines with social networking, and we are also seeing social cataloging.[9] We are seeing interesting innovations in how search results are being displayed.[10] Belmont Abbey College uses a visual map to browse for materials within Library of Congress subject headings. A common theme is this use of visual representations instead of text-based results lists.

We are seeing the economics of attention in action. A wealth of information creates a poverty of attention. The response to that is personalization, customization and delivering the information the user wants the way they want it.

CONCLUSION

What will libraries have to do to serve a world in which users expect information to be delivered to them, expect technology and interfaces to be highly personalized, and care more about convenience and community than privacy? We need to answer that because those are the fundamental values of the next generation of users. What does the library look like if the medium isn't a browser and the hardware isn't a PC?

We have administrators who are no longer seeing the value of the library. We have content providers who know we have no funding. We have user populations who do not know what we are doing. We have huge investments in current technology with all this new stuff on the horizon. We are committed to the medium and not the message. Does the

American Medical Association have a center for the stethoscope in the same way that we have a Center for the Book? We're committed to places not missions. We're building large central libraries instead of putting branches on each corner like Starbucks. We need to really think hard about our future.

We need to be user-focused, not library-focused. We need to rely on user technology, not library technology. What they have, not what we have. The message will be anywhere, anytime, any way you want it. Users who do not come to the library are not failures. Research from the dorm is the norm becomes research from the car or wherever you are. Our challenge for the next twenty years will be shifting from what we know to creating library services for a digital way of life.

NOTES

1. Theodore Modis, *Predictions: Society's Telltale Signature Reveals the Past and Forecasts the Future* (New York: Simon & Schuster, 1992).

2. *Buzznet.* http://www.buzznet.com/www/homepage.html.

3. *Friendster.* http://www.friendster.com.

4. *AQA–Any Question Answered.* http://www.aqa.issuebits.com.

5. *Earth Station 5.* http://www.es5.com/ (site now discontinued). "EarthStation 5." *Wikipedia.* http://en.wikipedia.org/wiki/EarthStation_5.

6. "Google Print." *Google.* http://print.google.com.

7. Michael Fitzgerald, "A Drive-Through Lane to the Next Time Zone," *New York Times,* July 18, 2004.

8. *Amazon.* http://www.amazon.com.

9. *Delicious Monster.* http://www.delicious-monster.com. Delicious Monster allows individuals to catalog their privately-owned books.

10. Examples of knowledge-mapping sites include: *KartOO* (http://www.kartoo. com), *Grokker* (http://www.grokker.com), and *Anacubis* (http://www.i2.co.uk/ anacubis).

CONTRIBUTORS' NOTES

Marshall Keys, PhD, is the Principal at MDA Consulting and adjunct professor at Simmons' Graduate School of Library and Information Science. Buddy Pennington is the Serial Acquisitions Librarian at the University of Missouri-Kansas City.

Painting America Purple:
Media Democracy and the Red/Blue Divide

Leif Utne

Presenter

Paul Moeller

Recorder

SUMMARY. This article is a condensed version of the presentation given by Leif Utne. In his presentation, Utne addresses the poisonous tone of U.S. political debate, what media is doing to exacerbate the problem, and what media can do to foster civil dialogue. He discusses some of the factors that contribute to the development of the red/blue ideological chasm and cites some examples of groups that are working to bridge this divide and fulfill their democratic duties. *[Article copies available for a fee from The Haworth Document Delivery Service: 1-800-HAWORTH. E-mail address: <docdelivery@haworthpress.com> Website: <http://www.HaworthPress. com>]*

Good morning. Thank you for inviting me here today. And thank you all for showing up on this last day of your conference. I am less interested in hearing myself speak than in hearing a little bit from all of you. I want this next hour to be a dialogue about our democracy and how we can not only protect it from the serious challenges it faces right now but

[Haworth co-indexing entry note]: "Painting America Purple: Media Democracy and the Red/Blue Divide." Moeller, Paul. Co-published simultaneously in *The Serials Librarian* (The Haworth Information Press, an imprint of The Haworth Press, Inc.) Vol. 50, No. 1/2, 2006, pp. 37-45; and: *Roaring into Our 20's: NASIG 2005* (ed: Margaret Mering, and Elna Saxton) The Haworth Information Press, an imprint of The Haworth Press, Inc., 2006, pp. 37-45. Single or multiple copies of this article are available for a fee from The Haworth Document Delivery Service [1-800-HAWORTH, 9:00 a.m. - 5:00 p.m. (EST). E-mail address: getinfo@haworthpress.com].

Available online at http://www.haworthpress.com/web/SER
doi:10.1300/J123v50n01_06

also how we can make it better and more inclusive. I'm going to talk about the role of the media in promoting democratic dialogue. How it's failing in that role, and what journalists like myself and librarians like you, as citizens and gatekeepers of information and stewards of public knowledge, can do to improve the situation. I'll cite some examples of where the media is doing it right and talk about several organizations that are promoting models of civic dialogue.

Let me start off by asking what is democracy? What are some words associated with democracy? Voting, free choice and free speech, participation . . . freedom of the press is a good one. Access to information might be one that you all feel strongly about. These are all essential ingredients to democracy. I'd like to offer my definition of democracy. Democracy is a conversation among members of the community that fosters peaceful resolution of conflict and creative solutions to shared problems that require an educated and informed citizenry, but even more importantly it requires free and open dialogue across boundaries such as race, class, gender, and especially political persuasion. A diverse, free, and democratic media is an essential ingredient to that conversation. The media doesn't just inform people of what is going on in the world but reflects communities back to themselves. A representative democracy requires a representative media. It requires opportunities for connections between people and for meaningful conversations among people with whom we may disagree. It's only through that dynamic of conversation, discussion, and debate that we're able to learn and to come up with creative new solutions. So the media should have a role in bringing us together in conversation and promoting democratic dialogue. More than any other institution in our society the media has the power to connect us to each other and to bring people together in meaningful conversation across ideological divides. It can do this by introducing their readers, viewers, and listeners to one another and by modeling for the public what civic dialogue looks like. This isn't done through jingoism and hyper-patriotism that glosses over our diversity, but rather by showing us the true diversity of voices that exists in our country and in the rest of the world. Informing us about the complexity of the issues and connecting us in civil and conclusive dialogue. But unfortunately the media is falling down on the job. They divide us more than they unite us for a variety of reasons. For one, controversy sells. The old axiom in the newsroom "if it bleeds it leads" means that important stories go overlooked every day because they have to cover car crashes, bombings in Baghdad, and whatever gets in the way of the real stories of democracy in our communities. Media consolidation is a huge problem. One of the most damaging aspects of consolidation is that it encourages self-censorship. Writers, producers, and editors are going to be less courageous in pursuing stories that might ruffle the feathers of those connected to the corporate conglomerate they work for, when only six companies own virtually all of the media that people consume.

There is also a shrinking of news holes. The news hole is the space between the ads. A study showed that in 1981 the average news hole in a half hour news broadcast was just above twenty-two minutes. By 2001, it was down to eighteen minutes and thirty-seven seconds. That puts incredible pressure on producers to reduce the news to sound bites, to say this is the position of the right and this is the position of the left. As a result public discussion and dialogue suffers. Also journalistic standards are eroding in the mainstream media. The over reliance on official sources, which we have seen in the coverage of the war in Iraq, in the debate over social security reform, and on environmental issues is damaging because journalists are not covering a story unless they can find a government spokesperson willing to comment on it. As a result dissident voices are not being heard in the media the way they once were. All of these pressures lead to the rise of partisan pundits and interest groups who derive a lot of their power from maintaining division. Activist groups on all sides of the issues derive much of their power from fundraising and mobilizing membership. Activities that motivate these members also are polarizing them more and more. So these are all ways that the media serves to divide us rather than to promote civil dialogue.

How many of you saw Jon Stewart on *Crossfire* last October accusing the hosts of the show of being partisan hacks? Stewart asserted that the hosts' partisanship was helping the politicians and big corporations and he asked them to stop hurting America. Within a week of the episode's airing, a clip of this interview was widely distributed on the Web and it became the most downloaded piece of Internet media in history. What Stewart did on *Crossfire* was speak a truth that many Americans feel very deeply. That mainstream media, in its incessant focus on conflict and controversy and their constant drive to dumb down political discourse to two-dimensional sound bites, is hurting America. This is how the dominant view of politics reduces the range of political discussion. Accordingly most media outlets portray a map of America as consisting of red and blue states. More responsible mainstream outlets might present this map with smaller parcels of widely dispersed sections of red and blue. You have to look to independent media to see more nuanced takes on the true diversity of political opinions in this country. My father published a map of America's political landscape in

Utne Magazine in 1991. It goes beyond the left/right divide by adding three other axes. There is centralized versus decentralized, liberty versus equality, and freedom versus order. There are many other axes one can put on a map but this is one suggestion for how we can break out of the left/right block. As a nineteen-year-old political science student, this map blew my mind. For the first time, I had a framework for looking at politics that wasn't just left and right. I saw that libertarians are actually closer to anarchists than they are to the Christian right even though we consider them both to be part of the right. And I saw that communism and fascism in some respects are not that far apart. I also noticed that environmentalists come from all over the map.

I'd like to give some examples of organizations and media that are doing it right. They are working to bridge the red/blue divide and represent the country in more of its diversity and unity. Remember that introducing readers, viewers, and listeners to each other is a powerful step that mainstream media can take but they don't often do it because it is a scary step. To step out of the role of brokers of information and actually introduce people to each other is difficult but it is one of the most powerful things that can be done to build a more vital democracy. *Utne Magazine* has been in the business of promoting conversation for a long time. In 1991, we ran a cover story about living room conversation groups called "Salons and Beyond," on how to revive that ancient art of conversation and start a revolution in your living room. My father had been obsessed with the idea that conversation could bring about a revolution. Inside the issue, he put an ad that said if readers would like to meet other *Utne Magazine* readers in their neighborhood, send your information in to *Utne* and we'll match you up. We thought we might get a thousand or two responses but over eight thousand people responded. Within a year and a half we had twenty-five thousand people on our mailing list and six thousand groups meeting monthly around the country. To this day, the development of these discussion groups is something that *Utne Magazine* is most known for. At the same time, we started *Café Utne* because we wanted to foster online conversation over the developing Internet. Actually one of your members has been a long time participant in this effort and she is the reason I'm here with you today.

An example of a group that is doing it right is Let's Talk America. Let's Talk America is an initiative of the Utne Institute, which is a nonprofit organization we started in 2004. Let's Talk America aims to revive the spirit of democratic dialogue across political divides by teaching people how to host conversations of their own in living rooms, libraries, and church basements around the country. This organization also aims to model what civil dialogue looks like and to push the media to cover these dialogues. Over the course of 2004, over two hundred dialogues involving several thousand people were convened around the country. The project received coverage in dozens of local and national newspapers and magazines. We were a bit of a blip in *Time Magazine*'s election day cover story in which it was said that this idea might be one campfire short of a Kum Ba Yah but more power to us. The most remarkable experience I had with Let's Talk America happened in 2004 when we partnered with the Public Democracy America Project to bring together two dozen thought leaders to explore the potential to bridge political differences through dialogue. The participants included prominent liberals as well as conservatives from the American Conservative Union and the Christian Coalition. This weekend gathering worked better than anyone had dared hope as issues of shared concerns and perspectives repeatedly bubbled up. We did this by stepping back to the level of personal stories. Starting out not by talking about our differences but rather about things like what it means to be an American or what democracy means to you. Together we signed the "We the People Declaration" calling for further dialogue across the political divide. This document is available on http://letstalkamerica.org.

Another organization I'd like to mention is the Council for Excellence in Government that has held town meetings across the country to discuss security. In these meetings, officials such as Tom Ridge, then Director of the Office of Homeland Security, were brought to a meeting in order to listen to the ideas of people from all walks of life on how to make people feel more secure. Through these meetings, officials were able to hear a wide range of ideas for improving security and the document "Homeland Security from Citizens' Perspective" was created.

Another effort to bridge the political divide that I'm excited about is the BothAnd Project. The BothAnd Project is a joint initiative of the Mainstream Media Project and the Harvard Global Negotiation Project. Its goal is to promote voices that can represent a both/and perspective and get people to think beyond taking a side and demonizing the opposition. The organization has had a good deal of success in preparing people to speak to issues using this both/and approach and placing them on radio programs.

An effort that's underway that I've just learned about is the National Coalition for Dialogue and Deliberation. This group is working on a news service that would provide stories to reporters about people who are working for the promotion of civil dialogue.

Another group I have written about is the Co-Intelligence Institute. This organization is something of a one-man think tank lead by Tom Atlee who wrote the *Tao of Democracy*. This book is a compendium of case studies about people who are creating new, experimental ways of doing deliberative democracy. Many of these studies are based on jury systems that get people to represent the whole community rather than individual constituencies. In Denmark, for example, when new legislation is introduced on sensitive subjects, a jury of citizens is convened to hear from a variety of interests who would be affected by the legislation. After testimony and deliberation, the jury has to come up with a consensus on how Denmark should proceed with the issue. The consensus is built into a piece of legislation the Danish Parliament has to vote up or down. This is just one of the many remarkable experiments that the Co-Intelligence Institute has gathered information on.

Here's something you should all know about if you haven't already heard of it. It is the September Project which is based at the University of Washington. The September Project is an attempt to organize libraries to utilize the space available to them as a place for dialogue to happen. Libraries are neutral ground and are loved by people from across the political spectrum. The project provides a toolkit for how to organize dialogue in your library.

I'd like to end with a quote from Abraham Lincoln's first inaugural address in 1861:

> We are not enemies, but friends. We must not be enemies. Though passion may have strained it must not break our bonds of affection. The mystic chords of memory, stretching from every battlefield and patriot grave, to every living heart and hearthstone, all over this broad land, will yet swell the chorus of the Union, when again touched, as surely they will be, by the better angels of our nature.

So if we can appeal to the better angels of those in our media, and to the citizens of this democracy all across our country, then we might see a media portrayal of our country looking a little red here and a little blue there, but mostly a vast sea of purple.

QUESTIONS FROM THE AUDIENCE

Question: Can you speculate on why the Right feels they have a lock on loving our country or how they have persuaded so many that those that disagree with them do not?

LU: In times of war and strife, we tend to think of things in terms of black or white. It's always been the case that an appeal to patriotism is an easy button to push when advocating a military adventure or misadventure. When the war in Iraq was about to start, I put up an anti-war sign in my yard and an American flag because I wanted my neighbors to see that the flag wasn't just theirs.

Question: I want to know why the Right is angry. They control the White House, the Senate, the House, and increasingly the judiciary. I saw Ann Coulter recently at my university. She was disrespectful and very angry. Why are they so angry?

LU: I think it has a lot to do with the fact that the message of the political right, to use that tired left right terminology, doesn't challenge established power structures. So they are able to get away with a fairly hateful and angry message much of the time because the media likes the salaciousness of people screaming at one another. That's why *Crossfire* was on for so many years. Every once in a while something like the Jon Stewart incident comes along and people take notice. I don't know if you've heard this but *Crossfire* has been cancelled. The new head of CNN has done at least one thing right so far.

Question: I want to know what evidence you have found in your career that those under the age of eighteen years of age can think deeply about democratic issues. I think they certainly can communicate in ways that I cannot but I'm interested in the teenage democratic dialogue.

LU: Well, this is where I draw inspiration from the local library we have here which has an incredible collection of alternative press. There is an explosion of underground zines and youth publications out there that are showing what kids are doing to get involved and participate in our democracy. Whether they are organizing protests at the meetings of the IMF, the World Bank, or the Republican National Convention, which was one of the largest demonstrations in our country's history, the lion's share of the people at these demonstrations were between the ages of sixteen and twenty-five. Just the fact that they are showing up is a pretty strong sign that they are willing and interested in getting involved. What we don't see much of is people sitting down and having conversations with people they disagree with whether those people are fifty or fifteen years old. A lot of the reason for this is that we are not taught or shown how to have a conversation. My wife is from Europe and when we go to a dinner party there, people from all over the political spectrum discuss politics. People will wear their political views like a hat but at the end of the night they are all still friends. People don't identify so deeply with their political views and they are also taught to criti- cally think and debate issues in a way we are not taught in our schools. I think these skills of conversational literacy are critically important. The Let's Talk America project is basically a literacy campaign.

Question: I am liberal and frequently find myself in discussion with conservatives who see their viewpoints coming from a moral position. How do I discuss these issues with them without the conversation being angry?

LU: There is a wealth of information on letstalkamerica.org that ex- plains how to host a conversation. I think the key is really in the ques- tions that you ask. Ask questions to start a conversation that get people to step out of their political identities and step down to the level of per- sonal stories. If you have to, set some ground rules for the conversa- tion. One of the key ground rules is to seek to understand not to persuade. Being open to questioning your own assumptions and changing your mind can be the scariest part. I have found, speaking here as a liberal, that the people on the right are more open to real dia- logue and to understanding how I came to my ideas and opinions than are many to the left I have talked to. I think the key to civil dialogue is the questions that are asked. You'll find a bunch of suggested conversa- tion questions at letstalkamerica. org that don't polarize.

Question: I find myself wishing we had a parliamentary system where everyone from the so-called "far left" and so-called "far right" could meet and talk. I find the two party system does turn us into Tweedledee and Tweedledum and we're always trying to find a middle and when we don't find a middle we splinter off into the four corners. Does the European system provide a petri dish for a more civil discourse?

LU: I think so. I wrote a piece about the different concept of choice and freedom between Sweden and the United States. In Sweden, when I was there a few years ago, there may only have been a couple of differ- ent toilets available and only a few different breakfast cereals in the stores but there were nine political parties in Parliament. I think a pro- portional representation system that involves a more diverse group of voices in the government beyond Election Day is a better way to go. The different voices in a party coalition remain involved throughout the pe- riod of governing. I'd like to again mention Tom Atlee's work with the Co-Intelligence Institute. He spends so much time talking about juries and new democratic processes based on models that don't draw people as representatives from specific constituencies because that, inherently, whether you have a two-party system like we have here or a parliamentary system, turns everyone into a special interest. When you bring people together as representatives of the whole community it changes the way they think. It invokes the sense of "We the People" that the founders of this country had hoped the Congress would be, but it sure hasn't turned out that way. I would encourage you to look at alternatives like that.

CONTRIBUTORS' NOTES

Leif Utne is the Associate Editor of *Utne Magazine*. Paul Moeller is Serials Cataloger and the Religious Studies Bibliographer at University of Colorado at Boulder.

STRATEGY SESSIONS

Access to Scholarly Literature: Publishing for an Extended Readership

John Cox

Presenter

SUMMARY. Access to scholarship and research has become controversial. It is described in apocalyptic terms as "open"–or good and moral, or "toll-gated"–with the life-blood of the system ebbing away. The real world is more complex. Publishing is not a homogenous activity, because it reflects the varied needs of scholars. This article will be based on evidence from surveys and from published inquiries. It will pose, and attempt to answer, some questions about the future of publishing scholarly information, including open access, in the context of what publishers are actually doing. It will describe the challenge that faces publishers and librarians in meeting both scholarly and societal needs. *[Article copies available for a fee from The Haworth Document Delivery Service: 1-800-HAWORTH. E-mail address: <docdelivery@haworthpress.com> Website: <http://www.HaworthPress.com>]*

THE COMPLEXITY OF SCHOLARLY JOURNAL PUBLISHING

The issue of access to scholarly journals has become a matter of considerable controversy. Online access is now widely available. The old payment models are being challenged by many who feel information

[Haworth co-indexing entry note]: "Access to Scholarly Literature: Publishing for an Extended Readership." Cox, John. Co-published simultaneously in *The Serials Librarian* (The Haworth Information Press, an imprint of The Haworth Press, Inc.) Vol. 50, No. 1/2, 2006, pp. 49-67; and: *Roaring into Our 20's: NASIG 2005* (ed: Margaret Mering, and Elna Saxton) The Haworth Information Press, an imprint of The Haworth Press, Inc., 2006, pp. 49-67. Single or multiple copies of this article are available for a fee from The Haworth Document Delivery Service [1-800-HAWORTH, 9:00 a.m. - 5:00 p.m. (EST). E-mail address: getinfo@haworthpress.com].

should be free. While this situation may be regarded as an extension of the "serials crisis," the debate is conducted in apocalyptic terms as a battle between good and evil. Information can never be free. To produce online information that readers will find searchable, informative and convenient takes time, effort and investment. Publishing is not a homogenous activity, because it reflects the varied needs of scholars. This article addresses a number of issues that are relevant to the debate, including the legacy of historical development, the overall market for journals, the importance of journal quality and reputation, the expectations arising from the Internet, the role of aggregators, and open access publishing. It is based on evidence from surveys and from published inquiries.

FACING THE FUTURE BY UNDERSTANDING THE PAST

Modern scientific enquiry and the modern journal have their roots in the sixteenth and seventeenth centuries, during which mediaeval explanations of the natural world, inherited from classical Greece, were challenged. Previously, all changes of matter could be explained by the interaction of the four elements, Earth, Water, Air and Fire, as the "self-evident" principles of solidity, wetness, volatility and heat endlessly mixed and separated.

The Greeks had devised a complete taxonomy of nature based on these principles by 350 BC. For the next 1,200 years, it proved capable of answering most of the questions that could be addressed to it. It saw its duty as recording and organizing what was known rather than exploring the unknown.

In the late fifteenth and sixteenth centuries these principles were overthrown by:

- the discovery of America in 1492, discrediting ancient geography;
- Galileo, whose observations shook classical astronomy;
- William Harvey, who discovered in 1628 that the heart was a pump, and not a furnace.

All of these discoveries were physical discoveries. In the words of Sir Francis Bacon, one of the progenitors of the Royal Society, nature must be "put to the torture," and made to yield its reluctant secrets to the astute investigator, through rigorous experimentation.[1]

The Royal Society was formally set up in 1662, but had existed as an informal group of experimenters and thinkers. Its ethos was practical. Robert Boyle simply wanted to report the results of his experiments and frequently lamented the lack of "histories," or collections of experimental results and accurate observations. In 1665, the Royal Society Council voted to allow Henry Oldenburg to commence publication of *Philosophical Transactions*–as his own private venture–"the first Monday of every month, . . . licensed under the charter by the Council of the Society, being first reviewed by some of the members of the same."

Philosophical Transactions set out the criteria by which new discoveries could be reviewed and published as the "minutes of science":

- *Registration:* the establishment of the priority and ownership of research work by a particular author.
- *Evaluation:* certification: quality control through peer review and rejection, so that the better papers are published. Appearance of a paper in a particular journal stamps that paper and by implication rewards its author as being of the same quality level as the journal.
- *Dissemination:* the broadcasting of authors' claims to like-minded peers around the world through the channel that the journal represents.
- *Archiving:* the establishment of a permanent record in the scientific literature for the work that was undertaken.

Philosophical Transactions was just the start. From the late seventeenth century onwards there is a steady stream of complaints concerning the mounting volume of print material that readers had to cope with. The number of book titles published annually in Britain increased four- or five-fold in the following century. The increase in the number of journals and periodicals was even more precipitous.

Scientific journals tended to become more specialized over the course of time, and to restrict access to their pages to qualified contributors. This tendency was brought to completion in the nineteenth century, when specialized technical journals became the preferred vehicles for detailed accounts of scientific research. Disciplines and faculties were definitively compartmentalized and professionalized. The job title of "scientist" became common currency.

Why is this history important? The functions set out by the Royal Society three hundred years ago are fully embedded in the professional practice of research and do not seem to have changed over time. They are fundamental to scholarship and research. They continue to drive researchers' motivations to publish. Understanding where we have come from is important in order to prepare for where we are going.

THE ECOLOGY OF JOURNAL PUBLISHING

Scholarly and scientific publishing is a global business. In its *Information Content Industry Market Size, Share and Forecast 2000-2007* report, Outsell Inc. estimates that the total global content industry was worth 184 billion dollars in 2002; scientific, technical and medical (STM) publishing comprised 11 billion dollars, or six percent of the total content industry world-wide. Investment analyst J. P. Morgan estimates that the global market is worth 6 billion dollars, of which 4 billion dollars is scientific and technical information, and 2 billion dollars is medical.[2] These estimates ignore the humanities and social sciences, where journals are filling the vacuum left by the decline in monograph publishing. They need to be treated with caution, as the industry is fragmented and data is not systematically collected.

A very rough estimate is that scientific and medical journals make up about 5 to 6 billion dollars, with a further 2 billion dollars for other disciplines. Seventy percent of the market is academic, while twenty-five percent is corporate, and five percent is "other."[3] To put it in context, the journal market is smaller than the global market for stamp collectors, which Stanley Gibbons, the United Kingdom stamp dealer and publisher, estimates at 10 billion dollars!

Although journal publishing is dominated by a small number of large commercial publishers, it is in essence a cottage industry comprising a large number of small publishers. Over half the market is in the hands of thousands of small publishers. The market for journals is dominated by the United States. J. P. Morgan estimates that the United States accounts for fifty-eight percent of STM literature, Europe twenty-six percent and the rest of the world a mere sixteen percent.

Journals operate in a dysfunctional market. Price signals do not reach the customer. The reader may select but does not bear the cost of acquisition, while the library deploys the budget but is driven by readers' requirements. Library budgets have continued to deteriorate in relation to the volume of information they are expected to acquire.

In the twenty-five years following the Second World War, investment in scientific research–"Big Science"–was substantial. Commercial journal publishers became significant players. They were much more innovative in reacting to the resulting demand for scientific publishing capacity than the learned societies. At the same time, university education was rapidly expanding. The abundant resources for scientific research were matched by abundant funds for libraries collecting the resulting literature.

In the 1970s, disillusionment set in. Science began to be seen as failing to deliver. It failed to solve the oil crisis in 1973. It had failed to show how we could avoid ecological disaster. The popular regard for science had declined. Government support had been reduced. Nevertheless, research and development manpower has continued to grow in the last quarter century, at around three percent annually. Today, twice as many scientists are doing research as compared to 1975, publishing twice as many papers per year. Library budgets have increased by only forty percent during the same period.[4]

In the 1970s, library expenditure as a proportion of total university expenditure in the western world was running at four percent of total university expenditure. Since that time, that proportion has steadily declined. It is currently well below three percent. University libraries have undeniably not been successful in selling the value of the library to the university community at large, and the faculty in particular. Faculty have failed to support the one facility that provides them with the literature they need for scholarship and research.

QUALITY AND REPUTATION

Quality is seen to reside in society journals. Society journals come out very well in Thomson ISI's citation rankings. The proportion of society journals with high Impact Factors outweighs titles from commercial publishers. Impact Factor is the accepted objective measure of quality. ISI indexes 5,400 scientific, technical and medical journals and 2,200 journals in the humanities and social sciences, out of a total universe of 19,000 active peer-reviewed academic and scholarly journals.[5] Impact Factor measures the frequency with which an article in a journal is cited as a reference in articles published subsequently. It is the ratio between citations and citable items published in the past two years. This measurement is used to assess the overall quality of each publisher's journals in each broad discipline.

Although Impact Factors are the generally accepted measure of journal quality in the academic community, they must be treated with some caution. In reality, the citations that drive Impact Factors are dependent not only on the inherent quality of the article cited but also on usage. Usage is driven by effective marketing by the journal publisher, and by widespread accessibility. Online availability in publishers' Big Deals improves accessibility and is likely to drive up the likelihood of articles being cited.

Impact Factors also vary by discipline. Any comparison of the Impact Factors of publications in different disciplines will be wholly misleading, as author behavior and custom and practice in citing other literature varies widely. They are useful only as a comparative measure of citation performance, and therefore quality, between individual journals within one discipline, or between publishers within one discipline.

In a project I undertook in late 2004 for an investment bank, the rankings of each major publisher's titles were calculated versus the other publishers in each of eight subject pools. The distribution of the rankings was studied and the percentages of each publisher's ISI-ranked titles that fall into each quartile were plotted. The following charts (Figures 1-3) show the number of titles indexed by ISI for each publisher featured in this study, and the proportion of each publisher's list currently indexed.

FIGURE 1. Number of ISI Ranked Titles for Each Publisher Studied

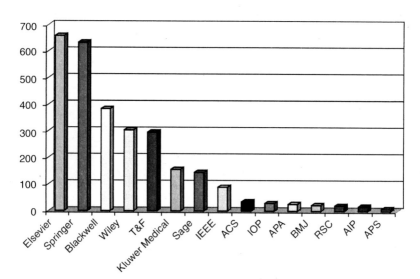

FIGURE 2. Percentage of Published Titles Indexed by ISI Citation Indices

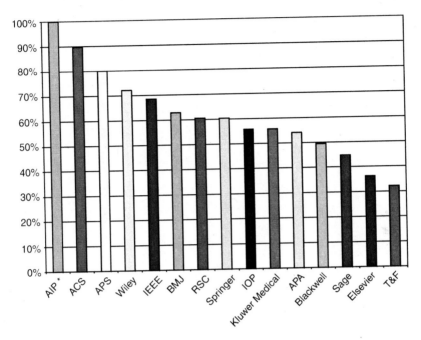

The specialist societies (American Institute of Physics, American Chemical Society, American Physical Society, IEEE, British Medical Journal, Royal Society of Chemistry, Institute of Physics and American Psychological Association) publish only in their specialist discipline, and publish fewer titles than the commercial publishers. They generally lead the field in their respective disciplines, and have a higher proportion of their titles indexed by ISI.

Wiley is particularly well indexed by ISI; this could be that their content is generally considered better, or that they are less aggressive in launching new titles which are therefore not yet covered by ISI.

Two subject examples illustrate the point.

Medicine

Wiley's overall Impact Factor in medicine is very high. It is ahead even of BMJ, a specialist non-profit medical society publisher. Its forty-eight indexed titles are more highly ranked than Elsevier's considerably larger list.

FIGURE 3. Percentage of Publishers' Titles Falling in Quartiles of Citation Rankings for Medicine

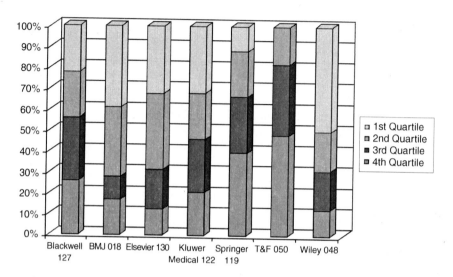

Kluwer Medical includes both the Lippincott Williams & Wilkins and Adis lists. The Adis list contains a high proportion of review journals. Review journals report on and review the latest important research published in the primary research journals, rather than publish the primary research papers themselves, which attract high citation levels.

Materials Science

Materials science journals are relatively few in number, compared with other scientific disciplines. The discipline is also notable for the absence of a dominant society. The specialist materials science society publishers have small lists. Elsevier and Springer dominate, as Wiley publishes only six titles, and SAGE, principally a publisher in the social sciences, has a small materials science journal program based in London.

Impact Factors have been compared in this report over the two-year period from 2001 to 2003. Within that period, trends in Impact Factors can be observed–which publishers are improving, and which are falling back. The following graph illustrates these trends (see Figure 4).

FIGURE 4. Percentage of Publishers' Titles Falling in Quartiles of Citation Rankings for Materials Science

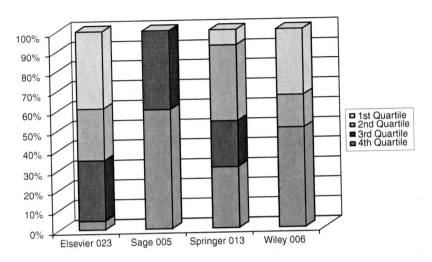

Since a general industry trend is to increased impact factor, no particular value should be attached to a rise for any particular publisher. The relative rises in Impact Factor between the commercial publishers is probably most significant, with Elsevier outperforming (in improvement terms) Springer and Blackwell. As can be seen, broad generalizations can be misleading.

TECHNOLOGY, EXPECTATIONS AND OPPORTUNITIES

The market for journals has been changed fundamentally by the adoption of online distribution of scientific journals by many publishers from the mid-1990s onwards. The benefits of online distribution are numerous, all of which improve the accessibility of published scientific research:

- Speed of delivery has been improved.
- Accessibility is regardless of location or time of day.
- Searching for and locating information has been transformed by the functionality of the technology, links to articles cited, and links to databases and other resources.

- The growing availability of usage data on journals, now based on international standards, provides hard evidence on which selection and acquisition decisions can be made.
- Overall access to journals has improved, as library consortia and major publishers have negotiated "Big Deals" by which all libraries within a consortium have online access to all of the publisher's output.

The benefits and disadvantages of the "Big Deal" lie outside the scope of this article, but the following evidence is an important indicator of where we are going.

The early anecdotal evidence, from organizations such as Ohio-LINK, the University of Toronto, the University of Warwick in the United Kingdom and Macquarie, Sydney and Australian National University in Australia, is that, where a package of journals is opened up to users, usage does not mirror what has actually been purchased by the library. OhioLINK has found, on the basis of usage over three years, that the fiscal difficulties that have been encountered by OhioLINK and others that have led to a partial retreat from the "all-in" deal does not detract from the attractiveness of buying in bulk:

- Eighty-five percent of usage came from forty percent of the titles available online via OhioLINK.

- Fifty-two percent of usage was from titles not previously held on subscription at the user's campus. At Ohio State, with a huge collection, the figure was thirty percent.[6]

However, many librarians contest the efficacy of offering large collections of journals to their readers that include many titles that would never have been held otherwise. In 2004, I conducted a survey of some fifteen academic librarians in the United Kingdom and the USA for a publisher client. I was struck by the explicit desire to return to individual title selection to more accurately reflect the needs of faculty and of research.

The other consequence of the Big Deal has been to put at risk smaller journal publishers by potentially excluding them from consortia purchases. The possible marginalization of such smaller publishers is a concern shared not only by the publishers themselves but also by academic libraries worried about the sustainability of important titles. A number of initiatives that are attempting to compete with such deals by forming coalitions of small publishers (e.g., Association of Learned and Professional Society Publishers' Learned Journal Collection, Project MUSE and BioOne.

On the customer side, a notable feature of the market has been the development of library consortia, in which libraries have pooled their resources and use their combined buying power to negotiate better deals from publishers. In my consultancy practice, the development of library consortia is important. Over 240 worldwide consortia actively buy scientific literature for their constituent libraries.

HOW ARE PUBLISHERS RESPONDING?

In 2003 I undertook a survey for the Association of Learned and Professional Society Publishers (ALPSP) of publishing practice of a cross-section of journal publishers in the United Kingdom, Europe, the United States/Canada and Asia.[7] Of the 275 publishers surveyed, which included all the major commercial and society journal publishers whose output dominates the acquisitions of most academic libraries, sixty-six percent responded, and their responses were analyzed. In relation to pricing and accessibility, the following practices were reported:

- Seventy-five percent of journals are available online; eighty-three percent of STM titles are online.
- Society publishers offer "bundles" of journals comprising the complete list more frequently than commercial publishers. Many, by definition, publish only in one subject. A significant number of commercial publishers offer subject bundles or sub-sets of their lists.
- Thirty-four percent of publishers allow the customer to select the titles they want, and then base the consortium offer on that aggregate selection.
- Most publishers provide active subscribers with access to the back volumes available online at no extra cost. Many small not-for-profit organizations make their journal archives freely available to non-subscribers once a set period after publication has elapsed.

ALPSP plans to repeat this survey to track significant changes in publishers' policy and practice, and to research their practice on issues such as open access and the growing significance of aggregators.

AGGREGATORS AND SUBSCRIPTIONS

For publishers, aggregated databases provide a means of reaching new markets and generating additional revenue:

- Institutions that will not normally maintain journal collections for primary research, but which can make good use of journal literature: four- and two-year institutions, public libraries, and schools;
- Universities with the need to provide for undergraduate teaching as well as research. A good deal of evidence–from libraries themselves, from the increased use of course packs and electronic reserve to support teaching, and from permissions facilitators such as HERON and Copyright Clearance Center–shows journals are increasingly in use in undergraduate courses.
- Under-funded markets that would normally not be able to subscribe to the primary journal. This applies to institutions where library budgets do not allow for truly comprehensive journal collections, and, particularly, in the rapidly developing economies of Eastern Europe. EBSCO Publishing's products have achieved substantial penetration of markets in Eastern Europe, where their initial acquisition was underwritten by the Soros Foundation.

As a consequence, aggregated databases extend readership. They serve the mission of many learned societies to improve awareness of the disciplines that they support.

In 2004, the conventional hypothesis that journals and aggregations are different and complementary was tested in telephone interviews with nine universities in the United Kingdom and Europe, and fourteen universities and similar higher education institutions in the United States, selected to be broadly representative of size and geographical spread. A remarkable consistency in librarians' view emerged.[8] The usage of journals clearly was primarily for research. In Europe, usage was sixty percent for research and forty percent for teaching. In the United States, the respective proportions were seventy percent for research and thirty percent for teaching. Comments made during the interviews by a number of librarians suggested that the use of journal content in teaching undergraduates is increasing as more becomes available online. Aggregated databases are used for both teaching and research which included Masters courses. In the United States, their use for undergraduate teaching predominates at fifty-six percent. In the United Kingdom and Europe, their use was more evenly split, with teaching at forty-nine percent. And finally, the majority of the librarians interviewed clearly stated that they viewed primary journals and aggregations of full text journal literature as essentially complementary:

- The primary journal has authenticity and completeness;
- The embargo in aggregated databases is a significant irritant and an important factor in persuading libraries to maintain journal subscriptions;
- In smaller, less well funded institutions, finance is a major driver which forces use of aggregations as the principal source of journal content if a full journal collection cannot be maintained;
- Aggregated databases cause cataloging problems for many libraries, and involve significant set-up work in establishing links with the OPAC, despite the availability of searching and linking tools.

Only two out of twenty-three librarians indicated that they would consider coverage in an aggregation as a substitute for a primary journal. The variability of content in aggregated databases was cited as a serious issue by seven out of the nine United Kingdom and European libraries interviewed, and by all fourteen United States libraries.

OPEN ACCESS

Is Open Access a rational response to the continuing inability of libraries to maintain complete and coherent journal collections? The concept of scientific information being freely available to everyone is a seductive one.

It describes a variety of publishing models driven by a desire for unfettered availability online to peer-reviewed research papers on publication. It involves a transition from the current subscription-based business model to a model where the financial burden falls on the author or his agent in the form of the university or research funding agency. Given that journal publishing serves the needs of authors, it would make sense to organize a publishing system where the burden of financing the process falls on the author rather than the reader. We do not have the luxury of designing a process from scratch. We have an existing system that has worked reasonably well for over three hundred years.

The publishing models fall into two general categories, the Open Access journal model and the Open Archive model, in which papers are posted to subject-based or institutional repositories.

The Open Access Journal Model

Access to the journal is entirely free online worldwide. Revenue is generated in one, or both, of two ways. Either the author's institution or research grant pays a publication fee, upon acceptance of the article, to cover the article selection process, peer-review, production and online publication, or institutions pay an annual membership fee to the Open Access journal, which allows an unlimited number of articles accepted for publication from authors at that institution.

The Open Access journal is, as yet, unproven. Its business model has yet to be shown to be sustainable. The enthusiasts for open access tend to describe its advantages in quasi-religious terms rather than in objective systemic and organizational terms, which makes a rational discussion on objective criteria somewhat difficult.

Open Access journals form a very small part of current scientific journal literature: 897 out of 19,310 active English-language peer-reviewed titles.[9] The Directory of Open Access Journals[10] lists 1,554 titles, comprising 72,878 articles; but some of those titles appear to be moribund. Moreover, an analysis reveals that eighty-six percent are either funded by grants, or are free online versions of subscription-based journals. Only fourteen percent are based on the author-pays model, of which two-thirds are published by two organizations: BioMed Central and Public Library of Science. In 2004, author paid articles published comprised 3,000 articles, or less than a quarter percent of the 1.2 million articles published annually.[11]

University league tables, research assessment audits and individual reward systems mean that authors, and their institutions, are reinforced in their desire to publish papers in the most prestigious journals–with high impact factors. The reward system is a significant disincentive to trying a new journal, open access or otherwise. A difficult proposition is to persuade an author to submit a paper to an unproven Open Access title and pay for the privilege, instead of an established high-impact journal that will publish the paper at no charge to the author. Furthermore, three issues must be addressed in judging whether a transition to open access journals will serve the scientific community well:

- At present, non-academic purchases comprise some twenty-five percent of journal revenues–corporate, government and other non-academic libraries–while non-academic authors are much less significant as a proportion of total authorship. If open access journals establish themselves, these libraries will access the literature free of charge. The academic community will have to bear almost the entire burden of financing the publishing cycle.

- Many learned societies depend on publishing revenues to finance other member activities. Open access has the potential to undermine the financial underpinning of most learned society activities.
- Much of the information infrastructure that publishers and librarians have developed over many years will remain necessary so that the literature emanating from a fragmented publishing industry can be indexed, navigated, searched, accessed and linked together in an effective information service.

In 2004, two reports were published that examined aspects of the efficacy of Open Access journals. The first was a report on author perceptions from CIBER, the Centre for Information Behaviour and the Evaluation of Research at City University in London.[12] E-mails were sent to 91,500 senior authors who had published in an ISI-indexed journal over the past eighteen months, inviting them to complete a Web-enabled questionnaire. The survey yielded 3,787 fully completed responses from ninety-seven countries and from every major discipline in the sciences and social sciences–a respectable response rate of four percent.

The report revealed that:

- Authors' reasons for publishing remain the same. Communication to their peers (rather than communication to the public) is the principal driver. This reason is reinforced by the institutional pressure to publish where most beneficial to the Research Assessment Exercise (RAE). This finding echoes what was published in a survey by ALPSP in the United Kingdom in 1999;[13]
- Only one in twenty feel they know much about Open Access;
- Most feel that access to the literature has improved in recent years, due to online availability;
- Fewer than one in five had published in any Open Access form, but the general feeling was that Open Access would enhance accessibility and mean fewer papers will be rejected;
- The least resistant to Open Access are authors in the life and earth sciences, while the most negative are in pharmacology, chemistry and engineering;
- Open access advocates maintain that research grants should include funds for publication. Thirty-five percent of United Kingdom-authored bio-medical papers have no external funding acknowledged, twenty-seven percent have one funding agency,

and thirty-eight percent have more than one. Attaching publication fees to funding will be ferociously complicated!

The second report was a White Paper published by ISI in 2004, examining the impact factors achieved by the Open Access journals already indexed by it.[14] ISI indexes a total of 7,800 journals. By June 2004, it had selected 239 Open Access titles, representing twenty percent of all Open Access journals, though they themselves represent only about two percent of the total literature. Open Access journals tend to be at the lower end of citation rankings, but that the percentage varies between disciplines. ISI found little to distinguish Open Access from conventional titles, except that the peak for citations occurs somewhat sooner after publication in the case of Open Access. Far more important is online accessibility–the online "Big Deal" looks "open" to the researcher at the desktop.

The Open Archive Model

Open archives appear in a number of guises. Authors simply post their articles as accepted for publication to their personal Web pages, they post them to an institutional depository, or they post them to an open depository established to cover a specific discipline.

The Open Archive model shows more promise, even though they have received much less publicity and comment than Open Access journals. Most journal publishers allow authors to post their papers to the institutional repository. The ISI report indicated that sixty-five percent of articles published in conventional journals indexed by ISI are openly accessible via self-archiving in subject-based or institutional repositories. This percentage is a significant segment of the published literature, and appears to complement existing publishing practice. The longer-term impact of the Open Archive on subscriptions remains to be seen, although most publishers appear to be relaxed over any impact on their future businesses. That is as true of Elsevier as it is true of university presses and societies.

The Institutional Archives Registry[15] lists a current total of 413 OAI-compliant Open Access Archives in universities and research institutes in over forty countries. But it has to be said that, after the very considerable publicity given to Open Access, extending well beyond the academic and research communities, this still represents only ten percent of the 4,000 universities and research institutes worldwide that journal publishers regard as their core market.

Moreover, uncertainty exists over the important issue of version control. The author's version of a paper has no status until it is published; the published version is definitive. This not only applies in the academy, but is also embedded in processes that apply research in the community. Drug regulators will not accept as evidence in support of a drug approval application anything other than the published version of a paper. The same applies to patent applications.

In the longer term, the Open Archive may be more subversive of the published journal than the Open Access journal. But they will have to become more like publishing entities and operate professionally and in a businesslike manner. Universities do not have an unblemished record in running publishing operations. The number of university presses that have become major players in publishing can be counted on the fingers of one hand. Some skepticism must exist about the proposition that with institutional repositories anything will be different.

ONE VIEW OF THE FUTURE

Where do we go with the journal in the future? Authors surveyed by ALPSP in 1999 publish because they want to communicate with their peers.[16] This reason remained true in CIBER's more recent and extensive survey. Speed of publication emerged as the most important factor in achieving their objectives. Other factors included publishing in journals with the highest impact factor in the field, quality of peer review and retrievability through abstracting and indexing services. The perceived reputation of the journal is a key driver of the decision where to publish, in all disciplines. Electronic availability was more important in the sciences than in the arts.

So the journal is still a "brand" of significance to authors. But what about readers? As online searching has become the norm, readers want to identify information of relevance at the article level. Whether this need can increasingly be satisfied by subject-based or institutional repositories remains to be seen. Universities do not have an unblemished record in publishing and the institutional repository is a publishing vehicle. Nevertheless, the prevailing complacency of most publishers about their authors posting papers to such repositories is most unwise. An underlying threat is that the academy could take back the scholarly communication and reporting process to itself and displace the industry to which this activity has been assigned for the past 300 years.

Authors still believe that the perceived reputation of the journal in which the article appears is a clear indicator of the quality of the content and the authority it confers on papers accepted for publication in it. That imprimatur of quality is important to authors, to their institutions and to readers searching for authoritative scholarship. The academic reward system at the institutional level, through the RAE, and at the individual level, through promotion and research fund awards, both reinforce the existing paradigm and inhibit the development of new journals and of communications structures. All the evidence suggests that authors' requirements and interests have not changed, and their behavior remains as it was.

The principal problem with the present system is economic. Collective purchasing by library consortia has developed in the last decade as a significant change in the way publishers and libraries do business. The business model on which journal publishing is based is one in which the reader pays, or his or her agent, the library. This continues to govern ninety-nine percent of scholarly publishing. Open Access journals will continue, but this effort is likely to be largely confined to bio-medical disciplines where research is grant-funded. The development of institutional repositories is more uncertain. The National Institutes of Health is encouraging any author whose research it funded to deposit the resulting paper in PubMed Central, a large life sciences repository in the United States, within twelve months of publication. NIH funds some twenty-five percent of United States biomedical research, and the United States represents thirty percent of world research activity in this area. In other words, NIH sponsors eight percent of world activity. This is not insignificant. The Wellcome Trust, a major United Kingdom life sciences research funder, is adopting the same policy and plans to establish a European "PubMed Central."

I believe that we will continue with a mixed economy for the foreseeable future. The impact on conventional publishing will be to act as a spur to greater efficiency. Publishers have neither explained the value that they have added to the journal publishing process nor have they kept their costs or prices as keen as they should. The value of the Open Access debate lies in its warning to the publishing industry that its value is not perceived to justify the prices, or the profitability many publishers enjoy.

There is an analogy in the airline industry. Low cost carriers like Virgin Blue, Ryanair and SouthWest have re-engineered the way they undertake the business of transporting people, and have put the legacy airlines like Qantas, British Airways and United under threat of extinction. If publishers do not change, and review and reform their publishing operations, they may be as much under threat as the airline industry.

NOTES

1. Allan Chapman, "England's Leonardo: Robert Hooke (1635-1703) and the art of experiment in Restoration England," *Proceedings of the Royal Institution of Great Britain*, 67 (1996) 239-275.
2. J. P. Morgan European Equity Research, *Scientific and Medical Publishing* (London, 2003).
3. Ibid.
4. C. Tenopir & D. W. Kind, "Trends in Scientific Scholarly Journal Publishing in the United States," *Journal of Scholarly Publishing* 28 (1997) 3.
5. *Ulrich's Periodicals Directory.* http://www.ulrichsweb.com (13 May 2005).
6. T. Sanville, *A Method out of the Madness: OhioLINK's Collaborative response to the Serials Crisis–a Progress Report*, UK Serials Group Conference, April 2001.
7. J. Cox & L. Cox, *Scholarly Publishing Practice (ALPSP 2003)*.
8. J. Cox, *Impact of Aggregated Databases on Primary Journals in the Academic Library Market and a Review of Publisher Practice* (ALPSP 2004).
9. *Ulrich's Periodicals Directory.* http://www.ulrichsweb.com (13 May 2005).
10. *Directory of Open Access Journals.* http://www.doaj.org (13 May 2005).
11. K. Hunter, "Critical Issues in the Development of STM Journal Publishing," *Learned Publishing* 18:1, 51-55.
12. D. Nicholas, I. Rowlands & P. Huntington, *Scholarly Communication in the digital environment: What do authors really want?* (CIBER, City University, London, 2004).
13. Alma Swan & Sheridan Brown, *What Authors Want* (Association of Learned and Professional Society Publishers, 1999).
14. M. McVeigh, *Open Access Journals in the ISI Citation Databases: Analysis of Impact Factors and Citation Patterns*, 2004. http://www.isinet.com/media/presentrep/essayspdf/openaccesscitations2.pdf
15. http://archives.eprints.org/eprints.php?action=browse (13 May 2005, 07 Nov. 2005, temporarily unavailable).
16. Alma Swan, Ibid.

CONTRIBUTOR'S NOTE

John Cox is Managing Director of John Cox Associates Ltd., which specializes in scholarly and research publishing.

Identifiers in Libraries:
ISSN Revision Unique

Regina Romano Reynolds

Presenter

SUMMARY. The world of unique identifiers can sometimes seem like an alphabet soup: SICIs, PIIs, ISSNs, DOIs, ISTCs, InfoURIs, and more. These standards will be explored, and questions raised related to unique identifiers as crucial keys to the new library environment, where information sharing requires the increased precision in identification and linking that can only come from development and use of unique identifiers. How do we uniquely identify a library or branches within a system? What about journals, articles within journals, books, chapters, component and other parts? Existing identifiers such as NUC symbols, ISBN, and ISSN are imprecise and may be inadequate in an age of machine parsing and processing. New identifiers are needed, and there are opportunities for library involvement and advocacy. *[Article copies available for a fee from The Haworth Document Delivery Service: 1-800-HAWORTH. E-mail address: <docdelivery@haworthpress.com> Website: <http://www.HaworthPress. com>]*

UPDATING AN ICON

With the advent of the digital era, unique identifiers have proliferated and have also taken on new uses and new importance. The world of

[Haworth co-indexing entry note]: "Identifiers in Libraries: ISSN Revision Unique." Reynolds, Regina Romano. Co-published simultaneously in *The Serials Librarian* (The Haworth Information Press, an imprint of The Haworth Press, Inc.) Vol. 50, No. 1/2, 2006, pp. 69-81; and: *Roaring into Our 20's: NASIG 2005* (ed: Margaret Mering, and Elna Saxton) The Haworth Information Press, an imprint of The Haworth Press, Inc., 2006, pp. 69-81. Single or multiple copies of this article are available for a fee from The Haworth Document Delivery Service [1-800-HAWORTH, 9:00 a.m. - 5:00 p.m. (EST). E-mail address: getinfo@haworthpress.com].

Available online at http://www.haworthpress.com/web/SER
doi:10.1300/J123v50n01_08

identifiers has become a veritable alphabet soup: DOI, URN, SICI, InfoURI, ARC, etc., including, of course, familiar and venerable identifiers such as the ISBN and ISSN. Are such so-called "legacy" identifiers still useful in the current environment? Have these identifiers kept pace with new forms of resources, and can these identifiers meet the new needs that have emerged in the digital environment? This presentation will explore the challenges facing the ISSN and how ISSN Network and the ISO Working Group revising the ISSN standard are working to meet those challenges.

What are the main challenges facing the ISSN? The first challenge—and in some ways the most difficult to solve—is also the most basic: What does the ISSN identify? In the late 1960s and early 1970s, when the ISSN was conceived and implemented, serials were fairly easy to identify and generally available in only one form, print on paper, so the question of what the ISSN should identify did not often arise. However, the digital environment has spawned new forms of resources as well as increasing the phenomenon of resources issued in multiple formats. Which new formats should be assigned ISSN, and how many ISSN should be assigned? Ever since the decision to assign separate ISSN to print, CD-ROM, and online versions of serials was made in the early 1980s, tension has existed between those user needs best met with a single ISSN per serial and those user needs best met with separate ISSN for each media version of a serial. The concern expressed by some that certain serials have too many ISSN contrasts with the concern expressed by others that too many serials have no ISSN! Finally, helping ISSN users to find and identify the correct ISSN for a given serial is an ongoing challenge, but one that has to be met if the ISSN is to remain a viable identifier for the future.

In 2003, when the current ISSN standard, ISO 3297, came up for what has been usually a routine 5-year International Organization for Standardization vote and affirmation, both the ISSN Network and the majority of ISO SC9 voting members favored revision of the standard. The ISSN Network had already agreed that ISSN should be assigned to the full range of "continuing resources" defined in revised Chapter 12 of AACR2, ISBD(CR), and the new *ISSN Manual*. Thus the ISSN standard needed to be updated to include this enlarged scope of resources that are eligible for ISSN. Additionally, many of the comments received during the voting mentioned some of the specific challenges noted above, particularly resolution of the questions about ISSN for resources issued in multiple media versions. Accordingly, ISO SC 9's Working Group 5 on the Revision of the ISSN Standard was established.

In between acknowledging the need for the ISSN standard to be updated and achieving that goal hangs the enormous question: "How do you update an icon?" Going back to the soup analogy, one could compare updating the ISSN to updating Campbell's soup, a staple of American cupboards for over one hundred years. During the ISSN's more than 30-year history, the ISSN has come to mean many things to many people. The ISSN is used by libraries, publishers, subscription agencies, abstracting and indexing services, union catalogs, newspaper and newsstand distributors, database producers, publications access management companies, digitizers, and many more. Some use a single ISSN to stand for a title, others use separate ISSN, still others group all ISSN any way associated with a serial. The answer to the question, "How do you update an icon?" could only be: "Very carefully!"

BACKGROUND

Before looking more closely at new uses for the ISSN in the electronic environment, some basic information about the ISSN will lay the groundwork. The ISSN is the premiere identifier for serials and, more recently, for other continuing resources, such as updating databases and updating Web sites. The ISSN uniquely identifies a continuing resource and distinguishes that resource from other resources with the same or similar titles. The ISSN is the numerical equivalent of the key title, a unique form of the resource's title. ISSN are assigned by seventy-seven ISSN national centers worldwide, and by the ISSN International Centre, located in Paris, France, which assigns ISSN to resources published by international bodies and to resources from countries with no ISSN centers. The ISSN International Centre also coordinates the ISSN Network, provides training and documentation to ISSN centers, and manages the ISSN Register, the official database of ISSN records. All continuing resources (that is, all serials and all ongoing integrating resources) are eligible for ISSN, with separate ISSN being assigned to each generic form in which a resource is published. For example, a serial issued in print, CD-ROM and online versions is assigned three ISSN. The ISSN assignment process requires that a cataloger perform title authority work to uniquely identify the resource, assign a key title and abbreviated key title, identify any relationships the resource might have to earlier and later titles, or to geographic, format, or language editions, and create a metadata record to document this information for the ISSN Register.

NEW ROLES FOR THE ISSN

In addition to the challenge of how to update an icon, the ISSN revision Working Group has to keep in mind the answers to the question: "Why update an icon?" Just as Campbell's has had to find new ways to package and deliver its soups to fit the current fast and portable food environment, so must the ISSN be updated to meet the needs of the current electronic environment. This environment has resulted in numerous new roles for the ISSN, roles that can be filled better by a revised and revitalized ISSN. Certainly, the ISSN continues to be central to the searching and identification of serials in OPACS, and to quick and unambiguous access to purchase and check-in records in integrated library systems. Increasingly, serials management includes interactions with publications access management companies (e.g., Serials Solutions or TDNet); ONIX transactions; and identification; file-matching, and deduplication in knowledge bases underlying Electronic Resource Management Systems and OpenURL resolvers; all of which involve situations where the ISSN has a major role to play.

In times of shrinking library budgets and growing numbers of resources to manage, libraries are being challenged to focus on the most basic tasks, and surely one of the most basic library tasks is connecting library users to the timely, valuable and expensive content represented by packages or aggregations of journals. Unfortunately for library budgets, not only is licensing this content expensive, but providing access to it has also proved to be more expensive than might have been anticipated. To lead a student, from a citation to an online article, the library has to be prepared to answer many questions, for all packages and all journals within packages: Does the library subscribe to this journal? In which aggregation(s) or package(s) can this journal be found? Which aggregations or packages contain the volume and issue in which this article appears? If the library does not have this article in online form, does the library have the article in its print collection? These questions are not easy for a library to answer, especially for those packages where the titles and dates of coverage of the respective titles are difficult to determine and frequently in flux. What's a library to do? Enter OpenURL and link resolution.

First, exactly what is OpenURL and how does link resolution work? OpenURL is a mechanism to achieve context-sensitive linking by packaging metadata describing a publication of interest to a user, along with other context information about the user or institution, into a URL (the "OpenURL"). The OpenURL is sent to a link resolver, a system that can interpret OpenURLs by taking into account local holdings and access privileges of the user's institution, and display links to appropriate resources (e.g., links to products to which the institution subscribes. For example, full text of an article that a student has discovered via a citation in an A&I database. Link resolution software, such as that used by SFX and other link resolvers, resolves OpenURL requests by (1) identifying the bibliographic elements of an OpenURL–especially the ISSN; (2) comparing those elements to institution-specific resolution tables; and (3) identifying the most appropriate "services" to present to a user. ISSN is a crucial part of the metadata identifying the desired article that the SFX server sends to the knowledge base. Link resolution is having a huge impact on the need for and use of ISSN in the electronic environment.

Of critical importance for any standard, and particularly for the ISSN revision process, is that the standard support interoperability, that is, the ability to operate within various environments and with various other identifiers and systems. Many essential and complex tasks are enabled by the interoperability of the ISSN. Importing and exporting data, such as takes place during exchanges among libraries, PAMS, A&I services, and others is made simpler and more accurate when ISSN identify all of the resources, and even better when ISSN is used as part of ONIX transactions. Database management tasks such as record merging, matching, and de-duplication in support of OPACs, and, increasingly Electronic Resource Management Systems (ERMS) are all facilitated when records contain ISSN. Migrating to new systems presents particular challenges of this nature. Finally, linking of all types within and among systems is often impossible without standard numbers, which for serials means ISSN. In addition to its use in OpenURL resolution described above, the ISSN is central to reference linking such as CrossRef provides, it is instrumental in "hooks-to-holdings" links from databases to the OPAC, and use of ISSN also allows linking from the OPAC to external files.

In revising the ISSN standard, the Working Group has kept clearly in mind the need to maintain the interoperability of the current ISSN with long-standing systems and users such as OPACs, union catalogs, newspaper or magazine subscription service databases, and A&I databases, while at the same time re-tooling the ISSN to improve its interoperability with emerging standards and systems such as OpenURL, ONIX for serials, PAMS databases, and link resolver knowledge bases. Just as Campbell's has gone about updating its iconic soups very carefully by adding new packages and flavors rather than removing old standbys, the ISSN Working Group is also trying to maintain the "classic" ISSN while updating the standard to provide for new uses in the current environment. Thus, a decision was made to make as few changes as possible in the basic format and meaning of the ISSN, to ensure functionality with the past, to respect usages of varied constituencies (e.g., library community, EAN community) and to make the benefits of any changes worth the cost of those changes.

THE REVISION PROCESS

Keenly aware of the above revision challenges, ISO SC9's Working Group 5, formally titled "Revising the International Standard Serial Number, ISO 3297," began work in January 2004 in Paris. The group is made up of representatives from national standards groups and, of great importance to the future success of the revised standard, the group is made up of representatives from all of the major ISSN user communities. Scholarly publishers, magazine and newspaper publishers, national libraries and national ISSN centers, subscription agencies, participants in related standards such as the ISBN, ISSN users such as CrossRef and the DOI are all represented on ISO SC9 Working Group 5. Of course, the variety of ISSN users and user needs represented on the Working Group has resulted in occasional conflicting opinions and potential impasses. However, each time such challenges have arisen, they have been resolved. The hope is that the result of resolving these conflicts will ultimately be a better standard.

The principal task of the working group is, of course, the revision of the ISSN standard, ISO 3297, itself. The areas of the standard that have been identified for specific revision are: updating the scope of the standard to cover all continuing resources, updating the ISSN assignment policy to provide for identification at multiple levels of granularity, and updating the ISSN Network's administrative organization to provide for an ISSN user group. Additionally, the Working Group recognized that the revised standard would be more effective if it were accompanied by new ISSN data distribution and look-up services, for which the Working Group is making recommendations. Two final tasks of the Working Group are the preparation of a background document to accompany the revised standard when it goes to ISO voting members, and planning for publicizing the revised standard, in particular, communicating and clarifying to the ISSN user community exactly what the ISSN identifies and how the new provisions in the revised ISSN standard should be used.

Clarifying and updating the scope of the ISSN is one of the ongoing issues raised during the revision process. The Working Group readily agreed that the scope of the present standard–serials–should be enlarged to cover those continuing resources that are not serials, that is, resources such as updating databases and updating Web sites. These "ongoing integrating resources" are the form which some print serials are taking in the electronic environment. All in the Working Group also easily agreed on the principle that comprehensive coverage of serials was a desirable goal and that coverage of updating databases and, especially, updating Web sites had to be more selective. However, the question of whether the standard should specify types of serials and types of other continuing resources not eligible for ISSN was a more difficult one to resolve. For example, calendars might seem to fit the definition of "serial," since they are published annually and carry a date designation. However, many ISSN centers do not feel calendars–especially those without any text–are appropriate for ISSN assignments. In the electronic realm, the question of whether to register personal blogs with ISSN has become a very contentious one between some bloggers and their respective ISSN centers. Because of these concerns, as well as issues relating to the scope of national bibliographies and the staffing of ISSN centers, some strong arguments were made for determining and listing in the standard categories of resources not eligible for ISSN (a similar list appears as an Annex in the ISBN standard). However, ultimately, the decision was made that the scope expressed in the revised ISSN standard should be as broad as possible to give the most flexibility, and the most "future-proofing." More specific information on exclusions–such as the exclusion of personal Web pages and personal blogs–will be given in the *ISSN Manual* and on the ISSN International Centre's Website.

ISSN ASSIGNMENT POLICY

The challenge of determining the scope of the ISSN paled in comparison to the challenge presented by determining the assignment policy for resources issued in multiple manifestations, particularly print and online versions of the same resource. Even before the Working Group began, strong opinions were being expressed both in favor of one ISSN being assigned to all manifestation of a resource and against any change to the existing policy of assigning separate ISSN to each manifestation. Additionally, some publishers were not applying for separate ISSN, some A&I services were using only one ISSN, and that some ISSN centers were uncertain about how to carry out and enforce the existing policy. Clearly, the Working Group had to come up with a solution for the revised standard!

Following its first meeting, the Working Group decided to survey the various ISSN user communities to better understand their needs and preferences regarding changing the ISSN assignment policy. A choice of scenarios was presented, including keeping the status quo and changing the ISSN to a title-level identifier. The results of the survey and of further discussions within the Working Group showed a need for identification at both the manifestation level–a level which can also be thought of as a broadly defined "product" level–as well as a need for identification at a higher level of granularity which can be thought of as a "title" level. These two needs were not much of a surprise to the members of the Working Group. However, they were surprised that the preferences for a higher or lower level of granularity for the ISSN did not group clearly along the lines of user communities. For example, within libraries, those involved in ordering and claiming serials preferred separate manifestation ISSN, while those implementing one-record policies for their OPACs and implementing link resolvers and ERMS systems preferred one ISSN at the title level. Addition of a medium suffix to a base ISSN was favored by some, but strongly opposed by others as so difficult and costly to implement that its adoption threatened to disenfranchise whole communities from use of the ISSN. What solution could the Working Group propose?

Identification at both a "product" level and a "title" level was being demanded of the ISSN. If possible, the revised ISSN standard should include a way to meet both needs. After much deliberation, the Working Group devised the concept that was first called the "t-ISSN" or "title-level ISSN" and is now being called (as of NASIG, May 2005) the "Collocating Number." However, some dissatisfaction within the Working Group and beyond still exists with this term, so the name "Collocating Number" should be regarded as provisional. Regardless of what the concept is called ultimately, the idea is that *in addition* to the manifestation-level ISSN that will continue to be assigned under the new standard, a single "Collocating Number" (cn) will also be assigned to all titles registered for ISSN, regardless of whether the title is issued in multiple manifestations or not. The cn will be the same for all titles in the cluster of titles linked by MARC 21 Field 776 (Additional physical form entry). The cn is a mechanism designed to support services such as OpenURL resolution that offer users search and delivery across all media versions. The cn is designed to be capable of being embedded in other identifiers and access mechanisms such as DOI, URN, and OpenURL to enable interoperability with systems using these identifiers and to enable title-level linking. The revised standard will include annexes giving instructions and examples of how to embed either the ISSN or the cn into other identifiers.

Many details about how the cn will be assigned and recorded have not been worked out as of this presentation. At its April 2005 meeting, the Working Group proposed that the first-assigned ISSN would also become the cn, and that all resources, both current and retrospective, whether issued in one or more media versions, would be assigned a cn. Furthermore, the cn would be recorded in MARC 21 field 024 (Other standard identifier) of the ISSN record. The ISSN International Centre would machine-assign a retrospective cn so that all ISSN records in the ISSN Register would also contain a cn. No separate records would exist for the cn, since what the cn identifies is really an abstraction, somewhat comparable to FRBR's expression level. The metadata pertaining to the cn can be regarded as a composite of the metadata pertaining to the separate medium-specific records. As an example, let's take *The Journal of Adhesion*, a journal that is published in print, CD-ROM, and online versions. The ISSN for the print version is ISSN 0021-8464, the ISSN for the CD-ROM version is ISSN 1026-5414, and the ISSN for the online version is ISSN 1563-518X. All three versions would have the same cn: cn 0021-8464, which was the first-assigned ISSN in this group of versions. The cn will likely not be printed on serial issues, or used by individuals as a look-up device. Rather, it is expected that the cn will be used primarily by systems and services, such as link resolvers that can be populated with data obtained by subscribing to products based on the ISSN Register.

One of the most significant unanswered questions about implementation of the cn is whether the cn will be assigned by individual ISSN centers at the time new ISSN are assigned, or whether cn will be machine-assigned by the ISSN International Centre when records from ISSN centers are entered into the ISSN Register. Centralizing assignment of cn would ensure systematic assignment by all centers, especially those centers who do not use MARC21 or UNIMARC and thus might not have a local field available to use for this purpose. Central assignment would also solve the problem presented by situations where the various medium editions of a serial are published in different countries. On the other hand, if cn were assigned by the ISSN International Centre, how would cn get into the national records maintained by individual ISSN centers? These and other questions related to implementing the cn are being explored by the Working Group and by the ISSN International Centre.

ISSN DATA DISTRIBUTION

The Working Group has proposed a two-pronged solution to the "multiple ISSN problem." The Collocating Number, just discussed, is one prong of that solution. The second prong is facilitating distribution and synchronization of ISSN data, cn data, and data about other kinds of relationships among serials with ISSN. Currently, especially in the United States, many databases, libraries, A&I services, providers of aggregations, and link resolver knowledge bases contain bad ISSN data. Unfortunately, the CONSER database is the source of much of this bad data, because purchasers of the CONSER database (e.g., ExLibris for its SFX knowledge base) expect that all ISSN in the database are correct, which is not the case. These purchasers disseminate these bad ISSN via their products, thus further distributing them and further adding to the problem of bad ISSN data and poor link resolution. In reality, the only ISSN in the CONSER database that can be considered authoritative are those assigned by two national ISSN centers, NSDP and ISSN Canada. These ISSN are authoritative to begin with and are systematically maintained. In many other cases (i.e., non-U.S. and non-Canadian imprints) ISSN have been added to records based on possibly incorrect ISSN printed by the publisher. Unfortunately, even if the ISSN was transcribed from the ISSN Register or checked in the ISSN Register by a CONSER library, that ISSN might later be cancelled and replaced by another ISSN without the correction being made in the CONSER database. The hope is that future ISSN distribution services will help to solve this problem.

At present, the only source of authoritative ISSN for all of the world's continuing resources is the ISSN Register. The ISSN Register is the official database of the ISSN Network and, as of the date of this presentation, the database contains over 1,125,500 records. Over 50,000 new records are added per year. The coverage is worldwide. For example, there are 193,000 records for continuing resources published in France; 31,000 records for resources published in Japan; and 24,000 records for resources published in Hungary. The ISSN Register is maintained with changes and corrections submitted from the ISSN centers and from diagnostic checks made by the ISSN International Centre.

Current ISSN products are the ISSN Portal (access to the Register via a Web interface), a quarterly CD-ROM, and data files.

When the cn was first proposed, it was recognized that this mechanism would only solve some of the need for collocation among continuing resources since the cn only collocates across medium versions. However, collocation among language editions, audience editions, geographic editions, or earlier and later titles will be desired in some situations. To answer this need, as well as the need to distribute ISSN and cn data, the Working Group is proposing that the ISSN Network develop a new product, a distribution service to send out to subscribers, perhaps on a monthly basis, ISSN data and data about relationships between and among cn and ISSN. This product would be a "push" service that would be offered in addition to the current ISSN Portal (a "pull" service). The ISSN International Centre is currently exploring technical issues, a business model, and pricing options for this kind of distribution service. The data would probably be supplied in XML as well as MARC 21, and the unique focus of the service would be on relationship data, for example, ISSN and the corresponding cn, earlier and later title ISSN, and various edition relationships. There might also be separate "look-up" (online access) and data distribution services.

ISSN USER GROUP

One of the very gratifying benefits of the ISSN revision process has been the fostering of better communications between ISSN users and the ISSN Network. Recognizing the benefits of such ongoing communications, an ISSN User Group has been established to provide regular input to the ISSN Governing Board from the various ISSN user communities. The membership consists of representatives from those communities involved in the ISO Working Group, plus others such as union catalog representatives. The first meeting of the ISSN User Group was held April 28, 2005 and it provided some valuable input to the Governing Board. In the future, the User Group can hopefully also serve as a sounding board for Governing Board proposals. In this way, the ISSN Network can better identify, meet, and hopefully even be able to anticipate user needs.

DRAFTING THE STANDARD

It is exciting and gratifying to realize that in rising to the challenge of revising an icon–the ISSN–the Working Group has also propelled the

ISSN Network forward on the development of an ISSN User Group and the exploration of new products and services. But how is work progressing on the revised standard itself? As of this presentation, work continues on the draft that will be presented to the directors of ISSN centers and then put forward for voting by SC9 member bodies. The standard will consist of three basic parts: the body, normative annexes, and informative annexes. The body of the standard will contain a foreword and introduction, plus sections on Scope, Definitions, Construction of ISSN, Assignment of ISSN, the Collocating Number, Printing and Display of ISSN, ISSN Metadata, and ISSN Administration. Normative annexes–annexes having the same force as the body of the standard–will cover the following: the Check Digit, the Collocating Number, Metadata, and ISSN Centres' Roles and Responsibilities. Informative annexes, while not having the same force as normative annexes, will be particularly important in the case of the revised ISSN standard, since these annexes will contain instructions and examples of ISSN use and Collocating Number use, respectively, in other identification systems. These two annexes will hopefully provide instructions to enable the ISSN to interoperate with or be part of existing or emerging systems such as OpenURL link resolvers. Finally, as previously mentioned, the revised standard will be accompanied by a background document that will describe the revision work and the evolution of the revised standard. The document will include information such as the goals the Working Group set out to achieve, the options that were considered and rejected in resolving issues such as that presented by the multiple ISSN assignment policy, and the reasons for the various decisions made by the Working Group. The background document will attempt to anticipate and to answer concerns that might be raised by the voting members.

When will the revised standard be available? Standards development is a long and sometimes tedious process, as is the revision of an existing standard, especially one as firmly rooted in various communities as the ISSN. Projected dates for the next steps in the revision process are as follows, although all dates are subject to change. Finalizing the Committee Draft (CD) including presentation and discussion at the annual meeting of directors of ISSN centers: May-October 2005; CD review: November 2005-January 2006; ISO voting period on the DIS (Draft Information Standard): May-September 2006; voting period, if necessary, on the FDIS (Final Draft Information Standard): Dec. 2006-January 2007; submission of the FDIS for publication: early 2007; and–finally–publication of the revised standard: April 2007!

CONCLUSION

Updating an icon like the ISSN is presenting significant challenges, but this effort also holds the promise of even more significant benefits. Care is being taken to preserve the make-up of the current ISSN so it will continue to function in existing systems, while updating it to interoperate in current and near-term future digital environments, especially in ERMS, ONIX and OpenURL applications–all exciting new uses for the ISSN. In fact, so important has the ISSN become in the emerging OpenURL and other digital contexts that it can truly be said, "If the ISSN did not exist, someone would have to invent it!"

SOURCES OF FURTHER INFORMATION

ISSN Network Web Site
http://www.issn.org

ISSN Revision
http://www.collectionscanada.ca/iso/tc46sc9/wg5.htm

OpenURL
http://www.niso.org/standards/resources/OpenURL_FAQ.html

ONIX for Serials
http://www.editeur.org/onixserials.html

http://www.fcla.edu/~pcaplan/jwp/

CONTRIBUTOR'S NOTE

Regina Romano Reynolds is Head of the National Serials Data Program at the Library of Congress.

FRBR and Serials:
An Overview and Analysis

Steve Shadle

Presenter

SUMMARY. This article provides an overview of the *Functional Requirements for Bibliographic Records* (FRBR) with an emphasis on issues of interest to serialists. The basics of the Entity-Relationship (E-R) model are used to introduce the aspects of FRBR which can be used to model serial publications. Special attention is paid to the attributes and relationships of the article (the individual contribution in a periodical) and the article's relationship to its "aggregated" work (the issue and the journal). This article includes a short discussion of the serial "work" and of outstanding issues in the application of FRBR to serial works. *[Article copies available for a fee from The Haworth Document Delivery Service: 1-800-HAWORTH. E-mail address: <docdelivery@haworthpress.com> Website: <http://www.HaworthPress.com>]*

In an informal show of hands taken at the beginning of two presentations I gave at the North American Serials Interest Group 2005 meeting, I discovered that roughly one-third of the 150 attendees were not at all familiar with the *Functional Requirements for Bibliographic Records* (FRBR). They had not read anything on it and had never been to a presentation about it. Nearly half the attendees had some FRBR awareness

[Haworth co-indexing entry note]: "FRBR and Serials: An Overview and Analysis." Shadle, Steve. Co-published simultaneously in *The Serials Librarian* (The Haworth Information Press, an imprint of The Haworth Press, Inc.) Vol. 50, No. 1/2, 2006, pp. 83-103; and: *Roaring into Our 20's: NASIG 2005* (ed: Margaret Mering, and Elna Saxton) The Haworth Information Press, an imprint of The Haworth Press, Inc., 2006, pp. 83-103. Single or multiple copies of this article are available for a fee from The Haworth Document Delivery Service [1-800-HAWORTH, 9:00 a.m. - 5:00 p.m. (EST). E-mail address: getinfo@haworthpress.com].

Available online at http://www.haworthpress.com/web/SER
doi:10.1300/J123v50n01_09

and understanding, but were not sure how it would be useful for serials. Given the fact that the model was published seven years ago and that there have been a number of experimental and commercial applications since then, I was surprised to find this proportion of attendees with such a limited knowledge of FRBR until I realized that very little work has been done to date that affects the serials community. FRBR applications have primarily focused on helping the user identify and select works in multiple editions, translations and versions (e.g., *Hamlet*) and works of performance available in multiple performances and recordings (e.g., *Brandenburg Concerto No. 1 in F Major*). I am guessing that because serial publications would contain relatively few of either of these situations and that they have an inherent complexity both because of the changing and aggregate nature of the serial work, the same interest has not been taken in modeling the serial work with FRBR. This article will attempt to provide background for the serialist by:

- Describing and illustrating the components of an Entity-Relationship (E-R) model in order to provide a background understanding of FRBR
- Providing a very broad overview of the FRBR model including examples of how books and articles can be modeled
- Illustrating the relationship between the article (as a single work) and the journal (as an aggregate work or *work of works*)
- Discussing the nature of the serial work and providing an overview of the current issues that are being discussed in the application of FRBR to serials

ENTITY-RELATIONSHIP MODELING

In the late 1970s, Peter Chen proposed a data modeling process that separated the logical data modeling from the physical database design. The idea being that the logical model would be independent from data processing storage and efficiency considerations, and that the logical model could be more easily developed and understood by people without a data processing background.[1] The Entity-Relationship model assumes that the purpose of a data system is to store data about things that can be distinctly identified and the relationships between these things.

To paraphrase:

- An *Entity* is a distinct identifiable thing for which a system must store data in order to perform some fundamental activities
- A *Relationship* is an association among entities
- An *Attribute* is a data element that describes an entity or a relationship
- A *Value* is a particular value of an attribute

For example, you may have a vehicle registration system that requires data modeling. Using an E-R modeling approach, one identifies the entities (*Owner, Vehicle*), any relationships between the entities (*Owns*) and the attributes of the entities and relationship. In this case, the *Owner* attributes might include: Name, Address, City, State, Zip Code; the *Vehicle* attributes might include: Make, Year, Model, Vehicle Identification Number; the *Owns* relationship attributes might include: Purchase Date, Purchase Price, Registration Date, and Registration Amount. Each of the real-world objects being modeled is represented by a set of data values. In Figure 1 you see that the author owns a 2002 VW Beetle that was purchased for $17,542 on August 1, 2002 with a registration in the amount of $247.36 that will need to be renewed on August 1, 2005. As shown in this E-R diagram, entities are generally represented by labeled shapes. Relationships between entities are usually represented as labeled lines between the shapes.

The E-R model also includes the concept of *cardinality*. For any particular relationship, one must determine whether that relationship is a one-to-one relationship, a one-to-many relationship, or a many-to-many relationship. Thinking about the car registration system, can an owner own more than one car? Can a car be owned by more than one owner? In Figure 1, this many-to-many relationship is expressed by the double arrows appearing on the relationship line between the two entities. In this model, an owner can own one or more cars and a car can be owned by one or more owners.

One more E-R modeling concept is useful in discussing FRBR. A relationship between two instances of the same entity type is called a *recursive* relationship (also known as a *reflective* relationship). Figure 2 illustrates a commonly seen recursive relationship that may need to be modeled in a human resource system. In this model, an *employee* is the entity and *supervises* is the relationship. In the first model, one employee supervises one or more employees (the cardinality of the relationship is reflected by the number of arrowheads). In the second model,

FIGURE 1. Entity-Relationship Model for Car Registration System

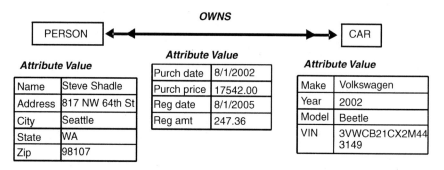

Attribute	Value
Name	Steve Shadle
Address	817 NW 64th St
City	Seattle
State	WA
Zip	98107

Attribute	Value
Purch date	8/1/2002
Purch price	17542.00
Reg date	8/1/2005
Reg amt	247.36

Attribute	Value
Make	Volkswagen
Year	2002
Model	Beetle
VIN	3VWCB21CX2M44 3149

FIGURE 2. Recursive Relationships

one employee supervises one or more employees *and* an employee can have one or more supervisors.

FRBR AS AN ENTITY-RELATIONSHIP MODEL

The Functional Requirements for Bibliographic Records is a model used to describe bibliographic resources. This model can be used to support the ability of users to find, identify, select and obtain bibliographic resources. FRBR's entities are grouped into three types:

- Group 1: Bibliographic resources (products of intellectual or artistic endeavor)
- Group 2: Responsible parties (individuals/groups responsible for content, production, custodianship)
- Group 3: Subjects (concepts, objects, events and places)

The four Group 1 entities that collectively represent the aspects of a bibliographic resource are of interest to a user. These four entities are:

- Work: A distinct intellectual or artistic creation
- Expression: The intellectual or artistic realization of a work
- Manifestation: The physical embodiment of an expression
- Item: A single exemplar of a manifestation

Each entity (except for work) is dependent upon the entity placed above it in the list. A dependency and to some degree, a hierarchy is represented in Group 1 entities. One also needs to note that work and expression reflect intellectual or artistic content, meaning they are intangible abstractions. Manifestation and item reflect the physical forms of those abstractions.

The E-R diagram in Figure 3 illustrates the relationships and cardinality between the Group 1 entities. As one can see in this diagram, a *work* may be realized through one or more *expressions*. However, an *expression* is the realization of only one *work*. An *expression* is embodied in one or more *manifestations* and a *manifestation* may embody more than one *expression*. A publication that includes both the original work and a translation of that work is an example of a manifestation that embodies more than one expression. A *manifestation* is typically exemplified by more than one *item* (e.g., copies of the same book) but an *item* can only exemplify one *manifestation*.

Examining the Group 1 entities from the "bottom up" can be a useful exercise in understanding the model. I am holding in my hand the single copy of FRBR that is owned by the University of Washington Libraries. It has a barcode and an ownership (represented by an ownership stamp)

FIGURE 3. Group 1 Entities

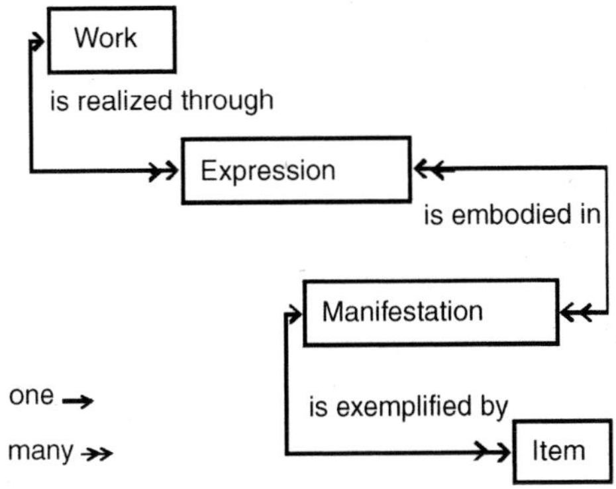

that make it unique in comparison to other copies of FRBR. This copy is an *item*. This item *exemplifies a manifestation* which was published by Saur in 1998 as part of the *UBCIM Publications Series*. When catalogers create bibliographic descriptions, unless they are noting specific information about their copy in hand (e.g., author's signatures, damaged pages), they are using the item as an exemplar of the manifestation to create a record that generally describes the manifestation. If you imagine that all of the words and figures from this manifestation (as exemplified by the book I have in my hand) have somehow floated off the page and are existing in some imaginary space (devoid of specific typeface, page layout, etc.), this collection of text and figures is an *expression* of FRBR. In fact, the 1998 Saur publication is a *realization of the expression* represented in the English-language 1997 final report. Earlier drafts of FRBR and translations of these drafts and of the final report are all different *expressions* (meaning different collections of text and figures) of the intellectual work known as the *Functional Requirements for Bibliographic Records*. Although some would argue that philosophically, having an abstract work without any physical embodiment or characteristics is possible, I would say that within the scope of FRBR's objectives (to help users find, identify, select and obtain bibliographic resources) something tangible is needed from which to identify and describe the four Group 1 entities. Now let's examine the entities and relationships in more detail.

A *work* is an abstract entity. One cannot point to a single material object as the work. When we speak of Shakespeare's *Hamlet* as a work, we are referring not to any particular presentation or text of the work. Instead, we are referring to the intellectual creation that lies behind all the various *expressions* of the *work*. Catalogers already recognize the concept of the work by the assignment of a uniform title to the catalog record for a bibliographic resource which appears in various expressions (e.g., editions, translations) or has appeared under various titles in the library catalog. Because a work is an abstract entity, defining precise boundaries for the entity can be difficult. FRBR states that (as a working assumption) revisions, updates, abridgements, enlargements and translations are considered to be different *expressions* of the same *work*. By contrast, when the modification of a work involves a significant degree of independent intellectual or artistic effort, the result is considered a new and different work. Thus paraphrases, rewrites, adaptations (either for an audience or from one literary or art form to another), abstracts, digests and summaries all represent new works. Tillett[2] provides a more complete taxonomy of bibliographic relationships that is useful in identifying the nature of the relationship between related works and/or expressions.

An *expression* is the "intellectual or artistic realization of a work in the form of alpha-numeric, musical, or choreographic notation, sound, image, object, movement, etc., or any combination of such forms."[3] An expression encompasses the specific words, musical notation, notes and phrasing, etc. that are independent of the physical realization of those words, notation, etc. Some would argue that translations actually create different *works* (due to the intellectual effort required and the inexact nature of translation). The authors of FRBR assume that translations are different expressions of the same work. Some examples of work and expressions can include:

> W_1 Charles Dickens' *A Christmas Carol*
> > E_1 the author's original English text
> > E_2 a Tamil translation by V. A. Venkatachari
> W_1 J. S. Bach's *Six Suites for Unaccompanied Cello*
> > E_1 1963 studio recordings by Janos Starker
> > E_2 1983 studio recordings by Yo-Yo Ma
> > E_3 1988 studio recordings by Yo-Yo Ma

In performance media (such as music), different performances of the same work are considered different expressions.

A *manifestation* is a physical embodiment of an *expression* of a *work*. As an embodiment of an expression, a manifestation represents all the physical objects that bear the same characteristics in respect to intellectual content and physical form. Changes in physical form, including changes affecting display characteristics, physical medium or carrier, result in a new manifestation. One example of this is a series of releases in different carriers of a single performance:

> W_1 J. S. Bach's *Goldberg variations*
> > E_1 performance by Glen Gould in 1981
> > > M_1 recording released on 33 1/3 rpm sound disc in 1982 by CBS Records
> > > M_2 recording re-released on compact disc in 1993 by Sony
> > > M_3 digitization of the Sony re-release as MP3 in 2000

In some cases, the determination of whether a characteristic is an attribute or an entity is a judgment call. FRBR considers a publisher to be an attribute of a manifestation. However, publishers are corporate bodies and in some ways could be considered entities with a relationship to a manifestation rather than as an attribute to a manifestation. Serials catalogers who are used to thinking of works as "emanating" from non-commercial corporate bodies might think it more natural to model publication as a "published by" relationship between a manifestation and a corporate body with the "published by" relationship having its own set of attributes (e.g., place, date). One advantage to modeling publication information in this fashion is that it allows for much better identification and selection of bibliographic resources by publisher information. Keyword searching of MARC 260, subfield b is much less reliable (because of variant forms of name) than searching using a relationship which exhibits some form of authority control.

An *item* is a single exemplar of a *manifestation.* In other words, a *manifestation* is *exemplified* by an *item*). The concept of an item is not new to libraries and is the basis of most library circulation systems:

W_1 Charles Dickens' *A Christmas carol*
 E_1 the author's original English text
  M_1 book published in 1996 by W.Morrow
   I_1 Bellevue Children's Fiction Barcode: 39352055996946
   I_2 Black Diamond Children's Holiday Books
             Barcode: 39352055996958
   I_3 Bothell Children's Fiction Barcode: 3935205599696X
   I_4 Burien Children's Holiday Books
             Barcode: 39352055996971
   I_5 Carnation Children's Holiday Books
             Barcode: 39352055996983

Now let's describe an example which is of more interest to the serialist. I wrote an article in 1988 that was published in *Serials Librarian.* As Haworth does, it simultaneously published that issue of *Serials Librarian* as a monograph. Four years later, the monograph was published in a second edition and I revised the article at that time. I also made a preprint of the revised article available in the University of Washington DSpace Web site. This article can be modeled in FRBR in the following way:

W_1 Steve Shadle. *A Square Peg in a Round Hole: Applying AACR2 to Electronic Journals*
 E_1 Original article
  M_1 *Serials Librarian* 33, no. 1-2 (1998)
   I_1 Copy in UW Libraries' periodicals collection

M$_2$ *E-Serials: Publishers, Libraries, Users, and Standards.* (New York: Haworth Press, 1998)

    I$_1$ Copy in UW Libraries' monographs collection

E$_2$ Revised article

    M$_1$ *E-Serials: Publishers, Libraries, Users, and Standards.* 2nd ed. (New York: Haworth Press, 2002).

    I$_1$ Copy in UW Libraries' monographs collection

  M$_2$ Electronic preprint

    I$_1$ Copy in UW Libraries DSpace collection

In this example, relationships are established between versions of the article and between the article appearing in a journal, monograph and independently on the Web. Another example of modeling different versions of an article might be a translation:

W$_1$ Н.В. Тупицын. *Новый Метод Отбора Хлебных Злаков На Потенциальную Урожсайность.*

  E$_1$ Original article

    M$_1$ *Доклады РАСХН*, 1995, №4, с.5-7

      I$_1$ Copy in UW Libraries' periodicals collection

    M$_2$ Electronic version: PDF scan

      I$_1$ http://selekciya.com/files/1995-04_New_method_for_selection_of_cereals_for_potential_cropping_power.pdf

  E$_2$ English translation: *New method for selection of cereals for potential cropping power*

    M$_1$ *Russian Agricultural Sciences,* 1995 no. 4, p. 6-8

      I$_1$ Copy in UW Libraries' periodicals collection

This Russian-language article appears in a Russian-language journal and is also made available (in Russian) as a PDF from a commercial Web site. The article was also translated into English and appeared in an English-language translation journal. This model shows the relationships between original Russian-language article (both in print and online) and the English-translation appearing in print.

Each of the four Group 1 entities has a set of defined attributes. For the sake of brevity, the lists following are a selected set of those attributes that will support discussion and examples in the article. These lists are far from complete. These attributes include:

Works

- Title
- Form (i.e., genre; *novel, play, poem, article*)
- Date
- Intended Termination (finite/continuing)
- Intended Audience

Expression

- Title of the *expression*
- Form of *expression (alpha-numeric notation (i.e., text), music notation, spoken word, musical sound, cartographic image, etc.)*
- Date of *expression*
- Language of *expression*
- Extensibility of *expression (expectation that content will be added)*
- Summarization of Content
- Expected Regularity of Issue (Serial)
- Expected Frequency of Issue (Serial)

Manifestation

- Title of the *manifestation* (all titles associated with the manifestation, appearing on piece or assigned)
- Statement of responsibility
- Edition/Issue designation (2nd ed., large print ed.)
- Publication information (Place and Date of publication, Publisher)
- Series statement
- Carrier information (material class of the *manifestation* [sound cassette, videodisc, microfilm cartridge, book], Extent, Dimensions)
- Manifestation Identifiers
- Source for Acquisition/Access Authorization and Terms of Availability
- Access/Use Restrictions on Manifestation
- Publication Status (Serial)
- Numbering (Serial)
- Reduction Ratio (Microform)
- Polarity; Generation (Microform or Visual Projection)
- System Requirements; File Characteristics (Electronic Resource)
- Mode of Access; Access Address (Remote Access Electronic Resource)

There has not yet been a discussion of modeling a serial publication (vs. an article) but the experienced serialist should immediately identify a problem with some of the attributes listed as Serial. Regularity and Frequency are identified as expression (but not manifestation) attributes but numbering is identified as a manifestation attribute. Apparently, in this world, the online, print and microform versions of a journal (different manifestations of the same expression) *must* have the same frequency and regularity, but can have different numbering. We know this assumption is not true. The numbering and "frequency" of an online journal can correspond to the article, while in the print journal it typically corresponds to the issue. On the other hand, depending on what is specifically reproduced, the microform may not carry any issue numbering and (as a cumulation) the frequency will typically differ from the print. Probably better to make these all manifestation attributes or at least identify frequency and regularity as both an expression and a manifestation attribute.

For the serialist, the only *item* attribute to be aware of is the item identifier (e.g., barcode, call number). The remaining item attributes listed in FRBR are characteristics such as provenance and item condition that support archival or preservation activities but that otherwise do not apply to serials.

Figure 4 represents an abbreviated E-R model for a 1996 Morrow edition of *A Christmas Carol,* illustrated by Carter Goodrich, with an afterword by Peter Glassman. There are two things to note in this model. First, the only title presented in these entities is that of the work *A Christmas Carol.* The reason for this is that FRBR (especially since it is a hierarchical model) allows inheritance. Thus, attributes of the work also apply to the expression, manifestation and item. Since no additional titles exist which are specific to the expression or manifestation, none are recorded in those entities. Second, the cataloger used to looking at the information in bibliographic records will observe the author is not appearing anywhere in this model and will probably wonder why the author is not an attribute of the work. The reason is that the author is a Group 2 entity which has a relationship to a work.

Why go through all this effort? The principal reason is to support the FRBR objectives of helping the user find, identify, select and obtain bibliographic resources. Figure 5 is one example of a "FRBR-ized" display of a public catalog. In this example of a VTLS demonstration catalog,[4] the catalog user searches on the title *Beau Geste.* The resulting displays in most library catalogs would display in a sort order based on

FIGURE 4. Partial E-R Diagram for a Book

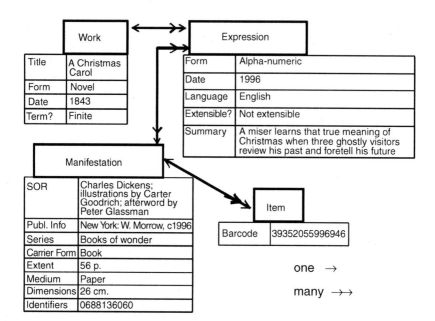

either an index (e.g., author, title), a specific MARC field or combination of fields (e.g., 1XX, 245) or possibly by date (most recent first is a popular choice). Most likely, none of these displays will display search results in an order or in groupings that will make sense to the user. Typically, the user may have to hunt and peck through any number of individual records before identifying the desired resource.

A display taking advantage of the FRBR structure can present search results in a manner more intuitive to the user. The search results list all of the *works* whose titles begin with Beau Geste. The first display lists resulting works by genre (comic book, motion pictures, novel, and radio drama). The display is hierarchically organized so that any of the work records can be opened up to see a listing of the individual expressions and manifestations. In this example, the user has selected the 1983 film version (work) in English starring Benedict Taylor, Anthony Calf and Jonathan Morris (expression) which was released on videotape by the BBC in 1983 (manifestation). In this display, one can also see that the library has the novel available in the original English, in five translations, and as two spoken word recordings. This type of hierarchical display

FIGURE 5. VTLS Display

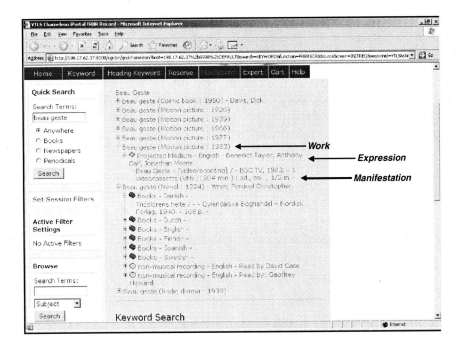

which groups individual resources together by shared characteristics of genre, format and language is much easier to navigate then a single listing of all the bibliographic records in a sort order that may not be intuitive or useful to the user.

Let's return to the E-R diagram of *A Christmas Carol.* We have yet to fill out the diagram with our Group 2 and Group 3 entities. Group 2 entities are individuals or groups that are responsible for intellectual content, production or custodianship of bibliographic resources. Currently, two entities are identified with the following attributes:

Person: Name, Dates, Title, Other Designation

Corporate Body: Name, Other Designation, Number (Meeting), Date (Meeting), Place (Meeting)

Group 2 entities have the following relationships with Group 1 entities:

Group 1		Group 2
A *Work*	is created by	a *Person/Corporate Body*
An *Expression*	is realized by	a *Person/Corporate Body*
A *Manifestation*	is produced by	a *Person/Corporate Body*
An *Item*	is owned by	a *Person/Corporate Body*

The four relationships all exhibit two-way multiple cardinality. A work is created by one or more persons/corporate bodies and a person/corporate body can create one or more works, etc.

The Group 3 entities are basically the subjects of works (i.e., what works are about). In addition to the existing Group1 and Group 2 entities (after all, a work can be about a work or a person), FRBR identifies the following as Group 3 entities:

- *Concept* (an abstract notion or idea)
- *Object* (a material thing)
- *Event* (an action or occurrence)
- *Place* (a location)

Each of these entities has one attribute labeled *Term*. Within FRBR, no context for authority control exists over names or subjects. There is a set of entities that have a single value. The IFLA Section on Cataloguing has established working groups associated with the Functional Requirements of Authority Records (FRAR) and the Functional Requirements for Subject Authority Records (FRSAR) that are charged with creating the models and identifying the needs for authority control and authority records. The Group 3 entities have only the following relationships:

Group 1		Group 3
A *Work*	has as subject	a *Work*
		an *Expression*
		a *Manifestation*
		an *Item*
		a *Person*
		a *Corporate Body*
		a *Concept*
		an *Object*
		an *Event*
		a *Place*

This relationship also exhibits multiple two-way cardinality. A Work can have many subjects and subject can be the subject of more than one Work.

Figure 6 shows a more complete E-R diagram for this edition of *A Christmas Carol*. Note the work, expression, manifestation, and item entities on the left side of the diagram, two Group 2 entities (Charles Dickens as the author and Carter Goodrich as the illustrator) and three Group 3 entities (Christmas stories, Ghost stories, England) as subjects to the work. The *Realized by* relationship also has an attribute associated with it (*Illustrator*). Since relationships can also have attributes, there is the possibility of modeling the type of relationship between Group 1 and Group 2 entities by having a relationship attribute consisting of a relator term indicating the contribution made or role taken by the person or corporate body.

Even though the E-R diagrams present a relational view of data, they do not say anything about how the data is stored (remember Peter Chen saying that the logical model of the data does not necessarily correspond to the physical data structure). This data could be stored in a series of relational files, or it could be stored as a flat file. OCLC users can think of

FIGURE 6. E-R Diagram with Type 2 and Type 3 Entities

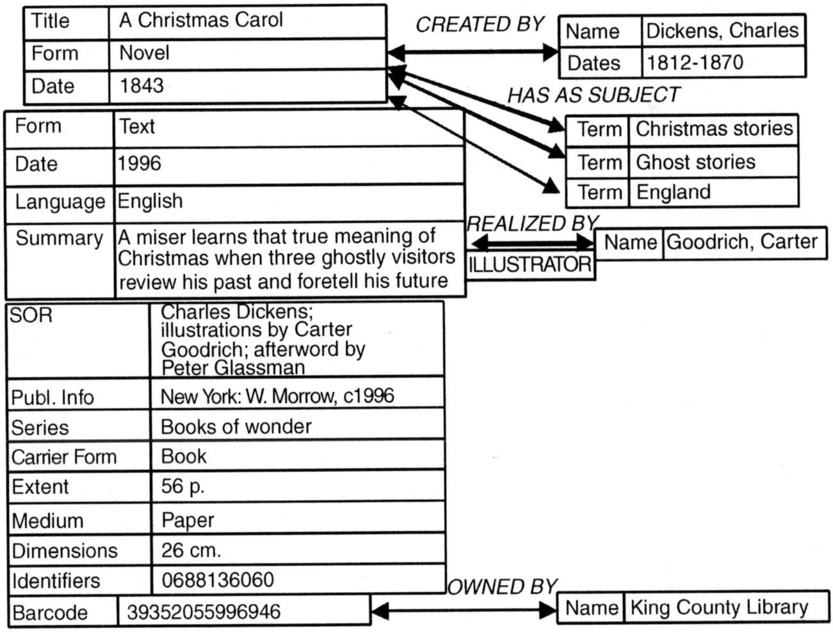

how bibliographic records appear to be flat records in Passport, but relational (with linked authority control) in Connexion.

THE SERIAL WORK AND RECURSIVE RELATIONSHIPS

The cataloging community is not in complete agreement that a serial is an intellectual work in the same sense that a work of single-authorship is. However, everyone is in general agreement that a serial can be considered a work of collected works or shared authorship and thus can be modeled in FRBR.[5] Most serialists would agree with the concept that a serial is an intellectual work. A journal is more than just a collection of articles. Editorial control shapes the scope and content, and peer review often revises the draft content or keeps content from appearing. Thus, the serial can be considered an intellectual construct of shared responsibility.

In addition to the entity relationships described so far, serials have recursive relationships that FRBR does not present in the E-R diagram of Group 1 entities,[6] most likely because the addition of these relationships to the diagram would make the diagram complex to the point of unintelligibility. One of these relationships is called *Has Part* and it is used to model the whole/part relationship between a serial and an issue of a serial, and between a serial issue and an individual article in that issue. Figure 7 is an E-R diagram showing the relationship of the serial, issue and article *works*. But is the *issue* a work?? NASIG presentation attendees agreed some issues (i.e., conference proceedings issues, theme issues) which have work-like characteristics could be thought of as an intellectual *work*. However, not everyone agreed on the fact that a typical issue of a typical journal could be considered an intellectual *work* from the FRBR perspective.

However, editors and editorial boards do not exhibit editorial control over *all* of the issues of a serial. They generally focus on a small number of upcoming issues. The relationship between the serial and the editor is not really a relationship between a person and a serial work, but instead between a serial and an issue work. Other attributes of a serial might be better associated with the *issue* rather than to the *serial as a whole*. Each of the work entities (serial, issue, article) will also be related to their own expressions, manifestations and items. In essence, the serial work will have relationships with its expressions, manifestations and items. The issue work will have corresponding relationships to its expressions, manifestations and items. The article will have corresponding relation-

FIGURE 7. The Whole/Part Relationships Between Serial, Issue and Article Works

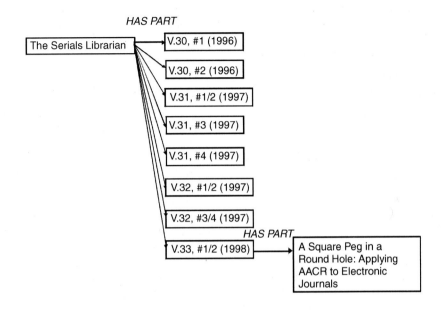

ships to its expressions, manifestations and item. One area that needs further exploration in the modeling of the whole/part relationship is what role *inheritance* can play in filling out these relationships. Including the title attribute at the expression or manifestation levels may not be necessary, if it is the same as the work title. Citing an issue title, with the exception of its numbering, may not be needed if it is the same as the work title.

Figure 8 illustrates a similar, but a more complex situation. The main work is the Russian-language journal, *Доклады РАСХН.* This journal has two expressions, the original Russian-language version and an English-translation called *Russian Agricultural Sciences.* Each of these *expressions* has a part (an issue numbered 1995, no. 4) and each of these parts has a part (an article either in Russian (*Новый Метод Отбора Хлебных Злаков На Потенциальную Урожайность*) or in English (*New method for selection of cereals for potential cropping power*)). So far, the situation is similar to the diagram in Figure 7 except the Whole/ Part relationship is modeled on the *expression* rather than on the *work.* The additional piece of modeling in Figure 8 is that *manifestations* of

FIGURE 8. E-R Diagram Illustrating Manifestation Whole/Part Relationship

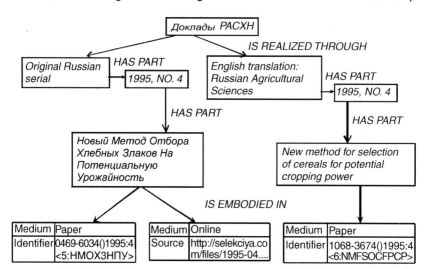

each article *expression* are also modeled. The Russian-language article has two manifestations (print and online) each with information unique to that manifestation. The English-language article has one manifestation (print) with a manifestation-level identifier.

As we see, the relationship of the individual article to the main work can be modeled in FRBR. How does this level of complexity and brain-twisting help us and the user? Currently abstracting and indexing services and citation/full-text databases provide description and access at the article-level. It does not seem that it will be of much help to the user (in terms of grouping or sorting) unless an article is available in multiple expressions or manifestations. Potentially, FRBR will radically change one aspect of the traditional library experience. In her presentations on metadata given for the 2002-2003 Metadata and AACR2 Institutes, Barbara Tillett enjoyed pointing out that in the late 1800s ALA had attempted to support the inclusion of journal articles in library catalogs by encouraging journal publishers to include back of the issue indexes that could be cut out and filed in library catalogs. After a pilot where ALA determined that providing article-level access in this manner was impractical, H.W. Wilson stepped forward and began producing commercial available abstracting and indexing services. At that point began a split in how libraries provide services to users that has never really been brought back together. "You're searching for articles? Oh, well you have to use *these* databases and not the library catalog." How many library catalogs display a warning along the lines of "The Library Catalog contains journal, magazine and newspaper *holdings*. To find an article, search a subject database."? For decades, libraries have had a split-file problem which users find confusing and invariably need help with.

What about the possibility of incorporating articles in the same search space as the catalog? Think about the FRBR catalog display presented in Figure 5 where results of a subject search are grouped by genre. If articles are included in the search space then they could be presented as a broad group, along with novels, motion pictures, radio dramas, comic books, etc. Users specifically interested in articles could expand that entry and go merrily on their searching way. Since most citation databases have article-level descriptions, how can we take advantage of that data (perhaps through broadcast searching) to incorporate the results of those searches into a more complete display of resources? FRBR could be a means to bring some sort of organization to that larger world of bibliographic resources.

OUTSTANDING ISSUES TO BE RESOLVED

In 2003, the IFLA FRBR Review Group appointed the Working Group on Continuing Resources to investigate whether the FRBR model is sufficient to account for all aspects of continuing resources. The Review Group's 2004 report[7] identified several areas of FRBR that needed revising to better account for continuing resources:

- FRBR needed to recognize a fourth mode of issuance: *streaming resources*
- FRBR needs to provide an additional *aggregate class* to better address serially issued resources
- The concept of seriality (change over time) needs to be addressed within FRBR manifestation attributes

The report also included discussion of how a different model (one that more specifically acknowledged the "issue") might be necessary. Patrick LeBoeuf presented a draft of an alternative model that could be used to model serial publications. Some changes in attributes (including frequency/regularity as a *manifestation* attribute and edition as an *expression* attribute) were also proposed.

The phenomenon of change over time is one that has vexed not only the FRBR folks, but all catalogers. As Judy Kuhagen points out in her presentation[8] at the FRBR in 21st Century Catalogues Invitational Workshop, the serials cataloging community has always had difficulties in determining how best to describe resource change over time and identifying at what point a serial becomes a new *work* (i.e., has a new record created due to a change in the resource). Kuhagen proposes that, in order to support the user objectives (to find, select, identify and obtain), a serial that changes title over time is best considered as a single serial work. Merger and splits would be an indication of new works. This conclusion is in agreement both with Tillett's proposal to use series authority records as *work* records[9] and with the CONSER Task Force on Universal Holdings report[10] that both suggest that a "super-record" which includes the sequential history of a serial title can be accommodated within the existing FRBR model.

If one agrees with the model and diagrams presented in Figures 7 and 8, seriality may already be expressible within FRBR. If an issue *work* or *manifestation* (in addition to the serial *work*) indeed exists, then changes in a serial over time can be expressed as *issue* attributes, rather than *serial* attributes. Or put another way, how does the serials cataloger recognize that a change has taken place over time? By comparing different issues against each other to see what has changed over time. So, if there is an issue *work* (remember Figure 7 showing a succession of issue *works* all of which have a *is part of* relationship to a serial work), then any change between issues is already described as an issue attribute (at the work, expression or manifestation level) and the *serial work* primarily serves as a collocating device. For example, a journal is published under Title ABC for its first two years, and then under Title DEF for its next two years. Now, why introduce the concept of seriality and change in the *serial work* when the two titles are attribute values associated with specific *issue* works? Seriality is already inherent in the FRBR model because there are successive issue works/expressions/manifestations, each reflecting the bibliographic description of that issue. Just as the serials cataloger does, by comparing the issues, a system can identify what changes happen when.

One goal that FRBR can help support is the ability to group serial families together so that the user can see the serial history at a glance and can then expand on any particular piece of the history to drill down to the desired resource. Existing MARC record linking fields can facilitate these groupings, but it is useful to think of it within the context of the FRBR model. VTLS has a demo available[11] that illustrates one approach to a FRBR-ized serial display in the library catalog.

CONCLUSION

Several significant benefits can be derived from applying the FRBR model to the serial work. However, one can easily get bogged down in the complexity of relationships, not only aggregate (whole/part) relationships but also relationships between expressions, manifestations and individual issues and items. In including the concept of a separate issue and article work, a level of complexity has been introduced into the FRBR model which can be powerful, but can also make it appear that in some respect everything is related to everything! I have one piece of advice (attributed to Einstein) to give to the leadership within the FRBR community: "Things should be as simple as possible, but not simpler."

NOTES

1. Peter Chen, *The Entity-Relationship Approach to Logical Data Base Design* (Wellesley, Mass.: Q.E.D. Information Sciences, 1977), 9-10.

2. Barbara B. Tillett, "Bibliographic Relationships," in *Relationships in the Organization of Knowledge*, edited by Carol A. Bean and Rebecca Green (Dordrecht: Kluwer Academic Publishers, 2001): 19-35.

3. IFLA Study Group on the Functional Requirements for Bibliographic Records, *Functional Requirements for Bibliographic Records: Final Report* (Munchen: K.G. Saur, 1988), 18.

4. *Virtual Demonstration Library Catalog*, http://www.vtls.com (9 May 2005).

5. Kristin Antelman, "Identifying the Serial Work as a Bibliographic Entity," *Library Resources & Technical Services* 48, 4 (Oct. 2004): 239-244.

6. IFLA Study Group on the Functional Requirements for Bibliographic Records, *Functional Requirements for Bibliographic Records: Final Report* (Munchen: K.G. Saur, 1988), 18: 63-81.

7. *Report on the FRBR Review Groups Meeting, Buenos Aires, August 27 2004* http://www.ifla.org/VII/s13/wgfrbr/FRBRRG_20040827_Report.pdf (20 June 2005).

8. Judy Kuhagen, *Modeling Continuing Resources in FRBR [and More]*, Powerpoint available at: http://www.oclc.org/research/events/frbr-workshop/presentations/kuhagen/Kuhagen_OCLC_FRBR.ppt (20 June 2005).

9. Barbara Tillett, *What is FRBR (Functional Requirements for Bibliographic Records)?* http://www.ala.org/ala/alcts/alctsconted/presentations/Tillett.pdf (20 June 2005).

10. CONSER Task Force on Universal Holdings, *An Approach to Serials with FRBR in Mind.* http://www.lib.unc.edu/cat/mfh/serials_approach_frbr.pdf (20 June 2005).

11. *FRBR Serials*, http://www.vtls.com/documents/FRBR12.PPT (20 June 2005).

CONTRIBUTOR'S NOTE

Steve Shadle is Serials Access Librarian at the University of Washington Libraries.

Negotiation for the Rest of Us

Joan E. Conger

Presenter

SUMMARY. The topic of this article is how to create sustainable relationships between librarians and vendors through cost- and benefit-based negotiation for mutual gain. Negotiation is the process of finding the highest benefit and lowest cost for *both* parties. The success of a negotiation process depends on three essential ingredients: effective communication, knowing what you (and they) want, and learning. Complementing an introduction to general principles and secret tips that reduce the stress of negotiating not just price but also service quality and basic relationship expectations, the instructor facilitated a participative learning experience that revealed the negotiation wisdom gathered in the room, from library professionals and vendors alike. *[Article copies available for a fee from The Haworth Document Delivery Service: 1-800-HAWORTH. E-mail address: <docdelivery@haworthpress.com> Website: <http://www. HaworthPress.com>]*

INTRODUCTION

Negotiation is about mutual gain. There, I feel better already.

If I am trained to treat negotiation as an I-(hopefully)-win-therefore-you-lose game, I am taken aback by this proposition. If I approach negotiation as a debate over whether you are going to give me what I think

[Haworth co-indexing entry note]: "Negotiation for the Rest of Us." Conger, Joan E. Co-published simultaneously in *The Serials Librarian* (The Haworth Information Press, an imprint of The Haworth Press, Inc.) Vol. 50, No. 1/2, 2006, pp. 105-117; and: *Roaring into Our 20's: NASIG 2005* (ed: Margaret Mering, and Elna Saxton) The Haworth Information Press, an imprint of The Haworth Press, Inc., 2006, pp. 105-117. Single or multiple copies of this article are available for a fee from The Haworth Document Delivery Service [1-800-HAWORTH, 9:00 a.m. - 5:00 p.m. (EST). E-mail address: getinfo@haworthpress.com].

I need, I am not only under pressure to win, I am also under pressure to convince you to give way. To complicate matters, I also assume that you approach our interaction with the same imperatives. I become fearfully determined that you will not "win" more than me.

The stage is now set for both of us to gain as little as possible. We both approach each other as an adversary and give out the least amount of information about ourselves, because information is power. With information, one side will know how to manipulate the interaction for personal gain. If, for example, I know you need a particular functionality, I can raise the price. As smart negotiators, we give each other very little information about ourselves, and seek instead to outwit the other side. Some thrill to play this game. For the rest of us, the game is stressful, time consuming, and not fun.

Negotiation[1] does not have to be about competition. It can be about relationship. Negotiation as competition may seem effective, especially for one-time exchanges, such as a car or house purchase. Most negotiations, however, are not one-time exchanges, but the establishment of an ongoing working relationship. What I will discuss in this article are ways to succeed within this relationship. This article may improve most of your working relationships, even your home life.

With attention to relationship, I choose to treat negotiation as a dialog designed to accrue as much gain to both sides as we can creatively manage. When I approach negotiation as dialog, I work with you to fully understand both our sets of needs. We collaborate to find the solution that best meets both our sets of needs. We work together for mutual gain, and in this working relationship information is, indeed, power. The essential elements in negotiation for mutual gain are:

- The free exchange of information, i.e., communication. Without effective communication our search for mutual gain ends before it begins.
- Clear knowledge about what I want and what you want. Without both of these pools of information, we cannot create a mutually advantageous solution.
- A commitment to learning. Through learning I am always curious, always seeking more explanation, and never accepting assumption as immutable fact.

This workshop explored these three essential elements both in terms of theory and from the viewpoints of those in attendance. This article will discuss the benefits of each essential element. It will present the results of workshop attendees thinking through these steps themselves in the roles of either library professional or vendor representative.

WHY ARE YOU HERE?

Before we began general discussion, attendees shared a few things they love and a few things they hate about negotiation.

- Love: "building relationships, learning the unexpected, the feeling of success after a positive outcome."
- Hate: "the conflict involved, needing to win, having to keep track of all the things a product must do for us, feeling alone, the pressure of making a good deal, having to do it again next year."

I was not entirely surprised to hear my course outline mirrored in these comments. These concerns are common, and the negotiation wisdom I wished to share addresses just these issues.

FIRST REQUIREMENT: COMMUNICATE EFFECTIVELY

The physicist turned communications philosopher David Bohm[2] defined dialog as the co-creation of new meaning. This act of co-creation, he writes, requires that each party relinquish our tight hold on our respective preconceived definitions of the world and work together to create a new understanding. Outside each of our own personal stories, emotions, and needs, a third point of coherence exists. This coherence creates from our respective stories and needs a new future more beneficial to both of us than one attained by protecting separate viewpoints.

Experts in interpersonal communication echo this assertion.[3] Differences are not resolved by establishing a position and defending it against encroachment from the other person's position. In the context of getting what one needs, this defensive posture can seem the most logical, but it only serves to entrench division—not to achieve resolution. Instead we most effectively resolve our differences when we find mutuality, not the absorption of one side into the other, but a third position that reflects the needs of the original two inside an enhanced solution.

If I try to communicate with you from an established position, I have already decided what outcome I need. I must now defend this position and its inherent requirements. By taking this position, I assume that I have all the information I need. I require no further refinement of this position, because that would mean losing ground, or losing face. I am not omniscient. Some of my knowledge will be grounded on assumption, but verifying all assumptions will take too much time and effort. I have staked my position and will insist on it against all comers. I will pull you into the future I desire by superior argument and by outwitting you as you defend the future you desire. Negotiation is an event, therefore, before which I do not have what I need and after which I hope to have what I came for. We are now in an adversarial negotiation.

In adversarial negotiation, I put all my effort into defending my position and eroding yours. Defending my position through debate is what my education, upbringing, and culture have trained me to do. Once I take my position, I save myself from having to learn more about my needs, understand more about your needs, explore the validity of my assumed knowledge, or contribute to a creative solution. I seem to have saved myself a lot of work, but somehow I feel stressed and frustrated. You are looking at me with a combative stare. I cannot go any lower in price, and you do not have that kind of money.

Let us back down and approach this from another angle.

I could try to communicate with you through dialog. This ground is new for me, and feels odd, but somehow it is exciting. I approach you with the expectation that together we will create an advantageous outcome not yet known to either of us. We pool our knowledge based on our respective experiences. From this pool, we create alternatives, build on ideas, receive epiphanies, and share frustrations. In short, we learn. We co-create a new future, by broadening our options to meet both our interests. Negotiation is not an event but a process. I approach our interaction as a student willing to learn about what I really need, what you really need, and what we can create with collaboration. What benefits of reasonable cost to me could sweeten the deal for you?

Before we examine how to learn about ourselves and each other, allow me to share what workshop attendees co-created as a foundation for the learning process.

ATTENDEES DIVE IN:
WHAT IS MUTUALLY BENEFICIAL?

I provided the shell of a Mutuality Worksheet for a role-play exercise. Workshop attendees divided into groups, took on the role of library professional or vendor, and used the Worksheet to reach mutuality. The first section of the Mutuality Worksheet allows us to clarify our purpose. Purpose is different from position. Our position defines the interests we must protect using the details of what our future must look like. Our purpose, on the other hand, defines our future by describing our desired contribution to the communities we serve. This future can be met any number of ways, none of which are specified in the statement of purpose.

Vendor's Main Purpose:

- Maximize profits
- Provide a service that people want
- Protect intellectual property from no profits
- Create sustainable customer relationships
- Improve, broaden product lines

Library's Main Purpose:

- Provide research sources to help customers
- Maintain a sustainable budget
- Protect our ability to provide services
- Protect users' needs
- Dependable access with minimum staff time
- Highest quality content for customer need
- Effective use of staff effort and time

Once we know our purpose, and are clear on the purpose of our negotiating partner, we have a well-defined set of parameters within which to be creative. Creativity with too much latitude has difficulty forming into a final conception. Our pool of knowledge needs sides to contain itself and against which we push to gain momentum. Within the broad parameters of organizational purpose, ours and theirs, we have a periphery against which to push and the room to create new possibilities.

Step two of negotiation for mutual gain means learning what you want and what they want in order to fill the pool of knowledge between you with possibility.

SECOND REQUIREMENT:
KNOW WHAT YOU (AND THEY) WANT

If I choose competitive negotiation, I seek a solution that best meets the needs of the position I have established for myself. My best solution is narrowly defined by how much I win for myself and, conversely, how much I do not give up to the other side.

However, if I choose to negotiate for mutual gain, I enter into a process with the other side that seeks to create a better solution. I am not compromising my best solution, because the better solution will not contain conditions I find unattractive. Together with my negotiation partner, I create a solution unimagined from the viewpoint of one position or the other.

A better solution contains an awareness of the thresholds of cost and benefit for both parties. In competitive negotiation, I create a position that I must achieve to claim success. I treat these costs and benefits as absolutes to be won or lost. I either protect my estimations of cost and benefit once negotiations begin or lose my estimations to compromise.

Costs are those elements of an agreement that reduce or expend my resources. Costs include the money libraries spend on, or vendors deduct from, the price of a product. Costs also include the time and staff effort required of both the library and vendor to improve, provide and maintain the product for the end user, or the costs in time and effort for the end user confronted with a less-than-easy interface or with restrictions in full access to content.

Benefits are those elements of an agreement that make the costs of the product worthwhile. In addition to an increase in service for the library's community, benefits of a product for libraries can include an expansion in active customers, greater remote access, or archival rights. In addition to making a profit, benefits of selling a product for the vendor can include greater name recognition, expanding the number of habitual users who ask for the product by name, and the expansion of market share through consortial relationships.

Thresholds of costs and benefits allow negotiating partners to creatively combine costs and benefits in the search for a better solution. If I know that the library cannot afford the prices I charge my corporate clients, but the library knows that this business database will be a required resource in students' coursework, a creative solution presents itself. We agree to license use of the database for a much reduced rate, knowing that the students in the university's number eight ranked business school will develop a life-long habit of turning to my database first when seeking information.

If I approach the defining of costs and benefits through negotiation for mutual gain, I am better off establishing thresholds of costs and benefits that I can refine over time as I gain more information about our respective realities. Within the process of negotiation for mutual gain, my options for success become richer as I and my negotiating partner learn more.

In the next section, I will suggest two ways to support this learning process, but first, let's hear from our attendees as they discover the costs and benefits of libraries and vendors.

ATTENDEES DIVE IN:
WHAT ARE THE COSTS AND BENEFITS?

Knowing your own costs and benefits is not enough. Commit to learning as much as you can about the potential costs and benefits of the product for your partner. With this mutual understanding, you can mutually create the better solution.

Vendor potential benefits:

- Librarian input on product development
- Customer loyalty
- Long term relationship with library
- Good name, recognition

Vendor potential costs:

- Overhead infrastructure, personnel
- Content, third party information sources
- Research and development, IT development and support
- Marketing costs

Library potential benefits:

- Having access for customers to good content with easy interface and consistent access
- Custom services for unique needs
- Good public relations for library
- Match activities of customers (course requirements, research needs)

Library potential costs:

- Personnel to support link resolver, etc.
- Troubleshooting
- Infrastructure: equipment, customer instruction, Web delivery
- Opportunity cost of one product over another

THIRD REQUIREMENT:
REMAIN CURIOUS

The difference between competitive negotiation and negotiation for mutual gain is the discovery of a better solution, one that contains within it recognition of the thresholds of costs and benefits for both sides. These thresholds are not absolute, established before and protected during a negotiation event. These thresholds are containers for continuous learning about our own realities and those of our negotiating partner. This continuous learning flows into a pool of knowledge from which a rich array of possible solutions emerges.

We have noted that negotiation does not have to be an event, dreaded in its coming then survived only to dread the next. Negotiation for mutual gain can be a process during which we learn about ourselves and the other party in time to navigate the creative search for a solution and prepare for the next creative search with more learning.

I suggest two toolboxes to help with this continuous learning.[4] The first toolbox is the art of collaboration through which we gather information from diverse sources. The second toolbox is a set of learning documents within which we capture, but do not hold too tightly, the information we collect.

Collaboration[5] allows us to tap sources of information we would not have access to if we were to define our costs and benefits alone. The costs and benefits of the products for which we negotiate licenses touch not only ourselves but a wide array of colleagues, customers, other stakeholders, and our negotiation partner's costs and benefits. Collaboration allows us to create a network of people to make the work lighter and the sources of information richer:

- The quantity and complexity of the information required to make intelligent decisions during negotiations means not only that we must directly ask, and never assume, the perspectives of each of these parties; but that we enlist the assistance of those particularly interested to help us condense the information into a usable format. (Read about learning documents below.)
- We need a wide diversity of perspectives, from user to library professional to vendor, to ensure that all costs and benefits are accounted for in the final solution. We need a diversity of analytic input to ensure that interpretations and priorities are set as objectively as possible and reflect the organization's (and not a politically motivated individual's) purpose in serving its community.

- The quantity and complexity of costs and benefits for a single product, and within the web of products and services of a library or a vendor, presents an almost overwhelming amount of learning for one person. Shared learning in groups means that we benefit from a multiplicity of learning styles, memory reservoirs, and analytical strengths.

Learning documents harness the agility and pervasiveness of online information sharing. The ancestor of the learning document is the policy statement. Usually these policies, if they are written at all, evolve into thick manuals that no one thinks of taking out to use on a daily basis. Learning documents are more like dossiers of helpful information, crib sheets we turn to as we use our professional expertise to navigate the complexities of meeting our needs during the negotiation process.

The essence of learning documents is their simplicity and dynamic ability to keep up with changing times. If you have sticky notes on your monitor with scribbled passwords and phone numbers, you have a collection of learning documents. Learning documents should easily capture new information and should also be subject to regular collaborative review to assure that they still reflect current reality. Learning documents should also be clear and concise, and distributed as widely as possible. Your customers and your negotiating partners will benefit as much as you from learning how you intend to meet your needs as you address theirs.

When we collaboratively collect, analyze, review, and update information available to us, these learning documents can capture the information and hold it ready for anyone who needs it. Because these dynamic learning documents are valuable both in their usefulness and accessibility by anyone needing to make or contribute to purchasing decisions, store them electronically in a location easily accessed from any desktop, even your customer's or your negotiating partner's.

The obvious solution is the Internet. A plethora of document storage solutions exist, from simple hypertext Web sites to blogs to wiki's that allow the editing and discussion of documents from any authorized user. Google Seedwiki is an example of a public wiki that can be made private.

Both of these toolboxes promote and amplify the work that goes into co-creating mutual gain. Collaboration and learning documents harness the information spread throughout the system. With this information, we learn about the costs and benefits of both parties in a negotiation. The negotiation turns into a creative search for the better solution.

ATTENDEES DIVE IN:
WHAT IS A CREATIVE SOLUTION?

A list of our needs and their needs is not complete until we have asked everyone who could give us input. The easier path is that of assumption. We could assume based on past experience and professional guesswork what needs must be met for our organization and their organization to meet our respective purposes for our communities.

The path to the better solution, however, is paved with real information. We ask our customers, our colleagues and our stakeholders to tell us what the needs of the organization look like now and should look like in the future. Informing the purchase of products is one of the fundamental tasks of Library Assessment. We also ask our negotiating partners what their needs look like now and what they would like for them to look like in the future.

Here are some questions shared by workshop attendees:

Questions from Vendors for Libraries:

- How can I help you with a better product? Better delivery to the customer? Better experience by the customer?
- What business models work best for you as you purchase resources?
- What license terms work best for you and help you best serve our mutual customers?
- What else can I do to help the price I'm asking be worth it?

Questions from Libraries for Vendors:

- Do you have working librarians on your development team?
- Can I invite you to watch me work? To watch me teach our customers how to use your product? To watch our customers use your product?
- What can I communicate to our customers about your product? How can you help me do this?

After learning about needs, we arrive at the point of success for negotiation. We are finally able to reach a better solution, a point of mutuality that addresses both our needs in a way unimagined from own narrow perspectives.

The best example of a negotiated mutual benefit that I have heard of over the years was the state library consortium who agreed to purchase an expensive product for statewide use if the vendor agreed to purchase billboards advertising the product, and the library, in each library's geographic area.

Appendix 1: Tips from an Expert

From Herb Cohen. 1980. *You Can Negotiate Anything*. New York: Bantam Books.
Test your assumptions (and the ones forced on you) at every chance:

- Just because the sign looks official, or the statement sounds official, or the document seems official, doesn't mean it's not negotiable.
- Most things are negotiable if both parties want a beneficial result (i.e., you want to buy something and they want to sell it).
- Learn to ask questions, even when you think you know the answers.

Give alternatives, never an ultimatum:

- Give two alternatives that work for you, but one will be more attractive to the other party.
- Not, "We can't pay you $50,000!" but "We can afford between $28k and $32k"
- From the other side, "I was paid $50k in my last job, but I'm willing to take a minimum of $42k given the cost of living differential." The recruit escaped a cap of $32k (above) because $42k sounded a lot better to the other side than $50k.)

Be a willing risk taker:

- When you *have* to do something, you pay top dollar. What do you *have* to do, and what can you do to change that?
- Be willing to walk away.

Legitimacy–people are trained to obey the official:

- Rules, signage, precedence (Again, always question the assumptions that these assert.)
- Expertise (Become expert, sound expert, don't be intimidated by experts' assumptions.)
- Morality (When your needs match those of the greater good, they're harder to dispute.)

- Attitude (When you look like you belong there, or are supposed to be doing it, people rarely question you.)

Time (in the form of deadlines) is the biggest pressure:

- Deadlines are always negotiable; always test any assertion or assumption.
- Concessions are made just before deadline, the tightest deadline loses.
- If they know your deadline, they can control your concessions.

Information wins the game (of finding mutual benefit):

- Negotiation is a process (beginning long before the talks) of learning, learning, learning.
- Give information in order to get it.
- Ask questions, even those you think you know the answers to.

NOTES

1. For more on successful negotiation read: Herb Cohen, *You Can Negotiate Anything* (New York: Bantam Books, 1980); and Roger Fisher, William Ury, and Bruce Patton, *Getting to Yes: Negotiating Agreement Without Giving In* (2nd ed. New York: Penguin Books, 1991).

2. David Bohm, *On Dialogue* (London: Routledge, 1997).

3. For more on effective communication read: Kerry Patterson, Joseph Grenny, Ron McMillan, and Al Switzler, *Crucial Conversations: Tools for Talking When Stakes Are High* (New York: McGraw-Hill, 2002); Marshal B. Rosenberg, *Nonviolent Communication: A Language of Compassion* (Encinitas, CA: PuddleDancer Press, 1999); and Douglas Stone, Bruce Patton, and Sheila Heen, *Difficult Conversations: How to Discuss What Matters Most* (New York: Penguin Books, 1999).

4. For more on negotiation, assessment, collaboration and learning documents in libraries read: Joan Conger, *Collaborative Electronic Resource Management: From Acquisitions to Assessment* (Englewood, CO: Libraries Unlimited, 2004); and Joan Conger, "Usage Statistics in Context: Develop Effective Assessment Practices Through Collaboration," *Usage Statistics of E-Serials*, edited by David Fowler (Binghamton, NY: The Haworth Press, Inc., forthcoming).

5. For more on learning organizations read: Ellen Gottesdiener, *Requirements by Collaboration: Workshops for Defining Needs* (Boston: Addison-Wesley, 2002); Peter Senge, Art Kleiner, Charlotte Roberts, Richard B. Ross, and Bryan J. Smith, *The Fifth Discipline Fieldbook: Strategies and Tools for Building a Learning Organization* (New York: Currency Doubleday, 1994); and Etienne Wenger, Richard McDermott, and William M. Snyder, *Cultivating Communities of Practice: A Guide to Managing Knowledge* (Boston, MA: Harvard Business School Press, 2002).

CONTRIBUTOR'S NOTE

Joan E. Conger is an organization development consultant and author of *Collaborative Electronic Resource Management* published through Libraries Unlimited in late 2004.

CROSSREF:
From Linking to Cross-Provider Search

Amy Brand

Presenter

SUMMARY. CrossRef's mission is to improve access to published scholarship through services that require consensus and collective initiative among publishers. The CrossRef citation-linking network today covers millions of articles and other content items from several hundred scholarly and professional publishers. This article looks briefly at CrossRef's attempt to develop a cross-publisher full-text search service and how this initiative relates to the launch of the Google Scholar service currently in beta format. *[Article copies available for a fee from The Haworth Document Delivery Service: 1-800-HAWORTH. E-mail address: <docdelivery@ haworthpress.com> Website: <http://www.HaworthPress.com>]*

CROSSREF

CrossRef is an independent membership association, founded and directed by publishers. CrossRef's mandate is to connect users to primary research content, by enabling publishers to do collectively what they cannot do individually. CrossRef is also the official digital object identifier (DOI) registration agency for scholarly and professional publications. It currently spans over 1,400 publishers and societies and 16

[Haworth co-indexing entry note]: "CROSSREF: From Linking to Cross-Provider Search." Brand, Amy. Co-published simultaneously in *The Serials Librarian* (The Haworth Information Press, an imprint of The Haworth Press, Inc.) Vol. 50, No. 1/2, 2006, pp. 119-124; and: *Roaring into Our 20's: NASIG 2005* (ed: Margaret Mering, and Elna Saxton) The Haworth Information Press, an imprint of The Haworth Press, Inc., 2006, pp. 119-124. Single or multiple copies of this article are available for a fee from The Haworth Document Delivery Service [1-800-HAWORTH, 9:00 a.m. - 5:00 p.m. (EST). E-mail address: getinfo@haworthpress.com].

Available online at http://www.haworthpress.com/web/SER
doi:10.1300/J123v50n01_11

119

million content items from journals, books, conference proceedings and other content formats. CrossRef operates a cross-publisher citation linking system that allows a researcher to click on a reference citation in a journal or book on one publisher's platform and link directly to the cited content on another publisher's platform, subject to the target publisher's access control practices.

THE DOI

A DOI, or *digital object identifier*, is a name (i.e., a string of letters and numbers) that is used both to identify an item of digital content and to link persistently to it. A DOI functions as an "actionable" link because it is keyed to the object's electronic address, or URL, in a central directory. Due to this resolution mechanism, DOI links do not fail when the content they link to changes location, as long as the DOI directory is updated to include the current address. Thus, the DOI as a unique identification scheme for online content combines the benefits of persistence and action ability.

WHY LIBRARIANS NEED TO KNOW ABOUT CROSSREF AND THE DOI

The CrossRef DOI has become the linking standard in scholarly and professional publishing. The vast majority of scientific, technical, and medical journal publishers employ the DOI. The adoption of DOIs is quickly spreading among publishers of humanities, social science, and professional material. DOIs are also being assigned to books, conference proceedings, and other content types, and several publishers assign DOIs to their legacy (back-file) materials as well as to current publications.

Although many primary and secondary publications already include DOIs, libraries can add DOIs to their own records for linking purposes. CrossRef makes unlimited DOI retrieval available to libraries free-of-charge. Several hundred libraries also use their CrossRef accounts for metadata retrieval in conjunction with their local (OpenURL) link resolvers.

HOW CROSSREF INTEGRATES WITH OPENURL

DOIs point to the authoritative version of content on the publisher's Web site and to publisher-designated resources. Yet, the user working in an institutional context is often directed to other resources. For example, the institution may not subscribe to the e-journal itself but may still be able to offer the user access to the desired article through an aggregated database or through print holdings. In addition, the library may wish to provide a range of linking options beyond what is available at the publisher's Web site.

The DOI and the OpenURL work together in several ways. First, the DOI directory itself–where link resolution occurs in the CrossRef system–is OpenURL-enabled. It can recognize a user with access to a local resolver. When such a user clicks on a DOI, the CrossRef system does two key things: (1) it redirects that DOI back to the user's local resolver, and (2) it allows the DOI to be used as a key to pull metadata out of the CrossRef database. This metadata is needed to create the OpenURL which targets the local link resolver. As a result, the institutional user clicking on a DOI is directed to appropriate resources. By using the CrossRef DOI system to identify their content, publishers in effect make their products OpenURL aware.

Secondly, since DOIs greatly streamline linking and data management processes for publishers, more of them are beginning to require that the DOI be used as the primary linking mechanism to full text. Link resolvers can use the CrossRef system to retrieve the DOI, if the DOI is not already available from the source (i.e., citing) document.

WHY CROSSREF HAS SUCCEEDED

CrossRef has been in existence for only five years. The CrossRef model rapidly took hold for several key reasons:

- Publishers were quick to recognize the importance of persistent links and the value of making their content discoverable for linking through a centralized database of DOIs and bibliographic data
- The CrossRef system is business-model neutral, which means publishers can participate regardless of whether and how they charge for access to their content
- Publishers are required to register only a minimal amount of metadata and are free to encode CrossRef links as they see fit (no branding); and
- CrossRef DOIs can be re-directed to OpenURL resolvers, as described earlier

CROSSREF SEARCH

In 2001, publishers participating in CrossRef first began openly discussing a cross-provider search service. CrossRef launched its first CrossRef Search pilot in 2002 based on full-text indexing of content from six participating publishers, in partnership with FAST Search & Transfer, Inc. Although early user feedback was quite positive, the CrossRef membership and Board of Directors could not reach consensus in support of the initiative, in the face of concern about development costs and about the potential of such a service to undermine existing secondary publishing platforms such as abstracting and indexing databases. In 2003, a small group of publishers *not* acting under official CrossRef auspices approached representatives of *Google*™, who agreed to provide technical services on a no-fee, no-contract basis. Many other publishers were quick to join the project.

In April 2004, CrossRef launched a second prototype CrossRef Search service in partnership with Google search technologies. Like the earlier version, this prototype was intended as a tool to solicit feedback from end-users, in particular to investigate the perceived value of an interdisciplinary search across publisher boundaries that results in free full-text access.

WHAT IS CROSSREF SEARCH NOW?

CrossRef Search is an interdisciplinary, inter-publisher search tool available as a pilot service. The pilot allows users to search the full text of high-quality journal articles, conference proceedings, monographs, and other resources covering a range of scholarly research from numerous leading publishers. Although a good deal of published content is now indexed by Google independently of this new initiative, what made CrossRef Search unique when it launched was that it provides a domain-restricted search. Through a special arrangement between Google and CrossRef, the service performs a normal Google search but filters the results set to the items from participating publishers, thereby reducing the noise produced by general Web searches and providing more targeted access to research material.

CrossRef Search is accessible to users, free of charge, via search boxes on the Web sites of participating publishers. As of June 2005, forty-two publishers are participating in the CrossRef Search pilot, contributing to an index of six million full-text content items. The index encompasses current content as well as back files of several journals. Results are returned using the standard Google search and ranking algorithms, filtering out all but the target publications, and using the item's DOI whenever possible to link from the search results to the full-text item. CrossRef itself does not host any content or perform searches. It works behind the scenes with Google to facilitate the crawling of content on publishers' sites, and sets the policies and guidelines governing participation in the initiative.

USER EVALUATION OF CROSSREF SEARCH

Over a thousand users responded to an online survey about their experiences using CrossRef Search. Eighty-five percent rated the pilot as "good" or "excellent" overall. Seventy-six percent were "successful" in their search endeavors. Eight-five percent were positive about the domain-restricted (published scholarly content only) feature. Seventy-nine percent found the full-text indexing feature useful.

The CrossRef Search pilot has, by design, several clear limitations, and many survey respondents commented on these limitations in their free-form feedback. It has no "destination" search page. The search boxes exist only on the Web sites of participating publishers. The coverage of the published literature is far from comprehensive. Currently, the pilot has no advanced search functionality, no citation indexing, and no citation export capability. Some users said they would like to see some indication in the search results of which resources are freely available.

THE LAUNCH OF GOOGLE SCHOLAR BETA

In early November 2004, the CrossRef Board of Directors voted to continue with the CrossRef Search pilot based on positive user feedback. Its success relies on attracting several major scholarly publishers to participate in the initiative. To the surprise of CrossRef and those publishers working with CrossRef and Google on the pilot, Google announced on November 18, 2004 the launch of its own scholarly search beta service.

Google Scholar replicates the key features of CrossRef Search by providing cross-publisher full-text indexing and search results that are mainly confined to the scholarly literature. Google Scholar also differs from CrossRef Search in several respects. Most significantly, Google

Scholar indexes unpublished papers that reside on institutional servers and returns search results that display alternative versions, both published and unpublished, of the same work. The ranking of results in Google Scholar is based largely on a work's citation frequency, as summed across all indexed versions of a particular work. Users can click on the "cited-by" count in the search results to see the list of works that cite the resource in question.

Given how much has been written in recent months about Google Scholar and how familiar many in the serials community are likely to be with it, an overview of its features or a review of its strengths and weaknesses will not be provided here. Whether the CrossRef Search initiative will continue remains to be seen. A role may still exist for a search service that indexes published research exclusively. Publishers who are allowing their full text to be indexed by Google are now seeing a tremendous amount of traffic coming from the main Google index (twenty to thirty percent of overall traffic, based on a small, informal sample; versus one to four percent from Google Scholar). This traffic is likely to increase the market for individual article sales. At the same time, publishers are understandably concerned about the potential of Google Scholar to cannibalize fee-based journal article sales and subscriptions by facilitating user discovery of free versions of published works.

Librarians and publishers alike are concerned about a loss of control over how scholarly information is accessed, faced with the growing popularity of the commercial search sites as the point of entry into the scholarly literature. Both groups should work together to ensure that Google Scholar and similar services evolve as value-added tools. In other words, they should steer development so new tools do not undermine existing services but instead add to the researcher's means of navigation and discovery. As more of the world's knowledge becomes full-text searchable, deep-text search across disciplines and content types becomes more feasible, opening the door to exciting new advances in research.

CONTRIBUTOR'S NOTE

Amy Brand is Director of Business Development for CrossRef/PILA.

Cross-Provider Search:
New Standards for Metasearch

Jenny Walker

Presenter

SUMMARY. This article, one of two in these proceedings addressing the issue of cross-provider search, concentrates on metasearch and the National Information Standards Organization (NISO) initiative to create and promote standards in this area. Metasearch is the process whereby a user can search heterogeneous resources simultaneously, through a single query form, and receive results back in a consistent way that will enable both merging of the results and general reuse of the results. The NISO Metasearch Initiative addresses three key aspects of metasearch–access management, collection description and search and retrieve. *[Article copies available for a fee from The Haworth Document Delivery Service: 1-800-HAWORTH. E-mail address: <docdelivery@haworthpress. com> Website: <http://www.HaworthPress.com>]*

INTRODUCTION

Libraries today are faced with the challenge of managing and providing access to growing collections of electronic resources. The providers of these collections make available their own separate presentation services. The user, in the course of their research, typically has to discover,

[Haworth co-indexing entry note]: "Cross-Provider Search: New Standards for Metasearch." Walker, Jenny. Co-published simultaneously in *The Serials Librarian* (The Haworth Information Press, an imprint of The Haworth Press, Inc.) Vol. 50, No. 1/2, 2006, pp. 125-135; and: *Roaring into Our 20's: NASIG 2005* (ed: Margaret Mering, and Elna Saxton) The Haworth Information Press, an imprint of The Haworth Press, Inc., 2006, pp. 125-135. Single or multiple copies of this article are available for a fee from The Haworth Document Delivery Service [1-800-HAWORTH, 9:00 a.m. - 5:00 p.m. (EST). E-mail address: getinfo@haworthpress.com].

Available online at http://www.haworthpress.com/web/SER
doi:10.1300/J123v50n01_12

access and interact with multiple presentation services. Each service may have its own unique user interface for discovery and its own access controls. The results that are retrieved may be difficult to merge, reuse and further manipulate.

Many disparate efforts have tried to address these issues. At one end of the spectrum is "just-in-time" metasearch and at the other end is "just-in-case" federated search. To date, these terms have frequently been used interchangeably. With the emergence of high-profile federated search tools such as Google™ Scholar, drawing this distinction is increasingly important. The term "cross-provider search," as in the title of this article, applies equally to metasearch and federated search. This article, one of two in these proceedings addressing the issue of cross-provider search, concentrates on metasearch and the National Information Standards Organization (NISO) initiative to create and promote standards in this area. It does not attempt to discuss the pros and cons of metasearch and federated search.

METASEARCH

Metasearch is the process whereby a user can search heterogeneous resources simultaneously, through a single query form, and receive results back in a consistent way that will enable both merging of the results and general reuse of the results. One example is the provision of an OpenURL for linking. Metasearch is often just one function of a library portal designed to enable the discovery of resources, which can then be used by the patron as targets for metasearching. Other key functions of a library portal include personalization such as alerts, personal resource lists and saved search histories, and a link resolver that leads the user, when relevant, directly to the appropriate copy of an item.

Over the past five years, we have seen a steady growth in the development and deployment of metasearch tools. [1] For a list of metasearch tools for libraries, see the Library of Congress Portal Applications Group Web site. [2]

The metasearch tool provides the interface between the user and the resources being searched. It translates the queries and manipulates and displays the results. The metasearch tool must understand and work with a variety of search and retrieve methods and manage the varied access mechanisms. For many years, library OPACs have supported the Z39.50 search and retrieve protocol. Despite the complexity of this protocol and the fact that it was not designed for article-level citations, a number of major information providers, particularly the abstracting and indexing vendors, followed suit in implementing Z39.50. [3] More recently, we have seen the emergence of the ZING initiative and the SRW/U search protocols. [4] Some vendors offer proprietary XML gateways for searching using metasearch tools. For those vendors who offer no standards-based search interface, the metasearch tool may use "screen scraping" or "html parsing" methods. These methods can and do work but are fragile, and highly susceptible to interface changes by the providers. It is labor-intensive to maintain the "screen scraping" programs or connectors.

THE NISO METASEARCH INITIATIVE

The absence of widely supported standards, best practices, and tools makes the metasearch environment less efficient for the metasearch system provider, the content provider, and ultimately the end-user. Much has been written on the challenges of metasearch including articles by Tamar Sadeh [5], Judy Luther [6], Andrew Pace [7] and others. An excellent bibliography can be found on the Library of Congress Portals Application Group Web site.

To move toward industry solutions, NISO is sponsoring a Metasearch Initiative to enable:

- metasearch service providers to offer more effective and responsive services
- content providers to deliver enhanced content and protect their intellectual property
- libraries to deliver services that are distinguished from those offered by Google and other free Web services.

Interestingly, unlike many standards initiatives that are librarian-led, this particular effort was prompted by information providers. At the 2003 American Library Association Midwinter Meeting, three vendors–EBSCO, Thomson Gale, and ProQuest–called a meeting to discuss the spikes in search activity that they were observing as a result of metasearch activity. Although these vendors all offered Z39.50 access to their databases, "screen-scraping" methods of access were being used, in some cases with a detrimental effect on the systems being searched. At this ALA meeting, NISO volunteered to take a leadership role in determining a solution.

In May 2003, a planning committee was formed to prepare for an initial meeting. Significant preparatory work by the committee, including the writing of white papers, ensured a productive meeting that uncovered the breadth of the problem from metasearch identification, authentication, and authorization to collection discovery and citation metadata. Three key areas were recommended for ongoing work. In January 2004, the NISO Metasearch Initiative was formalized.

Since these initiatives first got underway, a number of things have changed that make this initiative all the more important and urgent. Firstly, the number of electronic resources continues to grow exponentially. Increasingly these resources originate from outside the traditional library community that is already familiar with standard search and retrieve protocols such as Z39.50. Secondly, in the absence of clear direction from the community, information providers have been developing proprietary XML gateways. Metasearch vendors must develop and maintain different connectors for each such gateway. Thirdly, Google Scholar emerged in November 2004.

While the Metasearch group does not believe that Google Scholar can replace the need for metasearch, this topic has been greatly discussed and debated. Metasearch must work in the most optimal manner. In his April 2005 presentation to the NISO Metasearch group, "Google Scholar. Is Metasearch dead?" Roy Tennant of the California Digital Library suggests, "unless Google Scholar becomes something *very different* than what it is today, it will *never* provide the solution libraries seek in a metasearch tool." [8] Tennant advocates the need for libraries to target metasearch across specific resources tailored to a specific audience and purpose.

The NISO Metasearch Initiative, co-chaired by Andrew Pace of North Carolina State University and myself, drew a tremendous international response and sixty committee members were each assigned to one of three task groups to investigate access management (chaired by Mike Teets of OCLC), collection description (chaired by Juha Hakala of the University of Helsinki and the National Library of Finland) and search and retrieve (co-chaired by Sara Randall of Endeavor Information Systems and Katherine Kott of the DLF). The committee members include a mix of librarians, publishers, and library-software providers. The committee was charged with identifying, developing, and framing the standards and other common understandings that are needed to enable an efficient and robust metasearch environment. The goal, at a minimum, was to create a set of best practices. Committee members understood that the Metasearch Initiative could create new standards or endorse existing ones.

The first of two face-to-face meetings in North Carolina's Research Triangle Park in April 2004 was attended by nearly two-thirds of the committee members. Pace stated, "The success of the meeting is not only measured in the high level of participation and work accomplished, but also in the cooperative effort of disparate parties to solve the issues of metasearching for everyone–libraries, vendors, and publishers alike." Mark Krellenstein of Elsevier commented, "We believe that a standard which enriches the user experience through improved metadata and search capabilities while reducing the impact on content providers' systems is a benefit for all parties." [9]

ACCESS MANAGEMENT

The first of the three task groups addressed the issue of access management, covering both the authentication and authorization processes required for metasearch. Access management for academic institutions and other research organizations reaches far wider than metasearch. Most institutions are actively involved in deploying, or at least investigating, single sign-on environments that will make it easier for users to navigate between applications without being asked to repeatedly present their user credentials and yet provide the appropriate levels of security for the systems and the data being accessed.

Authentication is the process where a network user presents their credentials (explicitly by presenting username/password–or implicitly by IP address based on their location) and, thereby, establishes a right to an identity–in essence, the right to use a name. [10] Essentially, this process determines that the user is who they say they are.

The authorization process is whereby a network user, based on their attributes (which they received as a result of presenting their credentials), receives entitlements or authority to use a resource.

In a metasearch environment, authentication and authorization processes come into play between the user and the metasearch tool and also between the metasearch tool and the resources that are being searched. The access management task group focused their attention largely on the access controls required between the metasearch tool and the resources which itself is a multi-step process requiring the presentation and the checking of credentials and the retrieval of attributes for use in the authorization process. The AMP (Access Management Protocol) symbol created by this task group has become the unofficial mark of this group and illustrates the multi-step access process.

Because the significant work of this Metasearch task group, including a comprehensive environmental scan, is fully documented on the official NISO Metasearch Initiative Web site, this paper will focus only on the outcomes. [11] Proxy servers and username/password access methods scored highest in the report, both in terms of meeting the metasearch access management use cases and of the environmental factors such as ease of implementation, effectiveness, security, cost, and market acceptance. [12] After proxy servers, Shibboleth was ranked second highest because of its ability to meet the needs of the use cases. It scored very poorly on the environmental factors because it is not yet widely deployed and because few vendors currently support it. [13]

The NISO Metasearch Initiative Task Group on Access Management, therefore, recommends that institutions that are in the process of acquiring new electronic resources should implement either IP-authentication with a proxy server, or a username/password authentication system to control access to their electronic resources. These systems are the most widely supported by vendors, have the lowest implementation and maintenance costs, and are the simplest for smaller or less technically sophisticated organizations to install. They also ensure that remote users can access the resources of the institution with little difficulty.

This task group's final recommendations are surprising in their similarity to recommendations given by Cliff Lynch of the Coalition for Networked Information in 1998. He believed that ". . . most institutions will be forced to continue to support a proxy-based approach for the foreseeable future, if they are to manage access to a wide range of publishers." [14]

However, progress has been made in the intervening years. Shibboleth does hold the promise of providing the solution we seek. The current Shibboleth implementation model allows only for authentication between the user and the metasearch tool and does not allow for mediated access to controlled resources by the metasearch tool. Discussions are already underway between members of the Metasearch Task Group and the Shibboleth developers' community to ensure that Shibboleth 2, the next version of the specification, provides facilities that will allow surrogates to authenticate to service providers as the user that initiated the request. The Metasearch Task Group has recommended in its draft report that the metasearch implementation community continue to explore, and become involved with the development of, emerging authentication and access technologies to ensure that these new technologies can support the requirements of the metasearch environment. Regardless of the methods that prevail, the community must heed to the comments of Clifford Lynch. "Access management needs to be routine and easy to implement; once a contract is signed, lengthy technical negotiations between institution and content supplier should not be necessary before users can have access. In a world of networked information resources, access management needs to be a basic part of the infrastructure, and must not become a barrier to institutional decisions to change or add resource providers." [15]

COLLECTION DESCRIPTION

The discovery of collections and informational services is critical to effective metasearch, for end users to find relevant and available resources and for librarians to be able to find and group resources for easy access by end users using the metasearch tool.

The term "collection" can be applied to any aggregation of physical or digital items. It is typically used to refer to collections of physical items such as books, maps, compact discs, digital surrogates of physical items, and of "born-digital" items and catalogues of such collections.

Collection descriptions aid users in selecting the most relevant resources among those accessible via the metasearch tool they use. Data elements are, therefore, required that describe a collection for the purpose of resource discovery. Collection descriptions allow the owner of a collection to disclose information about their existence and availability to interested parties so that they can find and use the contents.

Associated with a collection is a set of services, one or more functions of interest to an end-user or a software application. Service descriptions will be used by applications in order to determine how to access remote services. Examples include structured network services like those based on a particular protocol (e.g., Z39.50, SRU/SRW, OAI-PMH, FTP). In the metasearch context, applicable services could be offered through protocols such as Z39.50 and SRW/U.

The second group's primary concern is the metadata needed in metasearch applications. The group has focused on two element sets, one for describing collections accessed by metasearch tools and another for depicting the services offered by the collections.

COLLECTION METADATA

Key criteria used in evaluating existing metadata schemes included the ability to:

- discover collections that meet a specified set of criteria
- obtain sufficient descriptive information to enable the identification of a desired collection
- obtain sufficient descriptive information to enable the selection of one or more collections from a number of discovered collections
- discover the services that provide access to the collection

Much work has been done in this area, in particular the work of the Research Support Libraries Program in the UK (RSLP). [16] The second task group benefited not only from the preceding work itself but also through a significant number of committee members well versed in this area and with cross-over membership of related standards initiatives. The second task group's recommendation is a schema based on the Dublin Core Collection Description Application Profile (DC CD AP) developed by the Dublin Core Collection Description Working Group. [17]

SERVICE DESCRIPTION METADATA

As with collection metadata, existing work was useful to the task group. It chose to use the ZeeRex explain schema as the starting point for a metadata element set for service descriptions. The ZeeRex origins in the Z39.50 Explain facility are clear in that ZeeRex stands for Z39.50 Explain, Explained and Re-Engineered in XML. [18] The first step in evaluating the viability of ZeeRex for metasearch was to create some ZeeRex records that described the variety of services that might be targeted by actual metasearch applications, and the outcome was successful.

RELATED ISSUES

Not directly addressed by the collection description task group is the exchange of collection description and service access descriptions. This issue is key to the success of the group's recommendations. The group is, however, following industry initiatives in this area such as the UK Joint Information Systems Committee (JISC) Information Environment Service Registry (IESR) project [19] and also the National Science Foundation (NSF) funded OCKHAM project [20].

SEARCH AND RETRIEVE

The search and retrieve methodology sits right at the core of metasearch. Metasearch tools use a variety of search and retrieve methods, including the Z39.50 and SRW/U standards, as implemented by interface providers. However, many of the interface providers with whom metasearch tools should interact do not yet support such protocols. Metasearch tools must rely on proprietary XML gateways or "screen-scraping" methods. Tools do exist to facilitate the implementation of Z39.50 and SRW/U. However, these protocols are still considered by interface providers to be too "heavyweight."

Many of the interface providers, especially the newer players serving the library market, are not familiar with the library-based standards. The third task group sought a simpler solution, proposed in the NISO Metasearch XML Gateway (MXG) protocol. It is based on the NISO SRU protocol and uses URL's sent via HTTP to retrieve XML responses.

This task group had significant overlap with SRW/U members who wanted the adoption of SRW/U as *the* Metasearch Initiative recommended protocol. One significant benefit for SRW/U that resulted from the task group discussions was the creation and publication of extremely useful "How to" documentation that helps demystify SRW/U, especially for implementers.

Although the search and retrieve task groups have concentrated their efforts on the search gateway, other key items have also been addressed:

- Results set metadata
- Citation level data elements

The results set metadata subgroup has provided recommendations on data elements for both results sets and records themselves as retrieved from the target resource. Results set metadata recommendations include elements that enable resource branding which is an issue for many information providers. A recommended set of citation level data elements will ensure the reuse of data retrieved by a metasearch tool, particularly vis-à-vis the provision of onward linking via the OpenURL. Not surprisingly, the recommended element set is based loosely on the OpenURL data elements, and also on Dublin Core elements for the description and subject fields, for example.

REACHING CONSENSUS

A September 2005 NISO workshop in DC marked the official launch of the MetaSearch Initiative standards and the recommendations for metasearch best practices. This workshop also provided an opportunity for information providers to learn how to implement these standards. Further, libraries and metasearch vendors that did not participate in the committee work were able to hear first-hand from the creators of these standards and to learn how library services can benefit from the implementation and adherence to these standards. The Metasearch best practice recommendations and the draft standards can be found on the NISO MetaSearch Initiative Web site.

Many thanks go to all those who contributed to this important work.

NOTES

1. Dick Boss, "Library Portal Sales Soar," *Information Systems Report* 3, no. 5, (October 2004).
2. *The Library of Congress Portals Applications Issues Group.* http://www.loc.gov/catdir/lcpaig/ (16 June 2005).
3. *International Standard Maintenance Agency Z39.50, The Library of Congress Network Development & MARC Standards Office.* http://www.loc.gov/z3950/agency/ (16 June 2005).
4. *SRW Search/Retrieve Web Services.* http://www.loc.gov/z3950/agency/zing/srw/ (21 June 2005).
5. Tamar Sadeh, "The Challenge of Metasearching," *New Library World* 105, no. 1198/1199 (2004): 104-112.
6. Judy Luther, "Trumping Google? Metasearching's Promise," *Library Journal* (October 1, 2003).
7. Andrew Pace, "Much Ado about Metasearch," *American Libraries.* (June/July 2004) http://www.ala.org/ala/alonline/techspeaking/techspeak2004/Junejuly2004muchado.htm (16 June 2005).
8. Roy Tennant, Google Scholar: "Is Metasearch dead?" NISO MI meeting. Raleigh, NC. (April 2005) http://escholarship.cdlib.org/rtennant/presentations/2005niso/ (16 June 2005).
9. See note 7 above.
10. Clifford Lynch, "Access Management for Networked Information Resources," *ARL Newsletter* 201 (December 1998), pp. 3-7. http://www.arl.org/newsltr/201/cni.html (15 June 2005).

11. *NISO Metasearch Initiative.* http://www.niso.org/committees/MS_initiative. html (21 June 2005).

12. Ranking authentication methods for use in a metasearch environment.

13. *Shibboleth, Internet 2.* http://shibboleth.internet2.edu/ (21 June 2005).

14. See note 10 above.

15. See note 10 above.

16. *The RSLP Collection Description.* http://www.ukoln.ac.uk/metadata/rslp (20 June 2005).

17. *Dublin Core Collection Description Application Profile.* http://www.ukoln. ac.uk/metadata/dcmi/collection-application-profile (20 June 2005).

18. *ZeeRex* http://explain.z3950.org/ (21 June 2005).

19. *Joint Information Systems Committee (JISC).* http://www.jisc.ac.uk/ (20 June 2005).

20. *The OCKHAM Initiative.* http://www.ockham.org/ (20 June 2005).

CONTRIBUTOR'S NOTE

Jenny Walker is Vice President of Marketing for the Ex Libris Group and Co-Chair NISO Metasearch Initiative.

Serials Industry:
Truth or Dare

Dena Schoen
Julia Gammon
Zac Rolnik
Bob Schatz

Panelists

Elizabeth Lowe

Recorder, Session 1

Donna Packer

Recorder, Session 2

SUMMARY. This panel, comprising experts from an academic library, a publisher and two vendor companies, engaged the audience and each other in a series of discussions on the problems and challenges currently facing each of the active members in the scholarly communication chain. The primary topics covered were: the recent flurry of cancellations of e-journal packages by libraries and consortia, evaluating vendor sustainability, jobbing orders (or "where do you put your eggs"), the cri-

[Haworth co-indexing entry note]: "Serials Industry: Truth or Dare." Lowe, Elizabeth and Donna Packer. Co-published simultaneously in *The Serials Librarian* (The Haworth Information Press, an imprint of The Haworth Press, Inc.) Vol. 50, No. 1/2, 2006, pp. 137-145; and: *Roaring into Our 20's: NASIG 2005* (ed: Margaret Mering, and Elna Saxton) The Haworth Information Press, an imprint of The Haworth Press, Inc., 2006, pp. 137-145. Single or multiple copies of this article are available for a fee from The Haworth Document Delivery Service [1-800-HAWORTH, 9:00 a.m. - 5:00 p.m. (EST). E-mail address: getinfo@haworthpress.com].

Available online at http://www.haworthpress.com/web/SER
doi:10.1300/J123v50n01_13

teria used to make acquisition or cancellation decisions, and standing orders. *[Article copies available for a fee from The Haworth Document Delivery Service: 1-800-HAWORTH. E-mail address: <docdelivery@haworthpress. com> Website: <http://www.HaworthPress.com>]*

What follows are accounts of the two Serials Industry Truth or Dare Strategy Sessions. The panel's exploration of the scholarly communication chain was fluid and consideration of some issues overlapped from one topic or session to another. Both sessions were broad ranging, freewheeling discussions, even chaotic.

SESSION 1

The panel began the Friday session by tackling the current backlash against perceived price gouging by large publishers. Observing the recent efforts by academic libraries and consortia to disentangle themselves from the Big Deals, Bob Schatz asked if the recent cancellations of e-journal packages made any difference in the way that large presses price and distribute their journals. Zac Rolnik answered that the Big Deal ultimately served to prohibit the introduction of new journals. Librarians perceive the need to stand up to publishers because, to some extent, they have lost control over their collection development, Rolnik suggested. In response to an inquiry from Schatz, one audience member indicated that, along with three other institutions, his institution had canceled their subscription to one of the Big Deals but they are feeling some pressure from faculty who want it back.

Despite the tumult, library reactions have not been limited to either submissive renewals or abrupt cancellations. A third approach is illustrated by the recent actions of OhioLINK. Julia Gammon explained OhioLINK's tactics. By employing usage statistics, Gammon explained that they were able to look at top and bottom percentage of journals and renegotiate as multi-year contracts come due.

One unexpected offshoot of the panel's first discussion was a consideration of how unaware professionals are of the demands and challenges facing their colleagues in other segments of the scholarly communication chain. Dena Schoen commented that the faculty still has an uphill track in understanding what librarians deal with and publishers do not always understand what librarians have to do vis-à-vis their clientele. Mentioning that faculty and students have more access to more journals on their desktops but do not see the cost, Rolnik postulated that the faculty, themselves, might perceive that it is a better world than it was ten years ago. Implying that all in Libraryland is not quite as rosy as our hypothetically access-satiated faculty might well believe, Schoen contended that the whole bibliographic world has suffered profoundly. Whole areas of the Library of Congress Classification scheme have been getting slashed and burned because librarians have to buy the rest of a journal collection (e.g., STM titles).

Prefacing their second question with the observation that libraries seem to be placing a moratorium on new journals unless another title is canceled, Rolnik asserted that new products come out which should be in library collections and asked the audience if they would share the metrics they use in evaluating journal cancellations and acquisitions. One audience member mentioned that, at her institution, the librarians would proceed on their own but would also present the faculty with a list of journals to evaluate for cancellations and purchases. With collection development policies driven by the realization of flat budgets, audience members expressed frustration with their lack of buying power. One audience member responded that their title cancellations were four percent of their journals. Another person said that their institution has to cut their approval program or bindery to compensate.

A similar sense of restrictions and the need for trade-offs was evident in the consideration of acquisitions. Bob Schatz asked if librarians took sustainability into account. The lack of audience response indicated that sustainability was not a primary consideration. Instead, audience members indicated that they looked at the research their faculty are doing, the number of ILL requests any particular title might receive, whether or not it was indexed and abstracted, whether it came from a good publisher and had an impressive editorial board, if it would support new academic programs, and if it was not covered in the e-journal packages to which they already subscribed.

This discussion of acquisitions criteria generated a side discussion on usage statistics and what they can tell us. Reflective of discipline specificity, one audience member observed that the best of the engineering titles do not get as much use as those in life sciences. Another audience member shared that her institution was currently looking at one of the Big Deals and while they have usage statistics for the last six months, she wondered what, if anything, they really tell us.

Beginning with the comment of one audience member that it was "very scary to see a journal we purchased get one or two uses, if we paid four to eight hundred dollars," the group then considered their reactions to journals with low usage statistics. Rolnik suggested that librarians should cancel a title if it was not being used. Schoen disagreed by stating that one use could have been by Einstein. She argued that libraries had a mission to preserve civilization and build collections for future use. Considering the more concrete realities, Julia Gammon, the librarian on the panel, said that her institution did not have that luxury. They were not an ARL institution and that, in practice, they just buy for the current user.

The questions of cost, of why prices keep escalating, and what can be done about it, captivated the attention of those present. Members of the audience groused about rising prices. One expressed the frustration felt by many librarians, saying that publishers raise prices because they can get away with it. Rolnik commented that he thought that increases were simply the nature of journal products. If you want a specific journal and if no substitute products will be suitable, you need to go to that publisher. Another librarian protested that libraries had dropped a lot of paper and then they would get calls from the publishers to see if they were getting the publication some other way. Then possibly embargoes would be placed on the release of content in the aggregators' packages. Rolnik acknowledged the problem, pointing out that aggregate purchases are not a substitute for primary journals because they do not have a lot of things that these journals have. What if, he asked, all of a sudden a primary journal was no longer in that database?

Schatz observed that while the goal of librarians is to meet the needs of faculty, they do not have enough resources to deliver. Another audience member said that Donald Trump was once asked about being 25 million dollars in debt and he replied that the problem was with the bank. If we do not have the money to buy journals that faculty need to do research and get published, he asserted, then that is the faculty's problem. Yet, as Rolnik pointed out, making faculty aware of the issues involved is difficult because, with products like ScienceDirect, they already have what they want when they want it.

The next topic was that of the economic indicators of vendors' financial health. Schoen stated the question was problematic: "Woe to any agent that talks about another agent's status." She urged the audience to recall that financial indicators can be cooked to look any way you want. In addition, Schoen said that, beyond the usual financial statements, other indicators include service behaviors. Schatz responded that these behaviors might or might not be indicators of a company's financial health. He pointed out that these sometimes really are due to flu epidemics or late customer payments.

Another issue that came up was the lack of financial analysis performed by libraries. One audience member pointed out that libraries had continued to put money into prepayment plans with *divine*, despite the company's shaky financial history. Schoen agreed and speculated that, despite seeing the financial indicators, many librarians do not want to contribute further to a company's demise by withdrawing their business. To which the audience member quipped that a line needed to be to drawn between continuing a relationship with a vendor and being fiscally responsible.

Shifting the conversation to the handling and assessment of vendor financial information, Bob Schatz asked whether anyone had requested financial information from vendors. After show of hands from audience, Schatz commented that about five percent have asked for information and fewer had received it. He then asked how the information was used. One audience member responded that, while her institution did require information from vendors, she had no idea what it meant, and the library handed it over to the financial people. Expressing a common concern of vendors, Schatz explained that many private companies do not wish to share information and lose control of it (i.e., let it fall into the hands of the competition). Gammon replied that, at her institution, vendor information was usually marked confidential. Not wanting the responsibility of interpreting this data, the library passed contracts and licenses back up the chain. Intriguingly, no one volunteered any responses to Schatz's queries on how the financial bona fides of vendors were employed within the library.

Gammon led the group in a dialogue on the practical aspects of the two theories of jobbing orders, namely those of putting "all of the eggs in one basket" or using multiple vendors. On the whole, the group preferred to use multiple vendors because, as one audience member stated, it resulted in greater leverage with the bigger vendors. Observing that fewer major vendors exist today than in the past, Schatz asked whether it was realistic for librarians to spread their business around. Various audience members illustrated the practical restrictions faced by small and mid-sized libraries: one library needed to put all their eggs in one basket on the monographs side to get the discount and stretch their budget; another institution was virtually forced to receive ninety-six percent of their serials from one big vendor because they had a one-person serials department.

Vendor service was a theme throughout much of the first session. Audience members expressed satisfaction with the service of vendors in the areas of law and other subjects. One audience member reported that she valued the relationships that she has with vendors because they will tell her if something is wrong on her side. In contrast, the audience attributed poor service to specific individuals and the absence of librarian-vendor communication. Schoen urged librarians not to withhold feedback from vendors, even if they were friends with the representatives or had worked with them for a long time. Pointing out libraries also have fluctuations in terms of service and budget, and none of us are immune to eccentric slips and arrears, Schoen argued that the withholding of information can contribute to the demise of a company. Instead, she advised librarians to spread their business around if they were worried about a vendor going bankrupt. Transfers are a challenge, she acknowledged, but asserted that the same could be said of approval programs.

SESSION 2

Schatz set the tone for Session 2 by stating the panelists' intention to give voice to controversial issues within the serials community, to allow us to challenge "what is being said." From their prepared list of ten discussion points, the panelists chose to question once again the role of subscription and standing order agents. Librarians, they proposed, state they want agents to survive. Given that libraries routinely by-pass agents by dealing through consortia or buying clubs, or going direct to publishers to get what appears to be a better bottom-line deal, do librarians really mean what they say? Gammon noted a library's responsibility is to save money wherever and whenever possible. Schoen pointed out that librarians continue to make these consortial and direct arrangements despite the hidden costs, including the extra work generated by widespread poor service, cutting and tracking extra checks, and so on. Audience comments confirmed Gannon's point about internal pressures to save costs, which sometimes negate pressures to streamline. At the same time, many vendors were slow to begin handling electronic subscription products. Some vendors still cannot or will not handle these subscriptions.

The panel returned to a question addressed in Session 1: given recent mergers and bankruptcies of some subscription agents, what indicators can librarians use to ascertain the financial health of their agents? How can librarians best protect their institution's money? The agents on the panel reminded us that the major vendors are all private companies, and have no legal obligation to make financial information public. Librarians, they charged, are often somewhat naïve in interpreting what financial information they can get. Schoen suggested that while all companies have service challenges, librarians can look to the range of services provided, and how they are delivered over time. Constant reshuffling of personnel can be one indication of turmoil within the company. She also stated that libraries must pay in advance with no guarantee they will ever receive the goods. The contrary is also true. Vendors sometimes provide the goods in good faith but they do not always get paid. Some libraries are extremely slow to pay, a serious problem in an industry where cash flow is critical. Schatz noted the economics of the information industry are of little interest to most librarians, and library schools do not teach it. Yet infrastructure costs continue to rise quite apart from the rising cost of content, and both librarians and vendors are often "winging it." The best advice the audience could provide was "Trust but verify." The verification often proves difficult or impossible.

Of special interest to publishers, the next question sought to ascertain how libraries decide to purchase new serial titles. Do librarians really place moratoria on purchasing new titles, or only purchase a new title if an existing subscription of equal or greater cost is canceled? Have library criteria for purchasing new titles changed in the digital environment? Audience responses indicated that practices vary with the size and the type of library. Many measure cost per use, and look at high costs overall. One medical librarian noted that her library must support new areas of research. They look at canceling what appear to be "dead wood" low use titles. They pay great attention to requests from users, and are reluctant to pick up new titles unless they are indexed. Rolnik noted indexing services could wait up to three years before picking up a brand. If the journal has few sales during those years, where will the capital come from to sustain the title during this very lean period? Academic librarians in the audience stated that the teaching faculty is extremely influential in making decisions on new titles, and that name recognition helps. For example, they have experienced immediate demand for the new *Nature* titles. Usage can be important in the decision; some libraries will not order a new title unless it has been requested on interlibrary loan a number of times (borrowing might be difficult if libraries are not buying new titles). Some institutions post proposed cancellations in various ways, and elicit feedback from various constituencies. Rolnik expressed some frustration when he asked "Should I hang it up because I'm a new company?" The one audience suggestion was that new publishers should get the most famous scholars they can find in the field to endorse the new publication and influence people to buy.

The discussion moved on to a question concerning standing orders for monographic series. Why do so many libraries send "standing orders" to subscription agents rather than to booksellers who are better equipped to handle them? Why do subscription agents accept "standing orders"? Schoen noted that some agents have both journal subscription and full-fledged standing order operations. Subscription agents who are really only set up to handle subscriptions will accept standing orders because they are more profitable. Gammon stated that sometimes where an order is placed would depend on the library's organizational structure at the time the order is placed. Audience members noted that decisions are also sometimes dependent on the way funds are set up for that particular purchase. The digital formats have also complicated things from a library standpoint. Some standing order agents could not handle electronic only formats, or they promised to handle them and did not follow through.

As the session moved into more general discussion, audience members returned to publisher Rolnik's issues. Librarians might put pressure on index publishers to take new titles earlier than three years. Many in the audience agreed the publishing market has room for "interesting niche players." The point was made again that librarians know very little about the economics of publishing and the agents' world, and that too many librarians are not interested in learning. The old rule of thumb that it takes five years for a journal to break even no longer holds; it can be much longer now. Library budgets are also threatened as the very large publishing houses move into the social sciences and humanities markets, driving up prices there. The industry is truly international, and the entrepreneurial traditions of other countries have a bearing. Some other issues for librarians, agents and publishers alike are that we still do not have a true machine-to-machine communication for necessities such as invoicing. Librarians find themselves working with auditors who still require paper trails, and often have trouble understanding the concept of the electronic journal or reference series. One audience member, in reminding us the problem is economics, not communication, was bold enough to suggest that SPARC "missed the boat." Competition means another title in the same specialty to buy; it does not resolve the underlying economic issues.

In the final moments of the session, a member of the audience asked the question that reflected a concern expressed throughout the conference. Why would a publisher come to NASIG? Rolnik stated that, for him, this was an opportunity to talk directly with his customers, and to learn. NASIG, in his opinion, should make a serious effort to reach out to publishers, especially the smaller ones. Schatz reminded the audience that publishers have many potential venues. They must look at the return on investment in sending staff to conferences, what will drive sales, and improve their credibility and visibility. Perhaps, NASIG could provide a "library advisory board" or focus group opportunities that might be especially helpful to smaller publishers.

The session was permeated with an overall feeling of frustration with the current environment, both from the supply side publishers and agents and the demand side libraries. While the session provided little in the way of satisfactory resolutions, the audience seemed truly to appreciate the panelists' willingness to participate, pose hard questions, tell a little of the situation from their side of the industry, and above all, to listen to the audience response.

CONTRIBUTORS' NOTES

Dena Schoen is Regional Manager-North America for Otto Harrassowitz. Julia Gammon is Head of the Acquisitions Department at the University of Akron. Zac Rolnik is Publisher for *Now–The Essence of Knowledge*. Bob Schatz is Director of New Business Development at Coutts Library Services. Elizabeth Lowe is a Catalog Librarian at Southern Illinois University Edwardsville. Donna Packer is Acquisitions Librarian and Head of Acquisitions/Serials Services at Western Washington University Libraries.

Ensuring Consistent Usage Statistics, Part 1: Project COUNTER

Oliver Pesch

Presenter

SUMMARY. This presentation provides a brief background on COUNTER, looks at changes brought on by Release 2 of the COUNTER code of practice and discusses the upcoming audit requirement to ensure and enforce compliance. It touches on the next area of focus of COUNTER before examining how technologies such as metasearch and pre-fetching by browsers can negatively affect usage reporting. *[Article copies available for a fee from The Haworth Document Delivery Service: 1-800-HAWORTH. E-mail address: <docdelivery@haworthpress.com> Website: <http://www.HaworthPress.com>]*

COUNTER RELEASE 1

According to the Project COUNTER Web site, "COUNTER (Counting Online Usage of NeTworked Electronic Resources) is an international initiative designed to serve librarians, publishers and intermediaries by facilitating the recording and exchange of online usage statistics." Its members, who include librarians, publishers and intermediaries, such as full text aggregators and subscription agents, share the common goal of providing credible and consistent measurement of usage statistics between vendors. The COUNTER Web site can be found

[Haworth co-indexing entry note]: "Ensuring Consistent Usage Statistics, Part 1: Project COUNTER." Pesch, Oliver. Co-published simultaneously in *The Serials Librarian* (The Haworth Information Press, an imprint of The Haworth Press, Inc.) Vol. 50, No. 1/2, 2006, pp. 147-161; and: *Roaring into Our 20's: NASIG 2005* (ed: Margaret Mering, and Elna Saxton) The Haworth Information Press, an imprint of The Haworth Press, Inc., 2006, pp. 147-161. Single or multiple copies of this article are available for a fee from The Haworth Document Delivery Service [1-800-HAWORTH, 9:00 a.m. - 5:00 p.m. (EST). E-mail address: getinfo@haworthpress.com].

Available online at http://www.haworthpress.com/web/SER
doi:10.1300/J123v50n01_14

at http://www.projectcounter.org. It contains details of the code of practice, lists of compliant vendors, and provides a history of COUNTER.

Unlike a formal standard like those created by NISO or ISO, the COUNTER Code of Practice (COP) is a voluntary set of guidelines that address terminology, layout and format of the report, processing of usage data, what categories or filters should be available, and delivery of reports. Each of these guidelines will be expanded on in this article.

COUNTER provides guidelines to ensure vendors are consistent in their use of terminology. Existing standards for definitions were used: NISO Z39.7 (Usage Statistics), ARL New Measures Initiatives, and ICOLC Guidelines for Statistical Measures.

COUNTER USAGE REPORTS

Listed below are examples of the reports that are identified in the COUNTER code of practice.

- **Journal Report 1:**

Full Text Article Requests by Month and Journal (Figure 1)

- **Journal Report 2:**

Turnaways by Month and Journal (Figure 2)

In the context of the COUNTER Code of Practice a turnaway occurs when an end-user's access to the site is denied because the maximum number of licensed simultaneous users has been reached. No other definition of turnaway applies.

- **Database Report 1:**

Total Searches and Sessions by Month and Database (Figure 3)

- **Database Report 2:**

Turnaways by Month and Database (Figure 4)

- **Database Report 3:**

Searches and Sessions by Month and Service (Figure 5)

FIGURE 1. Full Text Article Requests by Month and Journal

	A	B	C	D	E	F	G	H	I	J	K	L	M
		Print ISSN	Online ISSN	4-Jan	4-Feb	4-Mar	4-Apr	4-May	4-Jun	4-Jul	4-Aug	4-Sep	Calendar YTD
1													
2	Total for all journals			3942	10006	11093	14698	5346	5737	4563	4676	8301	68362
3	ABA Banking Journal	0194-5947		0	3	0	1	1	1	6	2	0	14
4	ABA Journal	0747-0088		1	6	4	25	5	2	5	0	2	50
5	Abacus	0001-3072		0	0	0	0	0	0	0	0	0	0
6	ABNF Journal	1046-7041		0	0	6	0	5	4	7	1	4	27
7	About Campus	1086-4822		0	0	0	0	1	1	0	0	0	2
8	Academe	0190-2946		0	0	0	1	0	0	0	1	0	2
9	ACADEMIC LEADER.	8750-7730		0	1	0	0	0	0	0	0	0	1
10	ACADEMIC QUESTIONS	0895-4852		0	0	1	3	4	2	0	0	0	10
11	Academy of Management Exec	1079-5545		10	27	4	13	10	9	0	26	17	116
12	Academy of Management Journ	0001-4273		4	0	8	4	3	18	2	27	3	69

FIGURE 2. Turnaways by Month and Journal

	Print ISSN	Online ISSN	Jan - 01	Feb - 01	Mar - 01	Calendar YTD
Total for all journals			6637	8732	7550	45897
Journal of AA	1212-3131	3225-3123	456	521	665	4532
Journal of BB	9821-3361	2312-8751	203	251	275	3465
Journal of CC	2464-2121	0154-1521	0	0	0	0
Journal of DD	5355-5444	0165-5542	203	251	275	2978

FIGURE 3. Total Searches and Sessions by Month and Database

	A	B	C	D	E	F	G	H	I
1			4-Jan	4-Feb	4-Mar	4-Apr	4-May	4-Jun	Calendar YTD
2	Academic Search Elite	Searches Run	1650	6072	7023	10765	3253	2816	31579
3	Academic Search Elite	Sessions	1065	3544	4126	4840	1644	1886	17105
4									
5	Academic Search Elite - Publications	Searches Run	0	0	0	0	0	0	0
6	Academic Search Elite - Publications	Sessions	0	1	0	1	0	2	4
7									
8	American Humanities Index	Searches Run	0	2	127	205	103	66	503
9	American Humanities Index	Sessions	0	1	54	60	26	28	169

FIGURE 4. Turnaways by Month and Database

	A	B	C	D	E	F	G	H
1			Jan-04	Feb-04	Mar-04	Apr-04	May-04	Calendar YTD
2	Total Database Record Turnaways for all Databases	Database Record Turnaways	17	13	0	0	0	30
3	Academic Search Elite	Database Record Turnaways	3	0	0	0	0	3
4	Academic Search Elite - Publications	Database Record Turnaways	0	0	0	0	0	0
5	American Humanities Index	Database Record Turnaways	0	0	0	0	0	0

FIGURE 5. Searches and Sessions by Month and Service

	A	B	C	D	E	F	G	H	I
1			4-Jan	4-Feb	4-Mar	4-Apr	4-May	4-Jun	Calendar YTD
2	Total for EBSCOhost	Searches Run	3555	10234	11560	17457	6123	5757	54686
3	Total for EBSCOhost	Sessions	3705	9881	11112	13792	5309	5316	49115

PROCESSING USAGE DATA

How and when usage is counted is something not addressed by other standards initiatives. The importance of consistent counting can be illustrated by using Web logs to count full text retrievals. Normally, PDFs are loaded "progressively" or a page at a time. Each time the Acrobat reader goes back to the server for more data, a transaction is recorded in the server's Web log. If the vendor were to merely count up the transactions, a large document could possibly appear as dozens of "full text requests." Fortunately, as these requests are logged, the first request has a distinctive "return code." Thus, the vendor must consider the return code and count only the first request and not subsequent ones. This area is covered by COUNTER.

Double, triple, quadruple clicking is also a major issue. On slow connections, users get impatient and click again. Each click is likely to be logged. These multiple clicks must be filtered to avoid over counting. Through some detailed testing done by Elsevier, a time window of ten seconds is optimal for HTML pages and thirty seconds for PDFs. If a user clicks the same link to an HTML page twice within ten seconds, only one click is counted. As you can imagine, improper handling of the data processing by vendors can lead to serious over-reporting.

WHO COUNTS THE FULL TEXT TRANSACTION

The next two diagrams demonstrate that the service that delivers the full text to the end user is the one responsible for providing the full text. In the first diagram (Figure 6), the user is linked from site to site until finally they are redirected to the publisher's site and the full text. The publisher counts the "full text request," whereas the other sites can only count the activity as link-outs. In the next diagram (Figure 7), the e-journal gateway has an authentication arrangement with the publisher and fetches the PDF from the publisher then redirects to the end user. The gateway is delivering the full text and thus the gateway is responsible for counting the "full text request."

DELIVERY OF REPORTS

The COUNTER Code of Practice dictates that a vendor must provide the reports as follows:

- CSV, Excel, or file that can be imported into Excel (XML version being tested)
- On a password controlled Web site
- Scheduled alert or automatic delivery of report via e-mail
- Provided monthly
- Available within four weeks of the end of the month
- Current and previous year's data is available

COUNTER RELEASE 2

With release 2 of the Code of Practice, COUNTER had several objectives in mind:

- Increase usability of reports
- Extend Journal Report 1

- Eliminate Level 2 reports in favor of "optional" reports
- Address the "non standard" implementation of the standard

Release 2 will be valid starting January 1, 2006.

MINOR FIXES TO EXISTING REPORTS

The following examples (Figures 8 and 9) show the changes in Release 2 as they relate to Release 1.

FIGURE 6

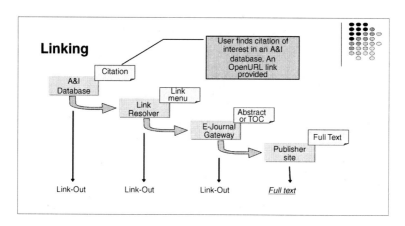

FIGURE 7

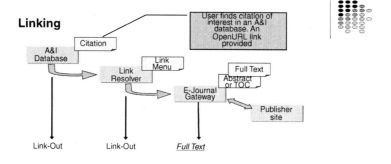

FIGURE 8

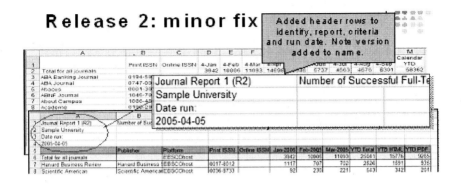

FIGURE 9

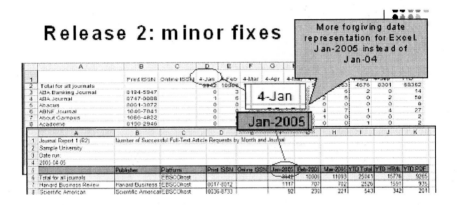

RELEASE 2 ENHANCEMENTS

Figures 10 to 13 show the enhancements made to the reports.

The total count of full text requests have often been viewed as a bit subjective. Some Web sites will automatically display the HTML full text with the citation. If a user is merely browsing the "detailed" display of a list of articles, they may well be accumulating the full text retrieval count by virtue of this being shown automatically. The user may not even have cared about the article, but the count is still accumulated. By separating out HTML and PDF, the institution can make better in-formed decisions related to a given journal . . . if the HTML displays au-

FIGURE 10

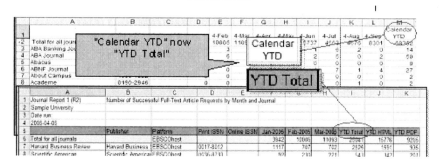

FIGURE 11

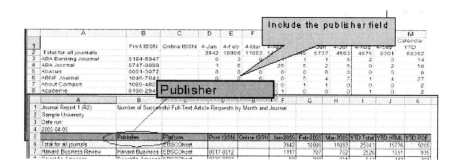

FIGURE 12

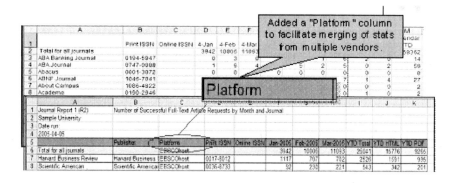

FIGURE 13

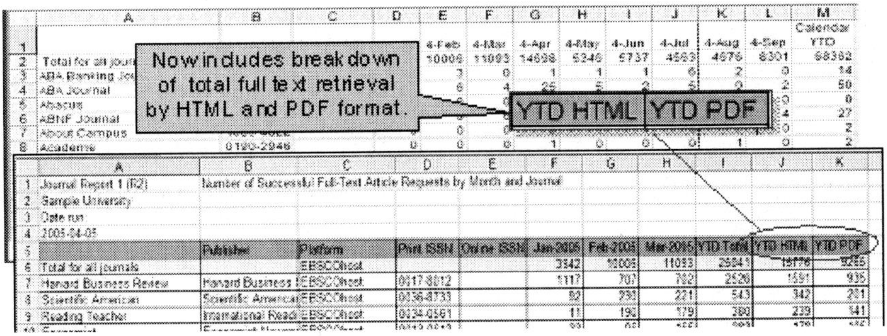

tomatically, then the PDF counts are probably a better indication of importance of the article because the user has specifically requested this format.

CLARIFYING THE ELIMINATION OF DOUBLE CLICKS

Double-click processing is a source of confusion when it comes to filtering more than two clicks in a row. If you have three clicks do you drop the second, then compare the third to the first (may now be over ten seconds), or do you drop the first and compare the second and third? Figure 14 provides an example of how to manage an HTML link being clicked several times.

As you can see we had a series of five clicks coming at six second intervals except for one with a fifteen second delay. The number of seconds between the transactions shows on the right. The first click is compared to the second, with the first being discarded because six seconds is less than ten. The second is compared to the third, with the second being discarded. The third is compared to the fourth, the third is retained. The fourth is compared to the fifth, etc. The net result is there are two "valid" requests, the first and the fifth.

CLARIFYING THE EXPECTATIONS FOR REPORTS LAYOUTS

Several ILS vendors are looking at providing modules for accumulating and consolidating usage from the various sources. COUNTER is viewed as the driving standard that can make this work. However, when

FIGURE 14

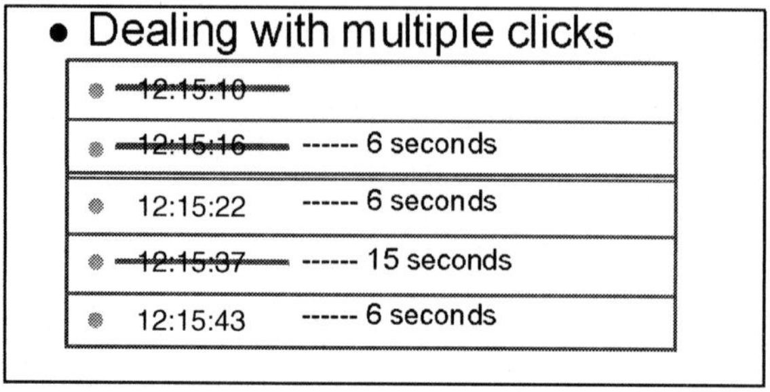

```
● Dealing with multiple clicks
  ● ──12:15:10──
  ● ──12:15:16── ────── 6 seconds
  ● 12:15:22      ────── 6 seconds
  ● ──12:15:37── ────── 15 seconds
  ● 12:15:43      ────── 6 seconds
```

the existing "standard" reports were gathered and compared, many were found to be different. Some of the issues were:

- Additional header rows added
- The column headings spread on two rows not one (for example the month on one row and the year on the one below)
- Additional columns included
- Some did not even resemble a COUNTER report

While we could lay blame on the vendors for getting it wrong, the COP must not have been clear about its rigidity. Therefore, in Release 2, all ambiguity and source of confusion has been removed. It explicitly states what must appear where, as indicated in Figure 15, an excerpt from Release 2 of the COP.

CLARIFY CONSORTIUM REQUIREMENTS

To eliminate confusion as to what kinds of reports are needed for consortia, COUNTER clearly states that:

- Only two reports apply:
  - Journal Report 1: *Number of Successful Full-Text Article Requests by Month and Journal*
  - Database Report 1: *Total Searches and Sessions by Month and Database*
- Vendor to provide (in separate files):
  - Aggregated reports for entire consortium
  - Individual reports for each member institute
- Aggregated reports include totals for the whole consortium

AUDITING COUNTER REPORTS

Initially COUNTER compliance was self-declared. A library panel performed basic testing to ensure compliance in format. COUNTER's plans include requiring vendors to pass an official audit before compliance is granted. This plan's implementation is slated for 2006 and will be conducted, at the vendor's expense, by a certified auditor–either a financial auditor or an organization approved by COUNTER. The auditors will be looking for:

- Layout: *Header rows; row and column placement; row and column labels*
- Formats: *CSV or Excel*
- Delivery of report: *E-mail notification of availability of reports; Access from password controlled Web site;*
- Accuracy of data: *Conduct series of tests for each report; Current tolerance is −8% to +2%*

COUNTER CODE OF PRACTICE FOR E-BOOKS AND OTHER REFERENCE WORKS

E-books and e-reference of the non-journal genre is COUNTER's next focus. Materials such as e-books, dictionaries, encyclopedias and almanacs are increasingly being digitized and included not only as stand-alone sites, but also as part of full text aggregations. How effec-

FIGURE 15

1. Cell A1 contains the text "Journal Report 1(R2)"
2. Cell B1 contains the text "Number of Successful Article Requests by Month and Journal"
3. Cell A2 contains the "criteria" as defined in the COP (eg "NorthEast Research Library Consortium" or "Yale University")
4. Cell A3 contains the text "Date run:"
5. Cell A4 contains the date that the report was run in yyyy-mm-dd format. For example, a report run on 12 Feb 2005 would show "2005-02-12".
6. Cell A5 is left blank
7. Cell B5 contains the text "Publisher"
8. Cell C5 contains the text "Platform"
9. Cell D5 contains the text "Print ISSN"
10. Cell E5 contains the text "Online ISSN"

tively this material is used is important to both the vendor and the library. Both can use the statistics to place a relative value on the material.

The challenge with this type of material is determining what the unit of retrieval is. With e-journals, one accepted measure is the requests for articles. However, with other e-reference material, the unit of retrieval may vary by user interface. For example, some services provide access to an entire e-book as a single PDF file, where others provide access at the chapter level, and still others provide viewing one page at a time. In order to address this issue, COUNTER is proposing two activity reports. One shows successful title requests by month and title and the other shows successful section requests by month and title. The former would be used by vendors providing only full-book access, whereas the latter is used for vendors providing access by a unit or section of the full content.

The proposed reports for E-Reference material are:

- Book Report 1
  - *Number of Successful Title Requests by Month and Title*
- Book Report 2
  - *Number of Successful Section Requests by Month and Title*
- Book Report 3
  - *Turnaways by Month and Title*
- Book Report 4
  - *Total Searches and Sessions by Month and Title*
- Book Report 5
  - *Total Searches and Sessions by Month and Service*

The code of practice for e-reference is out for comment. The latest version can be viewed at the COUNTER Web site. We encourage all interested parties to review and comment on it.

OTHER TECHNOLOGIES THAT MAY IMPACT USAGE REPORTING

In this section of the presentation, we discuss two technologies that are challenges to usage reporting, namely, metasearch and pre-fetching by browsers.

Metasearch

Metasearch technologies, sometimes referred to a broadcast or federated searching, work by providing a single user interface that performs simultaneous searching of multiple online services from different vendors. The goal is to give the end user a single access point to all information resources licensed by an institution. Figures 16 and 17 show the possible effect of metasearch on session and search counts.

As highlighted, the same basic amount of inquiry by a user produced vastly different results, the metasearch enabled site tallied up twenty sessions and searches compared to just two on the more traditional site. The good news is that the full text retrieval counts are not affected in the same way and remain relatively the same in both environments.

To combat this effect on searches and sessions:

- Libraries should try to isolate metasearch sessions and searches
  - Capture source of activity
  - Isolate metasearch IP address
  - Have metasearch access through separate account
- Support metasearch standardization activities through NISO
  - We need a standard way for a content provider to recognize a metasearch session

PRE-FETCHING

Google and other services are introducing pre-fetching of links to improve performance. Pre-fetching works like this:

- A user performs a search that results in a number of results.
- Google will introduce <link> tags for the first few results to cause the browser to fetch the pages in the background
- The pre-fetched pages are loaded into browser cache

If the results that are being pre-fetched were links to publisher full text then each pre-fetch is a full text request. When the user does click the link, another header request is made, that could be considered yet another full text request. Without some kind of control, this activity could result in significant over-counting.

Publishers and content providers can implement remedies for this situation. The pre-fetch action is identified in the HTTP header of the re-

FIGURE 16

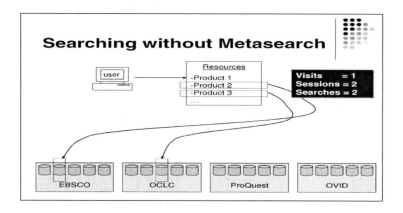

FIGURE 17

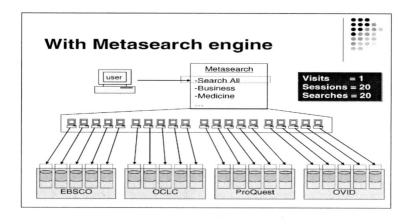

quest. Vendors can change systems to recognize pre-fetch and do one of the following:

- Simply return an error (do not deliver full text), the end user does not see this error
- Fulfill the pre-fetch request, but do not count the transaction
- Count only the request resulting from the actual click of the link

The bottom line being that unless pre-fetching and metasearch are handled by content providers, then some of the COUNTER statistics being provided may be significantly over counted. Through COUNTER and other standards organizations, libraries and content providers can work together to come up with common solutions to these challenges.

CONCLUSION

COUNTER is a collaboration of vendors and libraries. It is much more than a standards document. It is a code of practice with the added values of enforcement and registration of compliant services. It is about setting reasonable objectives with benefits that extend to all parties. It is an active organization that is forward looking. Broad participation by librarians, publishers and other intermediaries is not only encouraged, it is essential for COUNTER to meet current and future needs for usage reporting.

CONTRIBUTOR'S NOTE

Oliver Pesch is Chief Strategist for E-Resources at EBSCO Information Services.

Ensuring Consistent Usage Statistics, Part 2: Working with Use Data for Electronic Journals

Alfred Kraemer

Presenter

SUMMARY. A review of recent journal use data at the Medical College of Wisconsin Libraries showed a rapid shift in user preferences. The decline in print use was as dramatic as the increase in the use of electronic versions. Some of the unusual challenges of producing use reports for electronic journals are presented in this article. Last, but not least, some observations about the relationship between the access infrastructure and electronic journal use are discussed. *[Article copies available for a fee from The Haworth Document Delivery Service: 1-800-HAWORTH. E-mail address: <docdelivery@haworthpress.com> Website: <http://www.HaworthPress.com>]*

This presentation deals with "use data integrity," which may not at first be apparent. The word "integrity" has multiple meanings that can be found in any standard dictionary of the English language. Depending on context "integrity" may refer to the soundness or completeness of facts and the honesty in a person. According to the *Webster's Third New International Dictionary of the English Language*, it may also refer to "the quality or state of being complete or undivided."[1]

[Haworth co-indexing entry note]: "Ensuring Consistent Usage Statistics, Part 2: Working with Use Data for Electronic Journals." Kraemer, Alfred. Co-published simultaneously in *The Serials Librarian* (The Haworth Information Press, an imprint of The Haworth Press, Inc.) Vol. 50, No. 1/2, 2006, pp. 163-172; and: *Roaring into Our 20's: NASIG 2005* (ed: Margaret Mering, and Elna Saxton) The Haworth Information Press, an imprint of The Haworth Press, Inc., 2006, pp. 163-172. Single or multiple copies of this article are available for a fee from The Haworth Document Delivery Service [1-800-HAWORTH, 9:00 a.m. - 5:00 p.m. (EST). E-mail address: getinfo@haworthpress.com].

Available online at http://www.haworthpress.com/web/SER
doi:10.1300/J123v50n01_15

Working with use data can be described as making the best of various types of usage data to help make decisions on a set of current journal acquisitions. Complete as well as estimated or projected data requires a context before decisions can be derived from the data. Given the occasional contentiousness of journal budgeting negotiations, misrepresenting data unintentionally can have a lasting, damaging impact. The strength or weakness of data must be clearly identified. Even the best data is no substitute for communicating with user constituencies.

Historically, most studies of journal use in libraries were either based on sampling techniques or employed cumbersome procedures that often involved barcodes on journal issues, bound volumes, and sometimes even on journal shelves. A smaller number of libraries–invariably those with expensive journal subscriptions–devised more comprehensive methods of gathering use data for all subscribed journals. The advent of electronically accessible journals has produced much more journal use data than most of us anticipated. While keeping an eye on the source and quality of the data will be important, we also need to focus on analyzing and interpreting the available data so as to understand its meaning and relevance.

Since 1994, use data from an integrated library system has been a key element in the annual review of journal subscriptions at the Medical College of Wisconsin Libraries. Improvements in the decision-making process were made over the years, but by and large the same evaluation method was used year after year–as long as print journals were predominant.

After about two years of working with use data for a mostly electronic journal collection, some similarities between use data for print and that for electronic journals became clear–just as expected. The surprise was in what the use data from a variety of user access points showed about the extent of decline in print use, the speed of adoption of e-journals, and the importance of convenient access points. A few observations show some continuity between print and electronic use data. For the most part, journals which had the highest use as print journals have similar use as electronic journals.[2]

WHY DO WE NEED THE USE DATA?

We have become used to re-examining that question. For libraries with expensive journal subscriptions, use data has been a mainstay for justifying the purchase of new journals and the cancellation of no longer cost-effective subscriptions. However, this reason has never been the only rationale for working with use data. The use data has also been extensively utilized to support funding for other library functions, such as housing collections and providing services to library patrons. Last but not least, it has played an important role in the change of fund reallocations from monograph to serials acquisitions.

In short, the importance of use data was never just limited to renewal decisions for journals but also extended to a support and access infrastructure. In a print journal environment, patrons were offered access options that were tied to a physical location and specific, direct, and tangible library services. Electronic journals have changed the service and access needs of our patrons dramatically. While establishing how much of a journal's total use is facilitated by one of several access options is nearly impossible, the use data that we get from proxy servers, remote access portals, or databases with embedded links provides very good information about trends.

The fact that we may not be able to calculate the exact relationship between offering remote access and a specific growth margin in the total use of a journal does not imply that such relationships should not be reported together with overall journal use data. On the contrary, if the access infrastructure for electronic journals is overlooked and neglected, negative impacts on electronic journal use are bound to ensue. At the Medical College of Wisconsin, the growth in the use of PubMed LinkOut and the proxy server for remote access are very similar in timing and growth rate to the overall increase in electronic journal usage.

In summary, the following activities rely to a great extent on complete and reliable use data:

- Changes in journal collection:
    - "Rejuvenating" the collection
    - Making cuts while minimizing negative impacts
    - Quantifying the effect of changes
- Choosing among available access options
- Setting priorities in trouble-shooting e-resource problems
- Communicating with user constituencies

METHODS OF COLLECTING AND MERGING USE DATA

The formats and contents of publisher-provided use data reports vary widely, even if many of them comply now with the COUNTER requirements. Seemingly small variations, e.g., an unusual ISSN format (Figure 1) require special attention before that data can be merged with other data, for example, prices from invoices.

The basic sources for the annual review of current journal purchases at the Medical College of Wisconsin Libraries are:

- Combined use data reports for all journal titles
- Bibliographic data from the online catalog
- Price data from publisher and/or vendor invoices

For a shrinking number of electronic journals, locally gathered click-through counts from an A to Z list are the only statistics available. Since click-throughs represent only a fraction of the total use, that count is multiplied by a factor that has been derived from journals for which both click-through counts and publisher-provided COUNTER-compliant data was available. Any journal for which the total use data was estimated on the basis of click-through tallies is clearly marked in any final use data reports. The following list shows the stages of compiling and analyzing use reports:

- Combine all use reports that provide per-title full-text accesses
- Extrapolate locally generated e-use tallies (e.g, click-through counts)
- Merge with price data using the ISSN (Insist on price data/invoices with ISSN)
- Add calculated fields: price/use, increase/decrease rate compared to previous years
- Sort to filter out low-use, high cost-per-use titles
- Examine trends and develop scenarios

FIGURE 1

Title	ISSN	Total
American Heart Journal	'00028703	478
American Journal of Cardiology, The	'00029149	988
American Journal of Emergency Medicine, The	'07356757	181
American Journal of Gastroenterology, The	'00029270	784
American Journal of Hypertension	'08957061	542
American Journal of Infection Control	'01966553	125
American Journal of Medicine, The	'00029343	999

Managing large and diverse data files has its own set of challenges; guidelines for good data management are readily available. The key requirements for data files on electronic resource usage at the Medical College of Wisconsin Libraries are:

- Retain source data files and files with source data compilations. Follow retention guidelines from other administrative departments on campus, but keep data longer if needed.
- Ensure that basic procedures to generate reports exist and are updated–including information how derived data fields are created.

The flowchart below outlines the process of combining use data, importing price information, and creating reports on journals that should be given special attention because of their low use or their high cost-per-use ratio (Figure 2).

FIGURE 2

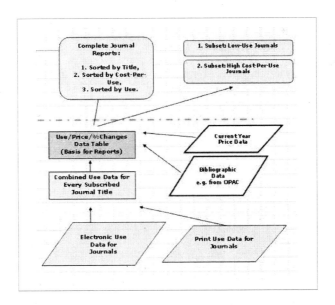

TIME IS OF THE ESSENCE:
RAPID CHANGE IN USER PREFERENCE

The quick transition from a predominantly print to a largely "electronic-only" journal purchasing paradigm at the Medical College of Wisconsin Libraries (Figure 3) is by no means unique. Because of a long-standing practice of tallying print data, we were able to see the dramatic decline in the use of print volumes at the same time when we were evaluating the first use reports for electronic journals. The actual numbers (Figure 4) were seen as a clear "mandate" to accelerate the pace of electronic-only journal acquisitions.

FIGURE 3

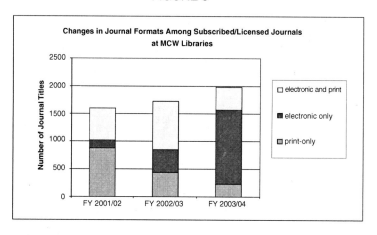

Changes in Journal Formats Among Subscribed/Licensed Journals at MCW Libraries

FIGURE 4

Journal Use at MCW Libraries by Fiscal Year (FY)			
	FY 2001/02	FY 2002/03	FY 2003/04
Electronic Journals	84,819	183,889	325,728
Print Journals	115,893	99,184	51,064
Total	200,712	283,073	376,792

Please Note: Print usage, based on reshelving statistics, tends to be undercounted compared to electronic full-text article accesses.

CORRELATED EFFECTS

Calculating or estimating the effect of the access infrastructure on the overall use of electronic journals is a great challenge. Even a cursory look at the growth rates in the use of more recent access options, e.g., remote access via proxy servers (Figure 5), embedded links in PubMed (Figure 6), and other similar "access facilitators" raises the question: What is the impact of the local access infrastructure on the use of a library's electronic resources? An article published in 2002 by Johan Bullen and Rick Luce was among the first to discuss that question.[3] The Association of Research Libraries' New Measures Initiatives Web site and the Web resource on administrative metadata management for electronic resources at Cornell University are good starting points to develop local strategies for capturing and analyzing metrics. [4,5]

A look at another statistic, the rate of increase in use for individual electronic journals, appears to show higher rates for those journals with advanced linking features, e.g., linked references, OpenURL

FIGURE 5

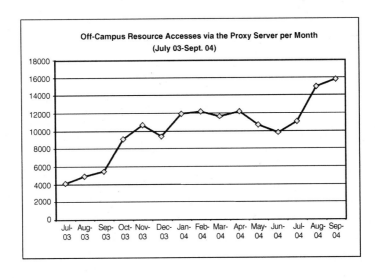

FIGURE 6

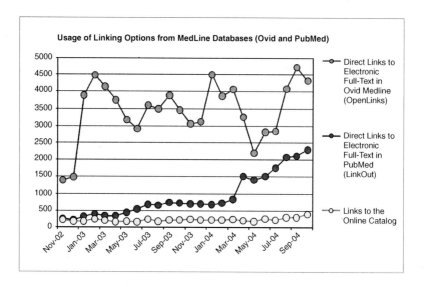

support, and other features that "enhance the presence" of a journal in an electronic environment. This observation deserves further investigation.

INDICATORS OF THE NEED FOR NEW JOURNALS

Obtaining any use indicators for new journals has become more difficult. Impact factors, interlibrary lending statistics, and patron surveys all have their flaws. Interlibrary lending statistics used to be an excellent predictor of a need for a new journal subscription. As highly requested journals are added it inevitably becomes harder to determine worthwhile additions as one reaches a point where the benefits of a new subscription might not be greater than those of another subscription that would have to be canceled.

No matter how obvious or difficult decisions on changes in journal subscriptions might be, patron participation is essential. Without it, even the best decisions can result in negative feedback and suspicion towards the library. The Medical College of Wisconsin uses a Web-based survey on the Intranet to solicit feedback on a list of journals for which requests have been tracked. Figure 7 shows an excerpt of the

FIGURE 7

	JOURNAL TITLE	# ILL Requests	Prev. Years over Copyright	Subscription Price 2004	Subscription Price/Ill-Requests
▾	ACCIDENT ANALYSIS AND PREVENTION +	10	2001-	$1,442.00	$144
Essential If funds permit	ADULT EDUCATION QUARTERLY	-	-	$206.00	-
▾	AMERICAN JOURNAL OF PSYCHOTHERAPY	-	-	$100.00	-
▾	ANTIVIRAL THERAPY	-	-	$672.00	-
▾	APPLIED CLINICAL TRIALS	-	-	$64.00	-
▾	ASSOCIATION FOR THE ADVANCEMENT OF AUTOMOTIVE MEDICINE, ANNUAL PROCEEDINGS	-	-	$40.00	-

survey. The names of those who requested a journal would be included in a column to the right of the excerpt but is omitted from this figure.

CONCLUSIONS

Use data does not always make decisions easier but it arguably makes them better. Making bad decisions with good data is not impossible but it appears to be more difficult. Furthermore, ongoing data evaluation would tend to reveal past mistakes in interpreting data. The most significant change appears to be that electronic journal use is more dependent on the range of access mechanisms available, than was the typical use scenario for print journals. If, for example, the access infrastructure for electronic journals is poorly developed, the data will show use levels well below their potential.

Most comparable, title-level use data can become a reasonable basis for determining the use ranking within an existing journal collection. The ranking sequence may not change much whether overall use of the collection is high or low. However, for the purpose of justifying fund allocations and for continued library support the information about use changes for the entire set of current subscriptions is vital.

NOTES

1. *Webster's New International Dictionary*, 3d. ed., s.v. "integrity."
2. David H. Morse and William Clintworth, "Comparing Patterns of Print and Electronic Journal Use in an Academic Health Science Library," *Issues in Science and Technology Librarianship*, no. 28 (Fall 2000). http://www.istl.org/00-fall/refereed. html (23 March 2005).
3. Johan Bullen and Rick Luce, "Evaluation of Digital Library Impact and User Communities by Analysis of Usage Patterns," *D-Lib Magazine* 8, no. 6 (June 2002), http://www.dlib.org/dlib/june02/bollen/06bollen.html (15 April 2005).
4. ARL–New Measures Initiatives. *Section: Best Practices: Collection Management and the Application of New Measures for Library Assessment Presentations from the ALCTS CMDS session at ALA, June 27, 2004 in Orlando, FL.* http://www.arl.org/stats/ newmeas/index.html (15 April 2005).
5. *A Web Hub for Developing Administrative Metadata for Electronic Resource Management.* http://www.library.cornell.edu/cts/elicensestudy/home.html (15 April 2005).

CONTRIBUTOR'S NOTE

Alfred Kraemer is Assistant Director at the Medical College of Wisconsin Libraries.

Talk About:
E-Resources Librarian to the Rescue?
Creating the Über Librarian:
Turning Model Job Descriptions
into Practical Positions

Katy Ginanni

Presenter

Susan Davis
Michael A. Arthur

Recorders

SUMMARY. Libraries are assessing the need for a separate electronic resource librarian and identifying where managing e-resources fits into the organizational structure. If such a position is warranted, what does it look like? Feedback from the 2004 conference evaluations suggested having a topical discussion session to hear many ideas and find out what has and has not worked. Questions pointed to the need for a better understanding of the responsibilities of these positions and the need to identify the knowledge required to perform at a high level. Salary concerns were also expressed, as was the prevalence of trial and error training. A good

[Haworth co-indexing entry note]: "Talk About: E-Resources Librarian to the Rescue? Creating the Über Librarian: Turning Model Job Descriptions into Practical Positions." Davis, Susan and Michael A. Arthur. Co-published simultaneously in *The Serials Librarian* (The Haworth Information Press, an imprint of The Haworth Press, Inc.) Vol. 50, No. 1/2, 2006, pp. 173-177; and: *Roaring into Our 20's: NASIG 2005* (ed: Margaret Mering, and Elna Saxton) The Haworth Information Press, an imprint of The Haworth Press, Inc., 2006, pp. 173-177. Single or multiple copies of this article are available for a fee from The Haworth Document Delivery Service [1-800-HAWORTH, 9:00 a.m. - 5:00 p.m. (EST). E-mail address: getinfo@haworthpress.com].

Available online at http://www.haworthpress.com/web/SER
doi:10.1300/J123v50n01_16

173

mix of librarians from various types of institutions participated in two
lively discussions exploring these and other issues related to the successful management of electronic resources. *[Article copies available for a fee
from The Haworth Document Delivery Service: 1-800-HAWORTH. E-mail address:
<docdelivery@haworthpress.com> Website: <http://www.HaworthPress.com>]*

This discussion session, described as a "talk about," was led by Katy
Ginanni. She opened the well-attended sessions, with about forty to
fifty people each day, by explaining how the topic developed into a
strategy session at the 2005 conference. One of 2004's conference evaluations suggested that talking about what an e-resources librarian is and
what the job entails would make a great program, especially with a
group discussion format to allow lots of ideas to be exchanged.

Ginanni polled the audience to see how many had electronic resources in their job titles. About half of them had the term as part of their
titles. A few people dealt with e-only in their jobs. The audience's level
of experience was about evenly divided between those with more than
ten years' experience and those with less. Of those with less experience,
about half were hired into an electronic resources position.

An audience member asked how many libraries have tried to incorporate managing electronic resources into existing workflows and organization. Valparaiso has print and electronic together. Yale's Medical
Library has distributed responsibilities for electronic among technical
services staff. The University of Texas at Austin has also distributed responsibilities over several departments, but is designing a new e-resources librarian position. The University of Derby in the United
Kingdom has a combined serials and interlibrary loan department
whose head will be retiring in fall 2005. The library is now faced with
restructuring the electronic component into existing staff responsibilities and determining what, if any, new staff might be hired. The University of Washington has mainstreamed as much as possible. The
University of Wisconsin-Whitewater has tried a combined print and
electronic serials operation, but this arrangement is growing increasingly unmanageable. The University at Buffalo (SUNY) also tried to
manage print and electronic together, but decided to form a centralized
electronic periodicals management department to handle e-journals for
both health sciences and general libraries. Temple University is recruit-
ing for an e-resource librarian. Furman University has centralized responsibilities in one position. Southern Methodist University uses a
team approach. Indiana University has had an e-resources librarian for
four years who has dealt exclusively with electronic.

From the discussion, libraries are clearly struggling to find the best organizational structure to deal with the management of e-resources. One person questioned the need for a separate e-resources position. Would the need for such a position based on format go the way of the Microform Librarian? Some commented that e-resources librarians are a passing trend, but re-examining workflows and position descriptions offers opportunities to try new things.

Ginanni moved the discussion toward position descriptions. She reviewed job ads from the archives of SERIALST and ERIL-L and found examples of serials librarian job advertisements from 1995 and 1996 that were very short (less than a page). After 1996, she noticed a significant shift with digital resources librarians being sought instead of serialists. The job ads grew to about two pages. She asked the question, what is different now? Responses included: paying attention to copyright issues, knowledge of license terms and license negotiation, customer service orientation, creativity, managing data loads, and educating other library staff about licensing and access issues.

Given the new expectations of managing electronic resources along with the added complexities involved, how are librarians being trained for these positions? Most talked about on-the-job learning, self-teaching, trial and error, and asking subscription agents for help. Others noted technical services operations have fewer librarians. They are busier than ever and may not have sufficient time to train newer staff. Because everyone is so busy, documenting procedures and policies is even harder. Others believed that change is so rapid that the best training is on a case-by-case basis. Others recommended taking advantage of professional development opportunities at library conferences. Everyone agreed few formal training opportunities are available at present. Because many different parameters that affect specific procedures come into play based on size and scope of one's institution, preparing a course or workshop to fit all situations is not easy. One suggestion was to develop a course based on theory or general principles with checklists of common skill sets. Another suggestion was to offer internships to library school students.

Next, discussion turned to what attributes libraries are looking for when hiring or creating e-resources positions:

- Flexibility
- Creativity
- Interest in learning
- Cooperative/collaborative approach
- Serials knowledge

- Big-picture thinker
- Ability to multi-task
- Excellent communication skills
- User-oriented
- Well-organized
- Ability to follow through

Someone noted that trying to hire these multi-faceted, complex positions at entry-level salaries would not attract well-qualified candidates. Expectations are so high that salaries need to be commensurate with the duties. Some libraries were very concerned about upgrading support staff since those jobs are also becoming more complex, and then trying to establish appropriate salary levels. Another issue is trying to determine the appropriate skill level necessary for staff positions.

Relationships with Information Technology (IT) staff, legal counsel, and public services were discussed. Libraries whose licenses are reviewed first by lawyers reported frustration at not being in control of the process. Some institutions have great IT support. Others reported difficulty educating IT staff about library concerns even after repeated attempts. Some electronic resource positions even report to IT. The audience raised the question of where best does an e-resource librarian fit in the organization, public or technical services. Comments included the fact that e-resource staff have much more contact with the end users and may also need to adopt a "sales" pitch philosophy to explain the value of e-resources to university faculty. Some libraries therefore use teams or working groups to handle e-resources to ensure that both technical and public services skills are included in the process.

The enthusiastic discussion which characterized each session is indicative of the interest in this topic. Many libraries are struggling to find the right fit, both administratively as well as with the position itself. It will be interesting to review what an e-resources librarian position looks like in five to ten years, or if it even still exists!

RESOURCES

Vicki Grahame, *Managing Electronic Resources*: Spec Kit no. 282 (Washington, D.C.: Association of Research Libraries, 2004)

Sarah E. George, "Keeping the Connection: Maintaining E-Journal Subscriptions," *Serials Librarian* 46 (2004): 309-14.

Karen Cargille, "Looking Forward, Looking Back: Views of Serials Librarianship in the New Millennium," *Serials Review* 25, no. 4 (1999): 29-43.

Susan Andrews, "Meeting End User Needs in the Electronic Universe: a Dialogue," *Serials Librarian* 36 (1999): 247-51.

N. Lewis, "Redefining Roles: Developing an Electronic Journals Collection at the University of East Anglia," *Information Services & Use* 21 (2001): 181-8.

David Burke, "From Catalogers to Ontologists: Changing Roles and Opportunities for Technical Services Librarians," *Serials Librarian* 46 (2004): 221-6.

Catherine Von Elm and Judith F. Trump, "Maintaining the Mission in the Hybrid Library," *Journal of Academic Librarianship* 27 (2001): 33-5.

Xiaoyin Zhang and Michaelyn Haslam, "Impact of Electronic Resources on Serials Acquisitions," *Serials Librarian* 46 (2004): 326-7.

CONTRIBUTORS' NOTES

Katy Ginanni is Training Specialist for Training Resources of EBSCO Information Services. Susan Davis is Head of the Electronic Periodicals Management Department at University at Buffalo, State University of New York. Michael A. Arthur is Acquisitions and Serials Services Librarian at Old Dominion University.

"We Own It":
Dealing with "Perpetual Access"
in Big Deals

Andrew Waller
Gwen Bird

Presenters

SUMMARY. This article presents the results of a survey of Canadian university libraries that investigated whether libraries have been able to stay abreast of the many changes that affect their access to paid-for e-content. This report emphasizes the publishers' obligations to notify licensees when ownership changes hands and libraries' need to actively pursue licensed content in ownership transfers. The meaning and application of "perpetual access" clauses in e-journal licenses under change-of-ownership situations is also discussed. *[Article copies available for a fee from The Haworth Document Delivery Service: 1-800-HAWORTH. E-mail address: <docdelivery@haworthpress.com> Website: <http://www.HaworthPress.com>]*

INTRODUCTION

Over the last few years, academic libraries have been steadily canceling print journals that are duplicated in large, publisher-based, bundled

[Haworth co-indexing entry note]: "'We Own It': Dealing with 'Perpetual Access' in Big Deals." Waller, Andrew, and Gwen Bird. Co-published simultaneously in *The Serials Librarian* (The Haworth Information Press, an imprint of The Haworth Press, Inc.) Vol. 50, No. 1/2, 2006, pp. 179-196; and: *Roaring into Our 20's: NASIG 2005* (ed: Margaret Mering, and Elna Saxton) The Haworth Information Press, an imprint of The Haworth Press, Inc., 2006, pp. 179-196. Single or multiple copies of this article are available for a fee from The Haworth Document Delivery Service [1-800-HAWORTH, 9:00 a.m. - 5:00 p.m. (EST). E-mail address: getinfo@haworthpress.com].

Available online at http://www.haworthpress.com/web/SER
doi:10.1300/J123v50n01_17

electronic journal packages, i.e., Big Deals. These cancellations have been carried out for a variety of reasons. For instance, libraries are unable to afford both print and online formats; libraries want to save space by canceling print; libraries want to make the conversion to the electronic environment; etc. These decisions are often underpinned by a belief that libraries *own* this e-content as a result of licensing conditions. They believe that they have "perpetual access" to the material. This article investigates this situation in the Canadian university library community.

BIG DEALS AND PERPETUAL ACCESS: SOME DEFINITIONS

The Big Deal first discussed by Ken Frazier in 2001,[1] is defined here as an agreement to acquire bundled full-text e-journals direct from the publisher of those journals. Most common in the university library world, the Big Deal often involves the complete, or nearly complete, corpus of e-journals from a publisher and is usually brokered at a consortial level. Participating libraries usually pay a bit more money for a lot more content and, consequently, reduce the per-title subscription cost. Big deals can also involve other elements such as multi-year contracts and negotiated annual price increases. The definition given here does not cover third party aggregators, such as EBSCO or Gale databases.

"Perpetual access" takes effect at cancellation or termination. When an e-journal, or bundle of e-journals, is no longer subscribed to due to cessation, sale, or transfer, the library, or licensee, should have access to the electronic content that falls into the years for which the licensee had a subscription, if that access was included in the license. For example, library X had a subscription to Journal Y for three years in a big deal. Journal Y ceased publication. Under the terms of the license, the publisher, or licensor, has to make available the three years of content to library Y in some way.

PERPETUAL ACCESS SCENARIOS

Potentially, many different scenarios exist where perpetual access could (or should) take effect, both for individual e-journals and journal packages. The following list is not exhaustive:

- *A library has a subscription to a journal that ceases publication*
- *A subscription to a journal is canceled by a library*
- *A subscription to a journal is sold or transferred to another publisher*

In this situation, who will honor the perpetual access, the new publisher or the old publisher? The answer may depend on where the backfile resides; does it move with the current issues or stay with the previous publisher. Libraries often have to pursue access to this content. Occasionally the publisher will send notification, as in the spring of 2005 when Oxford University Press (OUP) sent out a message to serials-related discussion groups calling for previous subscribers to the European Heart Journal, which had recently moved from Elsevier to OUP.

- *The publisher of a journal, or bundle of journals, goes out of business*
- *A bundle of journals has a fluid title list*

Journal packages may regularly have titles that are bought and sold. Many of the Big Deal publishers are of this nature.

- *The publisher of a bundle of journals is bought completely or partially by another publisher*

This situation is not uncommon in the journal publishing world.

- *A subscription to a bundle of journals is canceled or not renewed by a library or consortium*

This cancellation could occur mid-contract, which can be a tricky situation in terms of a library acquiring the licensed content.

Perpetual access is defined in licenses in many different ways:

- *The license states that perpetual access is included*

Nothing more is stated. To see this sort of simple statement is not uncommon.
How useful is it? Is specifying some method of delivery better than taking what comes from the publisher?

- *The license specifies a particular method of fixed media delivery*

  Frequently-noted formats include CD-ROM, DVD, and tapes. Sometimes a fee is specified. The search software is often not part of the perpetual access offer; often it can be a separate deal. Again, how much use will this be to library users? Will the licensee be able to do anything with the particular technology that encapsulates the content?

- *The license specifies that the content will be stored on the publisher's server (this service is often for a fee)*
- *The license specifies that the content will be stored on a third-party server (this service could also be for a fee)*
- *The license allows for local loading of the content*

  A Canadian example of this is the Scholar's Portal in Ontario. Most of the Big Deal content available to Ontario academic libraries is accessed through and hosted on the Scholar's Portal, which is physically loaded at the University of Toronto.

- *The license specifies that the content can be included in a distributed cooperative caching venture.*

  At present, the best example of this is the LOCKSS (Lots of Copies Keep Stuff Safe) project at Stanford University (http://lockss.stanford.edu/index.html).

- *The license specifies that the content can be archived by the licensee in some way.*

  These related archival rights are one way of safeguarding perpetual access.

BACKGROUND TO THE PROJECT

The authors work in collection management units in two Canadian university libraries where they are responsible for, among other duties, e-journals and Big Deals. Like many other academic institutions, both libraries have moved fairly aggressively to the electronic side of the journal world. Both libraries have signed agreements for many Big

Deals and have canceled large numbers of print subscriptions that are duplicated in these packages, mostly for financial reasons. Print is only retained under conditions such as the print version has material that is not replicated in the electronic, images are better in print, etc.). When only the electronic version is available to users, librarians diligently negotiate perpetual access clauses into licenses and reassure users, especially faculty members (who are often the ones who ask "Do we own it?"), that all is well and that the library does own this electronic content.

But is this truly the case? Do libraries own it? Serious questions exist about what perpetual access actually means and what it looks like in practice. How has it been implemented now that Big Deals are several years old? Simply stated, is it working? At the authors' libraries, keeping track of the titles that are being bought and sold in the various bundles of journals is difficult. How are other Canadian libraries dealing with this situation? In order to better examine this topic, the authors decided to survey the libraries participating in the six Canadian Research Knowledge Network (CRKN) licenses for full-text journal packages. The products covered by these deals are:

- Academic Press (AP, now part of ScienceDirect)
- American Chemical Society (ACS)
- Institute of Physics (IOP)
- Royal Society of Chemistry (RSC)
- ScienceDirect (Elsevier)
- Springer LINK (Springer)

THE CANADIAN RESEARCH KNOWLEDGE NETWORK

The Canadian Research Knowledge Network (CRKN) (http://www.crkn.ca) began as the Canadian National Site Licensing Project (CNSLP). In 1999, sixty-four Canadian universities from all parts of the country, ranging from the largest institutions to the smallest; representing English, French, and bilingual schools; applied for and received a $50 million grant from the Canadian federal government's Canadian Foundation for Innovation (CFI) to help build the Canadian research infrastructure. Building this infrastructure was to be accomplished by licensing online content for all participating institutions in science, technology, and medical fields, through CNSLP. The funding was set up in a diminishing manner over three years with the participants assuming full local funding by the fourth year. A competitive bidding process resulted in the signing of seven initial licenses, five of which were made up of full-text journal content (Academic Press, ACS, IOP, RSC, and Springer). Deals were also formed for Web of Science and MathSciNet. All of these agreements began in 2001. A deal was later made for the ScienceDirect journals, which began in 2003. All sixty-four libraries signed on for the first round of licenses. With the ScienceDirect deal, no additional federal money was available and funding had to come from the individual institutions. All but three universities participated.

The work of CNSLP has continued. With the end of central funding, the governance structure of CNSLP has changed and it is now a free-standing incorporated federal entity, the Canadian Research Knowledge Network or CRKN. Membership has opened up and several new members have been added. The original seven licenses have been renewed without any attrition of participants. CRKN has scaled up four regional licenses for the Kluwer e-journals to a national level, has purchased e-journal backfiles, and is looking at buying material in the social sciences and humanities, which could include some Big Deal content.

All CRKN licenses include perpetual access language, which was drawn from the CRKN model license, developed in early 2001. Section 12.4 of the model license covers perpetual access. The first part of this clause reads as follows:

> 12. 4   On termination of this Agreement, the Consortium, Authorized Users and Walk-in Users shall retain the right to access and use in archived form the content of the Database for the period of time set out in Schedule 3 up to the date of termination, except where such termination is due to a breach of the Agreement by the Consortium which the Consortium has failed to remedy as provided in clause 12.1.1 and 12.1.3, in which case such continuing access shall be provided in respect of Licensed Materials published up to the date of such breach. On termination of this agreement, the Publisher shall at its option:
> (a) provide each Member, on request, with an electronic copy of the content of the Database for the period of time set out in Schedule 3 up to the date of termination, or
> (b) provide for continued access to the Licensed Materials on the Server for the period of time set out in Schedule 3 up to the date of termination.[2]

This clause is, of course, designed to be adapted to a specific licensing situation but it is roughly comparable to what can be found in many other big deal licenses, especially model licenses.

BIG DEALS:
AMERICAN AND CANADIAN ATTITUDES

This article largely reflects the Canadian university library environment. While many parallels can be drawn between Canadian and American attitudes towards perpetual access and Big Deals, some notable differences exist, especially regarding the latter. In Canada, the Big Deal is generally viewed in a positive light and consortia are moving ahead with more purchases of bundled e-journal content. In the United States, a feeling has emerged from some libraries that the time of the big deal may have passed. Terms such as "orderly retreats" and "cost for content approaches"[3] have appeared and a number of large, well-known academic libraries have renegotiated their e-journal packages. The recent ACRL Scholarly Communication Toolkit reinforces this perspective by urging librarians to "consider rejecting bundled or aggregated license agreements."[4] This difference in perspective underlies the survey analyses presented in this article.

THE SURVEY

Methodology

In order to answer the research questions previously outlined, the survey examined sample serials holdings statements and solicited qualitative responses from the sixty-four original CRKN members, regarding the six full-text e-journal packages licensed consortially by this group. Several factors supported this approach. First, since CRKN had used an all-in model, determining which libraries should have access to which content was easy. With respect to this group of publishers, these libraries all have the same rights, with a very few exceptions. Second, the libraries are five years into these licenses. A good number of titles were bought and sold into and out of these packages during this time. Third, CRKN has an active listserv for implementers that includes at least one person from each library, which facilitates communication with the group.

The quantitative part of the survey sought to determine how well libraries have been able to keep their holdings up-to-date, as an indicator of how successful they have been at tracking these changes. The qualitative part asked librarians involved in tracking this activity for their comments. Comments were also solicited from the consortium and publisher perspectives.

The publishers involved were contacted and requested to provide lists of the titles in this category, that is, either bought into or sold out of the "all e-journals" package licensed by CRKN, during the period 2001-2005. The resulting list included over a hundred titles in all. A sample was chosen for this survey. The list of sample titles was hand-picked, not random, and included ten titles added and ten titles dropped, with representation from four of the six publishers. The titles were chosen deliberately to represent a range of scenarios. Of the titles dropped, two had been sold by the publisher some years earlier and the libraries had completely lost access to the backfile with the sale. This scenario is what libraries are trying to avoid with perpetual access rights. In these cases, the holdings survey sought to determine if libraries had updated their holdings to indicate they no longer had access. In other cases, titles had been sold and libraries were entitled to continue accessing years they had paid for, even though they no longer had current access from the original publisher. Here the goal was to see if libraries had closed their holdings from the original publisher. The sample titles also deliberately included a mixture of titles that involved transactions that had happened several years ago, and some that were very recent, with the sales taking effect only a few months before the research was conducted in early 2005. Some titles had been the subject of announcements from the CRKN office, while others had been discussed in publishers' newsletters, or Web sites.

For the holdings survey, the authors checked the libraries' holdings by going to their Web sites as a patron would. Where the library had a journals' A to Z list or other obvious database of electronic journals, it was searched first. If such a list was not linked from the library's home page, or one click away from there, the library catalog was used instead. An attempt was made to replicate the experience of a library patron as much as possible. Having the holdings check done by the researchers (rather than self-reported by the libraries) allowed more consistency in the responses, and eliminated a potential source of reporting bias. Because four of the libraries did not have a publicly accessible tool of any kind that could be checked, they were omitted from the survey.

Both authors sought ethics clearance at their respective universities, and the research plans were also cleared with the CRKN office. An early version of the survey tool was pilot tested with a small number of e-journals librarians, and the tool was refined. The questions in the qualitative part of the survey were sent via the CRKN listserv, requesting a single response from each institution. A literature survey was conducted, which turned up only a small number of related articles not cited elsewhere in this article.[5,6]

Holdings Survey

The table in Figure 1 shows the results of the holdings survey for the ten sample titles that were sold out of the packages during the study period. Out of the sixty libraries, titles ranged from a high of sixty libraries with correct holdings, for only one title, to a low of fourteen libraries with correct holdings. The two titles with the highest rate of correct holdings were the ones for which libraries no longer had any rights. Not surprisingly, this indicates that the potential is highest for someone to notice incorrect holdings information when libraries lose all access to a title. No direct correlation was found between the date of the sale and the accuracy of the libraries' holdings. The title with the lowest number of correct holdings was sold in 2003. Although slightly counterintuitive, the transaction was particularly complex. Getting the holdings statement right for this title was more difficult than for some of the titles that were sold subsequently.

Of course, since the titles in the sample were not chosen at random, these results are illustrative only, and are not statistically significant. The authors were only seeking a sense for how well libraries had been able to stay on top of these changes, and the results do provide that. The answer, if not surprising, is not very good news. Generally, the libraries are not doing very well. For example, library holdings are correct in only fourteen to twenty-eight libraries for the five titles with the least up-to-date holdings. In other words, for half of the titles checked in this category, less than half of the libraries were able to keep up-to-date.

The table in Figure 2 shows the results of the holdings survey for the ten titles that were added to the packages. Here, overall, the libraries were doing slightly better. With the titles sold, there were 341 correct holdings statements out of a possible 600, or fifty-seven percent accuracy. Here, in total, there were 362 correct holdings statements, or sixty percent accuracy. None of the titles were as low as fourteen, or as high as sixty on this side of the survey. The highest number of correct librar-

FIGURE 1. Titles Sold

Title	Publisher	Date	Perpetual access?	Library holdings updated (of 60)
Geochemical transactions	RSC	2004	√	36
Pesticide outlook	RSC	2004	√	28
Acta mathematica scientia	Springer	2002	χ	60
Computational statistics	Springer	2001	χ	57
Amer. journal of evaluation	Elsevier	2005	√	26
Cornell hotel & restaurant admin	Elsevier	2004	√	32
Review of radical political econ	Elsevier	2003	√	42
Thalamus & related systems	Elsevier	2004	√	23
Journal of turbulence	IOP	2005	√	24
Public understanding of science	IOP	2003	√	14

FIGURE 2. Titles Added

Title	Publisher	Date	Library holdings updated (of 60)
Accounting forum	Elsevier	2004	27
Applied & preventive psychology	Elsevier	2004	28
Focus on pigments	Elsevier	2002	49
Jrl of cosmology & astroparticle physics	IOP	2004	35
Journal of geophysics & engineering	IOP	2004	44
Organic & biomolecular chemistry	RSC	2003	41
Photochem and photobiological science	RSC	2002	29
EcoHealth	Springer	2004	45
Landslides	Springer	2004	44
Sleep & breathing	Springer	2005	20

ies for these titles was forty-nine, and it was for one of the oldest changes in the group.

Another interesting way to look at this data is library-by-library, rather than title-by-title. Figure 3 summarizes the accuracy of libraries' holdings. The number of libraries is on the vertical axis, and the number of correct holdings is on the horizontal axis. Reading from the left, of the sixty libraries surveyed, one library had only one title correct, three libraries had two correct, and so on. The bars on the far right represent the

FIGURE 3

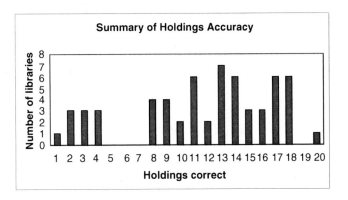

libraries with the most accurate holdings. Only one library had correct holdings for all twenty titles. In all, nineteen libraries had fifteen or more titles correct out of twenty, or just under a third of the libraries. At the lower end, ten libraries or seventeen percent that had four or fewer titles correct out of twenty. The average number of correct holdings was 11.7, indicating that the average library had just over half of these titles listed correctly in their catalogue or A to Z list.

Looking at this data begs the question, "What does it matter?" Some libraries take the position that it is fine to allow user inquiry to drive the updating of e-journal holdings in the big deal environment. The theory is that if a title is in demand, the library will hear from users about incorrect holdings. Other libraries firmly believe that inaccurate holdings lead to great frustration for library users, detracting from the credibility of libraries, electronic journals and library systems. While this philosophical debate cannot be resolved in this article, what is clear is that this group of universities is collectively spending many millions of dollars a year to provide access to these electronic journals. If new titles are not added into A to Z lists or catalogs, some patrons are likely not finding all the material that has been paid for. With the ubiquity of linking solutions, the libraries may also be generating and paying for ILL requests for items that should be available on the desktop, immediately. Finally, if libraries do wish to maintain current access to the titles in question and they do not know the titles that have been sold (as indicated by open holdings); the libraries will not know to pursue a current subscription with the new publisher.

Qualitative Survey

For this part of the survey, four questions were e-mailed to the CRKN implementers' listserv, asking for a single response from each institution (see Appendix 1 for full list of questions). The authors followed up to encourage response from non-responding libraries and received thirty responses, for a response rate of thirty-six percent.

The first question asked "Is your library actively tracking titles transferred into and out of electronic journal packages licensed directly from publishers?" Fourteen libraries responded "Yes," and nine responded "No." An interesting way to look at these responses is to correlate them with the accuracy of the holdings statements of these libraries. Among the fourteen libraries that said they were actively tracking such changes, the average number of correct holdings was 12.5 out of twenty. Among the nine libraries that said they were not actively tracking, the average number of correct holdings was 11.7. Although these numbers are not statistically significant, they are surprisingly close to one another, given the amount of labor that goes into this activity at the local level.

The second question asked "Have you ever claimed your library's perpetual access rights to a journal that has been *sold or transferred* by the publisher? If yes, please provide details (if responding from Ontario, please give examples outside of Scholar's Portal)." Eight libraries responded "Yes," thirteen responded "No," and two libraries responded "Not sure." The caveat about Scholar's Portal was included because the large scale local loading that comprises that project provides a province-wide perpetual access strategy for libraries. On the spectrum of ownership versus access that is the subject of this investigation, these libraries are much closer to owning the content in question.

The responses from libraries that said yes to this question included some good examples, many of which will be familiar to those who work with e-journals: *EMBO*, and the *Journal of Fish Biology* were mentioned, as were the Duke University Press journals that were withdrawn from Project Muse. Although the latter deals with distribution rights rather than an outright sale, it still raises issues about perpetual access.[7] In summarizing the responses to this question, it is worth noting that less than thirty-five percent of libraries surveyed had actively claimed perpetual access rights to sold titles. This illustrates the point that, to date, libraries have not pursued perpetual access rights on a grand scale.

The third question asked "Have you ever exercised your perpetual access rights under a license to journal content for which you have *canceled* the current subscription? If yes, please provide details (if responding from Ontario, please give examples outside of Scholar's Portal)." In response to this question, seven libraries said "Yes," eleven libraries said "No," three libraries said "Not sure," and two libraries wrote in "Not Applicable," because they had not canceled any journals during this period. Again, only thirty percent of libraries had exercised their perpetual access rights under these conditions, confirming the view that libraries do not have a lot of experience with this yet.

The fourth question on the survey asked "We welcome any other thoughts that you have on the issue of perpetual access and e-journal packages." Several libraries volunteered that perpetual access rights were very important to their libraries in considering acquisition of e-journals. More than one library responded that they had not known that the CRKN deals included perpetual access rights, and had, therefore, not been canceling print subscriptions. Because the license only covered termination, there is certainly room for ambiguity here. Finally, a number of libraries responded that tracking these kinds of changes was very difficult. A central effort to track changes, perhaps through the consortial office, would be very welcome. Some, but not all, of the changes that we tracked had been announced by the CRKN office via the implementers listserv. While these titles tended to have more accurate holdings than the ones that had not been announced, they were not perfect. Monitoring and responding to such messages involves considerable local labor.

Publisher and Consortium View

The Executive Director of CRKN had the opportunity to comment informally on the preliminary findings of the study. She observed that tracking these changes at the consortial level is as difficult as it is at the individual library level, and that this is a common refrain of consortia managers. She also remarked that consortium managers do not get the day-to-day input that individual libraries do from working directly with the journal collection, nor do they have the tools to manage the title changes, although some are now starting to utilize Electronic Resource Management systems for this purpose.

The publishers involved were also invited to comment on their role in providing perpetual access in this scenario. One publisher replied that the company places a high value on the stability and continuity of its journals publishing program, stating, "Stability and continuity make our lives and jobs much easier." In a reminder that the world of publishing is still very much a business venture, one publisher replied, "Occasionally journals are bought and sold for purely financial reasons, and there is no way to avoid this. We do not apologize for this." However, this same publisher stated that when they sell a title they always seek to allow, through the legal terms of the sale, continued access to back volumes for its prior subscribers. This practice would be a useful industry standard to enforce, and libraries are well positioned to advocate for it. Bilateral agreements are in place between some pairs of publishers to arrange this, but as yet no standard exists across all publishers. More than one publisher replied that they do what they have to do to stay in business and they try to be diligent about getting information out to subscribers about changes that take place in their title lists. Other publishers have made their position on perpetual access known via company newsletters or press releases.[8]

FURTHER RESEARCH

Two areas presented themselves as worthy of further investigation. One has to do with the size of the libraries. Several of the responses to the fourth, open-ended survey question indicated that smaller libraries found themselves unprepared to handle the work associated with maintaining holdings statements in the Big Deal environment. One typical comment was, "As a smaller institution we are having difficulty keeping up with the addition of new titles." Yet, it is not really known whether it is actually true that smaller libraries have more difficulty keeping their holdings up to date than larger libraries–on the surface, it appears that libraries of all sizes are struggling with this task. In this study there was no objective data available to measure the size of the libraries, but this question would merit further research.

The second area that deserves comment is the role of mechanically created lists in updating e-journal holdings. It was obvious to the authors in checking holdings that many of the libraries' A to Z lists were from commercial providers such as Serials Solutions, SFX or EBSCO's A to Z service. However, conclusions could not be drawn here either, since libraries may be using these tools behind the scenes, for example to update holdings in their library catalogue. It was not transparent what tool might have been used, but further investigation on this question would be useful.

CONCLUSION

We can conclude that all the players in the serials chain have roles in this situation. Librarians need to do their best to track down content to which they are entitled by contract; to do less is to shortchange the library user and engage in poor financial stewardship. The intermediaries in the serials world, especially providers of tools such as Serials Solutions and SFX, need to keep on top of the changing content in packages, getting accurate holdings information from libraries (i.e., what are you subscribing to exactly?) and getting accurate, frequently updated content information from publishers. Serials agents can be included with this group–on the question of how serials agents are repositioning themselves to add value in the age of e-journals, there may indeed be an important niche for them here, if they are not left out of the deals altogether. Publishers need to provide regular, clear information to libraries and to the intermediaries on the state of their title lists. This information should include titles that have transferred in and out of their lists. It should be provided in machine readable form, and sent to libraries that want it, rather than residing on a Web site. Lastly, publishers have to be prepared to honor their licenses and work with licensees to set up access to subscribed-to content. The development of an industry standard would be useful for the disposition of backfiles in the sales of journals from one publisher to another. In addition, broad observations can be made in three other areas.

Challenges Not Yet Faced

The library community has not yet faced some potentially interesting and/or troublesome situations involving perpetual access, at least not in a major way. For instance, libraries have not had to track down and claim large amounts of content from publishers that have gone out-of-business but have not been purchased by other publishers. It is still more or less a title-by-title situation. Also, publishers and libraries have not yet gone to court over perpetual access (at least not as far as the authors know). Lastly, perpetual access for individual articles that could be removed from e-journals has not been a concern. Libraries focus on perpetual access at the journal title level but their concerns may need to be at a finer level.

No Going Back

Clearly, users of academic libraries like e-journals and they like having access to many e-journals, quickly and easily. As a result, libraries will be dealing with issues relating to e-journals, including perpetual access for quite some time. As well, the academic library community has been through a flurry of Big Deals and other purchasing models in recent years. They will continue to exist and new opportunities will arise but this may also be the beginning of a time of maintenance, when libraries will have to put energy and resources into regularly tracking down e-content that they are entitled to by contract.

Early Days

In many ways, we are still in the early days of electronic journals. Paper journals are centuries old while e-journals, for all intents and purposes, are less than a decade old. Libraries are also dealing with the online environment, in which change is rapid and never-ending. The options for dealing with perpetual access are not yet time-tested or time-honored. On the bright side, libraries exist in interesting times and librarians can often make their own solutions.

NOTES

1. Kenneth Frazier, "The Librarians' Dilemma: Contemplating the Costs of the 'Big Deal'," *D-Lib Magazine* 7, no. 3 (March 2001), http://www.dlib.org/dlib/march01/frazier/03frazier.html (June 14, 2005).

2. Canadian National Site Licensing Project (CNSLP) License Agreement, http://www.cnslp.ca/pr/achievements/CNSLP-License-12Feb01.doc (June 13, 2005).

3. Jeffrey N. Gatten, and Tom Sanville, "An Orderly Retreat from the Big Deal: Is it Possible for Consortia?" *D-Lib Magazine* 10, no. 10 (October 2004), http://www.dlib.org/dlib/october04/gatten/10gatten.html (June 14, 2005).

4. Association of College and Research Libraries, "Scholarly Communication Toolkit," May 2, 2005, http://www.ala.org/ala/acrl/acrlissues/scholarlycomm/scholarlycommunicationtoolkit/librarians/librarians.htm (June 14, 2005).

5. Ellen Finnie Duranceau, "Archiving and Perpetual Access for Web-Based Journals: A Look at the Issues and How Five E-Journal Providers Are Addressing Them," *Serials Review* 24, no. 2 (Summer 1998) 110-115.

6. Brian Cameron, "Now You Own 'em, Now You Don't: E-Journals and the Academic Library," *Nexus: A Ryerson University Newsletter* 14 (May 2002), 1. http://www.ryerson.ca/library/info/nexus/2002apr.pdf (June 14, 2005).

7. Eleanor I. Cook, "Drinking from the Firehose–The 'Poof Effect': The Impact of E-Journals Bought and Sold," *Against the Grain* 16, no. 5 (November 2004), 93-94.

8. Tony McSean, "Post-termination Access Policy for Journals on Science Direct," *Library Connect*, 2, no. 4 (December 2004), 7. http://www.elsevier.com/framework_librarians/LibraryConnect/lcvol2no4dec2004.pdf (June 14, 2005).

APPENDIX 1

Dear Colleagues,

This is a message from Andrew Waller, at the University of Calgary and Gwen Bird, at Simon Fraser University. We're working on a project investigating perpetual access to electronic journals, with a particular focus on six packages that were licensed by the CNSLP/CRKN between 2001 and 2005. We are asking for your participation by inviting you to respond to a few brief questions below by **Friday, May 13**.

The results of our project will be presented at the 2005 NASIG conference under the title *We Own it: Dealing With "Perpetual Access" in Big Deals*, and will also be published in an issue of the *Serials Librarian* featuring the NASIG 2005 proceedings. All responses presented in our presentation and publication will be at the aggregate level. Neither you nor your library will be identified at the individual level. In addition, we will be glad to share aggregated data with any interested partners.

Please limit your response to one per institution, from the person who knows the most about this topic at your library. If you have any questions or comments about our project, please feel free to contact us:
Gwen Bird: gbird@sfu.ca
Andrew Waller: waller@ucalgary.ca

We are asking about perpetual access rights to electronic journals including, but not limited to the CNSLP/CRKN packages. Please feel free to provide examples from other licenses in which your library participates.

a. Is your library actively tracking titles transferred into and out of electronic journal packages licensed directly from publishers?
Yes/No

b. Have you ever claimed your library's perpetual access rights to a journal that has been *sold or transferred* by the publisher?
Yes/No/Not sure
If yes, please provide details (if responding from Ontario, please give examples outside of Scholar's Portal).

c. Have you ever exercised your perpetual access rights under a license to journal content for which you have *canceled* the current subscription?
Yes/No/Not sure

If yes, please provide details (if responding from Ontario, please give examples outside of Scholar's Portal).

d. We welcome any other thoughts that you have on the issue of perpetual access and e-journal packages.

Thank you for participating in our research on perpetual access to electronic journals in Big Deals.

CONTRIBUTORS' NOTES

Andrew Waller is Serials Librarian at the University of Calgary. Gwen Bird is Head of Collections Management at WAC Bennett Library at Simon Fraser University, Burnaby, BC.

If We Build It,
Will They Come (Eventually)?
Scholarly Communication
and Institutional Repositories

Carol Hixson

Presenter

SUMMARY. Specialists in serials have been dealing with the effects of an imbalance in the scholarly communication process for some time. The increase in scholarly output coupled with the decreasing ability of libraries to provide access to that output due to spiraling journal costs has created tensions for libraries and their communities. By advocating and providing a means to provide open access to scholarly output, institutional repositories have been promoted as one strategy for redefining the scholarly communication model. Since January 2003, the University of Oregon libraries have been exploring this approach. The article will discuss the challenges and opportunities that such repositories face and examine their effectiveness in changing the nature of scholarly communication. This will be done primarily through a case study of the experience of the University of Oregon Libraries. *[Article copies available for a fee from The Haworth Document Delivery Service: 1-800-HAWORTH. E-mail address: <docdelivery@haworthpress.com> Website: <http://www.HaworthPress.com>]*

[Haworth co-indexing entry note]: "If We Build It, *Will* They Come (Eventually)? Scholarly Communication and Institutional Repositories." Hixson, Carol. Co-published simultaneously in *The Serials Librarian* (The Haworth Information Press, an imprint of The Haworth Press, Inc.) Vol. 50, No. 1/2, 2006, pp. 197-209; and: *Roaring into Our 20's: NASIG 2005* (ed: Margaret Mering, and Elna Saxton) The Haworth Information Press, an imprint of The Haworth Press, Inc., 2006, pp. 197-209. Single or multiple copies of this article are available for a fee from The Haworth Document Delivery Service [1-800-HAWORTH, 9:00 a.m. - 5:00 p.m. (EST). E-mail address: getinfo@haworthpress.com].

Available online at http://www.haworthpress.com/web/SER
doi:10.1300/J123v50n01_18

INTRODUCTION

The rising costs of journals and the inability of libraries to buy access to formally published scholarly output for user populations have been forcing institutions to make changes to their journal collections for the past twenty or thirty years. Serials specialists, bibliographers, and library administrators are painfully aware of the fact that journal prices have been rising faster than could be accounted for by inflation for the past thirty-five years; they have actually increased four times faster than inflation since 1986. Library budgets have not been able to keep pace. In an attempt to cope, many libraries have selectively canceled journal subscriptions and increased the percentage of their materials budgets dedicated to serials. Some libraries have also made public announcements explaining their decisions to cancel all journals from specific publishers whose pricing models they considered especially prohibitive.[1] At the same time, scholarly content has been moving from exclusively paper-based media to electronic. Electronic journals account for twenty-six percent of library serial expenditures and spending on e-journals has increased 712% since 1994/95.[2]

As the content of scholarly journals has moved increasingly into electronic form, many publishers and aggregators have adopted what libraries consider restrictive pricing models for licensed access to these materials. Although the specific formulas vary from aggregator to aggregator and publisher to publisher, the end result is that libraries have been less able absorb the price increases, no matter how creatively they have approached the problem.[3] Scholarly serial and monograph output is also increasing. Between 1986 and 1999, *Ulrich's International Periodicals Directory*'s listing of titles increased by fifty-five percent.[4] Formally published scholarly output is more expensive to purchase or license than it was ten years ago, and there is an increasing amount of it. Libraries are able to provide access to an ever smaller percentage of the total.

Like other libraries, the University of Oregon Libraries took incremental steps to deal with the journal crisis, including several large serials cancellations projects. We have since acknowledged that the process is a continuous one and have renamed it "serials review."[5] We also began to educate ourselves and the campus about the changing nature of scholarly communication with a series of discussions on the relationship between traditional publishing models and costs, electronic-only options, and open access. We have likewise attempted to mitigate the effects of our reduced buying power through consortial purchases of licensed electronic resources and sharing selected journal collections with Oregon State University.[6] We have cataloged all of our electronic journals for many years and also did a one-time project to catalog all the titles available in the Directory of Open Access Journals (DOAJ), as well as the DOAJ site itself. In August 2003, we brought up SFX, a reference linking software designed to increase access to our electronic journal collection and maximize our investment. We are in the process of implementing Innovative Interfaces, Inc. Electronic Resource Management module to increase our efficiency in licensing, acquiring, and providing access to electronic content. One could argue that we have done such an effective job of shielding our users from the effects of the scholarly communication crisis that many of them are unaware of any significant problem.

THE INSTITUTIONAL REPOSITORY MOVEMENT AND OPEN ACCESS

In addition to efforts for increasing efficiency and sharing resources more widely, libraries have tried to reform the scholarly communication model through direct action. One example of such direct action is the Scholarly Publishing and Academic Resources Coalition (SPARC). SPARC is an alliance of universities, research libraries, and other organizations that was begun as an initiative of the Association of Research Libraries (ARL) in 1997 as a "constructive response to market dysfunctions in the scholarly communication system."[7] In 2002, a SPARC position paper outlined the definition, rationale, role, essential elements, costs, and benefits of institutional repositories (IRs). That paper defined institutional repositories as "digital collections capturing and preserving the intellectual output of a single or multi-university community" and postulated that "Institutional repositories can provide an immediate and valuable complement to the existing scholarly publishing model, while stimulating innovation in a new disaggregated publishing structure that will evolve and improve over time." In addition to the potential to help develop a new scholarly publishing paradigm, the report also suggested that IRs could increase institutional visibility and prestige, "by capturing, preserving, and disseminating a university's collective intellectual capital, [IRs] serve as meaningful indicators of an institution's academic quality." Another rationale cited in the report that resonated with us was the possibility of capturing output not otherwise archived.[8]

The Association of College and Research Libraries has also been working extensively in this area, presenting a position paper in June 2003 entitled "Principles and Strategies for the Reform of Scholarly Communication," in which they endorsed key principles and identified the development of IRs as one of the strategies for the reform of scholarly communication.[9] IRs, then, are seen as an important component of the open access movement. According to *Wikipedia*, open access "focuses on allowing all members of society to freely access relevant cultural and scientific achievements, in particular by encouraging the free (online) availability of such information."[10]

UNIVERSITY OF OREGON'S INSTITUTIONAL REPOSITORY EFFORTS

Among the actions taken by the University of Oregon Libraries to mitigate the effects of the scholarly communication crisis on our collections and our user population was the establishment of a task force in 2003 to study institutional repositories. The initial Institutional Repository Group (IRG), co-chaired by the author and including members from different functional areas of the library, was charged to gather background information, survey the campus for potential pilot projects and move forward on any opportunity for implementation. As well as researching the issues surrounding the IR movement as outlined above, the IRG investigated software options for mounting a digital archive of scholarly content for the campus. Since our group was small and we all had many other responsibilities, we were looking for software that would be easy to implement (since we had to do it without outside assistance); be OAI-compliant so that we would be able to join up with other repositories; not need a major investment of hardware to support it; be inexpensive; and, have been tested by other institutions.[11]

We chose DSpace because it met all of these criteria and seemed to have the functionality that we needed. Jointly developed by MIT Libraries and Hewlett-Packard Labs, DSpace is freely available as open source software that can be customized and extended. Libraries and other organizations around the world use the software for providing access to and archiving a wide variety of digital content. As an open source application, it depends upon its users to continue developing it. The community of users is active and helpful, sharing technical, policy, and procedural solutions freely.[12] The University of Oregon's DSpace implementation was first brought up as a test site in May 2003. Since then, we have been working on developing and refining policies, identifying and acquiring appropriate content, upgrading the software with new releases, establishing our local contextual wrapper, and publicizing the service.

Scholars' Bank is the name of the University of Oregon's institutional repository.[13] It is a digital archive of the intellectual products of the faculty, researchers, staff, and students of the University of Oregon that is accessible to end users both within and beyond the institution. Our vision for the archive has expanded over time to include materials that are either themselves scholarly or else support the University's scholarly mission. Our initial goal was to build a digital archive for faculty where they would submit their own scholarly work directly, without any mediation or intervention by the Libraries. We envisioned the library's role as setting up the infrastructure, working with academic units to establish the policy framework for their communities and collections, helping them get started, archiving the content, and then stepping out of the way. However, the vision of self-submission has not yet been borne out, as well over ninety-five percent of the current content has been added by UO library staff with the authors' permission. Acquiring content continues to be one of the most significant challenges facing the majority of institutional repositories worldwide. The University of Oregon Libraries now considers self-submission a long-term goal, rather than an immediate necessity.

Over the past two years, we have identified the policy issues that need to be addressed, including: submission policies; metadata standards; institutional commitment to the archive; position on copyright and licensing; who within the library would be responsible for setting up and coordinating the archive; and what role campus groups would play. Policies have evolved over time and continue to change based on our interactions with different academic departments or campus groups.

We have developed a series of Web pages that explain the issues, provide an overview of the repository's features; explain how it can meet the needs of faculty, students, and others; and answer the questions that are of greatest local interest in language that a non-specialist can understand. In discussing the archive, we no longer refer to it as an institutional archive, which has little meaning for our users, but rather as a digital archive for scholarly materials. In the overview, we explain that its mission is to preserve in digital form and make more widely available to the international scholarly community the intellectual output of the faculty, staff, and students of the University of Oregon. We cite the benefits of preservation of their work–availability on the open Web, stable and unique handles (which function like URLs), and full-text indexing of text-based content.

Utilizing the positions of ACRL, ARL, and other groups, we discuss scholarly communication, open access, and the role that an institutional repository can play. We also attempt to inform members of the campus community about their rights as authors or creators of scholarly content. Recognizing that few people have the time to research these complex issues thoroughly, we have created local pages on scholarly communication that summarize them in terms that our community can understand quickly and easily. We have to be able to reach our target audience quickly with a short, simple message–what's in it for them? Since the concept of the repository is evolving and the service is new, we have found it helpful to provide layers of information with varying amounts of detail. Whenever we summarize an issue, we also provide links to more complete discussions or to resource pages where people can investigate the issue more thoroughly. The positions on open access articulated by the Wellcome Trust and in the *Berlin Declaration on Open Access* help put our efforts into an international context.[14]

One of the biggest concerns for the faculty of the University of Oregon has been copyright and whether posting their work to Scholars' Bank will jeopardize their relationships with their publishers. To address this concern, we point potential contributors to sites where they can learn about their rights. Among other resources, we refer them to the SHERPA site on publisher copyright and self-archiving policies. SHERPA, part of the UK's Joint Information System Committee's Focus on Access to Institutional Resources Programme, has provided a site which lists the copyright policies of many commercial publishers.[15] Authors can use the site to find a summary of permissions that are normally given as part of each publisher's copyright transfer agreement. This site is always of great interest to faculty and can serve to inform them of the rights they may already have, without needing to negotiate special arrangements with their publishers.

Early on, our local license agreement for the archive proved to be another obstacle. We have opted thus far to have one standard license agreement that absolves us of responsibility for determining if authors actually have the copyright to what they submit to the archive and grants us the right to make the material publicly available, taking whatever steps may be necessary to preserve the files or present them appropriately. Although we attempted to avoid legal terminology, most individuals are unaccustomed to reading any license agreement and were unsure what we were asking them to agree to. To lessen their confusion and anxiety, we have created a Web page reproducing the entire text of the license agreement with an explanation at the top of what we are actually requesting. This allows authors to review the agreement and ask questions about it before they enter into the submission process itself.

STRUCTURE OF SCHOLARS' BANK

We have not yet attempted to modify the basic structure of the archive beyond what is provided in the general DSpace releases. The hierarchical structure reflects the assumptions of the DSpace developers about how such an archive would be deployed. The current structure requires communities at the top level. A community may contain sub-communities but it will always contain collections. Collections consist of works or titles; works are comprised of one or more files. Communities, sub-communities, collections, and titles are all automatically assigned a unique CNRI handle[16] as soon as they are created. The handle is stable, persistent, and can be cited and linked to like a URL.

In Scholars' Bank, individual faculty, academic departments, campus units, institutes or programs may establish a community. We discuss with community representatives the types of materials to be submitted, the average size of individual files, whether or not the community desires restrictions as to who can submit or access the materials within it, whether they want single or multiple collections, and who will be handling the actual submissions. The software supports a review process for newly submitted content, with specific individuals being authorized to review and modify submissions. However, this process has so far not been utilized by any community in our repository. Although a community's members often express concern about vetting the content of submissions, they have so far been unwilling to accept responsibility for reviewing individual submissions. At this time, the only review is being handled by library staff who consult with community representatives when they have questions about specific submissions. A community can have sub-communities and multiple separate collections with different guidelines, standards, workflows, and authorizations for each one.

Individual titles can be searched from within a community, a collection, or across the entire repository. As soon as a file is submitted, the metadata supplied about the work is indexed and searchable. Metadata is mapped to qualified Dublin Core and normally consists of fields such as author, title, publisher, keywords, series, description, and the like. A nightly indexing program provides full-text searching of each text-based file. Titles (works) may consist of one or multiple files. For instance, a title may contain a PDF file, some associated images, an HTML document, or any combination of files that make up the whole. The software permits the same title to appear in multiple collections, keeping the same handle. We have found this to be helpful for faculty who wish to appear as part of a larger community but who also wish to highlight their own work.

We have devised workarounds to some aspects of the software that we consider problematic, such as the way that license agreements are handled. Because the software was developed with the model of self-submission of works by authors, every submission requires a click-through license agreement. Clicking on the agreement button attaches a file that includes the text of the agreement as well as the e-mail of the individual who submitted it. In those cases where library staff are handling the submission for authors, we now require an e-mail verification or hard-copy of authors' consent to the archiving and distribution of their work in Scholars' Bank. From the e-mail or hard copy, we create an electronic file which we then attach as a second license file to the submission. Neither the system-generated license file, nor the one we create from an author's separate permission, is displayed to the public. While this is somewhat labor-intensive, we consider it an important step until the software is modified to accommodate different submission models. In the case of a serial, we store the editor's license agreement with the first issue.

SERIALS WITHIN SCHOLARS' BANK

Serial publications present a number of challenges within an institutional repository. Some challenges that we have identified and dealt with when archiving serial publications reflect problems that have plagued serials specialists for years, as well as others, that are unique to an effort to build a digital institutional repository using particular software. These challenges include locating appropriate content; getting permission to archive; converting to electronic form, if needed; migrating to different file formats, if needed; educating campus editors and authors about serial publishing; presenting them in a useable fashion within the archive; deciding on the appropriate metadata; and finally, deciding on links between the IR and the library catalog.

The first step in building an archive like this is to demonstrate its utility to the target group, in this case the campus community of the University of Oregon. Utility can only be demonstrated when there is content to search and access. With serials, as with everything else, our first step has been locating appropriate content on the campus. In the serials realm, campuses have a proliferation of locally developed content that could benefit from being organized, archived, and disseminated through an institutional repository, including newsletters, journals, newspapers, and integrating Web sites.

Once appropriate serial content is located on a campus, getting permission to make it available electronically and archive it in the repository is necessary. We explain the benefits, including full-text searching of the content, worldwide accessibility, stable and unique handles, and free archiving. The University of Oregon Libraries offer to do all the work of harvesting and submitting content. As Scholars' Bank gains wider acceptance, we will be strongly encouraging authors and editors to harvest and submit their own content.

Some content acquired in Scholars' Bank was distributed originally only in paper, although frequently someone on campus has the electronic files that were used to generate the hard copy. Sometimes the publications have been made available electronically as Web pages. In those cases, we harvest from the Web pages and convert them to PDF. We do this for several reasons: (1) to stabilize the content; (2) to better present the content within the archive.

The first serial publication that we archived in Scholars' Bank identified itself as a periodic broadside called *CultureWork*. In many respects, it was the ideal publication. The editors contacted us and asked us to archive the publication, rather than us having to contact them and try to convince them of the utility of the repository for them. It was already published electronically and available on the Web for easy harvesting. It was presented reliably like a serial, with distinct issues bearing consistent numbering. This publication existed in HTML and had been archived by the publishing unit on the Web that way. For archiving in Scholars' Bank, we have harvested and saved issues as PDF files. The PDF retains all the links from the HTML and preserves them as links internal to the document, rather than taking the reader outside the document, as long as we have harvested the linked pages.

Harvesting HTML-based publications raises a number of questions. One of these is how deeply to follow links and harvest the content of the linked pages. Ordinarily, we harvest the links to individual articles within the publication and all links one level down from each article page. The other links remain in the final document and are active, as long as the HTML address continues to exist. This procedure normally works reasonably well, allowing us to capture the primary content of an issue. However, a recent issue of one campus newsletter that focused on blogs and their growing use on campus stretched this model, resulting in an issue with 240 pages of content, rather than the more typical fifty pages. With such publications, it is necessary to consider what constitutes an issue of an HTML-based publication. Who makes that determination? At the University of Oregon, we have made these decisions on a case-by-case basis in consultation with the publishers or editors.

Another challenge in defining the nature of a publication arises when we harvest HTML-based serial issues that are not current. If the issue is not archived and stabilized when it is published, links may break or contain different content. The content of back issues of HTML-based online serials often does not remain static. If the issues had links out to other pages, often the links disappeared completely or had content that was different from what it was at the time of its original publication. Harvesting years after the fact produces an inaccurate picture of what the issue was at the time of publication. In one example of a 1995 issue of a newsletter, one of the links was still active but went to a page that had been revised in 2005. Although this approach is not ideal, we have had to draw the line at researching the earlier content in the Internet Archive's Wayback Machine and trying to capture what the content was at the time of original publication.

Campus publishers sometimes have little understanding of how to create effective serial publications. The concept of having volume or issue numbering or dates to facilitate an orderly display and consistent access is revolutionary to many campus publishers. The inconsistencies of the original publications in designating issues, coupled with the limitations of the software present several challenges. In the model we have followed, metadata is added for each issue of the serial. Unlike an online catalog, where issue numbers are captured in holdings or check-in records, in this model each issue has a separate metadata record and capturing issue numbers somewhere in that record is necessary to promote useful sorting. To enhance the sorting and logical display of the issues in a list, we include the full title, along with issue-specific information, in the metadata record for each issue. We have experimented with several ways of dealing with the metadata to get a useful display.

One serial publication we added to Scholars' Bank was particularly problematic. Earlier issues were numbered, but the numbering jumped suddenly from volume 8, number 1 to volume 11, number 1. Subsequently, all numbering of issues was discontinued and instead seasonal designations without any month of publication were used to differentiate issues. The problem was exacerbated by the software's inability to sort properly by issue number, incorrectly displaying volume 11 before volume 1 in the listing. Consultations with the Head of Serials Cataloging led to an approach that forced most issues to display in chronological order. It was accomplished by inserting the year before the issue numbering. The problem of how to handle seasonal designations when the original publication does not provide a volume or issue number still exists. To make sorting issues chronologically possible, we supplied a number for each issue in the calendar year in which it appeared.

Deciding how much metadata to provide at the issue level was also necessary. This decision was made in consultation with the community. In some cases, the titles and authors of individual articles have been included in an issue's metadata record. However, we prefer not to do in-depth indexing at the issue level given the full-text searching capability of the archive. We also catalog all of the campus serial publications that are in Scholars' Bank and provide the link to the Scholars' Bank version, as well as the original site archive, if there is one.

In addition to campus serial publications, Scholars' Bank includes faculty working papers, presentations, post-prints and pre-prints; student theses, dissertations and honors papers; archives for individual classes; electronic records for the campus; campus planning documents; finding aids to library collections; and more. Academic departments, research centers, interdisciplinary programs, individual faculty, research interest groups, and various campus organizational units make up the communities in Scholars' Bank.

NEXT STEPS

What are our next steps? We plan to continue to acquire content by responding quickly to any expressions of interest from faculty, staff, and students of the University of Oregon and by making unsolicited contacts to likely contributors. We must also continue to promote the archive by meeting with potential user groups and keeping it in the spotlight through articles in campus newsletters, special programs, and routine library instruction. Aligning more closely with instructional programs, including developing more archives for specific classes, is another ongoing strategy. Developing the self-submission model among some communities will be essential for scalability and sustainability of the archive. An advisory group consisting of faculty, staff, and students can help to identify likely contributors, understand better what they want and need from the archive, and help us be more responsive. Another useful step would be to develop searching guides and targeted search interfaces that can be utilized by a particular class or department. Contributing to development of the open-source software is another planned step, as well as developing mechanisms for reporting on usage of the archive both as a whole and specific items within it.

How do we measure success? At the University of Oregon, and at many other institutional repositories, we have not ignited a revolution within the faculty yet–although they are beginning to see potential in the repository. Certainly, one measure of success is the amount of content that we have in our archives. With 782 items deposited since the archive went into production between May 2004 and May 2005, the University of Oregon Libraries have been more successful than many other institutions who have embarked on this endeavor, but less successful than others who have been at it longer or who have more resources at their disposal. However, it is important to measure success by more than quantity. As we collectively acquire more content in archives that are built on the same open access standards, these materials are being indexed and harvested by a variety of commercial and non-commercial groups. This is making a greater volume of scholarly content available to the world at large outside of the traditional paid publishing model. Our success should also be measured by the degree to which we have opened discussions, raised awareness, and captured previously lost or hidden materials on our campuses–materials such as student work, presentations, working papers, conference papers, newsletters, journals with limited distribution, electronic archival materials, and the like. Collectively, these materials form a rich resource for continued research. More and more we are measuring our success by the degree to which we are able to collect, preserve, and provide access to such grey literature and other underrepresented research and primary source materials.[17]

NOTES

1. "University actions against high journal prices," *SPARC Open Access Newsletter*, 72 (April 2, 2004): 1. *http://www.earlham.edu/~peters/fos/newsletter/04-02-04.htm* (Oct. 25, 2005)

2. Case, Mary M. "A Snapshot in Time: ARL Libraries and Electronic Journal Resources," *ARL Bimonthly Report*, 235 (August 2004). http://www.arl.org/newsltr/235/snapshot.html (Oct. 25, 2005)

3. Wolpert, Ann J. "The future of electronic data," *Nature*, 420 (11/7/02): 17-18.

4. Shulenberger, David E. "Principles for a New System of Publishing for Science." *Proceedings of the Second ICSU-UNESCO International Conference on Electronic Publishing in Science held in association with CODATA, IFLA and ICSTI at UNESCO House, Paris 20-23 February 2001 (revised Dec. 7, 2000).* http://www.icsu.org/5_abouticsu/CDSI_web/EPS2/shulenburgerfin.htm (Oct. 25, 2005)

5. For more detail on the processes, visit the University of Oregon Libraries' Collection Development & Acquisitions site on the topic: http://libweb.uoregon.edu/colldev/review04/ (Oct. 25, 2005).

6. For more detail on the Shared Collection Project, visit the Web site: http://libweb.uoregon.edu/acs_svc/osuo/sharing.html (Oct. 25, 2005).

7. Information taken from the About SPARC Web site: http://www.arl.org/sparc/about/index.html (Oct. 25, 2005).

8. Crow, Raym. The Case for Institutional Repositories: A SPARC Position Paper. Washington, D.C.: Scholarly Publishing & Academic Resources Coalition, 2002. http://www.arl.org/sparc/IR/ir.html (Oct. 25, 2005).

9. Principles and Strategies for the Reform of Scholarly Communication. Chicago, Ill.: ACRL Scholarly Communications Committee, 2003. http://www.ala.org/ala/acrl/acrlpubs/whitepapers/principlesstrategies.htm (Oct. 25, 2005).

10. Information on open access found in: Suber, Peter. "Removing Barriers to Research: An Introduction to Open Access for Librarians," *College & Research Libraries News,* 64 (February 2003): 92-4, 113 and in the *Wikipedia* article on "Open Access": http://en.wikipedia.org/wiki/Open_access (Oct. 25, 2005).

11. For additional information on the work of the University of Oregon's Institutional Repository Group, visit the Web site: http://libweb.uoregon.edu/catdept/irg/ (Oct. 25, 2005).

12. Information available about DSpace software at: http://www.dspace.org/ (Oct. 25, 2005).

13. Visit the Scholars' Bank archive at *https://scholarsbank.uoregon.edu* (Oct. 25, 2005) for the latest information about the repository and its contents.

14. The Wellcome Trust's position on open access can be found at *http://www.wellcome.ac.uk/doc_WTD002766.html* (Oct. 25, 2005) and the Berlin Declaration on Open Access is available at *http://www.zim.mpg.de/openaccess-berlin/berlindeclaration.html* (Oct. 25, 2005).

15. SHERPA is at http://www.sherpa.ac.uk/romeo.php (Oct. 25, 2005) and more information on the Joint Information Systems Committee (JISC) and its activities is available from its home site at: *http://www.jisc.ac.uk/* (Oct. 25, 2005).

16. A CNRI handle is "a comprehensive system for assigning, managing, and resolving persistent identifiers, known as 'handles,' for digital objects and other resources on the Internet. Handles can be used as Uniform Resource Names (URNs)." For more information, visit the CNRI handle site at: *http://www.handle.net/* (Oct. 25, 2005).

17. The full presentation delivered at NASIG with slides illustrating many of the points talked about in the paper is available in the University of Oregon's institutional repository, Scholars' Bank, at: *https://scholarsbank.uoregon.edu/dspace/handle/1794/843* (Oct. 25, 2005).

CONTRIBUTOR'S NOTE

Carol Hixson is Head of Metadata and Digital Library Services at University of Oregon Libraries.

TACTICS SESSIONS

Using Customer-Service Software to Manage Serials Online Access Issues

Carol Ann Borchert

Presenter

Tonia Graves

Recorder

SUMMARY. Carol Ann Borchert described how the University of South Florida is using customer relationship management (CRM) software to manage serials online access issues. Originally, an internal e-mail listserv was used to report problems, but tracking problems was difficult. To better manage the workflow, customer-service software was implemented to monitor access problems. *[Article copies available for a fee from The Haworth Document Delivery Service: 1-800-HAWORTH. E-mail address: <docdelivery@ haworthpress.com> Website: <http://www.HaworthPress.com>]*

University of South Florida (USF), founded in 1956, is one of the United States' top metropolitan research universities. With campuses in Tampa, St. Petersburg, Lakeland, and Sarasota/Manatee, the USF Libraries support a student population of approximately 43,000. Approximately 35,000 of those students are at the Tampa campus. USF awarded 7,788 degrees in the 2003/04 academic year.

[Haworth co-indexing entry note]: "Using Customer-Service Software to Manage Serials Online Access Issues." Graves, Tonia. Co-published simultaneously in *The Serials Librarian* (The Haworth Information Press, an imprint of The Haworth Press, Inc.) Vol. 50, No. 3/4, 2006, pp. 213-215; and: *Roaring into Our 20's: NASIG 2005* (ed: Margaret Mering, and Elna Saxton) The Haworth Information Press, an imprint of The Haworth Press, Inc., 2006, pp. 213-215. Single or multiple copies of this article are available for a fee from The Haworth Document Delivery Service [1-800-HAWORTH, 9:00 a.m. - 5:00 p.m. (EST). E-mail address: getinfo@ haworthpress.com].

Available online at http://www.haworthpress.com/web/SER
doi:10.1300/J123v50n03_01

Like many academic libraries, the USF libraries have experienced much change in their serials operations over the past several years, including hiring a serials coordinator after being without one for over ten years, implementing SFX from Ex Libris, implementing MetaLib, and preparing to change integrated library systems. Prior to the implementation of the customer relationship management (CRM) software in summer 2004, an e-mail listserv was used to report serials online access issues.

Borchert believes that difficulties in implementing SFX may have given SFX an undeserved reputation for problems with the Reference Department. When the USF Libraries implemented SFX, problems resulted from an incomplete knowledge base, numbering over 6,000 subscriptions and 13,000 unduplicated aggregator titles. Access problems experienced during the implementation of SFX and the concern that messages were being lost in e-mail inboxes drove the decision to replace the e-mail listerv with CRM software to manage serials online access issues. CRM, better known in corporate literature than in library literature, includes the methodologies, strategies, software, and Web-based capabilities that help an institution organize and manage customer relationships. Since USF's Academic Computing Department as well as other library departments had already been using CRM software by RightNow, the USF Libraries' Associate Director for Technology suggested using the same software for serials issues.

A Web form, with fields for name, e-mail address, description of access problem, and a citation to replicate the problem, is available from the Libraries' online forms section as well as being a link from its Technology and Technical Services page. Originally titled as "Report an SFX Problem," the name of the link was recently changed to "Report a Problem Accessing an E-journal," since SFX is often the gateway patrons and librarians see, but is not in fact the problem itself. The completed form is delivered as an "incident" to the e-mail boxes of designated library staff involved with access resolution. Each incident is assigned a unique reference number with a distinct sender address and subject line.

Features of the software include options to search for specific incidents by subject line, reference number, or name of person who reported the incident. Incidents have a status of updated, unresolved, waiting, or solved. If an incident remains unresolved after three days, a reminder is e-mailed to the staff person to whom the incident is assigned. The software monitors tone with a scale from green (polite) to red (rude). Standard responses can be established and weekly or monthly incident statistics are available. The software addresses privacy concerns and e-mail SPAM.

The most immediate benefit of using CRM software is that patrons are acknowledged faster via an immediate auto-response advising patrons to expect a human response within twenty-four hours. Patrons appreciate the swift response time and are pleased to see that the service is not too impersonal. Human contact information is included in each staff response. Additionally, this software allows librarians to maintain transcripts of each incident, including vendor responses and internal notes among staff. Staff can also keep track of open incidents, thereby eliminating the possibility of incidents being lost in an e-mail inbox with either no response or an incomplete follow-up. The system also provides monthly statistics of the number of incidents and the response time for each one.

This service has not yet been officially publicized university-wide. All public services librarians know about and use the form to report online access issues. Evidence shows repeat patron use of the service. Plans for the future include making the service more visible. A link has already been added to the bottom of all SFX screens since the 2005 NASIG Conference, as suggested by an audience member.

This presentation generated a lively discussion amongst attendees. Questions from the audience included asking about what operating systems and browsers the software requires, how much RAM is necessary, and who implements and oversees the software. One audience member pondered why electronic resource management systems or integrated library systems were not providing this service. Another wondered if this expectation of integrated library systems was valid and whether libraries would be able to wait for vendor development in this area. An attendee noted that at least one electronic resource management system includes an incident reporting field, but does not contain components such as e-mail notification and statistics.

CONTRIBUTORS' NOTES

Carol Ann Borchert is Coordinator of Serials at the University of South Florida. Tonia Graves is Electronic Resources Cataloger at Old Dominion University in Norfolk, Virginia.

Metadata Management Design

Nathan Rupp

Presenter

Elizabeth L. Bogdanski

Recorder

SUMMARY. This session, presented by Nathan Rupp, focused on creating a central repository at Cornell University for metadata tools. Rupp hopes that by implementing a repository for metadata tools digital projects librarians across campus will be able to utilize the best tools available instead of recreating tools or spending time searching via telephone for tools. This process will be revolutionary, bringing together all of Cornell's libraries. It will create an efficient and valuable repository to facilitate better metadata management. *[Article copies available for a fee from The Haworth Document Delivery Service: 1-800-HAWORTH. E-mail address: <docdelivery@haworthpress.com> Website: <http://www.HaworthPress.com>]*

This session, presented by Nathan Rupp, focused on creating a central repository at Cornell University for metadata tools. Cornell has been working on digital projects for ten years but still does not have a systematic way to produce metadata. Rupp suggested that managing the available metadata across Cornell's libraries will streamline and sim-

[Haworth co-indexing entry note]: "Metadata Management Design." Bogdanski, Elizabeth L. Co-published simultaneously in *The Serials Librarian* (The Haworth Information Press, an imprint of The Haworth Press, Inc.) Vol. 50, No. 3/4, 2006, pp. 217-219; and: *Roaring into Our 20's: NASIG 2005* (ed: Margaret Mering, and Elna Saxton) The Haworth Information Press, an imprint of The Haworth Press, Inc., 2006, pp. 217-219. Single or multiple copies of this article are available for a fee from The Haworth Document Delivery Service [1-800-HAWORTH, 9:00 a.m. - 5:00 p.m. (EST). E-mail address: getinfo@haworthpress.com].

Available online at http://www.haworthpress.com/web/SER
doi:10.1300/J123v50n03_02

217

plify metadata creation. Structural metadata and metadata for images, texts and subjects has been created.

Digital library objects have bibliographic metadata. The collections of digitized texts also have metadata in MARC records that can be repurposed and converted to use in a digital library. Rupp stressed that the metadata does not need to be recreated for each project. It can be maintained in one place, such as a repository, and used for both MARC records and metadata. Complexity can vary. Inevitably, this process is not easy due to differing systems.

Converting metadata can be done in two steps. First, mapping the elements in the MARC records to the metadata elements, and second transforming the data or programming. Current national efforts to map metadata include mapping MARC to Dublin Core and MARC to Library of Congress's Metadata Object Description Schema (MODS). Working with Cornell's Information Technology Department (IT), Rupp determined where to find and map the metadata so it could be transformed from MARC. For example, in mapping the Cornell *Historical Math Monographs* digital collection, the MARC records for the texts have dates in two fields reflecting the print and the digital text. In order to map this information from MARC to metadata, the specific date related to the digital must be selected.

Rupp used the *Making of America* project to further exemplify the need for mapping metadata. Metadata for this project is held both locally and distributed to other sites. Metadata is maintained in both the catalog and in the digital system. For a later project, Rupp hopes to find a streamlined approach to updating the catalog and the digital system to end inefficient, dual maintenance.

In order to map and transform metadata, Cornell needed to begin to coordinate the staff of its twenty libraries with the digital projects professionals. They discussed Dublin Core because it is becoming standardized and is used in ENCompass, Endeavor's digital collection management system. The discussion moved from national to local to individual level project schemes. Rupp's goal in coordinating the digital projects is to go from conversion for each project to universal standards.

IT can develop tools such as style sheets so staff can create and update metadata independently. By reducing the need for programming staff, costs will decrease and flexibility will increase because metadata professionals can make changes without IT intervention. Once these tools from individual desktops are placed into a centralized repository they will be readily accessible and facilitate metadata management.

The metadata management system will bring together users, developers, and libraries. This repository project will be extremely valuable because it will provide a context for what individual libraries are doing and facilitate metadata resource sharing. It will mirror the collections of digital objects Cornell currently uses. Essentially, the repository will be metadata about metadata. The readily available tools will be searchable, increasing productivity and allowing researchers to pick the best tool for the job. Searching a central repository will end the need to make multiple phone calls across campus attempting to find tools. Additionally, as people move on to new positions the tools they created will be held in the repository instead of being lost. As the digital projects community begins to work together the culture of communication and collaboration will continue to improve. The community will have a clear picture of the overall development of metadata tools reducing duplication and allowing the creation of new tools.

Rupp's outline of metadata management has yet to be implemented at Cornell. Getting a large number of people working together that previously did not have projects in common is challenging. As the digital projects professionals begin to talk, they will determine if resources need to be diverted and where the responsibilities will fall. An audience member suggested support from the administration will help expedite the process. Rupp emphasized that this process is slow but revolutionary. It will require a culture change but the end result will be valuable. Rupp suggested a repository created by several institutions will be even more valuable. It will further enhance the development of new and better tools.

CONTRIBUTORS' NOTES

Nathan Rupp is Metadata Librarian at Cornell University. Elizabeth L. Bogdanski is a library holdings consultant for ProQuest Information and Learning.

Beyond Article Linking:
Using OpenURL in Creative Ways

Morag Boyd
Sandy Roe

Presenters

Sarah E. George

Recorder

SUMMARY. OpenURL link resolvers are a popular library technology that connects users to services related to a particular item, such as the full-text of an article, the location of a print journal, an interlibrary loan form, and a related Web search. Librarians at Illinois State University discuss applications of openURL linking beyond connecting citations in online databases to the full-text of the article. These applications include use in the library's online catalog, bibliographies, and usage statistics. *[Article copies available for a fee from The Haworth Document Delivery Service: 1-800-HAWORTH. E-mail address: <docdelivery@haworthpress.com> Website: <http://www.HaworthPress.com>]*

OpenURL link resolvers are a popular library technology that connects users to services related to a particular item, such as the full-text of an article, the location of a print journal, an interlibrary loan form, and a

[Haworth co-indexing entry note]: "Beyond Article Linking: Using OpenURL in Creative Ways." George, Sarah E. Co-published simultaneously in *The Serials Librarian* (The Haworth Information Press, an imprint of The Haworth Press, Inc.) Vol. 50, No. 3/4, 2006, pp. 221-226; and: *Roaring into Our 20's: NASIG 2005* (ed: Margaret Mering, and Elna Saxton) The Haworth Information Press, an imprint of The Haworth Press, Inc., 2006, pp. 221-226. Single or multiple copies of this article are available for a fee from The Haworth Document Delivery Service [1-800-HAWORTH, 9:00 a.m. - 5:00 p.m. (EST). E-mail address: getinfo@haworthpress.com].

Available online at http://www.haworthpress.com/web/SER
doi:10.1300/J123v50n03_03

related Web search. In this presentation, Morag Boyd and Sandy Roe from Illinois State University (ISU) review the function of openURL systems and discuss additional applications of openURL linking beyond connecting citations in online databases to the full-text of the article.

The 2005 NISO standard (Z39.88: The OpenURL Framework for Context-Sensitive Linking) defines openURL as "a syntax that creates Web-transportable packages of metadata and/or identifiers about an information object. OpenURL metadata packages are at the core of context-sensitive or open link technology."[1] In CONSER's "Summit on Serials in the Digital Environment," Steve Shadle describes openURL in this way:

> OpenURL is an "actionable" URL that transports resource metadata. OpenURL standard is designed to support access from an information resource (source) to library service components (targets). A link resolver parses the elements of an OpenURL and provides the appropriate services that have been identified by the library.[2]

Three primary components of an openURL are the base URL, the source ID, and the citation information. A simplified example of an openURL is the following link:

> http://www.linkresolver.edu/library?sid=aidb&genre=article&issn=07309295&title=Information technology and libraries&volume=22&issue=3&date=2003&spage=129&atitle=The development of the NISO committee AX's OpenURL Standard

The URL "http://www.linkresolver.edu/library" represents the base URL for a specific library's link resolver. The "sid" identifies where the citation came from. The rest of the openURL identifies parts of the citation and includes the journal title, ISSN, volume, issue, date of publication, start page, and article title.

OpenURL linking benefits users in numerous ways. The link resolver automatically identifies appropriate copies and services for each item. Using a link resolver simplifies the process of connecting a user from a citation source to the appropriate content. Consulting multiple tools to locate materials is no longer necessary because the link resolver uses different Internet browser windows to connect the user from the source to the target service. OpenURL systems also centralize the management of content coverage for a particular item, resource, or service.

Illinois State's implementation of an openURL link resolver occurred in two stages. ISU's Milner Library serves a student population of approximately 20,000. The Library's collection includes 1.6 million print volumes. The online catalog contains 26,682 electronic titles, which includes 4,200 e-journals and 16,987 government documents. ISU's link resolver contains 24,300 active electronic titles, of which 19,653 are e-journals. The differences in the two sources indicate challenges of linking to items that do not have an ISSN or ISBN and the growing number of e-books in Milner's collection.

The first implementation phase took place in spring 2004 and involved an implementation team and a customization group. Within one month after training by the vendor, the implementation team went live with menu services that provided links to electronic sources, the online catalog, and a bibliographic citation management software. The inclusion of the citation linking was a strong need for a small community of users. A link for interlibrary loan was not included at this stage. Boyd remarked that the most challenging part of the initial implementation was reaching consensus among the customization group about the color scheme and a name for the system. Marketing of the new "Find It" service was minimal and was restricted to an announcement and FAQ page posted to the library's Web site.

Phase 2 of the implementation occurred in August 2004. The implementation team and customization group reconvened to enhance the current service. First the team created an A to Z list of e-journals, which is generated from data within the link resolver. This list replaced the library's former A to Z service. Citation Linker was added to the library's Web site, which allows users to search for known items (e.g., a citation from a book's bibliography). Finally, the group added to the service menu the ability to copy and paste the citation for the item and the corresponding openURL. This feature has proved to be popular.

Maintenance of the openURL link resolver is ongoing. Boyd and Roe continue to make changes in the sources and targets as subscriptions to databases and other e-resources change. Troubleshooting service problems remains a common activity. The two librarians also spend time with outreach, to educate other ISU librarians about the service and to explain the current limitations of the system. Boyd and Roe will oversee a software upgrade of the link resolver, the development of a marketing plan, and the redesign of service pages (including the A to Z list and Citation Linker pages) to match the overall redesign of the Library's Web site. An option for interlibrary loan will also be added to the list of services that users will see for each item.

Boyd expressed an interest in further development of the link re-solver beyond even these improvements. Boyd and Roe would like to create a system for continual and systematic input from other library staff. Usability testing of the library's Web site and online catalog has provided some initial feedback, but additional testing will inform future enhancements of the "Find It" service.

Boyd and Roe are adding openURL links to the online catalog for e-journals. To begin with, links are added for journals with only one full-text option, which allows users to bypass the link resolver's menu of service options and connect directly to the full-text. The use of openURL links instead of standard links to the online provider allows the library to collect usage statistics for online access, eliminates the need to maintain URLs within the online catalog due to changes in the content provider, and accommodates changes in proxy methods without additional work. For example, ISU's catalog record for *Biotechnology Progress* instructs users to "Click here for online access" and the corresponding URL is http://sfx3.exlibrisgroup.com:9003/ilstu?&sid=sfx:opac_856&issn=8756-7938&pid=serviceType=getFullTxt. Holdings infor-mation is included within the online catalog because participants in a usability test commented that because the holdings are not specified, the participants assume that the library does not have any issues of the jour-nal.

ISU library staff are promoting openURL links through persistent linking in bibliographies. Roe worked with a graduate assistant to trans-form a professor's list of citations into an online bibliography with openURL links to the full-text. The links are routed through ISU's proxy server, which facilitates the use of the bibliography by off-cam-pus users. With additional marketing of the service, Roe expects that more faculty will use persistent openURL links in class syllabi and course reserves. To aid in training faculty to use Citation Linker to build openURLs, Roe has created an online tutorial.

OpenURL links can be valuable in any situation where a user is find-ing a known item. A Web form such as ISU's Citation Linker can build an openURL. A future application of this linking system is the inclusion of openURLs within a database of ISU faculty publications, which is maintained by the library.[3]

Boyd presented an analysis of the link resolver's usage statistics to indicate patterns of use, patrons' behavior patterns, and areas for possi-ble improvement of the services. Currently ISU is averaging approxi-mately 48,000 requests per month when classes are in session. Fifty-five percent of the items requested have full-text options available, yet only 43% of users select the full-text link. Overall, users select a link on the service menu 48% of the time. In spring 2005, almost half of the usage originated from a source that was not an abstracting and indexing database; other sources include Citation Linker and the A to Z list. Users are least likely to select a full-text option from the A to Z list. The most commonly selected services are links to full-text and to the online catalog. The options to contact the Reference Desk and to copy the citation are rarely used in comparison.

More extensive usability testing is necessary to explore the reasons behind these usage statistics. Among questions to consider, Boyd identifies three: do users intentionally not select available full-text, what barrier(s) prevent better use of the A to Z list, and what would users like to do with openURL? A spring 2005 informal survey shows that ISU librarians are very enthusiastic about the library's openURL system. Teaching faculty responded with positive comments to a query posted to a faculty listserv.

At the conclusion of their formal remarks, Boyd and Roe posed a few questions to initiate discussion among the conference attendees. Only a few in attendance have added openURLs to their online catalogs. Some expressed concern that the inclusion of the openURL within the online catalog would create a circular loop for the user in linking back to the online catalog. A display logic can be devised so that the link to the online catalog is hidden when the source of the openURL is the catalog.

Boyd inquired about the libraries' experiences with increases in interlibrary loan after implementing a link resolver. Some ISU library staff have been concerned that pre-populating an ILL form via openURL would result in a dramatic increase in demand. Yet others anticipate that the citations submitted to the interlibrary loan office would be more complete and is a convenient service for users. One member from the audience said that her campus had seen no increase in interlibrary loan. Others mentioned how much users love how the link resolver fills in the ILL form for them. Another librarian stressed the ordering of the menu services so that users would be walked through the process of checking for full-text and print holdings before submitting an ILL request.

NOTES

1. National Information Standards Organization. "ANSI/NISO Z39.88-2004." April 2005. http://www.niso.org/standards/standard_detail.cfm?std_id=783 (15 June 2005).

2. Shadle, Steven. "OpenURL." *Glossary: Summary on Serials in the Digital Environment.* August 2004. http://www.loc.gov/acq/conser/glossary.html (15 June 2005).

3. Schwartz, Vanette et al. "Illinois State Normal University Faculty Research: A Bibliography 1857-1957." April 2005. http://www.mlb.ilstu.edu/facpub/home.htm (15 June 2005).

CONTRIBUTORS' NOTES

Morag Boyd is Bibliographic Services Division Head at Illinois State University. Sandy Roe is Serials Librarian at Illinois State University. Sarah E. George is Serials Librarian, Illinois Wesleyan University.

Binding Journals in Tight Times: Mind the Budget

Lucy Duhon
Jeanne Langendorfer

Presenters

Sandhya D. Srivastava

Recorder

SUMMARY. Despite heavy reliance on electronic resources, academic libraries still need to manage print journal collections. Although archiving of online content is unresolved, declining library budgets are putting pressure on libraries to stop buying and binding print. Budget concerns are forcing libraries to review traditional binding decisions and their impact on collections and workflow. The University of Toledo Libraries developed a strategy to address a radical cut to its binding budget. Bowling Green State University Libraries, facing ongoing budget cuts and work redesign, are developing plans to cut binding expenditures. *[Article copies available for a fee from The Haworth Document Delivery Service: 1-800-HAWORTH. E-mail address: <docdelivery@haworthpress.com> Website: <http://www.HaworthPress.com>]*

The session began with a polling of the audience to find out who else was experiencing a binding budget cut. Of the forty people in the room,

---

[Haworth co-indexing entry note]: "Binding Journals in Tight Times: Mind the Budget." Srivastava, Sandhya D. Co-published simultaneously in *The Serials Librarian* (The Haworth Information Press, an imprint of The Haworth Press, Inc.) Vol. 50, No. 3/4, 2006, pp. 227-233; and: *Roaring into Our 20's: NASIG 2005* (ed: Margaret Mering, and Elna Saxton) The Haworth Information Press, an imprint of The Haworth Press, Inc., 2006, pp. 227-233. Single or multiple copies of this article are available for a fee from The Haworth Document Delivery Service [1-800-HAWORTH, 9:00 a.m. - 5:00 p.m. (EST). E-mail address: getinfo@haworthpress.com].

Available online at http://www.haworthpress.com/web/SER
doi:10.1300/J123v50n03_04

one-third raised their hands. Duhon asked "How many are faced with decisions on what to bind and what not to bind?" More than half the room raised their hand at this question. Two issues that have affected binding in recent years have been the switch to electronic format and the increasing budget restrictions. Duhon stated the session would include a discussion of the University of Toledo and Bowling Green State University experiences as well as a look at the overall picture of what is occurring in the state of Ohio.

Jeanne Langendorfer discussed the historical background of both institutions. The University of Toledo and Bowling Green State University are located within twenty-five miles of each other. The University of Toledo, a metropolitan university with 19,500 students offering 250 undergraduate and graduate programs, began in 1872 as a city college. Today, it is well regarded for its Colleges of Business, Education, Engineering, Pharmacy, and its new Health and Human Services and its leadership in the study of polymers and crystallographics. The University of Toledo has a Carnegie classification of doctoral/research university-extensive.

Bowling Green State University was founded in 1910. Today, it serves over 20,000 students in over 200 undergraduate and graduate programs in a college-town atmosphere. The university is well known for its programs in Education, Business, Photochemical Sciences, and the College of Musical Arts. It has a Carnegie classification of doctoral/research university-intensive.

The University of Toledo Libraries and the University Libraries at Bowling Green State University have collaborated with each other for many years. They considered coordinating acquisitions activities including approval plans, serials, and withdrawn titles years ago. In 1996, a shared depository, the Northwest Ohio Regional Book Depository was created as a regional storage facility for low-use materials from the libraries of the three state-assisted universities of northwest Ohio. This formal arrangement was for low-use materials to be stored. In 1998, the University of Toledo and Bowling Green State University Libraries agreed for the first time to work jointly in an agreement with the periodical vendor selected through an RFP process to gain better service fees. Both universities also collaborated in a joint contract for binding that gained them a lower per piece cost.

The Ohio Board of Regents reported that higher education funding declined by fourteen percent per full time equivalent college student from 1996 to 2004. When higher education budgets are cut in Ohio, it impacts individual institutions and their libraries, as well as OhioLINK.

OhioLink is a consortium of Ohio academic libraries, of which the University of Toledo and Bowling Green State University are members. In 1996, OhioLINK had 178 e-journals representing a charter publisher group (Academic Press) and eighteen databases. In 2005, the consortium provided access to 6100 e-journals and 132 databases. Access is provided through OhioLINK's Electronic Journal Center (EJC). The EJC includes the following major publisher groups: Association for Computing Machinery, American Chemical Society, American Institute of Physics, American Psychological Association, American Physical Society, Berkeley Electronic Press, BioMed Central, BioOne, Blackwell Publishing, Blackwell Science, Cambridge University Press, Elsevier, Emerald, Ingenta, Institute of Physics, Kluwer, Lawrence Erlbaum Associates, Optical Society of America, Oxford University Press, Project Muse, the Royal Society, Royal Society of Chemistry, Sage, Springer, Thieme, Transaction Publishers, and Wiley.

In 2005, local e-resources for Bowling Green State University consist of 1,752 e-journals, 33 local databases and full-text aggregators providing access to over 17,000 titles (including the EJC titles). Local e-resources for the University of Toledo consist of 2,315 e-journals, thirty local databases, and full-text aggregators providing access to over 12,000 titles (5,656 in EJC, and 6,593 in EbscoHost). Like its neighbor, local resources at the University of Toledo include Caliber, Highwire Press, PubMed Central, as well as OCLC Electronic Collections Online (about a hundred titles), and various individual online subscriptions and packages.

Duhon outlined the University of Toledo's experience with journal collection management. Over the last decade, the print journal collection declined steadily. This decline was due to major cancellation projects in 1992, 1994, and 1996 driven by mostly declining budgets, and later, by the shift to shared electronic resources. In fiscal year 1994, Carlson Library had about 6,300 journal subscriptions including microform. In 1996, the first group of e-journals (178 Academic Press titles) was added to their collection. By fiscal year 2000, the library had 4,178 print subscriptions and 3,413 electronic subscriptions. One year later, the ratio reversed. For the first time, Carlson Library had more electronic subscriptions than print–4,750 e-journals to 3,500 print subscriptions.

During this same time period, the binding budget had remained constant. However, a new incoming dean requested a cut in all binding, and where possible, conversion of print subscriptions to microform. The binding budget, which had remained at $55,000 since 1993, was cut in fiscal year 2004 by eighty percent to $10,000. The library in the following year requested a slight increase to $12,000.

Ten years ago the University of Toledo Libraries routinely bound 9,000 volumes a year, including journals, monographs and theses. Today, around one-sixth of the number of journals are bound, monographs are no longer bound, and only one copy of theses and dissertations are bound. In early 2004, the personal theses binding service was also temporarily discontinued. They have since found a way to reinstate this service. In terms of numbers, in fiscal year 1995, 7,973 periodical volumes were bound, 921 theses, and 787 monographs. By the end of fiscal year 2004, only 491 periodicals, 532 theses, and 10 monographs had been bound. Nearing the end of fiscal year 2005, 833 periodical volumes, 437 theses, and just a handful of books have been bound, even with the slight increase in the budget.

At the time that the binding budget was cut in mid-2003, Carlson Library had 3,065 total print subscriptions, 130 titles covered in JSTOR (3 collections), 527 titles covered in EJC (Electronic Journal Center), miscellaneous online titles, and EbscoHost titles (which were incorporated into the catalog at a later date). The binding file consisted of 1,900 titles. A binding budget of $10,000 meant that only 1,600 volumes could be bound. The main issues became which 1,600 should be bound, and how to keep a smooth workflow for the binding assistant. The binding cut forced the library to re-examine print subscriptions in relation to online holdings. The logical place to look was at the online holdings of the EJC. As a result, 527 corresponding print subscriptions were cancelled in 2004. The 130 titles covered by JSTOR were identified for cancellation as well. The EbscoHost titles were not yet in the library's catalog. Later, this aggregator was used (sparingly) to compare to print holdings. Identifying titles to stop binding based on online availability in reliable and stable archives like EJC was easily accomplished. JSTOR because of the moving wall was more difficult. This problem was complicated by the fact that some of the titles were currently in the EJC. Categories of review files were created to update the records with handling instructions (depending on the moving wall, 3 years or 5 years). The vast majority of JSTOR titles do not have current issues available online and so the decision had to be made whether to ThermaBind™, box until no longer needed, or keep on shelf for a limited time.

The library also looked at what titles they could cease binding altogether regardless of online availability; reviewed which titles could be retained until microform was received; what titles could be bound less frequently; what titles could be stored temporarily (Haworth titles made a good test sample because they were a discrete publisher group of about 30 titles to track and stored well in pam-boxes); what titles could be temporarily bound (ThermaBind™ nursing titles); what titles could be converted to online only; and what titles could be canceled. Even with all these venues for change, as of February 2004, 1,721 subscriptions had no accompanying online access. Even with the 2004 cancellation project, the library still had 2,421 print subscriptions, and 1,908 of them still had to be bound.

Another approach to the strategy was to identify titles that absolutely needed to be bound. Duhon had identified 110 titles that still needed to be bound which included high use items; Taylor and Francis titles (for which there was no online access); education and society titles; Sage titles (still lacking from the OhioLINK database); and medical and mathematics titles not yet online. These records were updated immediately to make sure the binding assistant would know to continue to bind these titles when doing the binding review search, and 457 titles were coded as "do not bind" for various reasons. One hundred of these titles were converted to stable online archive using OCLC's Electronic Collections Online Print Subscriber Program. Using this program, 155 binding units have been saved, translating to $1,000 savings in the binding budget. Duhon also stated that the library stopped binding gifts, made reference titles a low binding priority (since many are single units), postponed binding low-use items and identified online package titles not to bind anymore.

Some problems that arose from changing this process included: how to remember to tattletape items that previously did not need to be tattletaped, how to treat items that currently had no online equivalent but were going to within a short time period, and impact of EJC cuts. Low-use item cuts were based on a cost-for-content measurement. This four percent cut occurred in late 2004.

Another strategy was to look at ThermaBind™ as a final product for shelving. Historically, even when the budget had been good, ThermaBind™ was used as a temporary measure to store incomplete volumes on shelves. For example, in fiscal year 1995, 367 volumes were thermabound. In fiscal year 2004, to begin saving some money, 122 volumes were thermabound. In fiscal year 2005, 154 volumes have been thermabound so far.

The future strategy for Carlson Library as outlined by Duhon includes continuing to convert existing print subscriptions to the online equivalent. The second is when adding subscriptions to the collection–prefer the online to the print subscription. The third is to prefer online

packages to individual titles. They will continue to re-evaluate the binding files. A final step would be to use limited retention and temporary
holding measures when possible.

Langendorfer gave an overview of the Bowling Green State University situation. The University Libraries had a binding budget of $80,000
for a long time. In fiscal year 2003, the budget was reduced to $70,000.
A graph of binding from 2000 to 2005 shows that the University Libraries has been binding less than 10,000 units per year. Although some
changes were made in the number of titles, the impact of the cuts was
hard to see. For the 2003 and 2004 subscription years, cancellations
were made to the print collection due to online equivalent availability in
the EJC. In addition, low use titles were cut. The measure used was less
than six uses in the last five years. Other titles were also cut to meet budget targets. Bowling Green State University Libraries began purchasing
JSTOR collections, and currently own five collections.

Budget management strategies that were developed successfully
pushed back review of further periodical cuts to subscription year 2007.
The University Libraries cut some expensive print packages that were
in EJC early on and also prepaid some e-journal packages.

Although the binding budget is not being cut at this time, a slight decrease is expected due to the cancellations in 2003 and 2004. Bowling
Green State University began to bind incomplete volumes in 2004, and
2,200 incomplete volumes years were bound. These volumes were up to
forty years old and, by virtue of their presence in Jerome Library, were
not low use volumes. When the library budget declines, a cut in the
binding budget is expected. For fiscal year 2005, Bowling Green State
University had 2,450 subscriptions and 2,006 of these titles are
currently bound.

Langendorfer outlined the future strategy for the University Libraries. One step is to continue cancellations of print duplication of titles in
EJC. Cuts to more unique titles likely would occur if or when budget
cuts occur. Another strategy is to cancel print reference materials in favor of electronic resources when available. The University Libraries
will continue to cut standing orders. Other steps that might be considered include purchasing shelf ready pre-bound monographs, discon-
tinuing binding of JSTOR titles and dropping the personal binding
service.

Duhon sent out a survey to find out the binding situation at other
Ohio academic libraries. The response rate was seventy-three percent
with sixty-two out of eighty-five institutions responding to the survey.
The results showed that sixty percent of Ohio academic libraries now

have binding budgets under $10,000. Over sixty percent use limited retention relying on online archives. Over forty percent use limited retention with no permanent holdings. Forty-three percent reduced their overall serials subscriptions. Fifty percent use miscellaneous strategies. Almost seventy percent based their decisions on EJC coverage. Fifty-three percent based their decisions on other online aggregator coverage.

Other strategies for binding that libraries are using include reduction of binding frequency, using pam-boxes, shrink-wrapping titles and placing them in off-site storage, and covering paperbacks in-house rather than send them out for buckram binding. An interesting figure is that fifty percent of respondents stated no particular strategy for the future. Over one-third reported that up to one staff position had been affected. Over half of the respondents no longer bind popular or non-scholarly titles. Over forty percent no longer bind indexes, abstracts and trade journals. Some are relying on Electronic Theses and Dissertations in OhioLINK and binding fewer dissertations. Of those institutions not yet affected by binding budget cutbacks, fifteen percent expected up to a twenty-five percent reduction in the coming year. Most others did not expect reductions since they had already experienced budget cuts.

Binding is still the best alternative for some situations. When the online version is not a print equivalent and if it is not a user-friendly format, retaining the bound print volume is best. If the online access is restricted, it is better to have the bound print volume.

CONTRIBUTORS' NOTES

Lucy Duhon is Serials Librarian, Acquisitions, University of Toledo. Jeanne Langendorfer is Serials Coordinator, Bowling Green State University. Sandhya D. Srivastava is Assistant Professor/Serials Librarian, Hofstra University.

A Collaborative Checklist
for E-Journal Access

Rocki Strader
Alison Roth
Bob Boissy

Presenters

Wendy Robertson

Recorder

SUMMARY. Strader, Roth and Boissy introduced a checklist which they had developed which indicates the different roles of the library, the subscription agent, and the publisher in providing access to e-journals. It is intended to clarify the different tasks so that everyone will understand their responsibilities and not duplicate efforts. Their goal of the checklist is to provide a more efficient process with better communication between all parties. *[Article copies available for a fee from The Haworth Document Delivery Service: 1-800-HAWORTH. E-mail address: <docdelivery@ haworthpress.com> Website: <http://www.HaworthPress.com>]*

Strader provided an introduction to the joint project which investigated how libraries, agents and publishers could work together to manage electronic journal access. The idea developed because of a small fee

[Haworth co-indexing entry note]: "A Collaborative Checklist for E-Journal Access." Robertson, Wendy. Co-published simultaneously in *The Serials Librarian* (The Haworth Information Press, an imprint of The Haworth Press, Inc.) Vol. 50, No. 3/4, 2006, pp. 235-242; and: *Roaring into Our 20's: NASIG 2005* (ed: Margaret Mering, and Elna Saxton) The Haworth Information Press, an imprint of The Haworth Press, Inc., 2006, pp. 235-242. Single or multiple copies of this article are available for a fee from The Haworth Document Delivery Service [1-800-HAWORTH, 9:00 a.m. - 5:00 p.m. (EST). E-mail address: getinfo@haworthpress.com].

Swets Information Services charged for managing e-access. Strader felt Swets was duplicating efforts in providing electronic access, making it difficult to see the value of this extra charge. A colleague suggested that what she needed was a checklist. Based on colleague's suggestion, Strader worked with Roth and Boissy to develop a checklist, comprising broad task areas with responsibilities assigned to each party to serve as a flexible process guideline.

ROLES IN E-JOURNAL ACCESS

Strader stated the library's role is to provide access to materials needed by students, researchers and other users. The library initiates inquiries on selected titles, asking for quotes or pricing information, negotiates licenses, provides IP addresses, pays invoices, communicates problems, and collects usage statistics. The library may work directly with publishers or through agents. They may act independently or through consortia such as the Committee on Institutional Cooperation (CIC) or OhioLINK.

Roth summarized the agent role as one of serving as an intermediary for information needed by both libraries and publishers. They compile accurate title lists, prices, invoicing profiles, reference numbers, contacts, IP addresses, and license essentials. Agents also may be involved in license negotiation. Roth reminded the audience that agents are commercial entities seeking to make a profit and receive revenue both from publishers' margins and libraries' service fees. Roth believes the agents' tasks were not simple in a print environment and are even more difficult in the electronic environment.

Boissy explained the role of the publisher as one of selecting, preparing, packaging and presenting content. They also act as an intermediary with the authors. Publishers are in competition with each other for the best authors. Publishers select the best articles, usually turning away more than accepted, as part of the peer review process. Publishers set the price, offer license terms (often undercutting their own prices), provide invoicing, provide access control (possibly through a third party) and respond to access problems. The publisher's responsibility is also to provide usage statistics. Commercial publishers seek to make a profit, usually by offering a variety of purchase options, including subscriptions and pay-per-view. Non-commercial publishers seek viable business models to sustain their publishing role.

CHECKLIST

The checklist includes tasks roughly in process order through cancellations, with general tasks following (see Appendix A). Strader gave an overview of the librarian's section of the chart. The checklist has sample questions a librarian might ask during license negotiation. Many more issues could be listed, depending on needs at a specific institution. Strader commented that many of the most challenging problems occur in the access/claiming section of the chart. Internal communication should be viewed as anything that can happen that does not involve one of the other two parties. The troubleshooting category is meant to clarify "who do I talk to first?" Finally, she commented that the process improvement section includes any communication issues that cannot be classified in another category.

Roth highlighted portions of the agent/vendor section of the chart. The role of the agent has been communication between libraries and publishers, administration and record keeping, and price tracking, with these tasks primarily included in the pricing structure category. She also emphasized that agents can provide line-by-line invoicing, which most publishers are not able to provide. Roth indicated that agents are constantly looking at ways to improve how they do business as part of their process improvement task.

Boissy discussed publisher's sections of the checklist. He indicated the importance of publishers announcing their prices and pricing model as early as possible in the year. Hopefully if prices were announced by August 1 and the pricing structure announced in late spring, librarians could communicate to agents before the cancellation deadlines. He indicated publishers understand the importance of grace periods, particularly because of complex licensing situations that can make renewals late. He commented that the number of library initiated cancellations allowed varies with the terms agreed to in each license. The number allowed must be tracked for each contract. Boissy encourages publishers to automate their processes as much as possible so that as soon as the invoice is paid, access is established. His opinion is that when troubleshooting, publishers should turn on access as quickly as possible and then work to resolve problems. People want access within twenty-four hours, if not sooner. Boissy indicated that publishers need to understand the importance of giving clear information about title changes, preferably giving a history of title changes on the home page of the title.

The three presenters responded to questions from the audience. Strader was asked how Ohio State University had the money for the extra charges for Swets services and why this charge was not part of the normal service. She indicated that her institution considered the charge is a part of the inflationary increase of the titles. They use the extra services for selected titles, particularly those with publishers who are difficult to deal with. Strader commented that often the agent gets a margin from the publisher for the print version but not for the electronic version. This method helps keep subscription agents in business.

Boissy was asked why publishers contact libraries directly, trying to get libraries to order directly. He answered that publishers are interested in learning who their customers are and what they want. This approach has been standard practice for publishers of popular materials for some time, but not for scientific, technical and medical (STM) publishers. Publishers also originally thought that with e-journals, agents would not be needed. However, they are finding that information still needs to be tracked and agents are well suited to this task. Invoicing is a big role for agents because publishers are not set up to invoice title by title and using electronic dissemination of information (EDI). Further discussion indicated that if all libraries went directly to publishers, the publishers would need to hire more people and train them in customer service. Thus, they would be duplicating the agent's services. Boissy indicated that tracking price caps makes the whole process more difficult. Shadow systems are being created to deal with price caps for each contract. Consortia are complicit in this problem, with the consortia acting as the agent.

Questions were asked regarding title changes and how libraries can get updated information as quickly as possible. Publishers are starting to create ONIX data for books. They may begin to include serials and e-books. Boissy cautioned that libraries should not rely on publishers to provide good MARC records. The presenters commented that publishers need more education about why they need to request an ISSN for a new title. Strader indicated that Ohio State University updates what they can in regard to changes to titles, ISSNs and URLs. Coordination among the various parties involved remains an issue.

Roth reminded the audience that agents have Internet availability reports. These reports are snapshots in time and rely on information from the publisher being sent in a timely fashion for the report to be current and accurate. They present a clear, organized list of what is available, and should indicate if the agents can request access or if the library must work directly with the publisher. Agents are also the best source of pricing information for the library because they will know what was actually paid.

In response to a question about the place on the chart for other intermediaries, such as SerialsSolutions, TDNet or SFX, Strader indicated they considered including additional columns on the chart. These intermediaries need to keep up with all the changes to publisher's content and have their own role for each task. The group also considered a column to clarify the role of consortia. Strader encouraged all consortia to get a clear title list of what is available electronically to the consortia, including title, ISSN, URL and what titles were included in previous years.

CONTRIBUTORS' NOTES

Rocki Strader is Electronic Resource Manager for The Ohio State University Libraries. Alison Roth is Regional Sales Manager-Northeast, for Swets Information Services. Bob Boissy is Manager Agent Relations for Springer. Wendy Robertson is Electronic Resources Management Unit Head at The University of Iowa.

APPENDIX A

Task	Library	Agent/Vendor	Publisher/Vendor
Pricing structure/ business model	• Determine pricing structure and/or changes as soon as possible.	• Pass on price structure and/or changes to libraries. • Identify and track any deep discount pricing deals.	• Communicate prices as early as possible. • Announce changes in pricing and/or pricing structures well before renewal season (e.g., April-May).
Availability	• Initiate inquiry re: availability for selected title. • PREFER agent information over direct inquiry to publisher.		• Announce new/ current public price catalog; make available electronically. • Be willing to negotiate special rates to certain clients or consortia.
Quoting	• Expect current price to include inflation rate of 8%-10%.	• Provide estimated pricing to libraries.	• Must be based on prior year prices until upcoming year prices are released. • Quote to library or consortium as soon as possible.

APPENDIX A (continued)

Task	Library	Agent/Vendor	Publisher/Vendor
License negotiation	• Ask the following questions: - Does title require a license? - Who is contact at publisher for questions/negotiation? - Is there an e-access embargo? • Negotiate terms preferred/needed: allow walk-in patron access on library premises; IP access; remote access; ILL, course pack, reserve provisions; perpetual access to subscribed content in event of cancellation. • Communicate license/subscription start dates to agent.	• Ask the following questions: - Does title require a license? - Is there an e-access embargo? - What role will publisher allow agent to play in license negotiation?	• Define in license: IP access; remote access; ILL, course pack, reserve provisions; location; number of users; embargo periods; perpetual access. • Respond to library/agent re: license terms in a timely fashion.
Invoicing	• Provide p.o. numbers related to order. • Request other reference numbers (e.g., publisher number, subscription number) related to order. • Request line-by-line invoice (i.e., each title priced individually), if possible.	• Send invoices early (i.e., by September) to allow for payment processing time. • Provide additional reference numbers (e.g., publisher number, subscription number) to library as may be needed by 3rd-party providers. • Accommodate library's preference for line-by-line invoice over lump sum, including e-access fees or other service charges.	• Send invoices early to allow for payment processing time. • Provide reference numbers on every document issued related to library's order.
Access/ claiming	• Provide IP ranges to agent or publisher. • Communicate problems to agent as soon as possible. • Record start dates and terms of subscriptions.	• Keep library's IP ranges on file. • Record who is actually providing online access; track platform/provider changes. • Record URLs. • Record contacts at publisher and provider. • Record start dates and terms of subscriptions.	• Define scope of access. • Define "location" (often defined in license). • Provide URLs or instructions relating to 3rd-party provider. • Record start dates and terms of subscriptions.

Task	Library	Agent/Vendor	Publisher/Vendor
Authorizing renewals	• Establish renewals to be automatic.	• Act as buffer for renewals to allow for payment processing time.	• Make agreements on cutoff dates for renewals on license terms. • Err on the side of library and allow grace periods for late orders.
Cancellations	• Identify cancellations as soon as possible and communicate to agent/publisher as soon as possible.	• Investigate publisher policies on cancellations. • Process cancellations for library; keep library updated on status and publisher response.	• Define refund/credit terms for cancellation of single-title license by library or for sale or removal of licensed content by publisher. • Define number of library-initiated journal cancellations allowable during term of multiple-title and/or multiple-year license.
Internal communication	• Communicate with IT dept. to keep current IP addresses; have liaison for troubleshooting technical problems. • Assign liaison to legal dept. or business office for questions about licenses.	• Assign personnel to specific library accounts.	• Automate, to the extent possible, the interface between the order entry/ remittance receipt system and the access maintenance system. Do not rely on passive or informal communications between order entry staff and access maintenance staff.
Troubleshooting	• Expect agent to be first line of defense.	• Must serve as first line of defense.	• Upon inquiry from either library or agent, turn on access in good faith, then immediately confirm order status.
Usage statistics	• Determine what types of usage statistics are needed. • Determine frequency for collection (monthly, quarterly, etc.) • Request COUNTER-compliant statistics from publisher or provider.	• Serve as conduit from provider for instructions on accessing and interpreting usage statistics.	• Provide Web-accessible COUNTER-compliant statistics. • Provide instructions for accessing and interpreting statistics (even if that means to go to 3rd-party provider).

APPENDIX A (continued)

Task	Library	Agent/Vendor	Publisher/Vendor
Title changes	• Confirm changes with agent or publisher.	• Keep libraries informed. • Be open to library input–often libraries confirm title changes before agents are alerted by publishers.	• Confirm changes with annual price list. • Maintain online catalog with current titles and list of changes. • Provide Web-accessible mechanism to keep agents and libraries notified.
Record keeping	• Maintain current list of IP ranges. • Maintain order records with reference numbers, price and payment history. • Keep pertinent correspondence. • Secure a copy of countersigned/ executed license. • Record start dates and terms of subscriptions.	• Retain records of titles requiring license. • Record license and subscription start dates from library or publisher for completing order process and for later troubleshooting. • Maintain order records, reference numbers, and IP lists. • Record start dates and terms of subscriptions.	• Confirm that library has copy of fully executed license. • Retain copy of executed license and IP lists. • Maintain subscription records, including reference numbers. • Record start dates and terms of subscriptions. • Amend license for new titles, etc. as needed.
Process improvement	• Designate specific contact person(s) to initiate inquiries and collect responses. • Communicate and follow up with both agent and publisher as necessary.	• Assign specific reps to streamline response.	• Fit timing of price or business model changes with library budget cycle. • Have designated contact assigned to streamline response.

Issues in Scholarly Communications: Creating a Campus-Wide Dialog

Jennifer Duncan
William Walsh
Tim Daniels

Presenters

Joe Becker

Recorder

SUMMARY. The issues surrounding the crisis in scholarly communication are well known to librarians. However, academic faculty and administrators often do not have a similar understanding of these concerns, or what librarians are doing to deal with them. Developing dialog with campus groups to further their awareness of the current situation is important. During this session, three librarians describe different approaches to proactively engaging university communities in the discussion of current issues and options relating to scholarly communication. *[Article copies available for a fee from The Haworth Document Delivery Service: 1-800-HAWORTH. E-mail address: <docdelivery@haworthpress.com> Website: <http://www.HaworthPress.com>]*

The cost of serials continues to increase drastically. Academic libraries must therefore continue to cancel journal subscriptions to stay

[Haworth co-indexing entry note]: "Issues in Scholarly Communications: Creating a Campus-Wide Dialog." Becker, Joe. Co-published simultaneously in *The Serials Librarian* (The Haworth Information Press, an imprint of The Haworth Press, Inc.) Vol. 50, No. 3/4, 2006, pp. 243-248; and: *Roaring into Our 20's: NASIG 2005* (ed: Margaret Mering, and Elna Saxton) The Haworth Information Press, an imprint of The Haworth Press, Inc., 2006, pp. 243-248. Single or multiple copies of this article are available for a fee from The Haworth Document Delivery Service [1-800-HAWORTH, 9:00 a.m. - 5:00 p.m. (EST). E-mail address: getinfo@haworthpress.com].

Available online at http://www.haworthpress.com/web/SER
doi:10.1300/J123v50n03_06

within budget. On the other hand, the current development of alternative pricing and access models gives hope that positive changes can be made to improve or restore access to scholarly communication. In an effort to increase faculty awareness of both the positive and negative aspects of journal access, Jennifer Duncan of Utah State University described her library's implementation of a departmental visit program. The background that has motivated the visit program is typical: a modestly funded library attempting to support forty-one departments with 120 advanced degree programs, facing a serials cancellation project and foreseeable mistrust from faculty due to lack of communication during previous cancellations.

Utah State University's library has assembled a team to meet with faculty, rather than putting the burden of the communication effort solely with the subject selector or liaison librarian. Team members include the Electronic Resources, Collection Development and Acquisitions Librarians, as well as the Associate Director for Technical Services and the selector. In addition to providing diverse expertise, the team approach allows the selector to maintain a positive relationship with the department while other team members can be the bearers of difficult news or address any negative comments. Departmental faculty meetings are the most likely venues for discussions of library issues. The agenda for the meetings tends to fall into three areas: the serials crisis, budget and funding information, and proactive and positive measures undertaken by the library.

It is important to relay information on the general serials crisis, including inflation comparisons with standard economic measures such as the Consumer Price Index, and longitudinal analyses indicating national library trends, such as Association of Research Libraries statistics on serials costs. Data that shows inflation rates relative to Library of Congress subject areas can also indicate the broad nature of the pricing crisis.

At the same time, providing pricing details specific to the library is essential. Developing a "worst offenders" list of high cost titles in the collection or tabulating the price history of particular departmental journal collections can illustrate the impact of spiraling costs. Faculty often may not be aware of current journal costs and cost increases.

Budgeting and funding information is another area where details need to be communicated. Peer group budget data can give a comparative frame of reference for the library's allocation. A particular set of peer institutions is often defined by university administration. Funding streams should be explained. Since the library may have particular combinations of on-going funding and occasional or "soft" funding, providing a longitudinal analysis of these funding sources and clarifying possible misconceptions regarding actual available long-term allocations is important. Budget charts that display current expenditures and allocation streams are useful.

In response to details on serials costs and funding, faculty typically may want to know what the library is doing to address these problems. The library team can discuss proactive and positive measures they are involved in, including significant new purchases, fund-raising efforts, and purchasing partnerships with departments and consortia. Information on open access initiatives and other innovative publishing models can be provided. In the same vein, the library can explain how faculty can become proactive in this crisis. Faculty efforts can include library partnerships, and communication with journal editorial boards and publishers. They can also consider open access and self-archiving options for the publication of their work.

Duncan summarized the key results of the departmental visit program at Utah State University. The library has increased visibility and developed and solidified contacts with academic departments. Of the forty-one departments, twenty-one participated in the first year of the program, with thirty-three participants in the second year. Several departments have since requested sessions of their own volition. The journal collection has been re-shaped in a collaborative process. The program has solidified departmental partnerships, and identified purchase opportunities. Two departments are now funding database purchases directly. The visit program has also identified campus advocates, those who are interested in, and understanding of, current issues regarding scholarly resources. The meetings have provided an opportunity for the library to discuss many positive issues rather than solely cancellations. Perhaps most importantly, the library has demonstrated a proactive ability to make changes based on the establishment of a communication process that informs and educates.

William Walsh, of Georgia State University (GSU), also spoke of his institution's efforts to raise awareness of scholarly communication issues. His focus, however, is on Web-based initiatives to achieve this end, specifically a scholarly communications blog.

Walsh makes reference to the *Create Change* advocacy kit, developed by Association of Research Libraries (ARL), Association of College & Research Libraries (ACRL), and the Scholarly Publishing and Academic Resources Coalition (SPARC). Objectives for advocacy programs described in this document include:

- To make faculty, administrators and other stakeholders aware of the problems and issues in the scholarly communication system
- To foster understanding and engage support for library decision processes
- To stimulate discussion
- To motivate stakeholders to specific actions

Institutions using Web sites to further these objectives are becoming numerous; examples include University of Arizona, Rutgers University, and University of Kansas, as well as Georgia State University's Issues in Scholarly Communications Web site, launched in 2003.

In contrast to the *Create Change* document, Walsh also refers to the *Hype Cycle* theory, developed by Paul McFedries of the Gartner Group. This five-phase continuum is intended to apply to technology adoption, but may be a useful assessment tool for the state of change in the scholarly communication system. The phases include early enthusiasm, inflated expectations, disillusionment, further experimentation and development, and acceptance of change. Walsh notes that the scholarly communications debate is now fifteen years old, and sees the blog as one more tool to advance the cycle.

The advantages of a blog are several. It can be incorporated into an existing Web site. Excellent software is available and no knowledge of code is required. Multiple people can provide input. At GSU, technical services librarians maintain the scholarly communications blog. It can be updated from any Web connection. An RSS feed can be provided. Also, whereas a Web site devoted to scholarly communication issues may seem to have a complex amount of information, the blog may be able to provide more current and more accessible packets of materials.

Important online sources for information on scholarly communications issues include Peter Suber's *Open Access News*, University of Illinois/Urbana-Champaign's *Scholarly Communications Newsletter*, and Johns Hopkins University's *Forum on Publishing Alternatives in Science*. The blog can augment these sources, and also tailor discussions for a local readership. Entries for the blog can be on any topic judged to be of interest to the local audience. Initial posts to the GSU blog deal largely with open access issues. Recent topics reflect the effort to broaden the scope of the discussions, with subjects including the cost of textbooks and course packs, e-journal self-archiving policies, and the Google Print Library project. Topics affecting the humanities are included when possible, since the English faculty at GSU has expressed interest in this debate. The information must be updated regularly. Postings must not be so numerous as to overwhelm the readership. Since the blog's inception in December 2003, five contributors have posted nearly 400 entries. The site has received about 1,200 hits a month, with the large majority originating from IP ranges at the university.

Walsh concluded by noting that, while the aim of the site is to disseminate information, the blog is equally useful to those delivering that information. Librarians who post to the blog are by the very process extending their own research and developing stronger expertise and understanding on the issues, and also creating a searchable database for these topics.

Tim Daniels, Walsh's colleague at Georgia State University, focused his presentation on the university's institutional repository (IR). He noted that when efforts such as those mentioned by his co-presenters are successful in increasing faculty awareness of the spiraling problems of the scholarly journal and the need to change the system, alternative systems must be made available. The institutional repository can be one of these options.

Networking is an important part of this initiative. Daniels compared his role to that of a sales person. The product being marketed is the concept and infrastructure of the institutional repository. This effort entails pushing information on institutional repositories out to faculty, departments, and administrators and developing opportunities to meet this constituency to discuss the IR option. Librarians may need to be educated on the IR concept so that they can become part of the sales team. This team should include public services librarians, usually at the front line of faculty communication; technical services librarians, with extensive serials knowledge; as well as the digital services or systems librarians, with infrastructure expertise. Ideally, the initiative can draw on all these groups to carry the concept forward.

A needs assessment can be done to provide details on current institutional resources. The IR can be an important archival system for local scholarly materials. The repository can house much more than journal articles. It can include working papers, charts, presentations, course materials, datasets, and graduate materials. It can provide a dependable access point for Web-based resources that may otherwise become lost. The discovery of these materials combined with the offer to archive them properly can be a compelling and detailed argument for use of the institutional repository.

An institutional repository initiative should identify constituents who are receptive to the concept and who can become early adopters. By working closely with these participants to archive their materials, the library can both develop successful implementations and provide useful examples to corroborate future discussions. One example is the Electronic Theses and Dissertations program at Georgia State University. This program has been in effect for two semesters as an optional method. It had nine participants in the first semester and over forty for the second semester. Graduate school representatives are discussing the efficacy of this archival option. Some graduate programs may mandate this method in the near future.

In final remarks, Daniels stressed that the institutional repository is an initiative that is proceeding along its own cycle of maturation, with many aspects yet to be determined. This dynamic nature makes the institutional repository an exciting project to work on.

The workshop provided three distinct approaches to creating dialog on issues of scholarly communication. Participants at the presentation no doubt came away encouraged by these successful efforts, while yet realizing that all librarians must take a role in this communication process if profound change is to be accomplished.

CONTRIBUTORS' NOTES

Jennifer Duncan is Electronic Resources Librarian at Utah State University. William Walsh is Head of Acquisitions at Georgia State University. Tim Daniels is Digital Technologies Librarian at Georgia State University. Joe Becker is Head of Acquisitions at New Mexico State University.

Adding Value to the Catalog in an Open Access World

Anna Hood

Presenter

Mykie Howard

Recorder

SUMMARY. As serial prices rise exponentially and budgets plummet, serials aficionados can still increase access to information by adding bibliographic records for open access journals to library catalogs. Anna Hood
shared procedures and practices on how she is adding value to her library's
catalog by adding such records. Bridging the gap between users and open
access journals in such a manner allows for true openness. An open access
journal is not truly "open" unless we take the time to unrestrict and make
them available to all. *[Article copies available for a fee from The Haworth Document Delivery Service: 1-800-HAWORTH. E-mail address: <docdelivery@
haworthpress.com> Website: <http://www.HaworthPress.com>]*

If a tree falls in the woods and no one is around to hear it, does it make
a sound? Likewise, are open access journals really "open" unless information users know about them and how to get to them? According to
Dictionary.com, the word "open" means "accessible to all; unrestricted

---

[Haworth co-indexing entry note]: "Adding Value to the Catalog in an Open Access World." Howard, Mykie.
Co-published simultaneously in *The Serials Librarian* (The Haworth Information Press, an imprint of The
Haworth Press, Inc.) Vol. 50, No. 3/4, 2006, pp. 249-252; and: *Roaring into Our 20's: NASIG 2005* (ed: Margaret
Mering, and Elna Saxton) The Haworth Information Press, an imprint of The Haworth Press, Inc., 2006, pp. 249-
252. Single or multiple copies of this article are available for a fee from The Haworth Document Delivery Service
[1-800-HAWORTH, 9:00 a.m. - 5:00 p.m. (EST). E-mail address: getinfo@haworthpress.com].

Available online at http://www.haworthpress.com/web/SER
doi:10.1300/J123v50n03_07

as to participants: an open competition." Arguments could exist for either side. However, most in the library world that take their role of information intermediaries seriously would say, "No."

One such person who would say that open access journals are not really open unless value-added effort is applied to them is Anna Hood of
Kent State University. The presentation is a sequel to Hood's 2004
NASIG Conference poster session on the same topic. Hood believes
that the best way to add value to open access journals is by cataloging
and maintaining open access bibliographic records in our library catalogs, such as she is doing at Kent State with the Directory of Open Access Journals (DOAJ). Adding these records increases the currency and
relevance of the catalog, encourages access to e-resources through the
OPAC rather than separately maintained utilities, and legitimizes
"freely available" resources.

This project started for Hood at the end of 2003 when her supervisor
suggested that she include bibliographic records for open access journals in the library's catalog, KentLINK, a resource which the library
was committed to maintaining. Access to more electronic resources is
something Kent State library users had requested in a recent
LibQUAL+ survey. Actual work on the project began in early 2004 by
creating a title list from the DOAJ Web site. Each title was searched in
OCLC for copy and evaluated before it was imported into the local catalog. Constant data using the OCLC Connexion client was applied and
local edits were added as each record was imported. These local edits
included adding subject headings, a uniform title added entry "Directory of Open Access Journals (DOAJ)" for the purpose of collocation in
the catalog, and Persistent URLs (PURLs) when available. Use of
PURLs helps to ensure stability of the URLs in the catalog. Each title received an individual bibliographic record and purchase order (PO). In
addition, a collection level bibliographic record and PO were created.
Because open access journals are freely available to all, Kent State did
not add its holdings symbol to the OCLC record. For titles that did not
have cataloging copy available, original records were input and saved
into the OCLC database for other libraries to use.

Kent State takes the separate record approach to cataloging its e-journals, downloading a record for the print and a separate record for the
electronic if both formats are held. Of the titles added for this project before July 2004, 88% (which was 87% of the total DOAJ records) had
copy available in OCLC, and 12% required original cataloging. Of the
titles added from July 2004 through May 2005, 84% had copy available
in OCLC, and 16% required original cataloging. As of May 2005,

KentLINK included 90% of the total DOAJ titles. Even though a high percentage of copy was available for the DOAJ titles, corrections still had to be made to frequently occurring errors including errors in the 006 or 007, form/original coding, dates, 300 fields, and missed title changes or variations.

Once the initial project was underway, URL maintenance became ongoing. New titles were added to KentLINK every thirty days as the DOAJ was updated. User feedback, especially from public services staff, and URL error reports from automated link checking helped with this process. The automated checking was not scheduled, instead had to be requested every thirty days from the library's System Department. The automated checking identified DOAJ titles from the KentLINK catalog by searching for the collocation phrase, tested each link and reported the type of error message received. Each URL is then tested again and updated in the bibliographic record. One problem with the automated checking is that URL routing and textual unavailability messages are not detected. As the 2005 NASIG conference, per the automated link checking report, the Kent State catalog only contained twenty-seven broken links which totaled about 2% of the total DOAJ records in the catalog.

As one can see from the process just described and as Hood mentioned in her presentation, "anything you spend this much time on is no longer freely available." Therefore, in order to get a return on the library's invested time, Hood began to market her work on providing access to the DOAJ. She made announcements in local library discussion lists and published articles in her library's newsletter, *Footnotes*, distributed to Kent State students and faculty. Kent State constituents took notice and were thrilled. Hood now gets several requests a week to add new electronic resources to the catalog!

Projecting into the future, Hood talked about what challenges lay ahead for this project. Maintenance of records and URLs could prove to be an issue. Although currently only an average of 2% of the DOAJ titles in KentLINK have proven to be problematic, keeping up with them could nonetheless be time consuming, especially as the number of titles in the DOAJ continues to rise on a monthly basis. Continually adding records on a monthly basis for the additional DOAJ titles with limited staffing and decreased budgets could prove challenging as well. Predictable access would also be an issue. Although the DOAJ has a method to notify users of the titles added on a monthly basis, it does not have a way of letting users know what titles have been taken out of the DOAJ. To help combat user frustration due to loss of access, Hood has sought and is awaiting approval from her public services colleagues to add a subfield 3 to the 856 saying "Freely available/subject to change." In addition, users at Kent State have sometimes automatically assumed that a title cataloged in English will be in English once they click on the link and are surprised when they find out differently. The more the users get, the more they want. These desires could be especially difficult due to dwindling budgets and the lack of staff. Currently, Kent State does not have a collection development policy in place to handle open access journals. A policy could curb outrageous, out of scope requests that may be made by users and colleagues.

Nonetheless, Hood trudges on, making improvements to this project She intends to automate by harvesting Open Archives Initiative (OAI) metadata and batch searching via OCLC Connexion, and possibly semi-automate by generating place-holding bibliographic records from the OAI metadata for titles that need original cataloging wherever possible. In addition, she hopes to incorporate open access journals into a local open URL resolver. She also wants to be involved in creating an electronic resource collection development policy that includes open access resources. Finally, she would also like to add titles from other open access directories into KentLINK.

Hood, in addition to others who are investing a great deal of time in making these open access journals more open and accessible to information seekers and users, is making a tremendous contribution to the information profession as a whole. For, not only is she making the DOAJ more accessible to Kent State library users, she is also making the DOAJ more accessible to the library users of the eighty-four member OhioLINK consortium (which includes Kent State) as well as the users of other libraries who chose to export the records for which she provides updates and original cataloging. She is ultimately supporting the open access model of scholarly publishing. Words mean nothing, but actions mean everything. An open access journal is not truly "open" unless we take the time to unrestrict and make them available to all.

CONTRIBUTORS' NOTES

Anna Hood is Head of Serials and Electronic Resources at Kent State University. Mykie Howard is Leader, Serials Unit, at the National Agricultural Library.

Collection Development in Public Libraries

Tina Herman Buck
Stephen Headley
Abby Schor

Presenters

Susan M. Banoun

Recorder

SUMMARY. This panel discussion featured serials librarians from three different kinds of public libraries discussing collection development of periodicals. They presented their policies and information regarding practices in public libraries. Similarities and differences were highlighted between a large city system with a central library, a large suburban system without a main library, and a single-building library serving a medium-sized city. Exploration of the topic included questions such as–what's the same, what's different, and what can be learned from each other? Public Libraries serve everyone: college students, children, parents, scholars, business people, new immigrants. How can a periodical collection serve all of these groups? *[Article copies available for a fee from The Haworth Document Delivery Service: 1-800-HAWORTH. E-mail address: <docdelivery@haworthpress.com> Website: <http://www.HaworthPress.com>]*

[Haworth co-indexing entry note]: "Collection Development in Public Libraries." Banoun, Susan M. Co-published simultaneously in *The Serials Librarian* (The Haworth Information Press, an imprint of The Haworth Press, Inc.) Vol. 50, No. 3/4, 2006, pp. 253-257; and: *Roaring into Our 20's: NASIG 2005* (ed: Margaret Mering, and Elna Saxton) The Haworth Information Press, an imprint of The Haworth Press, Inc., 2006, pp. 253-257. Single or multiple copies of this article are available for a fee from The Haworth Document Delivery Service [1-800-HAWORTH, 9:00 a.m. - 5:00 p.m. (EST). E-mail address: getinfo@haworthpress.com].

Available online at http://www.haworthpress.com/web/SER
doi:10.1300/J123v50n03_08

SCOPE OF THE COLLECTIONS

Headley, of the Public Library of Cincinnati and Hamilton County (PLCHC), described the large public library system with a main library and forty-one branches, which serves a population of over 823,000 in Hamilton County. The collection is vast, serving popular and research interests. In 2004, the library system had 14,188 periodical and 469 newspaper subscriptions. The 2004 budget for the main library was approximately $1.2 million. The periodical and newspaper collection at the main library is almost all reference, with the exception of a small collection of popular titles that circulate. At the branch libraries, magazines circulate. Every magazine and newspaper title at the branches is also carried by the main library. Historical newspapers and magazines date to the 1700s in print and microform. Headley is responsible for collection development decisions for the materials in his department at the main library. The branches are free to choose their own titles based on what is available at the main library.

Buck described the Hennepin County Library System (HCLS) as a suburban county system with twenty-six agency libraries, but with no main library. While Hennepin County includes the city of Minneapolis, the Minneapolis Public Library is separately managed. The twenty-one community and five resource libraries of HCLS serve the 740 suburban and rural residents of the county. The libraries were without a director for more than a year and have consequently experienced a lack of scope and direction. The agency collections are eighty percent non-circulating. Currently, they have over 4,000 paper magazine and newspaper subscriptions, with about 700 titles. The 2005 periodical budget is approximately $200,000. The collection is primarily popular titles, geared to support students, the business community and life-long learning. Approximately 68% of the paper subscriptions circulate. Usage statistics are anecdotal and both selection and retention are carried out across the system. Currently the libraries are trying to get commonality across the system for circulation policies.

Schor discussed the Arlington Heights Memorial Library (AHML), located in a large suburban community twenty-five miles northwest of Chicago. The library has a total collection of more than 430,000 items, with over 1,600 magazines and newspaper subscriptions. The periodical collection budget is $101,800. While mainly a popular collection, the library strives to satisfy their many student users with electronic articles provided by aggregator databases. After a large weeding project and opening stacks for back issues, circulation of paper periodicals increased by almost 30%. Electronic access to titles has enabled the library to pare down their paper collection of specialized academic and technical titles.

CANCELLATIONS AND ADDITIONS

Each of the presenters also described the processes for additions and cancellations to their collections. Headley described how budget cuts in Ohio and for Hamilton County–10% in the periodical budget in 2002 and 10% across the board in 2005–necessitated a significant cancellation project. In order to determine which titles to cancel, without circulation statistics, he relied on personal observation, shelving carts and staff input, and availability of titles at area academic libraries. While cost was a concern, he also analyzed the nature of the periodical. For example, scientific and technical titles that he believed were outside the scope of public libraries and were available at local universities were canceled. Additions are based on the popularity of the content, such as the prevailing trend in electronic gaming, which is high enough to prompt new subscriptions. He also examines other factors such as patron and staff requests, and whether or not a title is indexed. He tries to select all local publications as comprehensively as possible including alternate press titles. Because the community looks to the public library to collect and archive, it often has one copy for display and one copy to archive.

Budget is also a prime consideration for HCLS. With a five resource library model, each getting the daily New York Times and two daily papers, the budget was strained. Decisions for cancellations were based on trying to balance the collection across the system, selecting titles to meet diverse populations in nationality, age and interests. Teen interests had been neglected and they worked to correct this situation by adding titles geared specifically for this age group. The demographics of the community by agency is a factor in selection, while at the same time, a core collection of twenty to forty titles every library has is maintained across the system to provide balance and stability. They rely on use statistics to determine canceling print titles that are available online. Requests, popular titles and local publications are always considered for additions.

At AHML, budget and use are prime considerations. Decisions are based on the scope of the collection, with low-use titles dropped. These low-use titles tended to be expensive technical and academic titles. Also canceled were low use paper titles that are available electronically, through subscription databases. A core collection of public library essential titles is maintained to support the library's mission of providing information and entertainment. Titles supporting leisure and research are also included in the collection. Serials Solutions data helps point patrons to full text access. Additional titles are selected by requests from patrons and staff, as well as personal observation of new publications.

FORMATS AND ARCHIVING

The PLCHC is viewed by some as a research library, partly because they have always archived a large number of periodicals in print and microform. Conserving space is a benefit of archiving via microforms. The library has an increasing concern regarding the financial difficulty in trying to maintain subscriptions to both print and microform. Using microforms to archive titles is not always the best solution. For example, art and photography titles are archived only in print to preserve the visual images. Because of the decreased binding budget, some titles are no longer bound, while others are bound less frequently with larger bind units. At Hennepin County, the microforms have been reduced to two dozen titles or less. Bound titles have also been cut to approximately two dozen titles. Cost and time are the major factors in reducing both. They continue to keep local papers in microform. At Arlington Heights, nothing is bound. Both the *Chicago Sun-Times* and *Chicago Tribune* are available in microform.

CONCLUSION

The last item discussed is the presenters' favorite collection development tools. For Headley, the *Wooden Horse Publishing News Alert*, received by e-mail from http://www.woodenhorsepub.com is a favorite. This Web site is for freelance writers who are looking for leads or help in finding where to get published and has news on the latest new publications, cessations of popular titles, and changes in popular publications. This site is where he found *Shop, Etc.* and *Figure*, two recent additions to the collection. Schor relies on *Ulrich's Periodicals Directory Online*, http://www.ulrichsweb.com/ulrichsweb, for reviews and publication URL's, and links to OCLC WorldCat to check holdings of other libraries. Buck uses *MediaWeek*, http://www.mediaweek.com, as her favorite collection development tool. The panel discussion high-lighted the similarities and differences in collection development in public libraries. While each of the three libraries has unique character-istics, the predominant factor remains serving the needs of the commu-nity within the constraints of budget, space, staff and time.

CONTRIBUTORS' NOTES

Tina Herman Buck is Reference and Serials Librarian, Hennepin County Library System. Stephen Headley is Manager, Magazines and Newspapers Department, Public Library of Cincinnati and Hamilton County. Abby Schor is Collection Specialist, Arlington Heights Memorial Library. Susan Banoun is Serials and Electronic Resources Cataloging Unit Head, University of Cincinnati.

Challenges of Off-Site Library Storage Facilities: Cataloging, Access and Management of Off-Site Serials

Susan Currie
Sarah Corvene
Zoe Stewart-Marshall

Presenters

Sarah John

Recorder

SUMMARY. This session presented several case studies of libraries facing challenges following a decision to move materials to an off-site storage facility. The presenters described the entire process of moving materials to an off-site location: from planning and selecting materials to organizing the collection off-site, with an emphasis on the unique problems created by serials. All three presenters shared strategies and decision-making methods with the audience. *[Article copies available for a fee from The Haworth Document Delivery Service: 1-800-HAWORTH. E-mail address: <docdelivery@haworthpress.com> Website: <http://www.HaworthPress.com>]*

[Haworth co-indexing entry note]: "Challenges of Off-Site Library Storage Facilities: Cataloging, Access and Management of Off-Site Serials." John, Sarah. Co-published simultaneously in *The Serials Librarian* (The Haworth Information Press, an imprint of The Haworth Press, Inc.) Vol. 50, No. 3/4, 2006, pp. 259-265; and: *Roaring into Our 20's: NASIG 2005* (ed: Margaret Mering, and Elna Saxton) The Haworth Information Press, an imprint of The Haworth Press, Inc., 2006, pp. 259-265. Single or multiple copies of this article are available for a fee from The Haworth Document Delivery Service [1-800-HAWORTH, 9:00 a.m. - 5:00 p.m. (EST). E-mail address: getinfo@haworthpress.com].

Available online at http://www.haworthpress.com/web/SER
doi:10.1300/J123v50n03_09

Many large libraries, and even some smaller ones in a consortial environment, will have to consider off-site storage at some point. Even with the growth of electronic materials, a demand for print still exists. Depending on the institution and the library that serves it, growing archival and special collections can also create a demand for space. Furthermore, many libraries demand larger spaces for computer labs and study areas in space previously designated for stacks. For many libraries, moving materials off-site can be more economical than building or renovating the library. Services at an off-site facility can also help make such an option more feasible and even attractive since efficiencies in collection management allow for some services such as electronic document delivery to be faster than a traditional library. A thorough assessment of a library's collections and shelf space measurement can help to determine a library's space capacity for print materials. Susan Currie from Binghamton University explained that generally once stack space reaches an 80% capacity libraries might need to consider and plan for a storage facility move.

Moving to a storage facility involves a large number of crucial decisions for library staff. A great deal depends on the particulars of the institution, its needs and existing resources. Currie shared her experiences at two different universities, a large, private research library system at Cornell and a medium sized research collection that is state-supported at Binghamton. With both institutions, Currie stressed the need for four key aspects of the off-site storage moving process: planning, communication, selection, and knowledge of facility. Institutional variability may determine the type of facility chosen. Cornell decided to build a high-density storage facility. The libraries had reached a 90% capacity in some of its libraries. The first high-density warehouse at Cornell was completed in 1998. A second addition is currently in progress.

Materials in a high-density warehouse are not shelved by call number but by size for maximum space efficiency. Location is maintained by an inventory control system, since call number is not used. In the first move at Cornell, they primarily moved a mix of monographs, large journal runs and some microfiche and microfilm in order to make space in the central campus libraries. Cornell had an existing facility at the site which was retained and housed a variety of materials moved in the late 1970s. Binghamton did not have an option to build a facility. They leased a warehouse when the existing collection reached 105% capacity. The Binghamton Libraries moved monographs, runs of bound serial volumes, microfilm and microfiche as well as LPs. No matter the type of library, prior to moving, the existing collections should be measured and anticipated growth rate identified. Establishing lines of communication with all affected parties is also essential. Visiting another library's facility and looking at floor plans can be helpful in planning. Identifying what is unique and specific to your institution is important too.

Other important aspects of planning include selection criteria, politics, communication and decision-making, and deciding how to move materials. For selection criteria, keep in mind the type of material and various formats and sizes. Monographs are relatively easy to plan for; serials are more complicated, naturally! Serials have varying sizes and formats and staff will need to plan for the release and continued growth of space. When deciding on unbound versus bound journals, consider the usage, completeness and run of the title, and how the journals will be housed. Additionally, think long and hard before sending active serial titles to an off-site storage facility, as it is not efficient to deal with pulling for binding, planning for traditional growth space, etc. Some good options for serial moves include ceased serials. Low use microform sets are also a good choice, although they will need special housing considerations. For example, consider NOT moving the cabinets with materials but using special boxes and developing a unique item record and barcoding scenarios. Most storage facilities will have regulations and building codes to consider when planning for the selection of materials. Microform and other audiovisual material may have fire regulations that have to be considered. Finally, consider languages during the selection process. What special training do staff responsible for paging and delivering need to identify non-English language materials? Are certain language materials important to the collection or student population?

Politics are an unavoidable factor in off-site storage issues. Moving library materials carries an emotional component. Library staff need to pay attention and keep everyone, both staff and library users, in the loop during the process. The research needs of the institution are primary. With a dynamic collection consider having a steady state footprint, where one item is taken out for every one added. The days of large on-site research collections may be numbered and libraries may need to take a more active role in working with the institution to determine on-site collection needs. A good way to organize an off-site moving project is to establish a committee with representatives from technical services, access services, collection development, stacks, preservation and a high-level administrator. The committee chair must have decision-making authority and know when to delegate up or down.

When planning for a move, consider the types of staff you can afford and anticipate their training needs. Cornell provided funding for a two year moving project, hiring special book movers and training workers on warehouse procedures and forklift operation to move roughly 2,000 volumes a day. The type of facility is also crucial in deciding placement of the materials. At Cornell, they used a high-density facility with a forklift based on the Harvard model. A template is used to size materials into trays, the barcode in each book is linked to the barcode on the tray and when shelved, and the tray barcode is linked to the shelf barcode. All this information is collected with hand-held scanners and uploaded into the inventory control system. At Binghamton, the move was completed using students and professional movers.

Organizing materials in the facility is the next step in the process, especially the details relating to access and retrieval. Barcoding is the key to organization. Library staff should carefully consider the placement of barcodes on materials. Putting the barcode on the outside of materials is advantageous because it allows for easy scanning and inventory work, and for use in self-checkout machines. Inventory control systems are good for large collections. A proper inventory control system should interface with a library's ILS and link to items by barcode. In the absence of an inventory control system, libraries can use call numbers as a retrieval method; using call numbers can be more complicated and less efficient depending on how the library decides to interfile items. Working with the Generation Fifth Applications software, an item to shelf option was developed, where materials were loaded in call number order directly onto shelves and the book barcodes linked to the shelf barcode. If institutions cannot afford a high-density warehouse, using conventional shelving with this item to shelf option is ideal.

Finally, Currie discussed how materials were prepared for moving, including the decisions that had to be made about microform (to barcode or not?), and cleaning materials. Library staff had to decide how to prepare materials with maximum efficiency and lowest cost. After relocation, decisions had to be made about evaluating the off-site collection and preparing for possible relocation back to campus. An inventory control system can track circulation rates. The library can identify collection development criteria that might allow some materials to come back on-site. At Binghamton, a recent project was completed to identify journal runs for which the Libraries have subscriptions to full text electronic journals. The print volumes have value for research but can be stored off-site if current full text access is available.

Corvene from Harvard University described their unique challenges with an off-site storage facility. Ultimately their approach, "The Harvard Way," became a standard for other libraries. In reality, there is no one "Harvard Way," as Harvard encompasses numerous different libraries with different needs and resources, some with their own ILS. A Collection Management Council aided much of the decision-making. In 1990, Harvard began sending monographs to storage due to an extreme lack of space. The plan was controversial and to overcome resistance the staff and student workers marked materials that had not circulated in over five years. Professors checked the selected material and made the decision to send to storage. In 1993, Harvard began sending journals in coordination with JSTOR and Project Muse. Journals scanned for these projects were sent to the depository after scanning. Harvard staff also looked at usage statistics and patterns to select materials, identifying subject areas where older information was less crucial. Eventually, everything pre-1990 was sent to storage, including partial runs of older titles. This shift in materials had a major impact on their online catalog, which could not handle the moving walls.

Harvard chose to use minimal selector decisions when formulating selection criteria, encouraging them to send large classes of material instead. Popular materials for storage included ceased microfilm sets, large journal runs, and "medium-rare" materials identified by Preservation. Since Harvard's on-site libraries had numerous climate-control and security issues, sending certain materials off-site held benefits for Preservation by letting them have more control in the off-site environment.

Because of so many materials stored off-site, Harvard staff had to deal with the ramifications for public service, cataloging and holdings issues. Students wanted to know "Why is half of it at Harvard Depository?" Current periodicals presented another challenge in deciding what and how much to bind and send to storage. Harvard is a CONSER library, meaning it has a significant cataloging commitment. Cataloging staff needed to decide how much energy to devote to cataloging off-site materials. They could choose higher-level cataloging since off-site materials suffered a lack of browsability, or lower-level cataloging since the materials were lower-use. In the end, they made decisions case-by-case because both approaches had compelling arguments for both approaches. Harvard considered moving a significant cataloging backlog to storage and using "deferred cataloging." This option proved to be unpopular with faculty. Finally, since Harvard uses level-4 holdings to describe current receipts (the most complete and detailed level in the

MARC Holdings format), they had to consider how to display holdings for off-site material. With older runs of journals and bound incomplete journals, they could either redo the holdings statement or use item records. They found a case-by-case basis approach worked best.

Stewart-Marshall talked about Cornell University, where she oversees retrospective conversion and barcoding of materials, in addition to withdrawals and transfers for the off-site storage facility. Cornell has made two different moves to off-site storage. In the first move, staff moved mainly monographs with converted online records. Moving materials from the Graduate Library proved more challenging since most records had not been converted. Records are not always necessary if you have an inventory control system. However, they are important for patron accessibility. Eventually all monographs and most serials were converted and barcoded.

For Cornell's second move, they had to do two separate planning processes, one for the main libraries and another for everyone else. During the move, the planning centered on balancing the needs of the main libraries and smaller libraries. For both moves, gaining support from library administration and university administration was crucial. The moves to storage were not necessarily motivated by the growth of print, but by the needs of the libraries to provide more space for computers, cafes and study areas. Cornell further boosted their case when they planned to become a regional depository, allowing them to share support and resources with other libraries. To garner even more support, the presenters stressed the need to have statistics to support a low-use material designation. Also, consider having a reading room at the facility; even if it requires staffing, it can be an efficient, secure and politically popular option for users.

Cornell found success in elucidating and balancing the short-term and long-term goals for the move to off-site storage. In the short term, they needed more space in the library and were able to provide a better environment and more security for "medium-rare" materials. These materials often have special binding and provenance information that need to be addressed before a major move. In the long-term, Cornell asked selectors to be part of the planning process to help achieve a goal of a "steady-state" collection whereby a balanced and systematic approach is used to maintain a regular inventory. This process involves identifying materials on an ongoing basis and has benefits for stack maintenance. Cornell encouraged selectors to identify large classes of materials, not including current serials, and explained processing costs to selectors to keep them in the loop. Cornell tried to balance the mix of monographs and serials, keeping in mind the circulation issues that serials present with multiple holdings and split titles. Cornell plans to move non-print items for its next module, bringing up complex housing issues such as fire regulations. They recommend giving people as much information as they have about shelving and floor plans.

Audience discussion followed the presentation. One person asked how to deal with off-site materials that go from low use to high use. Currie highlighted the benefits of an inventory control system for tracking and setting thresholds, as well as discussing classroom needs with faculty. Another audience member asked about the distance of off-site locations from campus. Harvard's is one hour south of campus and has a reading room. Binghamton's is a half-hour away with a reading room. Cornell's has bus service near the facility and free parking. To enhance services, the presenters suggested utilizing desktop delivery, either electronically or delivering materials to campus or possibly to faculty offices.

Additional discussions centered on the indexing of older journal runs and how to deal with reclassification projects that may impact off-site storage access and retrieval. Another audience member asked about vendors, and Currie recommended Generation Fifth Applications. Finally, the audience discussed how to handle print de-duplications off-site. The presenters discussed various strategies, including establishing of a "copy of record" for serials in consideration of the long-term access to electronic collections. This problem may have also quota and staffing issues. Stewart-Marshall advised keeping the weeding process separate from the moving process.

The presenters concluded by bringing up the essentials of managing a successful move to an off-site storage facility: planning, flexibility, communication, and administrative support. Most communication will take place in a group setting and whoever is leading the project needs to be able to overrule decisions as well as be accommodating. Remember to keep all of the pieces of the puzzle in mind at all times and that one size does not fit all!

CONTRIBUTORS' NOTES

Susan Currie is Associate Director of Public Services at Binghamton University. Sarah Corvene is Serial Cataloger at Harvard College Library Technical Services. Zoe Stewart-Marshall is Database Enrichment Librarian at Cornell University Library. Sarah John is Electronic Resources Serials Librarian at University of California, Davis.

The Big E-Package Deals: Smoothing the Way Through Subscription Agents

Tina Feick
Gary Ives

Presenters

Jo McClamroch

Recorder

SUMMARY. How does your library manage the Big Deal package? A subscription agent and a librarian defined Big Deals and discussed ways for libraries to manage them. Initially, Big Deal packages were handled directly between the publisher and subscribing institution. Over time, subscription agents have identified ways they can assist their customers in this complicated and complex enterprise. The speakers outlined prospective benefits to all parties when subscription agents and publishers partner with customers in managing Big Deals. *[Article copies available for a fee from The Haworth Document Delivery Service: 1-800-HAWORTH. E-mail address: <docdelivery@haworthpress.com> Website: <http://www.HaworthPress.com>]*

[Haworth co-indexing entry note]: "The Big E-Package Deals: Smoothing the Way Through Subscription Agents." McClamroch, Jo. Co-published simultaneously in *The Serials Librarian* (The Haworth Information Press, an imprint of The Haworth Press, Inc.) Vol. 50, No. 3/4, 2006, pp. 267-270; and: *Roaring into Our 20's: NASIG 2005* (ed: Margaret Mering, and Elna Saxton) The Haworth Information Press, an imprint of The Haworth Press, Inc., 2006, pp. 267-270. Single or multiple copies of this article are available for a fee from The Haworth Document Delivery Service [1-800-HAWORTH, 9:00 a.m. - 5:00 p.m. (EST). E-mail address: getinfo@haworthpress.com].

Available online at http://www.haworthpress.com/web/SER
doi:10.1300/J123v50n03_10

To set the context for this session, Gary Ives offered this definition of a Big Deal: one that provides access to all titles in a publisher's package, one that is accessible at all campuses, one whose pricing is based on historic print subscription base, and one that may be offered as a multi-year agreement with negotiated price caps for each year of the agreement.

Tina Feick offered a brief historical overview and shared observations about the evolution of the Big Deal from publishers and how this development looked from the perspective of a subscription agent. About a decade ago, publishers began to package and market aggregations of titles as Big Deals. As these new offers were not individual subscriptions, traditionally managed by an agent, subscription agents were initially excluded from the process of mediating such packages for institutions. Subscription agents wanted to be involved in this new activity, not only for their expertise in managing subscriptions but also for their ability to provide value-added services to their customers. To ensure themselves a niche in this new market, vendors and their agents had to become more proactive and to directly promote to publishers and to libraries the services they could bring to the enterprise.

While Feick spoke specifically of some initiatives undertaken by Swets, all subscription agents were addressing the same situation. Agents began to work more closely with their customers to develop a clear understanding of the needs of libraries. In addition, they were involved in a lot of back and forth communication with publishers to determine appropriate roles for each prospective partner. Feick characterized this exercise as healthy for all parties to enable them to pool their complementary strengths and provide a better outcome for their customers.

As Ives observed, libraries have genuine staffing concerns in the management of electronic resources in general and the Big Deal packages in particular. The perpetual lament that libraries often have more work to do than staff to do it is another factor in the growing partnerships between libraries and agents. Feick identified many tasks that agents can help libraries with, such as ensuring the accuracy of an e-package list, providing line-by-line invoicing including direct electronic invoicing from agent to library. Subscription agents are able to provide a variety of management reports such as a breakdown of spending by local budget or fund code. In general, agent oversight of Big Deal packages should save time and money for the subscribing library, particularly in billing and payment processing.

Every technological innovation brings new challenges. We have moved beyond the basic challenges of selecting and choosing electronic journal subscriptions over (or in addition to) print subscriptions. As publishers continue to aggregate their suites of titles, libraries may want to give consideration to assigning more of the day-to-day payment and access details to their subscription agents.

Ives provided a description of Texas A&M, his home institution. It has a main campus and eight regional campuses, an FTE enrollment of 80,000 across the system. It is an institution that has purchased several Big Deal packages. Ives reported on the good experience at Texas A&M of working with a subscription agent to ease the management burden. The College Station Campus has a total of 9,000 subscriptions, of which one-third are electronic-only. He also indicated that over 45.5% of the serials budget is dedicated to electronic-only subscriptions, making it essential to explore new approaches to managing these packages.

As most libraries know, a tremendous amount of detail is required to negotiate and set up Big Deal packages. Discrepancies are often found between the publisher's list of subscribed titles and the institution's list. Ives observed that the agent's records are the most authoritative, complete, and accurate record of local subscriptions. As the entity with the most comprehensive data, a subscription agent can provide many services to their customers. For example, at Texas A&M, the university negotiates and signs the license agreement. The subscription agent monitors that access is in compliance with the negotiated terms. He maintains up-to-date information on the content of the Big Deal, monitoring titles that are coming in or going out of a package, alerting customers to title changes, merges and ceases, and the like. For budget and accounting purposes, Ives had great praise for the agent's accurate invoices which include line item detail at the request of the customer.

He acknowledged that no management tool or system is without shortcomings or pitfalls. Nevertheless, the benefits outweigh the costs to his institution in using a subscription agent versus local staff to manage Big Deals. He gave three positive points of a library/agent partnership: single vs. multiple workflows for subscription management; on-demand subscription management and collection assessment reports; and reduced overhead for library operations, "giving us services that publishers cannot provide, and that we cannot provide for ourselves."

Attendees at this Tactics Session had many questions for the presenters. While each institution has to make the right choice for their circumstances, all libraries are encouraged to explore new partnerships for big deal packages and determine appropriate roles for each of the players:

publisher, agent, and librarian. Partnerships between libraries and subscription agents for acquiring and managing Big Deal packages is yet another method to respond to the continuing abundance of electronic journal packages and their attendant complications.

CONTRIBUTORS' NOTES

Tina Feick is Vice-President of North American Customer Service for Swets Information Services. Gary Ives is Assistant Director of Acquisitions and Coordinator of Electronic Resources at Texas A & M University Libraries. Jo McClamroch is Electronic Resources Acquisitions Librarian at Indiana University.

Subscription Cancellation Projects:
How to Quiet Some of the Roar

Clint Chamberlain
Beatrice Caraway

Presenters

Susan Andrews

Recorder

SUMMARY. When faced with yet another subscription cancellation project at Trinity University, a closer look at certain aspects of the budget was decided on by Caraway and Chamberlain as a way to determine price increases and possible cuts. A new way of deciding the amount to cut for non-United States titles was taken in this study, using projected inflation figures. During the project, an even more interesting discovery was made in working and communicating with faculty. *[Article copies available for a fee from The Haworth Document Delivery Service: 1-800-HAWORTH. E-mail address: <docdelivery@haworthpress.com> Website: <http://www.HaworthPress.com>]*

Trinity University's library has approximately 2,000 print subscriptions totaling about $680,000. E-resources were not considered in this project. The subscriptions are prepaid in June of each year to Trinity's

[Haworth co-indexing entry note]: "Subscription Cancellation Projects: How to Quiet Some of the Roar." Andrews, Susan. Co-published simultaneously in *The Serials Librarian* (The Haworth Information Press, an imprint of The Haworth Press, Inc.) Vol. 50, No. 3/4, 2006, pp. 271-278; and: *Roaring into Our 20's: NASIG 2005* (ed: Margaret Mering, and Elna Saxton) The Haworth Information Press, an imprint of The Haworth Press, Inc., 2006, pp. 271-278. Single or multiple copies of this article are available for a fee from The Haworth Document Delivery Service [1-800-HAWORTH, 9:00 a.m. - 5:00 p.m. (EST). E-mail address: getinfo@haworthpress.com].

Available online at http://www.haworthpress.com/web/SER
doi:10.1300/J123v50n03_11

subscription vendor, Harrasowitz. The nine librarians, including the university librarian, have liaison responsibilities for instruction, collection development, and outreach. They work collaboratively on many, if not most, projects.

Caraway began the session by reading a letter from 1976 that she had found while cleaning out old files. The letter's main point was that her library was once again facing the task of cutting subscriptions. She noted that after thirty years no resolution had been found to the serials crisis. Sessions on serials cancellation projects continued to be a perennial favorite at NASIG. The main focus in this particular session would be on the monetary exchange rates and their effects on pricing, and on the faculty and their response to the actions taking during the cancellation project.

In the spring of 2004, Caraway and Chamberlain were becoming aware of the downward slide of the dollar. According to Caraway, the value of the dollar against the Euro as of May 17, 2004 was $1.26. A year ago it was $1.19, and the year before that it was $1.06. She noted that the sharpest decline of the dollar, however, happened between January and June 2003, when it fell from $1.26 to $1.05 against the Euro. Her library failed to pay any attention to that plunge, and only noticed it a year later. The value of the dollar against the British pound is currently $1.84. One would suppose that the weak dollar would make imported journals more expensive to buy. During the course of this explanation, Caraway coined a new term–the "wussy dollar," which apparently is what the United States currently is experiencing. The question that Chamberlain and Caraway focused on was the effect on 2005 subscription prices due to the weakness of the dollar, as distinct from normal price inflation. With some research, they ventured that the Euro would be worth around $1.28 in the fall of 2004, when prices were most likely being set for 2005. In fact, they came pretty close. Chamberlain and Caraway decided to try to adjust the target amount for cuts, partly based on the strength and weakness of the dollar to the Euro. They informed their university's academic departments about these considerations and reminded them that these circumstances were beyond all of their control.

Chamberlain discussed their contact with the academic departments by referring to a letter that they had sent to the Classical Studies faculty in April 2004. It primarily explained the upcoming need to cut subscriptions with a paragraph which specifically discussed non-United States journals and a brief discussion of the weakening dollar compared to the Euro and the British Pound. A second memo was sent out in mid-August 2004, with more detailed information regarding the budget, with a focus on European titles and inflation, and with specific suggestions regarding cuts for taking these factors into account. The figures used came from the formula on a handout (Figure 1). First, he figured the normal inflation rate, giving the United States an 8% rate, and giving Europe (averaging the United Kingdom and Europe together) an additional 6%, to arrive at a total 14% inflation rate, based on the weakness of the dollar. Chamberlain and Caraway decided that the number of titles they purchased elsewhere in the world was not large enough to make a significant difference. Exchange rates for those countries were not taken into consideration in this study.

Simply, the formula took the percent of United States titles in a given departmental list and multiplied it by 8% (the projected basic inflation rate), then took the percent of United Kingdom and European Union titles in a given departmental list and multiplied it by 14% (the projected basic inflation rate plus the projected increase caused by the weak dollar). The two resulting figures were added together to give the anticipated 2005 cost of the given department's subscriptions. Departments with fewer UK or EU titles would, as a result of applying this formula, see a smaller projected increase in total costs than those departments with a preponderance of titles imported from the UK and the EU. Since the library's budget was going to benefit from a surprising 7% increase, they would be able to cover 7% of the subscription increases. The target

FIGURE 1

Assume basic (U.S.) price inflation to be 8%, based on recent history.

Assume European inflation to be on average 14% (basic 8% + 6% increase for exchange rate).

Sample problem: Our religion subscriptions are heavily tied to overseas publishers (38.5%), so we calculated the expected inflation rate as follows:

(% of Eur. titles x Eur. Inflation) + (% of US titles x US inflation) = <u>total inflation</u>

(38.5%   x   14   ) + (61.5%   x   8   )   =

     5.39%   +   4.92%   =

     <u>10.31%</u>

amount to cut for each department would be the difference between 7% and the projected increase derived from the formula just described. In spring 2005, after most of the journals titles had been invoiced and pricing was known, they decided to check to see how close their calculations came. For Classical Studies, the estimated increase due to inflation and the projected effect of the exchange rate was $460. The actual inflation figure was $140. In general, the projected increases were higher than the actual increases. The projected increases were underestimated for History and Chemistry.

Another exploratory part of the project was to break the titles into small and large publisher groupings. The informal and subjective method used to determine whether a publisher was small or large was based on whether Chamberlain and Caraway had heard of the publisher (large publisher) or not (small publisher). Based on this division, Chamberlain checked to see if he could find any correlation between publisher size and the amount of increase in the price. His hypothesis was that small publishers' prices would more accurately reflect actual increases in operating and production costs, and in fluctuations in the exchange rate. Large publishers might have the luxury of adjusting prices to accomplish other objectives, such as minimizing cancellations. This admittedly informal and incomplete analysis was unable to support this hypothesis.

While the increases they projected were high for about 75% of the titles, the average difference was small: $2 to $3 for the United States, $13 for the United Kingdom, and $10 for the rest of Europe. According to an excerpt Chamberlain read from "Choosing Sides–Periodical Price Survey 2005" in the April 2005 issue of *Library Journal*, subscription price increases for the 2005 subscription year were lower than expected,[1] which made him feel better about his projections. The main reason given was that publishers were more concerned about the potential number of cancellations than they were about exchange rates.

At the end of this part of the session, Caraway asked the audience how they had handled their imported titles. Did they make projections based partially on the exchange rate? One audience member said that they had cut their subscription budget by 10% across the board and that this solution had worked well for them. However, an across-the-board cut would not be sensitive to the varying preponderance of UK and EU titles in different departmental lists of journals.

Another audience member felt that libraries should not allocate their budgets by academic department. Someone else felt that assigning by departments caused battles because so many titles crossed disciplines, plus usage statistics can be different for different departments, due to discipline related variables. Caraway replied that they were working on moving their inter-disciplinary titles into a general library fund. When queried about non-responses to subscription cancellation requests, she said that all of the departments responded, thanks to persistence on the part of the library faculty, who serve as liaisons to the departments. Another method of encouragement is to provide budget allocations only when responses have been received. An alternative method is to have librarians make the selections, if faculty do not choose what they want to cut.

Another respondent wanted to know why a distinction was made between United States and European publications rather than between categories like STM and humanities titles. Caraway replied that it appeared that the rate of increase for humanities titles had, in fact, been higher in the very recent past than those for STM publications. The assumption of greater inflation rates for STM could not always be held without question. An audience member said that during a cancellation project at Stanford they had found that the inflation rate for STM titles appeared to be sinking recently, and it was the humanities titles that were going into the double digits lately.

Someone pointed out that many publications set their prices in both dollars and Euros, and some exclusively in dollars. Caraway acknowledged that large publishers, especially, engaged in this practice. However, the practice did not eliminate the effect of the exchange rate on costs to United States libraries, but merely obscured its effect.

Caraway questioned, what can we do with regard to exchange rates? Discussion and comments included follow trends and remember that subscription agents are a valuable resource and partner. Payment can be made in dollars or the currency of the country depending on the strength of the dollar. Pre-paying each year can provide an early payment bonus that can offset some price increases. Another response focused on cancellations as a strategy. Cancellation lists can be sent to all of the academic departments to reflect the cross-discipline nature of some publications. Comments can be weighted by the department or by other factors.

Caraway noted that, judging from articles written in the early- to mid-nineties, publishers set and released their prices in June and July of each year. She wondered if libraries would conduct their cancellation projects differently if they had this information as early as June or July. The consensus from the audience was no. One person commented that subscription agents have tried to get prices set earlier, with some success, but that both they, and the publishers, have other factors to consider that cause this solution to be a problem for them to do. Caraway noted that the Association of Subscription Agents Web site has a short piece called "Campaign on Late Pricing," in which publishers are urged to release their price lists by the end of July each year.[2] A publisher in the audience responded that they do start working on pricing in June, but they cannot release their prices any sooner than they do.

A former agent said that they used to get prices out earlier, but the number of cancellations has caused problems. When they look at price increases, they do not look at inflation percentages, they look at dollars. The work that Caraway and Chamberlain had done was interesting. However, subscription agents already have most of the information involved and even more. We should rely on their expertise.

An audience member wondered how the dollar price was set for a foreign title. A publisher representative said they set the price and do not worry about the exchange rate. She said that many countries used to set their prices and then convert other currencies. Many now set the price in dollars, Euros, and Pounds. They just bear the exchange rates risks.

The final portion of the session centered on departmental communications. Caraway and Chamberlain met with half of their department chairs to ask if the information about currency factors had any effect on their deliberations about cancellations. While the currency rate did not impact decision-making, the opportunity to have individual meetings to discuss this opened dialogue on a range of library related issues. For example, Chamberlain and Caraway learned different departments had different preferences about when to receive such requests. In the future, with very little effort, the library can tailor the distribution of these requests to academic departments. Chamberlain and Caraway were able to educate the chairs about the roles and deadlines of subscription agents, and how that dictated, to a great extent, the schedule of review and cancellation decisions. Many of the departmental chairs did not know much about document delivery, including desktop delivery of electronic articles. Others wanted to talk about the difficulty of getting students to use library resources, which offered an opportunity to pitch library instruction sessions. Still others expressed concerns about diminishing books budgets, or other more general library issues.

Based on their experiences, Caraway and Chamberlain suggested using your most recent correspondence on any topic to department chairs as a pretext for making an appointment, saying that you would like to get their reaction to a given element in order to improve your communications with them. They recommended finding a time to talk not only during the usual cancellation cycle. Another recommendation was to try to send someone other than the assigned library liaison (e.g., the head of public or technical services, the serials librarian, or the assistant director) to provide a different perspective. In all cases, the appointed liaison should be briefed on the conversation afterwards.

In conclusion, it would appear that inflation is not as major a factor in the budgeting process as originally thought, although projections using this premise did work well. At Trinity University, Caraway and Chamberlain felt that the most important outcome from the project was the enhanced communication with faculty. Having contact with the faculty, at least the departmental chairs, was an important and fruitful endeavor, from their point of view, and something to be recommended and encouraged.

NOTES

1. Lee C. Van Orsdel, and Kathleen Born, "Choosing Sides," *Library Journal* 30, no. 7 (Apr. 15, 2005): 43-48.
2. Association of Subscription Agencies and Intermediaries. "2005 Price Projections." *http://www.subscription-agents.org/news/PriceProjections.html* (15 May 2005).

SUGGESTED READINGS

Association of Subscription Agencies and Intermediaries. "2005 Price Projections." *http://www.subscription-agents.org/news/PriceProjections.html* (15 May 2005).

Duranceau, Ellen. "The Balance Point: Exchange Rates and the Serials Marketplace." *Serials Review* 21, no. 3 (1995): 83-96.
Although now a decade old, this column still provides clear, basic descriptions of the ways libraries, subscription agents, and publishers might deal with currency fluctuations. Different perspectives are provided by Knut Dorn, John Cox, Harry Hoffer, Allen Powell, and James Mouw.

EBSCO Information Services. "Serials Price Projections and Cost History." http://www-us.ebsco.com/home/printsubs/priceproj.asp (15 May 2005).

Strauch, Bruce, and Katina Strauch, "Foreign Exchange Rates and Journal Pricing," *Library Acquisitions: Practice & Theory* 13, no. 4 (1989): 417-422. Includes a clear explanation of how a foreign exchange option works (p. 421).

Van Orsdel, Lee C., and Kathleen Born, "Choosing Sides," *Library Journal* 30, no. 7 (Apr. 15, 2005): 43-48. The 2005 periodical price survey discusses the many factors that are presently affecting journal prices. Reviewing the last 10-15 years of the annual survey in *Library Journal* is an easy way to get a good handle on what effect exchange rates are thought to have had on journal prices over the last decade or more. The 1993 survey by Kathleen Born and Lee Ketcham is especially instructive. The survey, which always appears in the April 15 issue, usually wraps up with a very general prediction of prices for the upcoming subscription year.

CONTRIBUTORS' NOTES

Clint Chamberlain is Electronic Access and Serials Librarian, Trinity University. Bea Caraway is Head of Technical Services, Trinity University. Susan Andrews is Head, Serials Department, Texas A&M University-Commerce.

Examining Workflows
and Redefining Roles:
Auburn University
and The College of New Jersey

Jia Mi
Paula Sullenger

Presenters

Pat Loghry

Recorder

SUMMARY. Paula Sullenger, Serials Acquisitions Librarian at Auburn University and Jia Mi, Electronic Resources/Serials Librarian at the College of New Jersey discussed electronic resource workflow models at their respective institutions. Services are available from vendors that aid in streamlining workflow for handling print resources and electronic journals. In addition, in-house statistics are used to determine serials tasks to eliminate and job functions to realign. *[Article copies available for a fee from The Haworth Document Delivery Service: 1-800-HAWORTH. E-mail address: <docdelivery@haworthpress.com> Website: <http://www. HaworthPress.com>]*

[Haworth co-indexing entry note]: "Examining Workflows and Redefining Roles: Auburn University and The College of New Jersey." Loghry, Pat. Co-published simultaneously in *The Serials Librarian* (The Haworth Information Press, an imprint of The Haworth Press, Inc.) Vol. 50, No. 3/4, 2006, pp. 279-283; and: *Roaring into Our 20's: NASIG 2005* (ed: Margaret Mering, and Elna Saxton) The Haworth Information Press, an imprint of The Haworth Press, Inc., 2006, pp. 279-283. Single or multiple copies of this article are available for a fee from The Haworth Document Delivery Service [1-800-HAWORTH, 9:00 a.m. - 5:00 p.m. (EST). E-mail address: getinfo@haworthpress.com].

Available online at http://www.haworthpress.com/web/SER
doi:10.1300/J123v50n03_12

Jia Mi began the program with a description of the College of New Jersey, a four-year college with seven schools providing fifty undergraduate and six graduate programs to 6,147 FTEs. They currently subscribe to ninety-five electronic databases and 19,814 unique e-journals with an electronic resources budget of $278,249 (electronic databases only). The catalog has MARC records for databases but not e-journals. The library has a new Head of Cataloging and plans to purchase e-journal MARC records to load into its OPAC in the near future. The school uses EBSCO-EJS and EBSCO.NET to manage their e-journals.

In 2003, when Mi started her job as an electronic resources/serials librarian, it was a newly created position. Mi is responsible for collection development, budgeting, license negotiation (with signature authority at the Director level), set-up and maintenance of the electronic products, but not for cataloging. In addition, Mi works at the Reference Desk providing bibliographic instruction. She feels one of the benefits of this structure is the ability to see the whole picture, to observe the problems first-hand. She is able to monitor funds, track the publisher's yearly registration requirements to prevent loss of access, and identify the duplication of titles among the print, electronic and microfilm copies.

STREAMLINING WORKFLOWS

The creation of an Electronic Resources Librarian position centralized the budget and acquisitions process, distributed statistics and housekeeping needs, and enabled collaboration on the marketing and selection of products. The centralized budget simplified determining if the product was acquired through a consortia, aggregator, or publisher. Centralized trials establish the vendor relationship at an early stage and simplified the technical details and license negotiation for terms and price.

Policies and procedures for selection of electronic databases, gathering usage information and setting up trials are essential to standardize the process. Selection is a collaborative process; Mi works with the other subject librarians and the collection development coordinator. Once the decision to renew or cancel has been made, Mi controls the process. Marketing the database is also a collaborative process. The Web master controls the server for the entire college. Mi maintains the library Web page and makes updates as needed. Web maintenance is a collaborative process with their users, as they have neither manpower nor time to proactively find problems.

The College of New Jersey uses Serials Solutions and subscribes to its A to Z list. This service is used to maintain their electronic databases and their electronic journal holdings. The list includes their serial print holdings as well as their electronic journals. Mi also uses the journal linker to link to abstracts and citations to full text. Serials Solutions' Overlap Analysis indicates which journals are available in more than one database which aids the library's collection development decision. Their Click Through Statistics gives very detailed information on how each database, e-journal and print journal has been used. EbscoNet's OAR (Online Availability Report) indicates the library's order status, and shows which journals are available in print only, print plus online, or electronic only. In addition, the report provides a list of publishers who require registration. Ebsco EJS Admin Alerts provides information such as the subscription ID needed to register journals with publishers. The college uses several technical tools to assist the process. "Form Genie" is used to get feedback on trial databases from librarians, faculty and patrons. The results are easily converted into an access database. "Web Alerts" are used to publicize new databases. This combined model of centralized, collaborative and distributed functions concentrates on data and function flow. It streamlines workflow and applications, builds a collaborative environment with public service librarians and makes the most efficient use of the staff available.

Paula Sullenger is the serials acquisitons librarian at Auburn University, a large land-grant comprehensive university, with twelve colleges. The main library serves all the colleges with the exception of Architecture Design and Construction, and Veterinary Medicine. The University has 24,000 FTE students. At a NASIG conference, Sullenger attended a round-table on redesigning workflow for moving from print serials to electronic. Some of the questions she took home from that session were:

- What print work could be dropped as they moved from print to electronic?
- What parts of the electronic workflow could be passed to staff as print tasks decreased:
- Did the organization have the kind of staff, at the appropriate levels, that could adjust to the tasks required with electronic products?

The Acquisitions Department's responsibilities include firm orders, firm order receiving, approval, bindery/physical processing and Serials/ Electronic Resources. The Cataloging Department is responsible for cataloging and URL maintenance and link checking, which are handled by a catalog maintenance unit. Acquisitions knew they would be dropping the Elsevier print titles in 2005, knew they were getting more use from the electronic serials and databases, and knew there would be five retirements coming up in the department in the next three or four years. Sullenger felt the time was right to plan for those retirements and to determine justifications for the positions.

Looking for trends and workload distribution, Sullenger gathered data from 2000 to 2003. She started by examining the number of books and journals ordered, received and claimed. The underlying assumption was that with a decreased workload in print serials and an anticipated decreased workload in monographs, existing positions could absorb new tasks. She did find that the workload was less in monographs, not enough to cut positions at this time. Continuations, standing orders and memberships are centralized in one position. The workload had a twenty percent drop after a major cancellation several years ago. Journal issue check-in was steady over the time period. Serials claims had a big spike in 2001 and 2002, but were stable in 2003. The serials claiming person and the check-in supervisor were assisting each other when the workload was heavy. Sullenger determined that gift and exchange titles had many claims. Few issues were received as a result of these claims but demanded a large proportion of the work.

What is the print situation now? In 2003, Elsevier accounted for about fourteen percent of the issues received and about ten percent of the claims. With the Elsevier cancellation, a ten percent drop in claims would allow one person to handle the work without assistance. Since staff only check in problem titles, no impact was felt on the receiving workload. If the loss of Elsevier print is not a problem, Auburn plans to cancel other publisher print subscriptions (e.g., Springer, Blackwell, and Taylor and Francis). These packages represent an additional fourteen percent of issues received and ten percent of the claims.

Last fall, Sullenger, her Department Head, and the two librarians in the department began to talk to staff. They looked at workflows to determine problem areas and to see what tasks could be eliminated. They and the staff went through procedures step-by-step to see what no longer made sense, what was a waste of time, what was driving them crazy. Were there procedural problems or personnel conflicts? They found a few minor things could be tweaked in the monographic area. No other workflow adjustments were required. They met with other units that interacted with acquisitions to see if any problems needed to be addressed. The Bindery Unit was spending an excessive amount of time trying to obtain missing issues. They decided that if the material were available online they would no longer replace issues. Fall 2005, they will stop claiming for all electronic journals where the print will be cancelled in 2006. Bindery is requiring a smaller budget as well, and when one of the staff retires, the position will likely not be replaced.

A lively question and answer period followed.

CONTRIBUTORS' NOTES

Jia Mi is the Electronic Resources/Serials Librarian at the College of New Jersey. Paula Sullenger is the Serials Acquisitions Librarian at Auburn University. Pat Loghry is Audiovisual Catalog and Licensing Librarian at University of Notre Dame.

AACR3 Is Coming–What Is It?

Paul J. Weiss

Presenter

Molly R. T. Larkin

Recorder

SUMMARY. The Joint Steering Committee for Revision of Anglo-American Cataloging Rules (JSC) has been working on creating a new standard for cataloging. In this session, Paul Weiss provided a context for this new standard and explained the work that has been done by the JSC. The presentation covered the impetus behind the new standard, the process for development of a first draft, reaction to that draft, and the current direction of the JSC's work. *[Article copies available for a fee from The Haworth Document Delivery Service: 1-800-HAWORTH. E-mail address: <docdelivery@haworthpress.com> Website: <http://www.HaworthPress.com>]*

In response to the current confusion that exists in the cataloging community surrounding the revision of the *Anglo-American Cataloging Rules*, Second edition (AACR2), Paul Weiss presented this session, which looked at the current status and progress of these revisions. Weiss began the session by stating that AACR3 is not coming, but rather that work is progressing on a document that will replace AACR2. The developers now view it as a new work rather than a new edition of

[Haworth co-indexing entry note]: "AACR3 Is Coming–What Is It?" Larkin, Molly R. T. Co-published simultaneously in *The Serials Librarian* (The Haworth Information Press, an imprint of The Haworth Press, Inc.) Vol. 50, No. 3/4, 2006, pp. 285-294; and: *Roaring into Our 20's: NASIG 2005* (ed: Margaret Mering, and Elna Saxton) The Haworth Information Press, an imprint of The Haworth Press, Inc., 2006, pp. 285-294. Single or multiple copies of this article are available for a fee from The Haworth Document Delivery Service [1-800-HAWORTH, 9:00 a.m. - 5:00 p.m. (EST). E-mail address: getinfo@haworthpress.com].

Available online at http://www.haworthpress.com/web/SER
doi:10.1300/J123v50n03_13

AACR2. Records created under the instruction of this new work will be compatible with AACR2 records. In order to understand how the current proposals for a new work came to pass, Weiss provided the context in which they were formed.

HISTORICAL CONTEXT

Four major driving forces contributed to the decision to create a new cataloging standard. The first was a 1998 report which defined the functional requirements for bibliographic records (FRBR). This report was the result of a 1990 study commissioned by the International Federation of Library Associations and Institutions (IFLA).

A second driving force was the 1997 International Conference on the Principles and Future Development of AACR, held in Toronto and sponsored by the Joint Steering Committee for Revision of Anglo-American Cataloguing Rules (JSC).[1] The purpose of this conference, which became known as the Toronto Conference, was to review the underlying principles of AACR, with a view to determining whether fundamental rule revision was appropriate and feasible and, if so, advising on the direction and nature of those revisions. A number of outcomes resulted from the Toronto Conference. One of these outcomes was a study entitled *The Logical Structure of the Anglo-American Cataloguing Rules* which provided a review of the underlying principles of AACR2. Another outcome included changes to AACR2 with the complete revision of Chapter 12 and a revision to Rule 0.24 to emphasize the primacy of intellectual content over physical format. Work would also be done to determine the extent of AACR2 use beyond the Anglo-American community. The JSC developed a Web site, formed a mission statement, became committed to more open sharing of information, and adopted a proactive role.

The third driving force was the International Meetings of Experts for an International Cataloguing Code (IME-ICC),[2] a series of worldwide regional meetings that began in 2003. The impetus behind these meetings was a desire to know if the 1961 *Report of the International Conference on Cataloguing Principles*, commonly known as the Paris Principles, were still relevant or if changes were needed. Forty-four years later, these principles remain the basis of nearly every cataloging code used in the world. The goal of the IME-ICC was to increase the ability to share cataloging information worldwide by promoting standards for the content of bibliographic and authority records used in library catalogs. They examined cataloging codes currently in use around the world to compare similarities and differences to determine if the development of an International Cataloguing Code was possible. A draft statement of International Cataloguing Principles was produced from the first meeting in Frankfurt, with ongoing refinements at each annual international meeting.

FRBR, the Toronto Conference, and the IME-ICC all feed into the fourth driving force, the *Strategic Plan for AACR*.[3] The contents of this plan, developed in 2002 and revised in 2004, include: purpose, vision for future development, strengths, and goals.

The desire to have a document to replace AACR2 has also been influenced by the broader metadata community. In addition to the general library community, archives, museums, and other cultural heritage communities have been working on developing metadata standards. Librarians, and catalogers in particular, have expertise to offer to these efforts. Computer scientists are beginning to recognize this knowledge. Finally, an easy-to-use standard would hopefully encourage wider adoption outside the strict library communities, which would lead to increased sharing of information.

Finally, societal changes were a huge impetus behind a new standard. The Internet, with a deluge of information resources, led to an information distribution revolution while at the same time disrupting the established pattern of behavior associated with creating, publishing, distributing, purchasing and using information. Library catalogs moved to the Web, which allowed libraries to provide greater access to their resources. However, the catalog rule remained bound by card catalog concepts and practices that have no relevancy in the online world. In addition, user expectations changed rapidly because of the influence of other information systems such as Google and Amazon.

ADMINISTRATIVE CONTEXT

In addition to the historical context, understanding the administrative governance responsible for any revisions or new editions is also important. In particular, this provides perspective on why implementing new standards takes time. The overall governing body of the cataloging code is the Committee of Principals (COP) which is made up of constituents from the United States, Canada and the United Kingdom. This committee coordinates the following three subordinate groups: the Co-Publishers of AACR, the Joint Steering Committee for Revision of AACR, and the AACR Fund Committee (Trustees). For more information and an organizational chart see: http://www.aacr2.org/governance.html.

FROM AACR2 TO AACR3

Weiss discussed the motivation for AACR3, recent and ongoing JSC work, and the process that was implemented to achieve the publication of a new set of standards. The main principle behind AACR3 was to provide accountability to ourselves, our administrations, and our users. The objective of this new document was to facilitate cataloger judgment. In addition, AACR2 Part I needed restructuring because categories of materials were not logically defined and new types of content or carrier were not dealt with quickly or satisfactorily. Resources were often covered by more than one chapter. It was not always clear to catalogers on how to apply multiple chapters or how to resolve the conflicts in the rules. Rules in the later chapters often duplicated rules in chapter one. The cataloging community also wanted to integrate authority control and authority records.

With these objectives in mind, the JSC began its work to format a new standard. Pat Riva, McGill University, worked to include FRBR terminology. A Format Variation Working Group (FVWG) was created to address issues surrounding expression headings and general material designations (GMDs). The American Library Association's Committee on Cataloging: Description and Access (CC:DA) began work to establish consistency across AACR2 Part I. The Library of Congress was tasked with incorporating authority control.

The actual process of completing a new document occurred quickly. The JSC hired Tom Delsey as a consultant in early 2004 and then as the editor of AACR3 in August 2004. Delsey developed a draft of Part I (Description) by September 2004. The JSC discussed this draft in October 2004. In November 2004, a revised draft was completed by Delsey. The JSC distributed the draft to its constituencies on December 17, 2004. Responses to the new draft were expected quickly. The development of the draft for Part I was not widely known, nor was the distribution of the draft very wide. The JSC/COP purposely limited distribution because of some concern that readers would try to implement versions of the draft before it was finalized and they were also concerned about intellectual property rights. Delsey began work on a draft of Part II (Choice of Access Points) during the winter and spring of 2005. Part III

(Authority Control) was scheduled and publication was planned for 2007.

The contents of this draft AACR3 were very similar in structure to AACR2. The draft consisted of introductions that covered general principles followed by Parts I-III (Part I: Description, Part II: Choice of Access Points, Part III: Authority Control, including form of access points), and ending with the appendices. The development of each section was done separately with principles, not practice, driving the instruction. Development of AACR3 was infused with FRBR. In addition, some changes in terminology occurred in an attempt to modernize and remove jargon from the language. AACR3 was intended to shift the emphasis from creating catalog records to creating catalogs. AACR3 also set out to explicitly relate the principles and objectives to the instructions and to reduce compartmentalization. The document would include tables to help with clarification and the use of abbreviations would be examined, as conserving disk space was less important. The abbreviations are sometimes not understood by end users and even, in some cases, catalogers. A group to look into including real illustrations (similar to those found in CONSER documentation) would be formed as well as an outreach group that would work with other culture heritage and metadata groups. Finally, the document would continue to be available both in print and digitally.

Weiss explained the specifics and development of the draft version of AACR3. The JSC created a background document that discussed their objectives and principles for rules and for the descriptions created by the rules. Like AACR2, AACR3 was intended to be used to assist the cataloger with the focus of the description, sources of information, level of description, and then with recording the data. However, in AACR3 the cataloger would apply the general rules and only use special rules when directed to do so. The establishment of the rules in this manner would reduce the need for redundant rules, promote consistency across records for all types of resources, and facilitate efficiency in cataloger training and production.

At this point, work began on AACR3 Part II, and a plan for AACR3 Part III was developed. For Part II, Delsey completed a paper on the function of the catalog and the organization of this part was proposed. A proposal was made that the "rule of 3" become optional and more emphasis be placed on the role of persons and corporate bodies. This proposal would encourage the use of role designations and necessitate an enlarged set of terms, which could possibly be used in authority records. The plans for Part III called for the continuation of the work of the

FVWG on headings for works and expressions and the authority control work done by the Library of Congress. The FVWG had defined the functions of such headings as identification, collocation, and differentiation. They determined that expression citations should be based on work citations. Catalogers would be encouraged to add as much to a citation as was required. The Library of Congress worked on principles of authority control, defined data elements for authority records, which are tied to FRBR user tasks, and determined maintenance of authority records. AACR2 Chapter 26: References would be integrated into chapters on particular entities and would no longer be a separate chapter.

After the completion of the AACR3 Part I draft, ALA's representative to JSC, Jennifer Bowen, was able to distribute it to the entire membership of the CC:DA. CC:DA members were allowed to show the draft to other people at their institution, but they were not allowed to give out copies. The draft received considerable discussion at ALA Midwinter. The constituents who had received a copy of the draft submitted a lot of feedback.

Weiss detailed a few of the issues raised by the feedback. The objectives and principles laid out by the JSC were appropriate and useful, but the draft did not achieve them. A desire to take full advantage of the online environment was expressed as well as a concern that the draft itself was too text and print centric. Some were disappointed that the single-record approach was not included in the draft. Many agreed that the GMD split was good, but it should be made repeatable and moved out of area 1. In addition, opinions on transcription varied widely. For example, serial catalogers are usually less concerned than rare book catalogers who want transcription to be very exact. In the end, the feedback called for a standard that is compatible with our past, deals with the present, and prepares for the future–a standard for the 21st century. The current direction of the draft was not viewed as one that was worth pursuing. The JSC met April 24-28, 2005 in Chicago to consider the feedback and to plan for the future.

The outcome of the JSC meeting resulted in some significant changes. The JSC processed the feedback and found some general consensus with the comments. Although the feedback suggested that the JSC's objectives, principles, and goals were not met, they were validated as an appropriate concept, including the desire to have the rules used as a resource beyond the library community. The JSC acknowledged that the dissatisfaction with the arrangement of the rules and that the language needed to be clearer and more direct with library jargon eliminated. In addition, metadata standards used by other communities should be considered and in some cases serve as a model for some of the rules. Finally, the JSC affirmed that a new standard is still appropriate. However, with this new approach came a new working title, *Resource Description and Access* (RDA).

FROM AACR3 TO RDA

Along with the new working title came a change in direction, which Weiss explained. The content of the new standard will be built on AACR2. Records resulting from the use of the new standard will be AACR2-compatible. RDA will be a content standard, not a display standard so instructions for data and presentation aspects will be independent of each other. An emphasis will be placed on an online product, which will allow for some new functionality. In addition, the layout and formatting of instructions will be more cataloger-friendly with levels of description, access, and authority control linked to user tasks. Finally the structure will be aligned more directly with FRBR, functional requirements for authority records (FRAR), and functional requirements for subject authority records (FRSAR).

Another considerable change came with realizing a need for proactive consultation with the stakeholders throughout the development process. In order to facilitate consultations with the stakeholders and to provide context for constituency reviews, a prospectus that outlines the new approach and includes the table of contents for the General Introduction and the three parts, as well as sample text, will be written. Understandably, this major change in direction resulted in a revised timeline as detailed below:

May 2005-July 2005:	Development of prospectus
October 2005-April 2006:	Completion of draft of part I– Constituency review
May 2006-September 2006:	Completion of draft of part II– Constituency review
October 2006-April 2007:	Completion of draft of part III– Constituency review
May 2007-September 2007:	Completion of General Introduction, Appendices, and Glossary
2008:	Publication

Revisions to AACR2 may be considered since the publication date of the new edition has been postponed.

RESOURCE DESCRIPTION AND ACCESS

Weiss concluded the session with an overview of specific issues that were a result of the April 2005 JSC meeting, with the major caveat that any of the decisions or changes are subject to change. In order to make the standards more adaptable by those outside the library community, an implementation decision was made that metadata communities can use as much or as little of the new standard as needed. Likewise, the standard will have more terminology changes such as "access point" for "heading" and "citation" for "uniform title."

Weiss broke the issues down by different parts of the RDA. The introduction will be briefer than originally planned, but will include overall principles of the whole standard, functions of the catalog, and the conceptual framework including FRBR. More in-depth information on the theory and principles behind the rules may be developed as separate tools.

Part I will be organized to be more directly aligned with FRBR. All instructions for a particular data element will be centralized in one place. Each data element will also present the purpose, sources of information, information on how to record the data element, and suggestions on whether or not to include it as a controlled or uncontrolled access point. Concepts of digital media, such as in GMD terminology and URLs will be more integrated into the standard. Basically, the rules will be deconstructed and reassembled in a way that acknowledges differences between the sequence of ISBD areas and the sequence of capturing/recording data for the description.

Another issue addressed is the focus of the description and sources of information. The new standards will clarify the relationship between the selection of the focus of the description and the selection of the chief source of information and will refrain from over-generalizing instructions. The JSC will also pursue the Library of Congress's proposal to simplify and clarify instructions on what is being described and on the sources of information. Consideration will be given to the idea of eliminating the concept of "chief source" in favor of a prioritized list. A working group will be established to propose terms used in place of the current GMDs and specific material designations (SMDs). RDA will have more flexibility in recording and displaying information on the type and form of content and the type and form of carrier due to the separation of instructions for recording information from the guidelines for presentation. The question of resources issued in successive parts and integrating resources will be resolved by placing the instruction for them directly following the relevant general rule. In addition, the term "continuing resources" probably still will not be used.

The JSC also addressed some other issues relevant to Part I. The single-record or aggregator-neutral approach will not be pursued, although it may be mentioned in the introductory material. The JSC will also look at some of the Library of Congress's proposals such as the simplification of the instructions for ISBD area[4] and making the fuller form of publisher name an option. The Library of Congress will submit a proposal to include archival concepts at a basic level. Issues concerning levels of description will be deliberated. Such issues include adding description for the Library of Congress's access level and whether or not to mention non-RDA elements like subject. In terms of the specific rule revisions received from the feedback, the JSC will review them and if a consensus exists, the revisions will be given to the RDA editor to incorporate into the working draft of RDA. If a consensus does not exist, the JSC will discuss the suggestions at their October 2005 meeting.

Issues on the other parts of RDA will be pursued. Part II: Relationships will include a focus on the use of access points to reflect relationships among FRBR group 1 entities and between group 1 and group 2 entities. Another issue will be the exploration of the simplification of rules for choosing the primary access point when needed only on a record for another resource. The JSC will consider the simplification or elimination of detailed special rules for musical works, certain legal works, certain religious works, etc. Another possible change may be that not all access points will need justification in the description. In addition, the JSC will consider whether compilers and/or other roles should be part of the primary access point. Little change is planned for the instructions of Part III: Authority Control. It will present the principles and content standards for authority records with a focus on the formulation of access points to reflect both authorized and variant forms of names. In addition, other data elements will be used in authority control. Like Part II, the JSC will consider the simplification or elimination of detailed special rules. The appendices will be largely unchanged, but will pursue the Chartered Institute of Library and Information Professionals' (CILIP) ideas on the principles behind usage of abbreviations. The appendices on abbreviations, capitalization, and numbering will be revised to align them with the rest of RDA. Other issues that the JSC will study include the concept of self-describing (e.g., Books) and non-self-describing (e.g., Photographs) resources and the decision on whether other standards should be incorporated, given a brief mention, or removed.

The session concluded with the reminder that all the current proposals of RDA are subject to change. Weiss also acknowledged Kevin Randall who not only proposed the session, but also took detailed notes as an observer at the JSC April 2005 meeting. In addition, Weiss credited the following people for helping him to pull together this presentation through their conversations and presentations: Barbara Tillett, Library of Congress; Matthew Beacom, Yale University; John Attig, Pennsylvania State University; Jennifer Bowen, University of Rochester; Deidre Kiorgaard and Ann Huthwaite, Australian Committee on Cataloguing. Weiss also pointed to the JSC Web site (http://www. collectionscanada.ca/jsc/index.html) as an invaluable resource to keep abreast of the formation of a new standard.

NOTES

1. For more information on this conference see: http://www.collectionscanada.ca/jsc/intlconf.html

2. *IFLA Cataloguing Section.* "IME-ICC." http://www.ifla.org/VII/s13/index.htm#IME-ICC (accessed June 14, 2005).

3. *Joint Steering Committee for Revision of AACR.* "Strategic Plan for AACR." http://www.collectionscanada.ca/jsc/stratplan.html (accessed June 14, 2005).

4. The decision was made not to call this part of section A "Continuing Resources" for a number of reasons. First, renaming AACR2 Chapter 12 to "Continuing Resources" was not the original plan. Although these instructions primarily cover continuing resources, they also covered some finite resources such as finite integrating resources, reprints of serials, and serial-like multipart monographs. Finally, some constituencies did not like what they saw as a convoluted scope for Chapter 12.

CONTRIBUTORS' NOTES

Paul J. Weiss is Head, Monographs Cataloging Division, at the University of California, San Diego. Molly R. T. Larkin is Electronic Resources Cataloger, at Temple University.

Tracking Usage of E-Government Publications

Susan L. Kendall
Celia Bakke

Presenters

Lisa McDaniels

Recorder

SUMMARY. This workshop demonstrated how a multi-departmental team at a state university library devised a method of tracking their patrons' use of electronic federal government depository materials. Due to the increasing percentage of documents migrating to electronic-only format and the unusual joint use arrangement between the university and the local community, library staff saw the need to develop a new way of identifying which electronic government documents have been accessed via the library's online catalog. The presenters described how the usage statistics have enabled them to learn more about their patrons and their information needs and, therefore, how to make more informed decisions about collection management and programming. *[Article copies available for a fee from The Haworth Document Delivery Service: 1-800-HAWORTH. E-mail address: <docdelivery@haworthpress.com> Website: <http://www. HaworthPress.com>]*

[Haworth co-indexing entry note]: "Tracking Usage of E-Government Publications." McDaniels, Lisa. Co-published simultaneously in *The Serials Librarian* (The Haworth Information Press, an imprint of The Haworth Press, Inc.) Vol. 50, No. 3/4, 2006, pp. 295-303; and: *Roaring into Our 20's: NASIG 2005* (ed: Margaret Mering, and Elna Saxton) The Haworth Information Press, an imprint of The Haworth Press, Inc., 2006, pp. 295-303. Single or multiple copies of this article are available for a fee from The Haworth Document Delivery Service [1-800-HAWORTH, 9:00 a.m. - 5:00 p.m. (EST). E-mail address: getinfo@haworthpress.com].

Available online at http://www.haworthpress.com/web/SER
doi:10.1300/J123v50n03_14

INTRODUCTION

Tracking usage of library materials has traditionally been accomplished by one of three ways: analysis of circulation records, in-house shelving counts and surveys of patrons. At San Jose State University (SJSU), the first two methods worked just fine in the days of tracking items you could hold in your hand–print and various microforms and even CD-ROMs. With the advent of online electronic resources, however, the old rules no longer apply. Patrons accessing online library resources no longer pull items off a shelf to use them nor do they bring their "materials" to the circulation desk. Indeed, today's "shelf" often amounts to a MARC tag for a URL and the "checkout transaction" occurs via an exchange of bytes at a cyber circulation desk somewhere between the user and the library's server.

Two sets of circumstances converged to spur the SJSU library staff to find a new way to collect electronic government document usage information from their patrons. First, beginning in August 2003, the University and the City of San Jose launched an unusual collaborative arrangement, making all library resources and services available to both university and community users. When a patron checks out a book at the library's circulation desk, determining whether they are a community or a university patron is easy enough. Borrowing privileges still differ for some items. However, anyone with Internet access can access the SJLibrary.org catalog which links to free government documents, either from a computer inside the library or from anywhere in the world. In order to better serve their patrons, library staff wanted to learn more about which links were selected and how often, as well as whether the users were university or community patrons.

The increasing percentage of federal government documents available only in the online format was the second reason for developing a new tracking method. The United States Government Printing Office (GPO) has been alerting depository libraries recently of their plans to migrate a significant portion of their publications from print to electronic format–well over 50 percent, with some estimates running closer to 90 percent. SJSU has been a participant in the Federal Depository Library program since 1962 and continues as a partial recipient (over 50 percent). In addition, they have full bibliographic records for all print documents back to 1986.

However, as more documents are available only online, SJSU's traditional tracking methods would include a decreasing percentage of the documents collection. The resulting usage data would therefore become less reliable in making selection and other planning decisions. In order for usage statistics to continue to provide meaningful information about the needs of patrons, library staff recognized that they needed a new way to identify both the documents being used and who was using them.

METHOD

In 2003, shortly after the initial announcement from GPO, Kendall attended the GPO annual conference. She learned of the possibility of tracking hits on the GPO home page. However, this method would not provide information about individual documents that patrons accessed. She also heard University of Denver's Chris Brown's talk about a program he had written using ColdFusion and Microsoft Access to track usage of online documents. She was encouraged by the results but felt this method required more human intervention than would be feasible at her institution. Returning to SJSU, Kendall decided to contact Celia Bakke, Head of Technical Services, to see what could be done at her institution.

By the spring of 2004, a team was assembled. The primary members being Shirley Hwang, a database analyst in Technical Services and Lyna Nguyen, a programmer in the Information Technology department of the SJSU library. In consultation with Kendall and Bakke, they planned the steps and wrote the code that would ultimately provide the reference staff the information they needed.

TECHNICALITIES

Using a combination of ColdFusion, HTML and CSS programming languages as well as a Microsoft SQL database, the team members developed a tool that would store the identifying information about an online federal document into a text file each time a patron clicked on the hotlink in the catalog record. Basically, what they did was devise a program to (1) identify the bibliographic records for federal documents that contain an 856 field, (2) add the bibliographic record number (system number) to the end of a programmer-developed prefix, and (3) insert the prefix (tracking information) at the beginning of each MARC tag 856.

The next step was to move the appropriate records into a review file. It was accomplished by searching for records with "GPO" in the 856 field. This search identified 37,000 bibliographic records with 50,000

MARC 856 fields. Some records had more than one URL per record. Following several weeks of preliminary testing, approximately two additional weeks were required to run the initial database change. The process was further delayed by records containing non-standard URLs that required special handling. Exhibits A and B illustrate the structure and concepts embedded in the programs for both the client and the administrative aspects.

EXHIBIT A. Government Publications Architecture

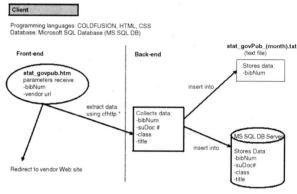

EXHIBIT B. Government Publications Architecture

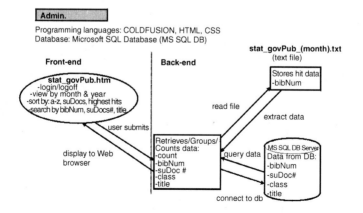

The final piece of code took care of searching and batch changing incoming records (from the MARCIVE program) on a monthly basis. New records with URLs are identified by an automatic search and e-mailed to the database analyst where problems can be sorted out prior to making the batch change. This on-going monthly maintenance takes approximately thirty to sixty minutes of the database analyst's time and about two to four hours of machine time. A flowchart of how the batch process program works is presented in Exhibit C.

REVEALING RESULTS

In return for this minor investment in staff time, library staff can now call up usage reports on demand on the library's Intranet site. The timeframe is customizable, single or multiple months can be selected. Results can be sorted by title, highest number of hits or by Superintendent of Documents (SuDocs) classification number.

The actual results over the nine month reporting period have confirmed some initial assumptions, namely that the quantity of total

EXHIBIT C. Government URL Batch Process (simplified)

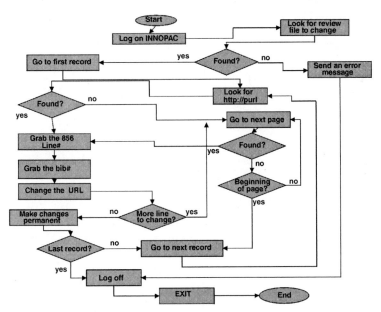

monthly hits follow the academic semester cycle very closely. August 2004, the first month of data, showed slightly fewer than 200 total uses. This total turned out to be the lowest total for the entire history to date. The numbers started climbing in September (just under 400), coinciding with an upswing in one-shot reference instruction sessions, followed by sharp increases in October (more than 800) and November (well over 900) when students tend to be more focused on conducting research for their courses. December and January dropped off dramatically, but the following three months, February through April, followed the same pattern as the previous semester with increasing high levels of use.

Bakke pointed out some of the unexpected outcomes, from a technical services perspective, from running the program through the bibliographic database and then later, reviewing the results. One important discovery was that approximately 1,000 records that should have been picked up by the searching function of the program were not included in the initial batch run. These records either did not have a PURL or had some other error in the URL. Not only did these errors prevent the records from being pulled into the review file for batch changing, they were preventing patrons from accessing the documents themselves. These records may require manual clean-up, and as a result of the usage project these problem records have been identified.

Another clean-up project was generated when Bakke sorted the usage statistics by SuDocs classification number. What she found were a number of bibliographic records that lacked SuDocs numbers altogether. The print versions of these documents had not been shelved in the documents department; instead they had been assigned a Library of Congress call number and shelved in the main stacks. As long as those documents remained in their present physical location, no one would likely have noticed that they lacked a SuDocs number, until these usage statistics brought the issue to light.

DEMOGRAPHIC CLUES

Without identifying information in hand it is impossible to say with absolute certainty who the users of e-government resources are but the data does yield some clues. The close matching of the usage numbers with the academic calendar as described above points to a strong likelihood that a large percentage of users come from the academic community, whether students, faculty or staff. A good portion of hits during the months when student research activity is known to dip (i.e., at the beginning and the end of the semesters, as well as during semester breaks) could be attributed to general community patrons.

These users could be students or faculty who also reside in the local community. Sometimes, they are seeking library resources in their role as university student or faculty and other times they may be seeking information to help them in their everyday lives. The presenters addressed the importance of determining user type during the workshop discussion period. They explained that, while the city and the university have merged in many ways, they still receive funding from separate sources. The primary mission of the university library remains to serve the SJSU patrons. Collections and services are funded and targeted primarily for university constituents and only secondarily for local community patrons.

ENHANCING THE COLLECTION

A closer look at the data reveals several ideas for collection management. For instance, the presenters felt obtaining an archival print copy for items that are accessed in higher numbers and for certain documents stored in large electronic files would be beneficial. Likewise, items of low use can be identified and selections adjusted accordingly.

This issue was described in more detail in the workshop discussion in regard to feedback from students about long download times. The students actually preferred coming into the library to view the print version of a 1000-page bill or lengthy congressional hearings. Students still appreciate the paper collection. On the other hand, for hot or controversial topics, the presenters stressed that the electronic copy is sometimes the only intact copy available. The usage data will, therefore, provide staff with the information necessary to respond to user preferences in building and maintaining the documents collection.

REACHING OUT TO REMOTE USERS

Outreach programming ideas also emerge from looking at particular topics with high usage. Topical reports sent out to subject liaisons, like one for health sciences which indicated a strong interest in osteoporosis, stem cell research and steroid use, point to possible topics for targeted workshops and closer coordination with curricular activities. Another example of a programming idea came from seeing the continual hits on the 1997 *Economic Census*, well after the 2002 *Economic Census* documents became available. A workshop or some other outreach mechanism might be useful to let patrons know which of the 2002 *Economic Census* materials have been released and how they can be accessed.

DISCUSSION AND NEXT STEPS

The presenters were encouraged by the number of online documents accessed so far and conclude that the data already demonstrates the viability of the online catalog as a useful resource for electronic documents, even in the age of Google. The preliminary data illustrates emerging patterns in usage as well as demographic trends, but they plan to look at a two-year cycle of data before attempting to draw any firm conclusions. The upcoming summer session will provide baseline information for yet another part of the academic cycle. They anticipate fewer students on campus (budget cuts have resulted in fewer summer classes than originally planned) but how much that will affect online document usage remains to be seen.

When asked about why they were only collecting usage statistics for federal documents and not for international, state, local and other types of documents, the presenters explained that they would like to expand the project to include other types of documents. However, the MARCIVE program is the only one that provides good maintenance of URLs. California state and other government entities currently have no such program to update their bibliographic records.

The presenters also discussed with the attendees their desire to attain more detailed user information as a tool for more effective resource management and program planning. They initially dismissed the idea of creating a pop-up dialog box which would ask users to self-identify as either university or community users. Privacy concerns as well as anticipated patron annoyance with (or blockage of) the pop-up feature weighed heavily in their decision not to query the users. However, as more studies indicate that users, especially users in the traditional undergraduate age range, are less concerned about privacy, the presenters indicated a willingness to reconsider a tactic they had previously assumed would be roundly rejected.

In addition to learning more about their patrons and their information needs, Kendall and Bakke noted another valuable outcome of the usage tracking project: it tells the success story of how library staff from three different departments came together to work towards the shared goal of improving services in the area of electronic government publications. The presenters expressed hope that by sharing both the process and the results of their project others will be inspired to use this partnership model at their institutions.

CONTRIBUTORS' NOTES

Sue Kendall is Reference Librarian and Government Publications Coordinator and Celia Bakke is Head of Technical Services at San Jose State University. Lisa McDaniels is Serials Cataloging Librarian at the University of Iowa.

Do You See RSS in Your Future?

Paoshan Yue
Araby Greene

Presenters

Lisa S. Blackwell

Recorder

SUMMARY. Paoshan Yue and Araby Greene from the University of Nevada, Reno Libraries presented a broad overview of RSS, an XML technology in widespread use by bloggers and commercial industries to facilitate easy sharing of Web content. Librarians at the University of Nevada, Reno have begun to explore applications of this technology in the library setting. Several Reno Libraries pilot projects utilizing RSS technology were discussed. Finally, future applications of RSS in the serials world were postulated. *[Article copies available for a fee from The Haworth Document Delivery Service: 1-800-HAWORTH. E-mail address: <docdelivery@haworthpress.com> Website: <http://www.HaworthPress.com>]*

WHAT'S THIS THING CALLED RSS?

RSS is an acronym variously translated as "Really Simple Syndication" (RSS version 2.0) or "RDF (Resource Description Framework) Site Summary" (RSS version 1.0). Both versions are applications of

[Haworth co-indexing entry note]: "Do You See RSS in Your Future?" Blackwell, Lisa S. Co-published simultaneously in *The Serials Librarian* (The Haworth Information Press, an imprint of The Haworth Press, Inc.) Vol. 50, No. 3/4, 2006, pp. 305-310; and: *Roaring into Our 20's: NASIG 2005* (ed: Margaret Mering, and Elna Saxton) The Haworth Information Press, an imprint of The Haworth Press, Inc., 2006, pp. 305-310. Single or multiple copies of this article are available for a fee from The Haworth Document Delivery Service [1-800-HAWORTH, 9:00 a.m. - 5:00 p.m. (EST). E-mail address: getinfo@haworthpress.com].

Available online at http://www.haworthpress.com/web/SER
doi:10.1300/J123v50n03_15

standard XML coding to facilitate sharing of frequently updated Web content. A Web content developer will choose to build with a specific RSS version based on what type of data utilization is intended. For example, RSS version 1.0 is often chosen to deliver content that is rich in metadata. RSS 2.0 contains additional features that may be of greater importance to the developer than the ability to encode metadata.

XML-based publishing formats that are essentially RSS "clones" are also beginning to appear. A new clone called "Atom" is rapidly gaining popularity. Google, for example, utilizes Atom to create syndicated feeds for its Blogger.com service, a popular tool to allow users to easily create their own Web sites with RSS feeds. These sites are referred to as "Weblogs" or "blogs."

Typical uses of RSS include:

- Monitoring news
- Current awareness for professionals
- Tracking Weblogs
- Sharing technical information, link lists, and photos

In order to view RSS feeds without seeing raw XML markup, the user must acquire a "feedreader." A feedreader is an aggregator that gathers chosen RSS feeds and formats them for display. The user is ready to select "feeds" (RSS files) available on specific Web sites of interest once a feedreader is installed. A wide variety of feedreaders is available on the Internet:

- Web-based aggregators (free)–*Bloglines, NewsGator Online Edition, My Yahoo!, Pluck Web Edition*
- Readers that plug into other applications–*Pluck* (Internet Explorer), *NewsMonster* (Mozilla), *NewsGator* (MS Outlook)
- Standalone readers installed on the user's computer–*FeedDemon, AmphetaDesk, Awasu, RSSReader*

The ability to read RSS feeds is not dependent on the specific reader that is chosen, but readers differ on various extra features included. CNet reviews (*http://www.cnet.com/4520-6022-5115113.html?tag=rss*) and RSS Compendium (*http://allrss.com*) are two good Internet resources to assist the novice RSS user with understanding RSS technology, feedreader options, tools and other useful tips.

EXPLORING RSS

How does the new user begin to add feeds to his feedreader? Finding a feed is the first task. Fortunately, Web sites with RSS feeds can be found in a number of different ways. One of many such indexing Web sites, Syndic8.com (*http://www.syndic8.com/*), lists thousands of categorized feeds. Many of the feedreaders themselves contain searchable feed directories. Another option is to use a specialized search engine. Feedster is an example of such a search engine (*http://www. feedster.com/*). It indexes millions of feeds and they are also fully searchable. Finally, many Web sites already indicate that they have RSS feeds available.

Any site with feeds will usually have an instantly recognizable orange button labeled "XML" or "RSS." Clicking on the button allows the user with a browser-integrated reader to preview the feed and subscribe or, alternatively, copy the link and paste it into the "add feed" section of a desktop reader. After subscribing, the user is notified by the feedreader when new content is added to the Web site. The user chooses a convenient time to read the content, subscribe or unsubscribe, and is even able to read feeds from mobile devices that receive text. Goodbye overstuffed e-mail boxes!

LIBRARY APPLICATIONS

The library world is taking notice of RSS technology. According to a 2004 article, forty-nine libraries worldwide were producing fifty-five Weblogs by October of 2003.[1] A later report in April 2005 listed 245 libraries producing hundreds of Weblogs.[2] A quick check of blogwithoutalibrary.net just one month later reported 430 libraries producing "who knows how many" Weblogs.[3] Clearly, this is a trend to monitor! Blogwithoutalibrary.net (*http://blogwithoutalibrary.net/*), created and maintained by a librarian, is a useful resource to track what libraries are doing with blogs and RSS technologies.

Examples of how libraries are using RSS for information dissemination include the following:

- library news:
  University of Nevada, Reno Libraries *http://www2.library.unr. edu/infoedge/*

- subject blogs or guides:
  Georgia State University Library *http://www.library.gsu.edu/news/*
- new acquisitions:
  University of Alberta Libraries *http://www.library.ualberta.ca/ rss/index.cfm*
- book reviews:
  Colorado College Library *http://library.coloradocollege.edu/ bookends/*
- catalog search queries and personalized circulation information:
  Hennepin County Library *http://www.hclib.org/pub/search/RSS.cfm/*
- staff communication:
  Oregon Libraries Network *http://www.oregonlibraries.net/staff/*

The publishing world has also noted the potential for RSS technologies to enhance visibility, usage and convenience for users. Many e-publications now include the capability to subscribe to their content via RSS feed. BioMed Central (*http://www.biomedcentral.com*), a pioneering open-access publisher, has placed several feed links in focused sections of the site allowing the user to monitor areas of particular interest. Commercial publishers such as Oxford (*http://www3. oup.co.uk/jnls/online/*) offer feeds for many of their publications.

Commercial media outlets have been some of the earliest adopters of RSS technology. CNN news (*http://www.cnn.com/*) is only one of hundreds of news sources that includes RSS feed for news headlines. Others include the *Wall Street Journal* (*http://online.wsj.com/public/page/ 0,,2_0323,00.html?mod=TFFP1OSM01*), the *New York Times* (*http:// www.nytimes.com/*), and *USA Today* (*http://www.usatoday.com/*). Even the government has adopted the technology. PubMED (*http:// www.ncbi.nlm.nih.gov/entrez/query.fcgi*) has recently added a new RSS feature that allows the user to send search results to their desktop feedreader.

IMPLEMENTING A PROJECT AT RENO LIBRARIES

The University of Nevada, Reno Libraries has created a number of pages with RSS feeds. One such page is an index of their journals that offer RSS feed for their users: *http://www.library.unr.edu/ejournals/ alphaRSS.aspx*

Another page, "New Electronic Journals," alerts subscribers to new e-journals added to the collection: *http://www.library.unr.edu/ ejournals/new.aspx*

The process of creating the new electronic journals page is fairly uncomplicated. ASP.NET is utilized and dynamically creates the contents of the page and RSS 2.0 feed from information stored in an SQL server database. Each file contains an .aspx extension to allow the Windows-based Web server to process the embedded ASP.Net script. The script itself is written in Visual Basic.Net language. It connects to the SQL server and requests data from a stored query. Thus, the ASP.Net script creates an e-journals RSS feed from the SQL server and outputs the feed to a memory stream (ejrss.aspx).

The library employs an essential tool to alert site visitors to the existence of RSS feed on a page, the RSS auto-discovery tag. The link included at the head of any document with RSS feed would look like: <link rel="alternate" type="application/rss+xml"title="University of Nevada, Reno Libraries–New Electronic Journals" href=http://www. library.unr.edu/ejournals/ejrss.aspx/>

Almost any Web site can easily be RSS-ified. Serials librarians deal with constantly changing subscriptions, publication contents, changes at the publisher level, database changes, and so on. The opportunities to utilize RSS technology in the serials environment are endless.

CONCLUSION

RSS is an innovative, exciting new technology with a wide array of potential applications. Publishers, news media outlets, bloggers and libraries are only a few of the users eagerly responding to opportunities to use RSS. It is becoming increasingly popular with an Internet audience that demands personal, immediate, and customized information delivery. Perhaps most convincingly, it is an easy technology both to implement as a Web developer and to adopt as a user.

NOTES

1. Clyde, Laurall A. "Library Weblogs." Library Management 25, no. 4/5 (2004): 183-189.
2. 4-12-05 post at *http://blogwithoutalibrary.net* (June 9, 2005)
3. 5-15-05 manual count at *http://blogwithoutalibrary.net*

RECOMMENDED READINGS

ARTICLES

Cohen, Steven M. *RSS for Non-Techie Librarians.* June 3, 2002.
  http://www.llrx.com/features/rssforlibrarians.htm. (June 5, 2005).
MacLeod, Roddy. "RSS: Less Hype, More Action." *FreePint* (June 17, 2004).
  http://www.freepint.com/issues/170604.htm#feature (June 9, 2005).
Wusteman, Judith. "RSS: the Latest Feed." *Library Hi Tech* v. 22 no. 2 (2004): 404-
  413. *http://juno.emeraldinsight.com/vl=7775505/cl=36/nw=1/rpsv/cw/mcb/07378831/*
  v22n4/s10/p404 (June 9, 2005).
Reichardt, Randy. "RSS: Moving into the Mainstream." *El Update: Engineering Information Online Newsletter* v. 3 no. 1 (Mar./Apr. 1, 2003)
  http://www.ei.org/eiupdate/03_librarians_corner/index.html (June 9, 2005).

BOOKS

Hammersley, B. *Developing Feeds with RSS and Atom.* Sebastopol: O'Reilly, 2005.
Fitzgerald, M. *XML Hacks.* Sebastopol: O'Reilly, 2004.
Ayers, D. and A.Watt. *Beginning RSS and Atom Programming.* Indianapolis: Wiley,
  2005.
Tennison, J. *Beginning XSLT.* Berkeley: Apress, 2004.
Morrison, M. *Sams Teach Yourself XML in 24 Hours.* 2nd ed. Indianapolis: Sams,
  2002.

CONTRIBUTORS' NOTES

Paoshan Yue is Electronic Resources Access Librarian and Araby Greene is Web
Development Librarian at the University of Nevada, Reno Libraries. Lisa Blackwell is
Serials/Electronic Resources Librarian at Grant Morrow III, M.D. Library, Columbus
Children's Hospital.

Analyzing How Much
Publisher Packages Are Worth?

Nancy Macomber

Presenter

Julie C. Harwell

Recorder

SUMMARY. The session provided a how-to for analyzing the value of publisher packages. Macomber's project took approximately three months to produce a public relations tool for her library, an aid for self-study within academic departments as well as the serials unit, and a mechanism to increase accuracy in fund reporting and allocation. The session included basic information on how to design such a project, a discussion of available resources, recommendations for data to gather, and suggestions for application. *[Article copies available for a fee from The Haworth Document Delivery Service: 1-800-HAWORTH. E-mail address: <docdelivery@haworthpress.com> Website: <http://www.HaworthPress.com>]*

The session's roots can be traced to a straightforward list that Macomber developed when e-journals were first added to the collection at Benjamin Rosenthal Library of Queens College where she is cur-

[Haworth co-indexing entry note]: "Analyzing How Much Publisher Packages Are Worth?" Harwell, Julie C. Co-published simultaneously in *The Serials Librarian* (The Haworth Information Press, an imprint of The Haworth Press, Inc.) Vol. 50, No. 3/4, 2006, pp. 311-314; and: *Roaring into Our 20's: NASIG 2005* (ed: Margaret Mering, and Elna Saxton) The Haworth Information Press, an imprint of The Haworth Press, Inc., 2006, pp. 311-314. Single or multiple copies of this article are available for a fee from The Haworth Document Delivery Service [1-800-HAWORTH, 9:00 a.m. - 5:00 p.m. (EST). E-mail address: getinfo@haworthpress.com].

Available online at http://www.haworthpress.com/web/SER
doi:10.1300/J123v50n03_16

rently the acquisitions librarian and government documents coordinator. Initially, the simple list was a basic management tool. As its
complexity mushroomed, it began to demand increasing resources and
time. Like many serials colleagues, Macomber was initially frustrated
by the demands of e-resources and lack of standards. Inspiration came
to her in the form of "The Glad Game" from Eleanor H. Porter's *Polly-
anna.* She resolved to maximize the use of the project and explore every
possible benefit. Her efforts yielded a public relations tool, an aid for
self-study within academic departments as well as the serials unit, and a
mechanism to increase accuracy in fund reporting and allocation.

Macomber opened the session with an overview of Queens College.
Part of the City University of New York and established in 1937,
Queens College has approximately 12,000 FTE students. It is a member
of several consortia, including Nylink (http://nylink.suny.edu/) and
Westchester Academic Library Directors Organization (WALDO)
(http://www.waldolib.org/). In 1994, the Rosenthal Library cancelled
approximately one third of its journal subscriptions, and prior to that
cancellation project were two other "big cuts." The result was that the
journal collection was compromised. Patrons had low confidence in the
collection. In fact, faculty referred students to other colleges. The library's reputation has since had a complete turnaround. It has a high
profile as well as the respect of faculty, and is viewed as a partner during
accreditation reviews. Currently, the library utilizes the ALEPH integrated library system and has access to about 2,700 online journals
through individual subscriptions and packages such as Science Direct
and JSTOR and access to over 20,000 titles when aggregated databases
such Academic Search Premier and LexisNexis are included.

Macomber posed two questions which guided the evolution of the
list. The first was "How many e-journals do we have in a given subject
area, and how much are they worth?" The second was "How much is the
library spending for periodicals, including e-journals, for any given
subject/department?" With these questions, Macomber examined what
to include in her list: all vendors and databases, scholarly or peer-reviewed titles only, only titles where a current issue is accessible (not
those with an embargo, but titles with a current (not previous) subscription), and open access titles.

The next step was to identify sources to construct the new list and
which fields to include. Microsoft® Access was selected to store and
manage the data. To populate the database, Macomber utilized her original list, subject browse results from the library's Serials Solutions list,
ulrichsweb.com™, vendor price and subject lists, their OPAC and

OCLC WorldCat™. Suggested fields for the database include: title of journal, publisher, vendor, subject, Library of Congress classification code (LC class), usage, price and fund code. Macomber gathered vendor, LC class and fund code information from her original list. Subjects and pricing were pulled from ulrichsweb.com. Macomber encouraged caution when gathering pricing information. For example, one should not simply convert prices listed in euros from search results pages within ulrichsweb.com. Instead, you must go to the item page to obtain the United States price. Nor should you rely on pricing within your subscription agent's catalog. She strongly encourages using invoices and contracts whenever possible to factor in consortial and other price discounts. When these resources are not available, an average price can be calculated from a combination of sources.

Once the data is collected, the next step is to count the total number of titles, total the price column for dollar value of journals, and add up the total usage. Macomber experimented with several sorting options to address multiple questions: by title (Which titles are in multiple databases?); by use and then vendor (Which titles show the least and most usage?), by call number or subject (Which fund code can be assigned to each title?). With their integrated library system, only one fund or budget code can be assigned. Macomber's suggested formula was to combine the uses of titles in a subject, divide it by total uses for a database, and finally multiply the figure by the cost of the database. A sample calculation was for four anthropology titles with total usage of 420 counts (based on COUNTER, http://www.projectcounter.org/) within a database which had total usage of 2,200. The anthropology titles had 19.1% of the use of the database (420 divided by 2,200). The cost of the database was $25,000. Therefore, the Anthropology Department would be "charged" 19% of the total cost of the database, or $4,775. Macomber noted that, while this method is the most effective and accurate means to assess costs to a fund code, it does require retro-calculation and allocation which is not conducive to the budget process. Therefore, she does not actually charge back departments; rather, this data is used for assessment.

The project took approximately three months to complete and yielded several positive results. As a public relations tool, it assists with recruitment of faculty for the library and other academic departments and is a talking point for subject specialists to help build a rapport with faculty members and instill confidence in the library, its collection and management. The project has stimulated discussion regarding budget allocation for multidisciplinary titles and format choices.

Macomber acknowledged that every project has strengths and weaknesses. She closed the session by sharing some of the advantages and disadvantages with her approach. She felt the advantages were:

- Cost is charged to subjects in proportion to actual, not anticipated, use
- More of the library's expenditures are tied to specific rather than general funds
- The library does not have to stay within the same subject when exchanging titles due to duplication in consortial packages.

Some weaknesses were:

- Interdisciplinary titles do not fit into a single subject
- Due to widely varying prices and different average prices for different subjects, can we say that each use carries the same weight?
- There is resistance to allocation changes
- One cannot assess who the actual user is (Is it a history major using a chemistry journal, for example?)
- Should centrally purchased packages be included?

CONTRIBUTORS' NOTES

Nancy Macomber is Acquisitions Librarian and Government Documents Coordinator at Rosenthal Library, Queens College, City University of New York. Julie C. Harwell is Training Resources Manager at EBSCO Industries, Inc.

Presentations That Keep Your Audience Interested and Awake

Beth Bernhardt

Presenter

Karen S. Fischer

Recorder

SUMMARY. Presentation style has a great impact on the effectiveness of conveying a message to an audience. Bernhardt presented basic tips on presentation style, visual aids, and tactics to engage the audience. The session was conducted as a class, with audience participation. *[Article copies available for a fee from The Haworth Document Delivery Service: 1-800-HAWORTH. E-mail address: <docdelivery@haworthpress.com> Website: <http://www.HaworthPress.com>]*

Bernhardt began with an illustration of what *not* to do when you giving a presentation. She held her notes in front of her face and read in a monotone voice. Her role playing got laughs from the audience and served as the first tip in presentation style! The session was conducted as a class, with lots of audience participation. It started with video clips

[Haworth co-indexing entry note]: "Presentations That Keep Your Audience Interested and Awake." Fischer, Karen S. Co-published simultaneously in *The Serials Librarian* (The Haworth Information Press, an imprint of The Haworth Press, Inc.) Vol. 50, No. 3/4, 2006, pp. 315-318; and: *Roaring into Our 20's: NASIG 2005* (ed: Margaret Mering, and Elna Saxton) The Haworth Information Press, an imprint of The Haworth Press, Inc., 2006, pp. 315-318. Single or multiple copies of this article are available for a fee from The Haworth Document Delivery Service [1-800-HAWORTH, 9:00 a.m. - 5:00 p.m. (EST). E-mail address: getinfo@haworthpress.com].

Available online at http://www.haworthpress.com/web/SER
doi:10.1300/J123v50n03_17

of famous speakers and concluded with discussion of presentation style and tips and visual aids.

To get the audience thinking about different styles of presentation, four video clips were viewed. The audience was asked to think about the following questions:

- What techniques do the speakers use to get their message across?
- How does the audience get involved?
- How does the speaker hold the audience's attention?
- How does the speaker use verbal and non-verbal techniques?

The excerpted video clips were: "I Have A Dream" by Martin Luther King, "Some Chicken Speech" by Winston Churchill, "Keynote Address" by Barbara Jordon, "Inaugural Address" by John F. Kennedy.

Bernhardt asked, "What presentation techniques did you observe the speakers using?" The audience gave the following answers:

- KING: repetition, rhythmic quality, use of hands, tone and voice, emphasis and tone, know the audience, metaphors, goes with the momentum
- CHURCHILL: vocal–stress points, quiet during the cheering of the crowd, gestures with hands, humor, engaging, pacing
- JORDON: humor, historical perspective, personalized, stated the obvious, dignity, distinct speech, head movements, took logical steps in the content, posed questions
- KENNEDY: distinct speech, questions, sequence, challenging others, repetition, eye contact

PRESENTATION TIPS AND STYLE

The audience paired up and Bernhardt distributed an exercise. Each person read a 140 word paragraph and their partner timed them for one minute. After the exercise was completed, people shared observations. They mostly noted that they read too fast. Bernhardt said you should not say more than 140 words per minute. You should take pauses and breathe.

Maintaining eye contact is an important aspect of connecting with the audience. In response to the question "How should a speaker/presenter maintain good eye contact?" the audience responded: speak to both sides of the room, look away from your notes and to the audience, read notes while pausing, keep eyes moving, use an outline rather than prose for your notes.

Additionally, the use of hand movements can be distracting. The following tips were noted: hold on to podium if needed, don't play with anything (like a pen), don't be jerky, videotape yourself if you're brave enough, do meaningful movements, use hands for emphasis, and keep hands in plain view. The class brainstormed on other tips that are helpful. They suggested asking a question and waiting for the answer, avoiding fillers such as "um" (or any other repetitive word), using a roaming microphone so you can get out from behind the podium, using facial expressions, breathing deeply, and knowing your content! Bernhardt noted that body language is an integral part of any presentation and it has the most effect on the audience.

VISUAL AIDS

The knowledge conveyed to the listeners increases when there is audience participation and the presenter's style is dynamic and engaging. Any kind of participation or discussion greatly enhances the learning experience. A session becomes more of a teaching experience rather than simply reading one's ideas.

Bernhard next posed the question "Why do we use visual aids?" Some ideas shared by the audience were: pictures are worth a 1000 words, draws the attention of the audience away from you, provides an outline for the audience, addresses different learning styles, adds variety, reinforces ideas, and helps the presenter keep on track with the content. Be sure to avoid including too much text on a given slide and try not to read the words on the visual aid exactly, but vary the words.

Effective visual aids techniques include having a mixture of words and images, using charts and graphs, being consistent with colors. If you are presenting a complex image, build it gradually so the audience can follow along. Unless you have a handout for your listeners to take with them, ninety percent of what is said in a presentation will be forgotten within twenty-four hours. Bernhardt suggested giving handouts at the end of a presentation so that attention is paid to the presenter and not the handout. She offered a checklist for visual aids:

- Is it essential?
- Is it simple?
- Is it large enough?

- Is it labeled well?
- Is it interesting?

CONCLUSION

In conclusion, the audience compiled a list of tips and techniques of presentation style that will help them with future presentations:

- Use questions to involve the audience
- Have fun and humor
- Breathe!
- Practice out loud
- Be prepared and practice
- Always have a backup
- Slow down
- Don't use hands too much
- Look away from notes
- Keep the structure simple
- Clearly thought out ideas
- Summarize at the end
- Use of stories
- Look at evaluations
- Know your subject

Two handouts were available to be picked up at the end of class.

Abernathy, Donna J. "Presentation Tips from the Pros," *Training & Development*, October 1999: 19-25.

Wilder, Claudyne. "8 Basic Guidelines for Visuals," *Presenters University*. 2005. *http://www.presentersuniversity.com/visuals_visuals_8basic.php* (May 26, 2005).

CONTRIBUTORS' NOTES

Beth Bernhardt is Electronic Journals/Document Delivery Librarian at the University of North Carolina, Greensboro. Karen S. Fischer is Information Resources Librarian at Hardin Library for the Health Sciences at the University of Iowa.

The RFP Process
at the University of Memphis:
A Work in Progress

Elizabeth McDonald

Presenter

Jerry R. Brown

Recorder

SUMMARY. McDonald reported on the process the Memphis area library consortium is following in order to develop an RFP (Request for Proposal) to choose a new integrated library system. The consortium is required by state law to write an RFP for major purchases. The workshop focused on the basic organization needed to achieve their goals and concluded with a question and discussion period. *[Article copies available for a fee from The Haworth Document Delivery Service: 1-800-HAWORTH. E-mail address: <docdelivery@haworthpress.com> Website: <http://www.HaworthPress.com>]*

BACKGROUND

Since 1994, the University of Memphis has been a DRA customer. Most consortium member libraries are located within the Memphis area and serve a widely varied student community. The University of

[Haworth co-indexing entry note]: "The RFP Process at the University of Memphis: A Work in Progress." Brown, Jerry R. Co-published simultaneously in *The Serials Librarian* (The Haworth Information Press, an imprint of The Haworth Press, Inc.) Vol. 50, No. 3/4, 2006, pp. 319-323; and: *Roaring into Our 20's: NASIG 2005* (ed: Margaret Mering, and Elna Saxton) The Haworth Information Press, an imprint of The Haworth Press, Inc., 2006, pp. 319-323. Single or multiple copies of this article are available for a fee from The Haworth Document Delivery Service [1-800-HAWORTH, 9:00 a.m. - 5:00 p.m. (EST). E-mail address: getinfo@haworthpress.com].

Available online at http://www.haworthpress.com/web/SER
doi:10.1300/J123v50n03_18

Memphis is a metropolitan university with approximately 20,000 students, granting bachelor's, master's, doctoral, and law degrees. Its branch libraries are Audiology and Speech Language Pathology, Music, Mathematics, and Chemistry.

The partner libraries are LeMoyne-Owen College, an historically black liberal arts bachelor degree granting college in Memphis, with a student population of about 800, and Jackson State Community College in Jackson, Tennessee, granting associate's degrees, with an enrollment of about 2,700 students. The University of Memphis' Cecil C. Humphreys School of Law is managed separately from the rest of the University's library system. It serves about 425 law students and is counted as a partner library.

METHODOLOGY

The University of Memphis Dean of Libraries announced the RFP project at the fall 2004 library retreat, stressing the need for excellent and on-going communication among all the concerned libraries. The Dean sees the project as a high priority project that would affect the libraries for years to come. A task force was formed with representation from all the departments of the University library, except for Interlibrary Loan. The partner libraries decided that they did not have enough staff to assign someone to the project. To facilitate communication among all the consortia libraries, a dedicated Web site was designed to be accessible only by the University and partner libraries in order to maintain confidentiality of discussion, proposals, and decision-making. Meeting minutes were available within forty-eight hours, reports were posted for review and comment, and a timeline maintained to show the task force's progress. An advisory group of faculty and students was also created to solicit input from the wider university community.

The RFP task force was formed and began its work in September 2004. A timeline of one year was developed to guide the project. The process was divided into phases for clarity and control. Everyone recognized that the effort would be a lengthy and time consuming. However, the value of the process was recognized in that the new ILS is expected to be used for about ten years and must suit the needs of all the member libraries as closely as possible.

The task force was initially composed of general members and one co-chair from each sub-committee. It grew from nine to fourteen members as both sub-committee co-chairs participated. The sub-committees are: Acquisitions and Periodicals, Circulation and Reserve, Cataloging, Public Services, and Systems. Each sub-committee has two co-chairs, with at least one from that specific area. The membership of the task force and subcommittees covers a cross section of library faculty and staff, with the subcommittees composed of 42% faculty and 57% staff. The Dean wanted people who work hard, are discrete and accountable, and are willing to do the research the project requires.

Phase I was scheduled from September to December 2004. This time was devoted to setting up procedures, training the members of the task force, developing committee charges, organizing the subcommittees, and drafting planning documents. Early in the process, team-building workshops facilitated understanding of the writing process and how it would work. Charges were drafted by the subcommittee co-chairs, presented to the task force for further input, and then given to the University of Memphis' Dean of Libraries for final approval. This process helped the entire group appreciate how each task related to the whole, facilitating a more collegial approach to the process.

Phase II was scheduled for January through April 2005 and devoted to task force review and revision of the subcommittee reports. Careful editing for content, meaning, and document design resulted in some sections of the reports being returned to the originating sub-committee for revision and clarification.

Phase III is scheduled for May through August 2005. When the documents are complete to the satisfaction of the task force reviewers, they will be posted on the Web site for comment from all of the member libraries faculty and staff. Notification will go out via e-mail of the postings and include the deadline for comments and suggestions. After the deadline passes, the task force will make decisions concerning the suggested changes and those decisions will be explained to the entire consortial community.

By July 1, 2005, the final draft will be prepared by the task force and submitted to the Dean of Libraries. The Dean will seek funding, and the RFP document will be distributed. The RFP is expected to be ready for dissemination by fall 2005.

The processes the cataloging sub-committee went through in drafting their report were presented to illustrate the processes used by each of the sub-committees. Information about the requirements for a cataloging module were obtained by interviewing staff, consulting department heads and groups who catalog on the system, reading sample RFP's, posting a question to AUTOCAT discussion list, and surveying other Universities' catalog departments. The document was placed on the

University of Memphis' file sharing drive to provide open access. This committee is ready to weigh the list of potential specifications for the ILS to determine what are "must haves," "really wants," and "can live withouts."

WHAT WE LEARNED

Due to the large commitment of time by a substantial number of faculty and staff, this process is expensive. The Phase I time frame did not allow for the time lost to various holidays and other member commitments during the fall semester. Motivating the entirety of the consortia libraries' faculty and staff to carefully review the documents and respond with their comments and suggestions in a timely manner has been challenging. Clarifying issues at an early stage of the process (i.e., the difference between system driven parameters and policies; and when and how input from outside the task force and subcommittees is needed and wanted) would have enabled more useful input from all concerned. Site visits are a priority. A mechanism to increase faculty and student input is needed.

More than anything, the process has resulted in enhanced communication among the participating libraries, faculties, and staff. The opportunity for staff to discuss their frustrations with the current system helped clarify what they wanted from the new system. It also allowed assessment of the current processes and workflow within departments and led to discussions of how they could be improved in the future. Discussion over a period of time allows everyone to participate and bring their expertise to the table in order to suggest improvements. The process helps prepare everyone for the changes that are inherent in migrating to a new system and increases faculty and staff buy-in to the new system because they participated in determining the libraries' wants and needs from the beginning of the process.

CONCLUSION

The consortium's work is not finished. The exercise has been beneficial in building relationships among the consortia libraries and internally among faculty and staff. The partner libraries have clarified what their wants and needs are from a new ILS, and that will help them choose the system that best suits their libraries without having too many second thoughts about the decision.

DISCUSSION

The audience questioned the benefits of a consortial approach. Mc-Donald highlighted benefits and challenges that come with consortium membership. One advantage is that students are able to share the resources of the consortium members. Merging different institution's desires into the final product can be difficult. Customization becomes critical to successful implementation. Distance users need to have access to all the resources of the consortium via the ILS. Flexibility becomes important with the environment of rapid change–predicting the consortium's needs five to ten years out is difficult. Adding libraries to an existing consortia ILS can be difficult. The needs of students and faculty across each campus are likely unique and affect priorities in the ILS selection. Meeting those diverse needs in one system is challenging. Ways to develop the system so these needs can be meshed must be considered from the beginning.

CONTRIBUTORS' NOTES

Elizabeth McDonald is Catalog Librarian, Serials Specialist at the University of Memphis. Jerry R. Brown is Assistant Professor of Library Services and Public Services Librarian at Central Missouri State University.

POSTER SESSIONS

DEVELOPING A CUSTOMIZED DATABASE SYSTEM FOR MANAGING ELECTRONIC RESOURCES

Maggie Wineburgh-Freed
Janis F. Brown
Janet L. Nelson

Norris Medical Library, University of Southern California

As the number of electronic journals the medical library acquired exploded, we envisioned a database solution to manage licensed electronic resources. Paper management systems were no longer functional. Staff needed to access information simultaneously, to eliminate inputting similar data into multiple systems, and required an effective data tracking method.

When the University decided to revise the database used to create Web pages of electronic resources, the Library took the opportunity to add management functions. Through an iterative process, the Medical Library and the University Library worked with a programmer from the University's Web Services Group. Needs were determined. Fields and records were discussed. Search interfaces and results pages were developed. The system is maintained in a MySQL relational database with a Web-based administrative module created with PHP.

[Haworth co-indexing entry note]: "Poster Sessions." Mering, Margaret, and Elna Saxton. Co-published simultaneously in *The Serials Librarian* (The Haworth Information Press, an imprint of The Haworth Press, Inc.) Vol. 50, No. 3/4, 2006, pp. 325-330; and: *Roaring into Our 20's: NASIG 2005* (ed: Margaret Mering, and Elna Saxton) The Haworth Information Press, an imprint of The Haworth Press, Inc., 2006, pp. 325-330. Single or multiple copies of this article are available for a fee from The Haworth Document Delivery Service [1-800-HAWORTH, 9:00 a.m. - 5:00 p.m. (EST). E-mail address: getinfo@haworthpress.com].

Available online at http://www.haworthpress.com/web/SER
doi:10.1300/J123v50n03_19

Library staff can easily manage changes in vendors, gateways, and licenses that affect many journal titles by simply revising one global record. Although electronic journals were the driving force in the new database's creation, it includes both licensed and free electronic resources in all formats. Data revisions and additions are on-going. System modifications are made as necessary.

This new system is a vast improvement over the previous paper system. All management information is now conveniently available to multiple internal users, and informational notes can be included that are easily accessed. The database also provides much more flexibility and searching functionality for the public electronic resources Web site.

ELECTRONIC OR PAPER FORMAT? ISSUES INFLUENCING DECISIONS

Michelle Grace
Victoria Peters

Minnesota State University

This poster session was based on an April 2005 survey of serials librarians. They were asked what issues they consider when deciding to purchase electronic, paper, or combined serials formats. No single concern (archival access, patron preference, budgeting, etc.) makes the decision easy. The presenters identified a common set of issues that guide purchasing and policy matters.

DE-STRESSING FOR SERIALISTS

Wendy Baia

University of Colorado

This poster session was based partially on "Stress and the Library," a section of a chapter called "Succeeding as a Non-Tenure-Track Librarian," which Baia wrote for the book *The Successful Academic Librarian: Winning Strategies from Library Leaders*. The book was scheduled to be published summer 2005.

Although this section of the book discussed stress in general in academic libraries, Baia narrowed the focus for the poster session to cover current sources of stress for librarians who work with serials and included suggestions on how to decrease that stress. Baia provided a bibliography of pertinent articles and books on this topic.

USING INNOVATIVE INTERFACE'S MILLENNIUM SOFTWARE, EXCEL AND OLD FASHIONED TEAMWORK TO CHANGE SERIALS VENDORS

Kathy Kobyljanec

John Carroll University

The poster session's purpose was to trace the process of changing serials vendors, using the Innovative Interface's Millennium system and Excel software. When the decision was made to switch vendors at John Carroll University, many issues and problems were considered. The Periodicals Librarian and Acquisitions Assistant in charge of periodicals and standing orders, and vendors were involved in the process. At the same time, a periodicals cancellation project was in process. Approximately 300 titles were canceled and 1,300 subscriptions were renewed with the new vendor.

The poster session presented the steps taken in changing vendors and the cancellation program, which included identifying titles to be canceled by academic departments, developing lists for each liaison librarian, removing the canceled titles from the title list, reviewing the renewal list from the "old" vendor, creating lists in Millennium to generate a list for the "new" vendor, reviewing subscription start and end dates, sorting bibliographic records by record number and ISSN, and identifying problem titles and membership complications.

Other steps in the process were loading dummy invoices to change vendor ID and title number fields in both the Innovative Interface's acquisitions and serials modules, deciding when to change the information in the check-in records as issues were received from the old vendor and how to handle claims during overlap. Finally, the issue of "free online with print" complicated the turnover since the old vendor had provided an electronic journal service, which was lost in the transition.

SUNCAT:
BUILDING A SERIALS UNION CATALOG FOR THE UK

Liz Stevenson

The University of Edinburgh

SUNCAT (*http://edina.ac.uk/suncat*) is an exciting new initiative in the UK. Its purpose is to build a national union catalog of serials holdings of research libraries in higher education public and national libraries. Research and consultation with the academic and library communities highlighted a requirement to improve access to serials holdings information and the quality of serials records. Government funding was provided for a two year project to set up a pilot service. The contract was awarded to the University of Edinburgh, led by EDINA, one of the two national data centers in the United Kingdom. The project partner is Ex Libris, who provides the Aleph 500 software for the catalog database. As well as ensuring that users can better locate serials titles, a key aim of the project is to provide contributing libraries with high quality bibliographic records to download to their local catalog databases.

In February 2005, the pilot service was successfully launched and includes the holdings of twenty-two largest research libraries in the United Kingdom, including nineteen university libraries and three national libraries, as well as the CONSER and ISSN databases. Funding has been secured for a further two years. Phase 2 of the project is underway to incorporate holdings from another sixty libraries, including special libraries.

The Poster Session highlighted serials union catalogs, the United Kingdom context collaboration with project partners, and challenges of the project.

MOVING E-SERIAL HOLDINGS AND URLS
OUT OF THE CATALOG USING SFX

Jonathan David Makepeace

University of Windsor

The University of Windsor's Leddy Library is moving e-serial holdings and URLs out of its Voyager catalogue using SFX. URLs in holdings records will point to a table, which will point to an SFX menu for the serial, eliminating the need for holdings and URL maintenance in the catalog.

E-JOURNAL TRAINING IN A TIME-CRUNCH: A TEMPLATE TO RE-TOOL ACQUISITIONS/ SERIALS DEPARTMENTS

Wendy Highby

University of Northern Colorado

In the increasingly complex electronic library environment, stagnant staffing levels and traditional workflow patterns are becoming untenable. At the University of Northern Colorado, solving this staffing and workflow dilemma has been challenging and positively transformative. This poster session provided an innovative training template that actively engages acquisitions and serials staff of all skill levels.

Team-based assignments boost confidence and collaboration by pairing more experienced e-serialists with less experienced and/or experienced but print-oriented staff. The innovative team orientation is combined with a traditional classroom structure. This setting provides the familiar and helpful discipline of deadlines, homework, and a nurturing atmosphere. Hands-on activation, information-gathering, and troubleshooting exercises build the trainees' abilities to apply local policy, quickly identify essential information, and navigate through various publisher platforms, the integrated library system, and electronic resource management interfaces.

This poster session was particularly helpful for the librarian leading staff out of a traditional, territorially defined workplace into a team-oriented environment. It also aided the manager who is charged with guiding mid-career staffers from the stability of print formats into the fluidity of e-journals. Success of the template is measured qualitatively through candid feedback from trainees.

TRACKING AND "CHECK IN" OF ELECTRONIC JOURNALS: A HOMEGROWN SOLUTION

Amanda Yesilbas

Florida Atlantic University

Florida Atlantic University's Serials Department is in the grips of major change. Last year's renewal saw the University move over 400 journals from print subscriptions to online journals with more being added every day. FAU has also begun preparations for moving to a new integrated library management system. The Serials Department has created a Serials Management Database to track all aspects of serials management. To cope with the major migration of materials from print to electronic and an antiquated ILS, the department has developed a special module for the tracking and the "check in" of electronic material. By using their new database module, FAU is insuring access and registration to a large number of online resources. The poster session demonstrated the daily workflow and "check in" operations and provided ideas to other libraries on how to cope and handle major changeovers in format. Essentially, the database program generates a daily list based on the frequency of publications of online titles. Based on this daily list, access to journal issues is checked down to the .pdf level and then "checked in" to FAU's database and cataloged in a manner very similar to print titles. This system has helped in finding and correcting many problems in registration and initial access of online resources. It also insured that FAU continued to have access in the changeable world of online journals.

20th ANNUAL
NASIG CONFERENCE REGISTRANTS

NASIG Conference 2005–
Registrants by Last Name

Abaid, Teresa L.	Florida Atlantic University
Acreman, Bev	Taylor & Francis
Acton, Deena	National Library of Medicine
Adam, Darlene H.	Karolinska Institute University Library
Aitchison, Jada	University of Arkansas, Little Rock
Alan, Robert	Pennsylvania State University
Albee, Barbara	Indiana University School of Library and Information Science India
Allen, Mary	Lawrence Livermore National Lab.
Allen, Norene	Swets Information Svcs.
Allman, Miriam	Tufts University
Alvarez, Josefa	University of Texas at El Paso
Anderson, Rick	University of Nevada-Reno
Andrews, Sarah	University of Iowa Libraries
Andrews, Susan	Texas A&M University-Commerce
Arcand, Janet	Iowa State University Library
Ard, Allyson R.	EBSCO Industries, Inc.
Aro, Carlene	South Dakota State University
Arthur, Michael	Old Dominion University
Aufdemberge, Karen	JSTOR
Baden, Marla	Indiana University Purdue University Fort Wayne
Badics, Joe	Eastern Michigan University

Available online at http://www.haworthpress.com/web/SER
doi:10.1300/J123v50n03_20

Baia, Wendy	University of Colorado at Boulder
Bailey, Mary	Kansas State University
Baker, Jeanne	University of Maryland, College Park
Baker, Mary Ellen	California Polytechnic State University
Bakke, Celia	San Jose State University Library
Ballard, Rochelle	Princeton University
Banoun, Susan M.	University of Cincinnati
Barba, Claudia Haydee	Universidad Nacional Autonoma de Mexico
Barrett, Ariella	National Academies
Basar, Ivan	Library and Archives Canada
Basch, N. Bernard	Basch Subscriptions, Inc.
Becker, Joe	New Mexico State University Library
Beidler, Susan	Lycoming College
Beky, Endre L.	Elsevier Inc.
Bellinger, Christina	University of New Hampshire
Belskis, Sandy	Absolute Backorder Service, Inc.
Benevento, Jenny	University of Illinois at Urbana-Champaign
Bernards, Dennis	Brigham Young University
Bernhardt, Beth	University of North Carolina at Greensboro
Bethel, Jane	St. Olaf College
Bird, Gwen	Simon Fraser University
Blackwell, Lisa S.	Columbus Children's Hospital
Bogdanski, Elizabeth	ProQuest Information and Learning
Boissy, Robert W.	Springer
Boone, Cecelia N.	MINITEX Library Information Network
Borchert, Carol Ann	University of South Florida Tampa
Bordeaux, Abigail	Binghamton University Libraries
Born, Kathleen	EBSCO Information Svcs.
Boyd, Morag	Illinois State University
Brady, Chris	
Brand, Amy E.	
Branham, Janie	Southeastern Louisiana University
Brannon, Kathy	Swets Information Svcs.
Brass, Evelyn	University of Houston
Brau, Jessica	Eastview Information Services
Breed, Luellen	University of Wisconsin, Parkside
Breton, Gabriel	Library and Archives Canada
Brewster, Paula J.	EBSCO
Bright, Alice	Carnegie Mellon University
Broadwater, Deborah	Vanderbilt University
Brown, Elizabeth W.	Project Muse
Brown, Jerry R.	Central Missouri State University

Brubaker, Jana	Northern Illinois University
Buck, Tina H.	Hennepin County Library
Bukralia, Rajeev	Black Hills State University
Bulger, James	Allina Hospitals & Clinics
Burk, Martha	Babson College
Burke, David	Villanova University
Burris, Christian	Wake Forest University
Buttner, Mary	Stanford University Medical Ctr.
Bynog, David	Rice University
Byunn, Kit S.	University of Memphis
Callahan, Patricia	Massachusetts General Hospital
Canepi, Kitti	Southern Illinois University Carbondale
Cannon, Heather	Loyola Health Sciences Library
Cannon, Martha	Drexel University
Caraway, Beatrice	Trinity University
Carey, Ronadin	University of Wisconsin, Eau Claire
Carlisi, Marietta	Federal Reserve Bank of Atlanta
Carlson, Amy	University of Hawaii at Manoa
Cascio, Diane	Santa Clara University
Castrataro, James	Indiana University
Celeste, Eric	University of Minnesota (Twin Cities)
Chamberlain, Clinton	Trinity University
Champagne, Thomas	Thomas Jefferson School of Law
Chang, Linh	Stanford University
Cheng, Daisy T.	University of Mississippi
Chisman, Janet	Washington State University
Christensen, Carol M.	Utah State University
Clanton, Christina	Sun Microsystems, Inc.
Clark, Stephen	College of William and Mary
Cleary, Robert	Syracuse University
Cleavenger, Patricia M.	Hanford Technical Library
Cochenour, Donnice	Colorado State University
Coffman, Ila	University of Oklahoma Libraries
Cohen, Joan	Bergen Community College
Cole, Kerry	Portland Press Ltd.
Collins, Jill M.	Boise State University
Collins, Maria	Mississippi State University
Conger, Joan	
Conger, Mary Jane	University of North Carolina at Greensboro
Congleton, Robert J.	Rider University
Conrad, Marc A.	Chicago Public Library
Conway, Linda M.	St. Cloud State University
Cook, Eleanor	Appalachian State University

Copnick, Andrew B.	Nova Southeastern University
Corvene, Sarah	Harvard College Library Technical Svcs.
Courtney, Keith	Taylor and Francis Ltd.
Cousineau, Huguette	Cisti/NRC
Cowan, Friedgard	George Mason University, Fenwick Library
Cox, John E.	John Cox Associates Ltd.
Creamer, Marilyn	Haverford College
Creech, Anna	Central Washington University
Cronin, Margot	R.R. Bowker, LLC
Crooker, Cynthia	Yale University
Cross, Rubye J.	Ga Tech Library & Info Center
Crowder, Travis	FBIS
Culmer-Nier, Lessie	Drew University
Currie, Susan	Binghamton University
Cyr, Mariann	3M Company
Daniels, Tim	Georgia State University
Darling, Karen	University of Missouri-Columbia
Dausch, Linda S.	Chicago Public Library
Davies-Venn, Rebecca P.	University of Maryland
Davis, Jennifer K.	US Government Printing Office
Davis, Susan	University at Buffalo, SUNY
DeBlois, Lillian	Arizona Health Sciences Library
Degener, Christie T.	University of North Carolina at Chapel Hill, Health Sciences Library
Del Baglivo, Megan	University of Maryland, Baltimore
Deyoe, Nancy	Wichita State University
Doescher, Starla	University of Oklahoma Libraries
Doig, Margaret R.	University of Derby
Dong, Sophie Zhihui	University of Georgia
Dowdy, Beverly	University of Central Oklahoma
Dudley, Virginia	MINITEX, University of Minnesota
Duhon, Lucy	University of Toledo Libraries
Duncan, Jennifer	Utah State University
Duxbury, Janell	University of Wisconsin, Madison
Dyas-Correia, Sharon	University of Toronto
Dygert, Claire	American University
Edwards, Jennifer L.	MIT Libraries
Edwards, Michael A.	Pentagon Library
Elmore, Eric	Sam Houston State University
Emery, Jill	University of Houston
Endres, Ellen	Brill/De Gruyter
England, Deberah	Wright State University Libraries
Ercelawn, Ann	Vanderbilt University

Essency, Janet	Bridgewater State College
Eyler, Carol	Carleton College Library
Fahey, Barbara J.	University of Wisconsin Oshkosh
Farber, Anita	University of Texas at Austin
Feick, Tina	Swets Information Svcs.
Feis, Nathaniel	School of the Art Institute of Chicago
Ferguson, Christine L.	Furman University
Ficken, Carol	University of Akron
Fields, Cheryl	National Library of Medicine
Fischer, Karen	Hardin Library for the Health Sciences
FitzGibbon, Kerry	Richard Stockton College of NJ
Fletcher, Peter V.	Tulane University
Folsom, Sandy	Central Michigan University
Fons, Theodore A.	Innovative Interfaces
Foster, Connie	Western Kentucky University
Fowler, David C.	Iowa State University
Freeman, Christine	Texas A&M University-Corpus Christi
Frick, Rachel	University of Richmond
Frohlich, Anne	McNeese State University
Gabrio, Katy	Macalester College
Gammon, Julia	University of Akron
Gardner, Gene	University of Colorado Health Ctr.
Garner, June	Mississippi State University
Geckle, Beverly	University of Baltimore Law Library
Geer, Beverley	YBP Library Svcs.
Geller, Marilyn	
Genereux, Cecilia	University of Minnesota
George, Sarah	Illinois Wesleyan University
Gibson, Jessica	Illinois Library Computer Systems Office
Gilbert, Mary	Towson University
Gillespie, E. Gaele	University of Kansas
Ginanni, Katy	EBSCO Information Svcs.
Gold, Debra	Lakehead University Library
Goodwyn, Tony W.	St. Olaf College
Gordon, Martin	Franklin and Marshall College
Grace, Michelle A.	Minnesota State University, Mankato
Grant, Maureen	University of Wisconsin, Madison
Graves, Tonia	Old Dominion University
Green, Carol	The University of Southern Mississippi
Greene III, Philip E. N.	Greene Consulting LLC
Greene, Araby Y.	University of Nevada, Reno Libraries
Grenci, Mary	University of Oregon
Grieme, Fariha	University of Minnesota Libraries

Griffin, JoAnne	Tufts University Health Sciences Library
Griffith, Jan	Hamline University-Bush Library
Grogg, Jill	University of Alabama
Grönvall, Karin	Karolinska Institutet University Library
Gurevich, Konstantin	University of Rochester
Hagan, Timothy	Northwestern University
Hamilton, Gloria	University of Chicago
Hansen, Colleen	Linda Hall Library
Ha'o, Kimberly	Brigham Young University
Harmon, Joseph	Indiana University Purdue University, Indianapolis
Hamish, Kathryn B.	Endeavor Information Systems
Harrell, Karen	Nelson-Atkins Museum of Art
Harvell, Tony	University of California, San Diego
Harvey, Phyllis J.	Palmer College of Chiropractic
Harwell, Julie C.	EBSCO Industries, Inc.
Hasan, Syed	Springer
Haslam, Michaelyn	University of Nevada, Las Vegas
Hawthorne, Dalene	Emporia State University
Hay, Marie	Trinity International University
Headley, Stephen	Public Library of Cincinnati and Hamilton County
Hebard, Jeanne	Babson College
Heminger, Sharon	JSTOR
Henderson, Kittie S.	EBSCO Information Svcs.
Henle, Alea	Colorado State University
Hensler, Matthew	Sirsi
Hiatt, Derrik	Brigham Young University
Highby, Wendy	University of Northern Colorado
Hijleh, Renee	University of Wisconsin-Eau Claire
Hinger, Joseph	St. John's University
Hixson, Carol G.	University of Oregon
Hogan, Karen	Augsburg College
Holley, Beth	University of Alabama
Holloway, Trina	Georgia State University
Holmberg, Melissa	Minnesota State University, Mankato
Hood, Anna	Kent State University
Hopkins, Sandra	Harvard Law School Library
Hovorka, Carolyn	East View Information Services
Howard, Bob	
Howard, Mykie	National Agricultural Library
Howland, Jared	Brigham Young University
Hoyer, Craig	Swets Information Services

Hoyer, Rob	Swets Information Services, Inc.
Huenniger, Jim	Swets Information Services
Hulbert, Linda	University of Saint Thomas
Hutchinson, Robin	St. Lawrence University
Imre, Andrea	Southern Illinois University Carbondale
Irvin, Judy	Louisiana Tech University
Iverson, Cyndi	Harley E. French Library of the Health Sciences
Ives, Gary	Texas A&M University
Ivins, October	Digital Content and Access Solutions
Jaeger, Glenn	Absolute Backorder Service, Inc.
Jamal, Yasmin B.	SFU
Jander, Karen	University of Wisconsin, Milwaukee
Jayes, Linda	University of New Hampshire
Jenner, Margaret R.	University of Washington
Johansen, Kathy	Brigham Young University
John, Sarah	University of California, Davis
Johnson, Kay	University of Tennessee, Knoxville
Johnson, Sue-Ellen	Stanford University
Jones, Janie	Tarleton State University
Joshipura, Smita D.	Arizona State University-West
Julian, Gail	Clemson University
Jurries, Elaine	Auraria Library
Kane, Julie	Stanford University
Kaplan, Michael	Ex Libris, Inc.
Kara, William	Cornell University
Kaste, Ann M.	University of Nebraska Medical Center
Keith, Paul	Chicago Public Library
Kelley, Steve	Wake Forest University
Kendall, Susan L.	San Jose State University
Keys, Marshall	Principal, MDA Consulting
Khosh-khui, Sam	Texas State University, San Marcos
Kiker, Douglas P.	University of Florida
Kilzer, Rebekah	Drexel University
King, Paula	Scripps Research Institute
Kirby, Colleen M.	South Dakota State Library
Kirk, Tamra M.	Mayo Clinic Libraries
Klimley, Susan	Columbia University
Knapp, Leslie	EBSCO Information Svcs.
Knight, Sharon	University of Wisconsin, Whitewater
Kobyljanec, Kathleen	John Carroll University
Koehler, Tom	3M
Koller, Rita	Lake Forest College

Koppel, Ted	The Library Corp.
Kowalska, Ewa H.	R.R. Bowker
Kraemer, Alfred	Medical College of Wisconsin Libraries
Kreitzer, Amy S.	College of St. Catherine
Krieger, Lee	University of Miami
Kropf, Blythe	New York Public Library
La Rooy, Pauline	National Library of New Zealand
Lamborn, Joan	University of Northern Colorado
Lamoureux, Selden Durgom	University of North Carolina at Chapel Hill
Lampley, Michael	Texas Christian University
Landesman, Betty	National Institutes of Health Library
Lang, Jennifer	Princeton University
Langendorfer, Jeanne	Bowling Green State University
Larkin, Molly	Temple University Libraries
Latchney, Jim	Michigan State University
Laurence, Helen	Florida Atlantic University
Le, Jia	Fondren Library Ctr.
Leadem, Ellen	National Inst. of Environmental Health Sciences
Lee, Rachel	University of California Press
Lee, Sheila Y.	Louisiana State University
Lentz, Janet	University of Pennsylvania
Lenville, Jean	Harvard University
Limaye, Asha	University of Illinois at Chicago
Lin, Selina	University of Iowa
Lin, Weina	Business Library of Brooklyn Public Library
Lindquist, Janice	Rice University
Linton, Dave	University of MN-MINITEX Library Info Network
Liu-Spencer, Hsianghui	
Loghry, Pat	Univ. of Notre Dame
Long, Bradley	Thomas Jefferson University
Lowe, Elizabeth	Southern Illinois University Edwardsville
Lu, Wen-ying	Michigan State University
Luckman, Liane	St. Edward's University
Luther, Judy	Informed Strategies
MacLennan, Birdie	University of Vermont
Macomber, Nancy	Queens College Library
Maestretti, Danielle	Utne
Makepeace, Jonathan David	University of Windsor
Malinowski, Teresa M.	California State University Fullerton
Manahan, Meg	American Museum of Natural History
Markham, Scott C.	Hennepin County

Markley, Susan	Villanova University
Markovic, Marija	Abbott Laboratories
Matson, Linda F.	University of Massachusetts Amherst
Maull, Nicole	Swets Information Services
Maxwell, Kimberly	Massachusetts Inst. of Technology
McAphee, Sylvia	University of Alabama, Birmingham
McCawley, Christina	West Chester University
McClamroch, Jo	Indiana University
McCracken, Peter	Serials Solutions
McCraw, Cheryl D.	CCLA
McDaniels, Lisa C.	University of Iowa
McDanold, Shana	Saint Louis University
McDonald, Brian	State University of New York, Oswego
McDonald, Donna S.	Texas Tech University
McDonald, Elizabeth	University of Memphis
McElroy, Emily	New York University
McEwan, Carole	University of California, Berkeley
McFadden, Scott	Ball State University
McGinty, James P.	Cambridge Information Group
McGough, Meg	The Journal of Histochemistry and Cytochemistry
McGrath, Kat	University of British Columbia
McGuire, Ruth A.	Northwestern College
McKee, Anne	Greater Western Library Alliance
McManus, Jean	University of Notre Dame
McSweeney, Marilyn G.	Massachusetts Inst. of Technology
Medeiros, Carolyn	Lawrence Livermore National Lab
Meneely, Kathleen	Case Western Reserve University
Menefee, Daviess	Elsevier Science
Mering, Margaret	University of Nebraska, Lincoln
Merz, Mildred	Oakland University
Mi, Jia	College of New Jersey
Miller, Bridget	George Mason University
Miller, Judy	Valparaiso University
Mitchell, Anne	University of Houston
Mizer, Sam	Brown University Library
Moeller, Paul	University of Colorado at Boulder
Moeller, Ulrike	Harrassowitz
Molto, Mavis	Utah State University
Montgomery, Debbie	University of Texas at Dallas Library
Moon, Young J.	Georgetown University
Moran, Sheila	Massachusetts General Hospital
Morse, Carol	Walla Walla College

Mudrick, Kristine E.	St. Joseph's University
Murden, Steven H.	Virginia Museum of Fine Arts
Murphy, Sandra B.	Harvard University
Nash, Anita J.	U. S. Postal Service
Nelson, Catherine	University of California, Santa Barbara
Nesta, Frederick	Lingnan University
Neuville, Amy	JSTOR
Newsome, Nancy	Western Carolina University
Nicholas, Pamela J.	University of Notre Dame
Novak, Denise	Carnegie Mellon University
Nowak, Michelle	Phoenix Public Library
Noyes, J. C.	Bridgeport National Bindery Inc.
O'Connell, Jennifer	EBSCO Information Svcs.
O'Hara, Lisa	University of Manitoba
Oliver, Marina	Texas Tech University Libraries
Oostergetel, Natasha	Palgrave Macmillan
Owen, Vanessa (Vandy)	Tennessee State University
Packer, Donna	Western Washington University Libraries
Page, Mary	Rutgers University Libraries
Paldan, Diane	Wayne State University Libraries
Palmer, Joy J.	Mayo Clinic
Parang, Elizabeth	Pepperdine University
Paratore, Amy	Swets Information Services
Parkhe, Smita	Arizona State University
Parks, Bonnie	Oregon State University
Parthasarathy, Kalyani	University of New Orleans
Pennington, Buddy	University of Missouri-Kansas City
Pesch, Oliver	EBSCO Information Services
Polakowski, Betsy	University of St. Thomas
Poorman, Kathy	University of Texas at El Paso
Powers, Susanna	Tulane University Library
Prentice, Brian	Elsevier
Rais, Shirley	Loma Linda University
Randall, Kevin M.	Northwestern University
Ranger, Sara	University of Houston
Razo, Ginny	Argonne National Laboratory
Reeder, Vern	Southwest Missouri State University
Resch, Peter T.	University of Regina
Reynolds, Elvira L.	Boston College
Reynolds, Regina Romano	Library of Congress
Rhoades, Alice J.	Rice University
Ricker, Karina	State University of New York, Albany
Riding, Ed	Dynix

Riley, Cheryl A.	Central Missouri State University
Rioux, Margaret	MBLWHOI Library
Ripley, Erika	Southern Methodist University
Roach, Dani	University of St. Thomas
Robertson, Wendy	University of Iowa
Robinson, Trina	Tulane University Law Library
Robischon, Rose	United States Military Academy Library
Roe, Sandra	Illinois State University
Rogers, Marilyn	University of Arkansas Libraries
Rolnik, Zachary	now publishers
Romaine, Sion	University of Washington
Roos, Carol A.	EBSCO Information Services
Rosenberg, Frieda	University of North Carolina at Chapel Hill
Roth, Alison C.	Swets Information Svcs.
Rudowsky, Catherine	Slippery Rock University
Rumph, Virginia A.	Butler University
Rupp, Nathan	Cornell University
Ryan, Allan	St. John's University Law School
Sanders, Laurel E.	Houston Academy of Medicine-Texas Medical Ctr. Library
Sandy, Stella M.	University of the West indies
Sapp, Masha	Olin Library, Washington University
Sappington, Jayne A.	Texas Tech University Libraries
Satzer, Patricia A.	University of St. Thomas
Savage, Steve	San Diego State University
Saxton, Elna	University of Cincinnati
Schatz, Bob	Coutts Library Svcs.
Schleper, Susan	Saint Cloud State University
Schlutt, Jayne E.	University of Notre Dame
Schmitt, Stephanie	Lillian Goldman Law Library
Schoen, Dena	Harrasowitz Library Svcs.
Scholl, Miki	University of St. Thomas Schoenecker Law Library
Schoofs, Bob	Grand Valley State University
Schor, Abby	Arlington Heights Memorial Library
Schorr, Andrea N.	University of North Texas
Schwartz, Marla	American University Law Library
Schwartzkopf, Rebecca	Minnesota State University, Mankato
Seamans, Marsha	University of Kentucky
Seeley, Joan L.	Lakehead University
Seifrid, Andi	Aurora University
Seikel, Michele	Oklahoma State University
Seymour-Green, Marie	University of Delaware Library

Shadle, Steve	University of Washington
Sheffer, Rena	University of Arkansas for Medical Sciences
Sheffield, Rebecca	Ball State University
Shelly, Susan C.	Goshen College
Showalter, Mike	Serials Solutions
Shriver, Jane	University of St. Thomas
Simpson, Esther	Library of Congress
Simser, Charlene	Kansas State University
Singh, Frances	Hamline University Law Library
Sinkler-Miller, Christina	Macalester College
Slagell, Jeff	Delta State University
Slater, Bill	Brigham Young University
Sleeman, Allison M.	University of Virginia
Smith Griffin, Linda	Louisiana State University
Smith, Merrill	EBSCO Information Svcs.
Smith, Sally	Bethel University Library
Smulewitz, Gracemary	Rutgers University, New Brunswick Libraries
Song, Liping	Falk Library of the Health Sciences, Univ. of Pittsburgh
Sorensen, Charlene	CISTI
Sorrell, Eva	UC Irvine
Spicuzza, Martha	Hillsdale College
Spring, Martha	Loyola University Chicago
Srivastava, Sandhya D.	Hofstra University
Stack, Bryan	Creighton University
Stamison, Christine	Swets Information Svcs.
Stanton, Victoria	University of North Florida Library
Steele, Patrick	Cuyahoga County Public Library
Steinle, Tammy	
Stevenson, Liz G.	The University of Edinburgh
Stewart, Brenton	Kansas State University
Stewart-Marshall, Zoe	Cornell University
Stickman, Jim	University of Washington
Stigall, Mary L.	LOUIS: The Louisiana Library Network
Stone, Evalyn	Metropolitan Museum of Art
Strader, C. Rockelle	Ohio State University
Strube, Kathy	Aurora Health Care
Su, Julie	San Diego State University
Sullenger, Paula	Auburn University
Sutherland, Laurie	University of Washington
Sutton, Sarah	Mary and Jeff Bell Library
Swetman, Barbara	Hamilton College
Swope, Cynthia D.	Himmelfarb Health Sciences Library

Taffurelli, Virginia	New York Public Library
Tarango, Adolfo R.	University of California, San Diego
Tawney, Sheila	Williamsburg Regional Library
Taylor, Marit	Auraria Library
Teel, Kay	Stanford University
Tenney, Joyce	University of Maryland, Baltimore County
Terrill, Lori	University of Wyoming
Thomas, Dana	Ryerson University Library
Thompson, Joan C.	EBSCO
Thunem, Carol	Carleton College
Tokoro, Shoko	Southern Methodist University
Tong, Dieu	University of Alabama, Birmingham
Tonkery, Dan	EBSCO Information Svcs.
Torbert, Christina	J.D. Williams Library
Toyota-Kindler, Yumiko	University of Minnesota Libraries
Tribble, Cole	FBIS
Trish, Maggie	University of Missouri-Rolla
Turitz, Mitch	San Francisco State University
Tusa, Sarah D.	Lamar University
Urrizola, Manuel	University of California Irvine
Vent, Marilyn	University of Nevada, Las Vegas
Vezina, Kumiko	Concordia University
Vital, Sarah M.	San Jose State University
Vukas, Rachel	EBSCO Information Svcs.
Waite, Carolyn	MIT Lincoln Laboratory
Walker, Dana	University of Georgia Libraries
Walker, Jenny B.	Ex Libris Inc.
Waller, Andrew	University of Calgary
Walsh, John C.	George Mason University
Walsh, William	Georgia State University
Waltz, Marie	Center for Research Libraries
Wang, Jane	University of Scranton
Wang, Jue	California State University at Northridge
Washburn, Judith	Stanford University
Way, Harold	EBSCO
Weiss, Paul J.	University of California, San Diego
Wesley, Kathryn	Clemson University Libraries
Wheeler, Karen	Elsevier
White, Joycelyn	University of Memphis
Whiting, Peter	University of Southern Indiana
Wierucki, Karen	Ontario Legislative Library
Wiggins, John W.	Drexel University
Wiley, Glen	North Carolina State University

Williams, Cynthia	Thomson Gale
Williams, Danielle	University of Evansville
Williams, Geraldine	Northern Kentucky University
Williams, Mary	Minot State University
Williams, Sheryl L.	University of Nebraska Medical Ctr.
Williams, Sue	University of Colorado at Boulder
Wills, Faedra M.	University of Texas at Arlington
Wilson, Jenni	Swets Information Services
Winchester, David	Washburn University
Wineburgh-Freed, Maggie	University of Southern California
Wingenroth, Brian	Johns Hopkins University Press
Winward, Kyle	Southwest Missouri State University
Wishnetsky, Susan	Northwestern University Medical School
Wuorinen, Louise I.	Lakehead University Library
Yaples, Jill	Binghamton University Libraries
Yesilbas, Amanda	Florida Atlantic University
Young, Jennifer	Northwestern University
Young, Naomi	University of Florida
Yu, Ying	Gallaudet University
Yue, Paoshan	University of Nevada, Reno
Zhang, Xiaoyin	University of Nevada, Las Vegas
Zhou, Don	William Mitchell College of Law
Zimmerman, Sara	LOUIS: The LA Library Network
Zoller, Amanda	Serials Solutions
Zuriff, Susan R.	University of Minnesota-Twin Cities

NASIG Conference 2005– Registrants by Affiliation

Brady, Chris
Brand, Amy E.
Conger, Joan
Geller, Marilyn
Howard, Bob
Liu-Spencer, Hsianghui
Steinle, Tammy

3M   Koehler, Tom
3M Company   Cyr, Mariann
Abbott Laboratories   Markovic, Marija
Absolute Backorder Service, Inc.   Belskis, Sandy
Absolute Backorder Service, Inc.   Jaeger, Glenn
Allina Hospitals & Clinics   Bulger, James
American Museum of Natural History   Manahan, Meg
American University   Dygert, Claire
American University Law Library   Schwartz, Maria
Appalachian State University   Cook, Eleanor
Argonne National Laboratory   Razo, Ginny
Arizona Health Sciences Library   DeBlois, Lillian
Arizona State University   Parkhe, Smita
Arizona State University-West   Joshipura, Smita D.
Arlington Heights Memorial Library   Schor, Abby
Auburn University   Sullenger, Paula
Augsburg College   Hogan, Karen
Auraria Library   Jurries, Elaine
Auraria Library   Taylor, Marit
Aurora Health Care   Strube, Kathy
Aurora University   Seifrid, Andi
Babson College   Burk, Martha

Available online at http://www.haworthpress.com/web/SER
doi:10.1300/J123v50n03_21

Babson College   Hebard, Jeanne
Ball State University   McFadden, Scott
Ball State University   Sheffield, Rebecca
Basch Subscriptions, Inc.   Basch, N. Bernard
Bergen Community College   Cohen, Joan
Bethel University Library   Smith, Sally
Binghamton University   Currie, Susan
Binghamton University Libraries   Bordeaux, Abigail
Binghamton University Libraries   Yaples, Jill
Black Hills State University   Bukralia, Rajeev
Boise State University   Collins, Jill M.
Boston College   Reynolds, Elvira L.
Bowling Green State University   Langendorfer, Jeanne
Bridgeport National Bindery Inc.   Noyes, J.C.
Bridgewater State College   Essency, Janet
Brigham Young University   Bernards, Dennis
Brigham Young University   Ha'o, Kimberly
Brigham Young University   Hiatt, Derrik
Brigham Young University   Howland, Jared
Brigham Young University   Johansen, Kathy
Brigham Young University   Slater, Bill G.
Brille/De Gruyter   Endres, Ellen
Brown University Library   Mizer, Sam
Business Library of Brooklyn Public
     Library   Lin, Weina
Butler University   Rumph, Virginia A.
California Polytechnic State University   Baker, Mary Ellen
California State University at Northridge   Wang, Jue
California State University Fullerton   Malinowski, Teresa M.
Cambridge Information Group   McGintly, James P.
Carleton College   Thunem, Carol
Carleton College Library   Eyler, Carol
Carnegie Mellon University   Bright, Alice
Carnegie Mellon University   Novak, Denise
Case Western Reserve University   Meneely, Kathleen
CCLA   McCraw, Cheryl D.
Center for Research Libraries   Waltz, Marie
Central Michigan University   Folsom, Sandy
Central Missouri State University   Brown, Jerry R.
Central Missouri State University   Riley, Cheryl A.
Central Washington University   Creech, Anne
Chicago Public Library   Conrad, Marc A.

Chicago Public Library	Dausch, Linda S.
Chicago Public Library	Keith, Paul
CISTI	Sorensen, Cherlene
Cisti/NRC	Cousineau, Huguette
Clemson University	Julian, Gall
Clemson University Libraries	Wesley, Kathryn
College of New Jersey	Mi, Jia
College of St. Catherine	Kreitzer, Amy S.
College of William and Mary	Clark, Stephen
Colorado State University	Cochenour, Donnice
Colorado State University	Henle, Alea
Columbia University	Klimley, Susan
Columbus Children's Hospital	Blackwell, Lisa S.
Concordia University	Vezina, Kumiko
Cornell University	Kara, William
Cornell University	Rupp, Nathan
Cornell University	Stewart-Marshall, Zoe
Coutts Library Svcs.	Schatz, Bob
Creighton University	Stack, Bryan
Cuyahoga County Public Library	Steele, Patrick
Delta State University	Slagell, Jeff
Digital Content and Access Solutions	Ivins, October
Drew University	Culmer-Nier, Lessie
Drexel University	Cannon, Martha
Drexel University	Kilzer, Rebekah
Drexel University	Wiggins, John W.
Dynix	Riding, Ed
East View Information Services	Hovorka, Carolyn
Eastern Michigan University	Badics, Joe
Eastview Information Services	Brau, Jessica
EBSCO	Brewster, Paula J.
EBSCO	Thompson, Joan C.
EBSCO	Way, Harold
EBSCO Industries, Inc.	Ard, Allyson R.
EBSCO Industries, Inc.	Harwell, Julie C.
EBSCO Information Services	Pesch, Oliver
EBSCO Information Services	Roos, Carol A.
EBSCO Information Svcs.	Born, Kathleen
EBSCO Information Svcs.	Ginanni, Katy
EBSCO Information Svcs.	Henderson, Kittie S.
EBSCO Information Svcs.	Knapp, Leslie
EBSCO Information Svcs.	O'Connell, Jennifer
EBSCO Information Svcs.	Smith, Merrill

EBSCO Information Svcs.   Tonkery, Dan
EBSCO Information Svcs.   Vukas, Rachel
Elsevier   Prentice, Brian
Elsevier   Wheeler, Karen
Elsevier Inc.   Beky, Endre L.
Elsevier Science   Menefee, Daviess
Emporia State University   Hawthorne, Delene
Endeavor Information Systems   Hamish, Kathryn B.
Ex Libris, Inc.   Walker, Jenny B.
Ex Libris, Inc.   Kaplan, Michael
Falk Library of the Health Sciences,
    Univ. of Pittsburgh   Song, Liping
FBIS   Crowder, Travis
FBIS   Tribble, Cole
Federal Reserve Bank of Atlanta   Carlisi, Marietta
Florida Atlantic University   Yesilbas, Amanda
Florida Atlantic University   Abaid, Teresa L.
Florida Atlantic University   Laurence, Helen
Fondren Library Ctr.   Le, Jia
Franklin and Marshall College   Gordon, Martin
Furman University   Ferguson, Christine L.
Ga Tech Library & Info Center   Cross, Rubye J.
Gallaudet University   Yu, Ying
George Mason University   Miller, Bridget
George Mason University   Walsh, John C.
George Mason University, Fenwick
    Library   Cowan, Friedgard
Georgetown University   Moon, Young J.
Georgia State University   Daniels, Tim
Georgia State University   Holloway, Trina
Georgia State University   Walsh, William
Goshen College   Shelly, Susan C.
Grand Valley State University   Schoofs, Bob
Greater Western Library Alliance   McKee, Anne
Greene Consulting LLC   Greene III, Philip E. N.
Hamilton College   Swetman, Barbara
Hamline University–Bush Library   Griffith, Jan
Hamline University Law Library   Singh, Frances
Hanford Technical Library   Cleavenger, Patricia M.
Hardin Library for the Health Sciences   Fischer, Karen
Harley E. French Library of the Health
    Sciences   Iverson, Cyndi

Harrasowitz Library Svcs.	Schoen, Dena
Harrassowitz	Moeller, Ulrike
Harvard College Library Technical	
Services	Corvene, Sarah
Harvard Law School Library	Hopkins, Sandra
Harvard University	Lenville, Jean
Harvard University	Murphy, Sandra B.
Haverford College	Creamer, Marilyn
Hennepin County	Markham, Scott C.
Hennepin County Library	Buck, Tina H.
Hillsdale College	Spicuzza, Martha
Himmelfarb Health Sciences Library	Swope, Cynthia D.
Hofstra University	Srivastava, Sandhya D.
Houston Academy of Medicine-Texas	
Medical Ctr. Library	Sanders, Laurel E.
Illinois Library Computer Systems Office	Gibson, Jessica
Illinois State University	Boyd, Morag
Illinois State University	Roe, Sandra
Illinois Wesleyan University	George, Sarah
Indiana University	Castrataro, James
Indiana University	McClamroch, Jo
Indiana University Purdue University	
Fort Wayne	Baden, Marla
Indiana University Purdue University,	
Indianapolis	Harmon, Joseph
Indiana University School of Library	
and Information Science India	Albee, Barbara
Informed Strategies	Luther, Judy
Innovative Interfaces	Fons, Theodore A.
Iowa State University	Fowler, David C.
Iowa State University Library	Arcand, Janet
J.D. Williams Library	Torbert, Christina
John Carroll University	Kobyljanec, Kathleen
John Cox Associates Ltd.	Cox, John E.
Johns Hopkins University Press	Wingenroth, Brian
JSTOR	Aufdemberge, Karen
JSTOR	Heminger, Sharon
JSTOR	Neuville, Amy
Kansas State University	Bailey, Mary
Kansas State University	Simser, Charlene
Kansas State University	Stewart, Brenton
Karolinska Institute University Library	Adam, Darlene H.
Karolinska Institute University Library	Grönvall, Karin

Kent State University	Hood, Anna
Lake Forest College	Koller, Rita
Lakehead University Library	Seeley, Joan L.
Lakehead University Library	Gold, Debra
Lakehead University	Wuorinen, Louis I.
Lamar University	Tusa, Sarah D.
Lawrence Livermore National Lab	Allen, Mary
Lawrence Livermore National Lab	Medetros, Carolyn
Library and Archives Canada	Basar, Ivan
Library and Archives Canada	Breton, Gabriel
Library of Congress	Reynolds, Regina Romano
Library of Congress	Simpson, Esther
Lillian Goldman Law Library	Schmitt, Stephanie
Linda Hall Library	Hansen, Colleen
Lingnan University	Nesta, Frederick
Loma Linda University	Rals, Shirley
LOUIS: The LA Library Network	Zimmerman, Sara
LOUIS: The Louisiana Library Network	Stigall, Mary L.
Louisiana State University	Lee, Shella Y.
Louisiana State University	Smith Griffin, Linda
Louisiana Tech University	Irvin, Judy
Loyola Health Sciences Library	Cannon, Heather
Loyola University Chicago	Spring, Martha
Lycoming College	Beidler, Susan
Macalester College	Gabrio, Katy
Macalester College	Sinkler-Miller, Christina
Mary and Jeff Bell Library	Sutton, Sarah
Massachusetts General Hospital	Callahan, Patricia
Massachusetts General Hospital	Moran, Sheila
Massachusetts Inst. of Technology	Maxwell, Kimberly
Massachusetts Inst. of Technology	McSweeney, Marilyn G.
Mayo Clinic	Palmer, Joy J.
Mayo Clinic Libraries	Kirk, Tamra M.
MBLWHOI Library	Rioux, Margaret
McNeese State University	Frohlich, Anne
Medical College of Wisconsin Libraries	Kraemer, Alfred
Metropolitan Museum of Art	Stone, Evalyn
Michigan State University	Latchney, Jim
Michigan State University	Lu, Wen-ying
MINITEX Library Information Network	Boone, Cecilia N.
MINITEX, University of Minnesota	Dudley, Virginia
Minnesota State University, Mankato	Grace, Michelle A.

Minnesota State University, Mankato — Holmberg, Melissa
Minnesota State University, Mankato — Schwartzkopf, Rebecca
Minot State University — Williams, Mary
Mississippi State University — Collins, Maria
Mississippi State University — Garner, June
MIT Libraries — Edwards, Jennifer L.
MIT Lincoln Laboratory — Waite, Carolyn
National Academies — Barrett, Ariella
National Agricultural Library — Howard, Mykie

National Inst. of Environmental Health
 Sciences — Leadem, Ellen
National Institutes of Health Library — Landesman, Betty
National Library of Medicine — Acton, Deena
National Library of Medicine — Fields, Cheryl
National Library of New Zealand — La Rooy, Pauline
Nelson-Atkins Museum of Art — Harrell, Karen
New Mexico State University Library — Becker, Joe
New York Public Library — Kropf, Blythe
New York Public Library — Taffurelli, Virginia
New York University — McElroy, Emily
North Carolina State University — Wiley, Glen
Northern Illinois University — Brubaker, Jana
Northern Kentucky University — Williams, Geraldine
Northwestern College — McGuire, Ruth A.
Northwestern University — Hagan, Timothy
Northwestern University — Randall, Kevin M.
Northwestern University — Young, Jennifer
Northwestern University Medical School — Wishnetsky, Susan
Nova Southeastern University — Copnick, Andrew B.
now publishers — Rolnik, Zachary
Oakland University — Merz, Mildred
Ohio State University — Strader, C. Rockelle
Oklahoma State University — Seikel, Michele
Old Dominion University — Arthur, Michael
Old Dominion University — Graves, Tonia
Olin Library, Washington University — Sapp, Masha
Ontario Legislative Library — Wierucki, Karen
Oregon State University — Parks, Bonnie
Palgrave Macmillan — Oostergetel, Natasha
Palmer College of Chiropractic — Harvey, Phyllis J.
Pennsylvania State University — Alan, Robert
Pentagon Library — Edwards, Michael A.

Pepperdine University	Parang, Elizabeth
Phoenix Public Library	Nowak, Michelle
Portland Press Ltd.	Cole, Kerry
Princeton University	Ballard, Rochelle
Princeton University	Lang, Jennifer
Principal, MDA Consulting	Keys, Marshall
Project Muse	Brown, Elizabeth W.
ProQuest Information and Learning	Bogdanski, Elizabeth
Public Library of Cincinnati and Hamilton County	Headley, Stephen
Queens College Library	Macomber, Nancy
R.R. Bowker	Kowalska, Ewa H.
R.R. Bowker, LLC	Cronin, Margot
Rice University	Bynog, David
Rice University	Lindquist, Janice
Rice University	Rhoades, Alice J.
Richard Stockton College of NJ	FitzGibbon, Kerry
Rider University	Congleton, Robert J.
Rutgers University Libraries	Page, Mary
Rugters University, New Brunswick Libraries	Smulewitz, Gracemary
Ryerson University Library	Thomas, Dana
Saint Cloud State University	Schleper, Susan
Saint Louis University	McDonald, Shana
Sam Houston State University	Elmore, Eric
San Diego State University	Savage, Steve
San Diego State University	Su, Julie
San Francisco State University	Turitz, Mitch
San Jose State University	Kendall, Susan L.
San Jose State University	Vital, Sarah M.
San Jose State University Library	Bakke, Cella
Santa Clara University	Cascio, Diane
School of the Art Institute of Chicago	Fels, Nathaniel
Scripps Research Institute	King, Paula
Serials Solutions	McCracken, Peter
Serials Solutions	Showalter, Mike
Serials Solutions	Zoller, Amanda
SFU	Jamal, Yasmin B.
Simon Fraser University	Bird, Gwen
Sirsi	Hensler, Matthew
Slippery Rock University	Rudowsky, Catherine
South Dakota State Library	Kirby, Colleen M.

South Dakota State University	Aro, Carlene
Southeastern Louisiana University	Branham, Janie
Southern Illinois University Carbondale	Canepi, Kitti
Southern Illinois University Carbondale	Imre, Andrea
Southern Illinois University Edwardsville	Lowe, Elizabeth
Southern Methodist University	Ripley, Erika
Southern Methodist University	Tokoro, Shoko
Southwest Missouri State University	Reeder, Vern
Southwest Missouri State University	Winward, Kyle
Springer	Boissy, Robert W.
Springer	Hasan, Syed
St. John's University	Hinger, Joseph
St. John's University Law School	Ryan, Allan
St. Lawrence University	Hutchinson, Robin
St. Cloud State University	Conway, Linda M.
St. Edward's University	Luckman, Liane
St. Joseph's University	Mudrick, Kristine E.
St. Olaf College	Bethel, Jane
St. Olaf College	Goodwyn, Tony W.
Stanford University	Chang, Linh
Stanford University	Johnson, Sue-Ellen
Stanford University	Kane, Julie
Stanford University	Teel, Kay
Stanford University	Washburn, Judith
Stanford University Medical Ctr.	Buttner, Mary
State University of New York, Albany	Ricker, Karina
State University of New York, Oswego	McDonald, Brian
Sun Microsystems, Inc.	Clanton, Christina
Swets Information Services	Hoyer, Craig
Swets Information Services	Huenniger, Jim
Swets Information Services	Maull, Nicole
Swets Information Services	Paratore, Amy
Swets Information Services	Wilson, Jenni
Swets Information Services, Inc.	Hoyer, Rob
Swets Information Svcs.	Allen, Norene
Swets Information Svcs.	Brannon, Kathy
Swets Information Svcs.	Feick, Tina
Swets Information Svcs.	Roth, Alison C.
Swets Information Svcs.	Stamison, Christina
Syracuse University	Cleary, Robery
Tarleton State University	Jones, Janie
Taylor & Francis	Acreman, Bev

Taylor and Francis Ltd.	Courtney, Keith
Temple University Libraries	Larkin, Molly
Tennessee State University	Owen, Vanessa (Vandy)
Texas A&M University	Ives, Gary
Texas A&M University–Corpus Christi	Fresman, Christine
Texas A&M University–Commerce	Andrews, Susan
Texas Christian University	Lampley, Michael
Texas State Univeristy, San Marcos	Khosh-khui,Sam
Texas Tech University	McDonald, Donna S.
Texas Tech University Libaries	Oliver, Marina
Texas Tech University Libraries	Sappington, Jayne A.
The Journal of Histochemistry and Cytochemistry	McGough, Meg
The Library Corp.	Koppel, Ted
The University of Edinburgh	Stevenson, Liz G.
The University of Southern Mississippi	Green, Carol
Thomas Jeferson School of Law	Champagne, Thomas
Thomas Jefferson University	Long, Bradley
Thomson Gale	Williams, Cynthia
Towson University	Gilbert, Mary
Trinity International University	Hay, Marie
Trinity University	Caraway, Beatrice
Trinity University	Chamberlain, Clinton
Tufts University	Allman, Miriam
Tufts University Health Sciences Lilbrary	Griffin, JoAnne
Tulane University	Fletcher, Peter V.
Tulane University Law Library	Robinson, Trina
Tulane University Library	Powers, Susanna
U.S. Postal Service	Nash, Anita J.
UC Irvine	Sorrell, Eva
United States Military Academy Library	Robischon, Rose
Univ. of Notre Dame	Loghry, Pat
Universidad Nacional Autonoma de Mexico	Barba, Claudia Haydee
University at Buffalo, SUNY	Davis, Susan
University of Akron	Ficken, Carol
University of Akron	Gammon, Julia
University of Alabama	Grogg, Jill
University of Alabama	Holley, Beth
University of Alabama, Birmingham	McAphee, Sylvia
University of Alabama, Birmingham	Tong, Dieu

University of Arkansas for Medical Sciences	Sheffer, Rena
University of Arkansas Libraries	Rogers, Marilyn
University of Arkansas, Little Rock	Aitchison, Jada
University of Baltimore Law Library	Geckle, Beverly
University of British Columbia	McGrath, Kat
University of Calgary	Waller, Andrew
University of California Irvine	Urrizola, Manuel
University of California Press	Lee, Rachel
University of California, Berkeley	McEwan, Carole
University of California, Davis	John, Sarah
University of California, San Diego	Harvell, Tony
University of California, San Diego	Tarango, Adolfo R.
University of California, San Diego	Weiss, Paul J.
University of California, Santa Barbara	Nelson, Catherine
University of Central Oklahoma	Dowdy, Beverly
University of Chicago	Hamilton, Gloria
University of Cincinnati	Banoun, Susan M.
University of Cincinnati	Saxton, Elna
University of Colorado at Boulder	Baia, Wendy
University of Colorado at Boulder	Moeller, Paul
University of Colorado at Boulder	Williams, Sue
University of Colorado Health Ctr.	Gardner, Gene
University of Delaware Library	Seymour-Green, Marie
University of Derby	Doig, Margaret R.
University of Evansville	Williams, Danielle
University of Florida	Kiker, Douglas P.
University of Florida	Young, Naomi
University of Georgia	Dong, Sophie Zhihui
University of Georgia Libraries	Walker, Dana
University of Hawaii at Manoa	Carlson, Amy
University of Houston	Brass, Evelyn
University of Houston	Emery, Jill
University of Houston	Mitchell, Anne
University of Houston	Ranger, Sara
University of Illinois at Chicago	Limaye, Asha
University of Illinois at Urbana-Champaign	Benevento, Jenny
University of Iowa	Lin, Selina
University of Iowa	McDaniels, Lisa C.
University of Iowa	Robertson, Wendy
University of Iowa Libraries	Andrews, Sarah

University of Kansas	Gillespie, E. Gaele
University of Kentucky	Seamans, Marsha
University of Manitoba	O'Hara, Lisa
University of Maryland	Davies-Venn, Rebecca P.
University of Maryland, Baltimore	Del Baglivo, Megan
University of Maryland, Baltimore County	Tenney, Joyce
University of Maryland, College Park	Baker, Jeanne
University of Massachusetts Amherst	Matson, Linda F.
University of Memphis	Byunn, Kit S.
University of Memphis	McDonald, Elizabeth
University of Memphis	White, Joycelyn
University of Miami	Krieger, Lee
University of Minnesota	Generaux, Cecilia
University of Minnesota (Twin Cities)	Celeste, Eric
University of Minnesota Libraries	Grieme, Fariha
University of Minnesota Libraries	Toyota-Kindler, Yumiko
University of Minnesota-Twin Cities	Zuriff, Susan R.
University of Mississippi	Cheng, Daisy T.
University of Missouri–Kansas City	Pennington, Buddy
University of Missouri-Columbia	Darling, Karen
University of Missouri–Rolla	Trish, Maggie
University of MN–MINITEX Library Info Network	Linton, Dave
University of Nebraska Medical Center	Kaste, Ann M.
University of Nebraska Medical Ctr.	Williams, Sheryl L.
University of Nebraska, Lincoln	Mering, Margaret
University of Nevada–Reno	Anderson, Rick
University of Nevada, Las Vegas	Haslam, Michaelyn
University of Nevada, Las Vegas	Vent, Marilyn
University of Nevada, Las Vegas	Zhang, Xiaoyin
University of Nevada, Reno	Yue, Paoshan
University of Nevada, Reno Libraries	Greene, Araby Y.
University of New Hampshire	Bellinger, Christina
University of New Hampshire	Jayes, Linda
University of New Orleans	Parthasarathy, Kalyani
University of North Carolina at Chapel Hill	Lamoureux, Selden Durgom
University of North Carolina at Chapel Hill	Rosenberg, Frieda
University of North Carolina at Chapel Hill, Health Sciences Library	Degener, Christie T.

University of North Carolina at Greensboro	Bernhardt, Beth
University of North Carolina at Greensboro	Conger, Mary Jane
University of North Florida Library	Stanton, Victoria
University of North Texas	Schorr, Andrea N.
University of Northern Colorado	Highby, Wendy
University of Northern Colorado	Lamborn, Joan
University of Notre Dame	McManus, Jean
University of Notre Dame	Nicholas, Pamela J.
University of Notre Dame	Schlutt, Jayne E.
University of Oklahoma Libraries	Coffman, Ila
University of Oklahoma Libraries	Doescher, Starla
University of Oregon	Grenci, Mary
University of Oregon	Hixson, Carol G.
University of Pennsylvania	Lentz, Janet
University of Regina	Resch, Peter T.
University of Richmond	Frick, Rachel
University of Rochester	Gurevich, Konstantin
University of Saint Thomas	Hulbert, Linda
University of Scranton	Wang, Jane
University of South Florida Tampa	Borchert, Carol Ann
University of Southern California	Wineburgh-Freed, Maggie
University of Southern Indiana	Whiting, Peter
University of St. Thomas	Polakowski, Betsy
University of St. Thomas	Roach, Dani
University of St. Thomas	Satzer, Patricia A.
University of St. Thomas	Shriver, Jane
University of St. Thomas Schoenecker Law Library	Scholl, Miki
University of Tennessee, Knoxville	Johnson, Kay
University of Texas at Arlington	Wills, Faedra M.
University of Texas at Austin	Farber, Anita
University of Texas at Dallas Library	Montgomery, Debbie
University of Texas at El Paso	Alvarez, Josefa
University of Texas at El Paso	Poorman, Kathy
University of the West indies	Sandy, Stella M.
University of Toledo Libraries	Duhon, Lucy
University of Toronto	Dyas-Correla, Sharon
University of Vermont	MacLennan, Birdie
University of Virginia	Sleeman, Allison M.
University of Washington	Jenner, Margaret R.

University of Washington	Romaine, Sion
University of Washington	Shadle, Steve
University of Washington	Stickman, Jim
University of Washington	Sutherland, Laurie
University of Windsor	Makepeace, Johnathan David
University of Wisconsin Oshkosh	Fahey, Barbara J.
University of Wisconsin, Eau Claire	Carey, Ronadin
University of Wisconsin, Madison	Duxbury, Janell
University of Wisconsin, Madison	Grant, Maureen
University of Wisconsin, Milwaukee	Jander, Karen
University of Wisconsin, Parkside	Breed, Luellen
University of Wisconsin, Whitewater	Knight, Sharon
University of Wisconsin–Eau Claire	Hijleh, Renee
University of Wyoming	Terrill, Lori
US Government Printing Office	Davis, Jennifer K.
Utah State University	Christenson, Carol M.
Utah State University	Duncan, Jennifer
Utah State University	Molto, Mavis
Utne	Maestretti, Danielle
Valparaiso University	Miller, Judy
Vanderbilt University	Broadwater, Deborah
Vanderbilt University	Ercelawn, Ann
Villanova University	Burke, David
Villanova University	Markley, Susan
Virginia Museum of Fine Arts	Murden, Steven H.
Wake Forest University	Burris, Christian
Wake Forest University	Kelley, Steve
Walla Walla College	Morse, Carol
Washburn University	Winchester, David
Washington State University	Chisman, Janet
Wayne State University Libraries	Paldan, Diane
West Chester University	McCawley, Christina
Western Carolina University	Newsome, Nancy
Western Kentucky University	Foster, Connie
Western Washington University Libraries	Packer, Donna
Wichita State University	Deyoe, Nancy
William Mitchell College of Law	Zhou, Don
Williamsburg Regional Library	Tawney, Sheila
Wright State University Libraries	England, Deberah
Yale University	Crooker, Cynthia
YBP Library Svcs.	Geer, Beverley

Index

A lower case n following a page number refers to a note. A number following an n refers to a note of that number. A lower case f refers to a figure. Titles are italicized.

AACR2
forces driving revision of, 286-87
replacement by new work, 285-86
revision emphasizing content over
form, 286
AACR3. *See* RDA
AACR Fund Committee, 288
abbreviations in RDA, 289,293
access infrastructure for e-journals,
165,169-70,171
access management
in academic and research
institutions, 129
proxy servers for, 130
username/password authentication
for, 130
ACRL. *See* Association of College and
Research Libraries
agendas for meetings, 22
aggregators, 60-61
Amazon.com, 35,287
AMP (Access Management Protocol),
129-30
AmphetaDesk (feedreader), 306
Anacubis, 36n10
Anglo-American Cataloging Rules.
See AACR2
AQA-Any Question Answered,
32,36n4
ARL, 245-46
Arlington Heights Memorial Library,
254,255-56
article-level access in catalogs,
100-101

ASP.Net, 309
Association of College & Research
Libraries, 245-46
Association of Learned and
Professional Society
Publishers, 59
Association of Research Libraries,
245-46
Association of Subscription Agents,
276
Atlee, Tom, 42,44
Atom (RSS clone), 306
attributes (entity-relationship model),
85
in FRBR, 92-93
audience participation in presentations,
317
authentication of network users
in the metasearch environment,
129-31
by proxy server, 130
by username/password, 130
authority control
and FRBR, 96
incorporation into RDA, 288,
290,293
authorization of users in metasearch,
129-31
authors in FRBR, 93
Awasu (feedreader), 306

Bacon, Roger, 50
barcoding of materials, 262

Berlin Declaration on Open Access,
     202
Big Deals, 138,194
     accuracy of library holdings,
          186-89,190,192-93
     American and Canadian attitudes
          on, 185
     analyzing value of titles in, 312-14
     and cancellation of print journals,
          179-80
     effects of purchasing, 58-59
     and perpetual access, 180-82
     services of subscription agents for,
          268-70
binding
     budget cuts for, 227-28,229-33
     impact of e-journals on, 282-83
BioMed Central, 62
Blogger.com, 306
bloggers, 31
     and community, 31-32
     and privacy, 31
     See also blogs
Bloglines (feedreader), 306
blogs
     and ISSN, 75
     produced by libraries, 307
     produced by publishers, 308
     on scholarly communication,
          245-47
     See also bloggers
Blogwithoutalibrary.net, 307
Bohm, David, 107
BothAnd Project, 41
Bowen, Jennifer, 290
Boyle, Robert, 51
Brown, Chris, 207
Bullen, Johan, 169
Buzznet, 31, 36n2

Canadian National Site Licensing
          Project (CNSLP), 183-84
Canadian Research Knowledge
          Network (CRKN), 183-85

captions and patterns fields (MARC),
     8-9
cardinality (entity-relationship model),
     85
cataloging
     open access journals, 249-52
     promoting a worldwide standard
          for, 286-87
CC:DA, 288,290
cell phones
     as information appliances, 32
     library uses for, 32-33
Centre for Information Behaviour and
          the Evaluation of Research,
          63,65
chaotic transitions, 30-31
     for information content providers,
          34
     in information seeking behavior, 35
     in information technology, 32-33
     in intellectual property, 33-34
     in libraries, 31, 35-36
checklist for e-journal access, 239-42
Chen, Peter, 84
Churchill, Winston, 316
CIBER, 63,65
citation ranking, 53-56
civic dialogue. *See* democratic
          dialogue
claiming, impact of e-journals on, 232-
     83
CNet Reviews, 306
Co-Intelligence Institute, 42,44
Cohen, Herb, 115
ColdFusion, 297,298f
collaboration in negotiation, 112-13
collection development
     collaborative, 228
     patron participation in, 170-71
     in public libraries, 254-57
     usage statistics in, 301
collocating number (ISSN), 76-78
Committee of Principals, 287,288
Committee on Cataloging: Description
          and Access, 288,290

communication in negotiation, 107-8
community
    Amazon.com as a, 35
    and emerging library users,
        31-32,35
CONSER database, quality of ISSN
        data in, 78
CONSER Publication Pattern
        Initiative, 10
consortia. *See* library consortia
continuous learning in negotiation,
        112-13
conversational literacy, 43-44
COP, 287,288
copyright and institutional repositories,
        202
Coulter, Ann, 43
Council for Excellence in Government,
        41
Create Change, 245-46
CRM software, reporting e-journal
        access problems with, 214-15
cross-provider search, 125-26
    See also metasearch
Crossfire (television program), 39,43
CrossRef, 119-21
    and ISSN, 73
CrossRef Search, 122-24
CSS (programming language),
        - 297,298f
currency fluctuations
    effect on journal prices, 13,14,
        272-74,275
    estimating for serials cancellations,
        272-74
customer relationship management
        software, 214-15
customer service software, 214-15

Delicious Monster, 36n9
Delsey, Tom, 288,289
democracy, 38
democratic dialogue, 38-42

hosting at the local level, 40-41,
        42,44
    of teenagers, 43
digital object identifier. *See* DOI
digital repositories. *See* institutional
        repositories
digital shoplifting, 33
Directory of Open Access Journals, 62
    benefits of cataloging, 250
    procedure for cataloging, 250-52
DOAJ. *See* Directory of Open Access
        Journals
DOI, 119
    and CrossRef, 120
    and ISSN, 74,77
DSpace (digital repository software),
        200-201, 203
Dublin Core metadata, 132,134,218

e-books usage statistics for, 157-58
e-journal access
    problem management with CRM
        software, 214-25
    role of library in, 236,237
    role of publisher in, 236,237
    role of subscription agent in,
        236,237
e-journal prices, 19,138,140
    determining for foreign, 313
    faculty awareness of, 138-39,140
    impact on library collections, 138
    See also journal prices
e-journals
    analyzing value of packages,
        312-14
    and cancellation of print
        subscriptions, 228,282
    expenditures by libraries for, 198
    impact of access infrastructure on
        use of, 165,169-70,171
    impact on binding, 228
    impact on journal publishing, 57-59
    and improved access to research,
        57-58

selection criteria for, 143
tracking by checking in, 329-30
usage statistics, 164
See also e-journal access; e-journal
    prices
e-reference works, usage statistics for,
    157-58
e-resources
    specialized or distributed
        responsibilities for, 174-75
    tools for managing, 281, 325-26
    vendor services for, 281
    workflows for, 174,280-83,329
    See also e-journals
e-resources librarians
    changes in job ads for, 175
    complex responsibilities of, 175-76
    job duties of, 280
    job titles of, 174
    relations with colleagues, 176
    salaries for, 176
    training of, 175,329
Earth Station 5,34,36n
Electronic Resource Management
    Systems
    and ISSN, 72,73
    and tracking titles in packages, 191
entities (entity-relationship model), 85
entity-relationship data model, 84-86
exchange rates. *See* currency
    fluctuations
expression (FRBR entity), 87,89
eye contact (presentation technique),
    316-17

facilitating meetings, 24-25
faculty, communicating about serials
    crisis with, 244-45,276-77
FAST Search & Transfer, Inc., 122
FeedDemon (feedreader), 306
feedreaders, 306
Feedster, 307
flow in meetings, 23-24

Format Variation Working Group,
    288,289-90
Forum on Publishing Alternatives in
    Science, 246
FRAR (Functional Requirements for
    Authority Records), 96
Frazier, Ken, 180
FRBR, 83-84,86-103
    applied to serials, 90-91, 93,101-3
    and article-level access in catalogs,
        100-101
    attributes of Group 1 entities, 91-93
    authority control and, 96
    authors in, 93
    entity groups in, 86
    expression in, 87,89
    Group 1 entities, 86-91
    Group 2 entities, 95-96
    Group 3 entities, 96-97
    inheritance of attributes in, 93,99
    item in, 87,90
    manifestation in, 87,89
    OPAC display based on, 93-95
    revision of AACR2,286,287
    serial issue as a work in, 98,102
    work in, 87,88
Friendster, 32,36n3
FRSAR (Functional Requirements for
    Subject Authority Records),
    96
Functional Requirements for Authority
    Records, 96
Functional Requirements for
    Bibliographic Records. *See*
    FRBR
Functional Requirements for Subject
    Authority Records, 96

general material designations,
    288,290,292
Generation Fifth Applications
    (inventory control system),
    262,265
gesturing (presentation technique), 317

GMDs, 288,290,292
Google, 287
    and CrossRef Search, 122-24
    pre-fetching of links in, 159
Google Print, 34,36n6
Google Scholar, 123-24,126,128
government publications
    migration to electronic format, 296
    tracking use of electronic, 297-302
Grokker, 36n10

Hakala, Juha, 128
handles in DSpace software, 203
handouts for presentations, 317
Hennepin County Library System,
    254,255,256
holdings statements
    accuracy for e-journal packages,
        186-89,190,192
    compression and expansion of, 9
hooks-to-holdings linking and ISSN,
    73
html parsing as a metasearch tool, 127
hype cycle theory, 246

ICOLC Guidelines for Statistical
    Measures, 148
IFLA, 286
IME-ICC, 286-87
impact factor (citation ranking), 53,
    55,56-57,64
    factors affecting, 54
    as motivating authors, 62
    variation by discipline, 54
Information Environment Service
    Registry project, 133
information seeking behavior, 35
inheritance of attributes, 93,99
Institute for Scientific Information,
    53,54-55,64
Institutional Archives Registry, 64
institutional repositories, 64,65,66

functions of, 199
and open access movement, 200
process of establishing, 247-48
software for, 200
types of materials in, 247
integrating resources and ISSN, 75
intellectual property, 33-34
International Conference on the
    Principles and Future
    Development of AACR, 286
International Federation of Library
    Associations and Institutions,
    286
International Meetings of Experts for
    an International Cataloguing
    Code, 286-87
inventory control systems, 260,
    262,265
ISI, 53,54-55,64
ISO 3297,70,74
ISSN, 71, 72-73,81
    accuracy in CONSER database, 78
    assignment process, 71
    distribution services for, 78-79
    and the electronic environment,
        72-73
    and interoperability, 73
    and multiple manifestions, 70,71,
        75-78
    need to revise, 70-71
    revision process, 74-75,80
    scope of resources eligible for,
        70,74,75
    title level, 76-78
    user group established, 79
ISSN centers, 71, 77-78
ISSN Network, 70,71, 74,78-79,81
ISSN Register, 71, 77,78-79
item (FRBR entity), 87,90

Joint Steering Committee for Revision
    of AACR, 286,287,288,294
Jordan, Barbara, 316
journal prices, 16,19,53,140,198,276

dates set by publishers, 275-76
effect of currency fluctuations on,
    13,14,272-74,275,277-78
effect on library budgets, 243-45
faculty awareness of, 244-45,
    276-77
two-tier, 13,14
See also e-journal prices
journal publication process, 16-17
journals
    binding, 282-83
    claiming, 282
    deciding on formats, 326
    factors affecting authors' choice of,
        65,66
    indexing of new, 143,144
    quality measures of, 53-54
    selection criteria for, 138,143
    subscription cancellations, 138,
        198,272-75
    See also e-journals; journal prices
JSC. *See* Joint Steering Committee for
    Revision of AACR
jury system of representation, 42,44

KartOO, 36n10
Kennedy, John F., 316
King, Martin Luther, Jr., 316
knowledge mapping, 35,36n10
Kott, Katherine, 128
Krellenstein, Mark, 129
Kuhagen, Judy, 101-2

learning documents in negotiation, 113
LeBoeuf, Patrick, 101
Let's Talk America, 40-41, 44
librarians
    confusing job titles of, 18
    relations with publishers, 18-
        19,236-38
    relations with subscription
        agencies, 18-19,142,236-38

role in e-journal access, 236-42
libraries as sites for public dialogue, 42
library budgets
    compared to growth in journal
        publishing, 53
    creating dialogue with faculty
        about, 244-45
    and declines in binding,
        227-28,229-33
    expenditures on e-journals, 198
    and journal cancellations, 138,198
    as percentage of university budgets,
        53
library consortia, 296
    purchasing by, 58-59,66,142,
        180,198-99
    sharing of ILS by, 323
    and tracking of titles in packages,
        191
    usage statistics for, 156
Library of Congress Portal
    Applications Issues Group,
    126,127
library portals, 126
library users, emerging, 31-32,35
licensing of e-journals and perpetual
    access, 181-82
LOCKSS (Lots of Copies Keep Stuff
    Safe), 182
*Logical Structure of the Anglo-
    American Cataloging Rules,*
    286
Luce, Rick, 170
Luther, Judy, 127
Lynch, Clifford, 130,131

manifestation (FRBR entity), 87,89
MARC Format for Holdings Data,
    8-10
    captions and patterns fields, 8-9
    compression and expansion of
        holdings statements, 9
    textual holdings fields, 9
McFedries, Paul, 246

media
  consolidation in, 38-39
  reliance on offical sources, 39
  role in civil public dialogue of, 38-39
  role in democracy of, 38
MediaWeek, 256-57
meetings
  achieving flow in, 23-24
  agenda development for, 22
  analyzing problems of, 24
  controlling discussion in, 25
  facilitating, 24-25
  generating ideas in, 24
  minutes for, 23
  protocol for, 22-23
metadata
  centralizing management of, 217-19
  mapping MARC to, 218
  in metasearching, 132
Metadata Object Description Schema, 218
metasearch, 126-27
  access management in, 129-31
  collection descriptions in, 131-32
  impact on usage statistics, 159,160f
  metadata schemes used in, 132
  NISO initiative on, 127-29
  search and retrieve methodology, 133-34
  service descriptions in, 131-32
  tools for, 126-27
Metasearch XML Gateway protocol, 133
MFHD. *See* MARC Format for Holdings Data
microforms, 256
Microsoft SQL database, 297,298f
  See also MySQL database; SQL database
minutes for meetings, 23
Modis, Theodore, 30,36n1
MODS, 218
MXG, 133
My Yahoo! (feedreader), 306

MySQL database, 325-26
  See also Microsoft SQL database; SQL database

National Coalition for Dialogue and Deliberation, 41
negotiation
  collaboration in, 112-13
  communication in, 107-8
  as competition, 105-6
  continuous learning in, 112-13
  costs and benefits in, 110-11
  learning documents in, 113
  mutual knowledge in, 108-11
  as mutually beneficial, 105, 107,108-11
New Measures Initiatives (ARL), 148,169
news holes, shrinking, 39
news media. *See* media
NewsGator (feedreader), 306
NewsGator Online Edition (feedreader), 306
NewsMonster (feedreader), 306
NISO Metasearch Initiative, 127-29,130
NISO Z39.7, 148
NISO Z39.50, 133
NISO Z39.88, 222
non-self-describing resources, 294

OCKHAM project, 133
off-site storage, 228
  cataloging issues in, 263-64
  climate control and security in, 263,264
  and fire regulations, 261, 265
  organization of materials in, 260,262
  planning for, 260-61, 264
  political considerations of, 261, 263
  preparation of materials for, 262

reading rooms in, 264
reasons for, 260,264
selection criteria for, 261
staffing for, 262
OhioLINK e-journals, 229
Oldenburg, Henry, 51
ONIX, 81, 238
and ISSN, 73
online journals. *See* e-journals
open access, 200
open access journals, 62-64
authors' perceptions of, 63-64
challenges to adoption of, 62-63
including in OPACs, 249-52
Open Access News, 246
open archives, 64-65
impact on publishers, 64-65,66
support by National Institutes of
Health, 66
types of, 64
and version control, 65
OpenURL, 81, 134
components of, 222
and CrossRef, 120-21
impact on interlibrary loan, 225
innovative uses of, 224
links in online catalog, 224
NISO standard, 222
OpenURL resolvers, 221-22,
223-24,328
benefits of, 222
and ISSN, 72-73,76-77
and usage statistics, 224-25
outsourcing of service work, 34

Pace, Andrew, 127,128,129
Paris Principals, 286
perpetual access, 180-82,193-94
in CRKN licenses, 184-85
defined in licenses, 181-82
libraries exercising rights to, 190-91
personalization of technology, 32,35
Philosophical Transactions, 51
PLoS, 62

Pluck (feedreader), 306
Pluck Web Edition (feedreader), 306
political dialogue. *See* democratic
dialogue
political diversity in America, 39-40
organizations promoting, 40-42
political polarization, media's role in,
38-39
POP (meeting effectiveness strategy), 22
portable information technology, 32-33
pre-fetching and usage statistics, 159
*Predictions: Society's Telltale
Signature Reveals the Past
and Forecasts the Future,*
30,36n1
presentation techniques, 315-18
privacy
blogger attitude toward, 31
and emerging library users, 35
and undergraduates, 302
Project COUNTER, 147,148,313
auditing of reports, 157
Code of Practice, 148,151-52,165
counting of full text requests, 151,
152f, 153-55
and e-books, 157-58
and library consortia, 156
and metasearching, 159,160f
and pre-fetching, 159-61
processing of return codes, 150
treatment of multiple clicks in,
150,155,156f
usage reports, 148,149f-150f, 151,
152f-53f, 155-57
protocol for meetings, 22-23
proxy servers, 130
Public Democracy America Project, 41
public dialogue. *See* democratic
dialogue
Public Library of Cincinnati and
Hamilton County,
254,255,256
Public Library of Science, 62
public library serials collections,
254-57

public speaking techniques, 315-17
publishers, 15,16-17,144-45
    citation rankings of, 53-57
    e-journal publishing practices of, 59
    economic factors affecting, 17
    effect of Big Deal purchasing on,
        58-59,138
    impact of e-journals on, 17
    impact of open archives on, 64-
        65,66
    mergers and acquisitions of, 34
    and provision of perpetual access,
        191-92,193
    relations with librarians, 236-39
    role in e-journal access, 236-42
    and tracking of Big Deal titles, 193
    universities as, 65
    See also scholarly publishing
PubMed Central, 66

Randall, Sara, 128
RDA
    and abbreviations, 289
    and authority control, 290,293
    and continuing resources, 292-93,
        294n4
    distribution of first draft, 288,290
    distribution of second draft, 291
    first draft of, 288-90
    focus of description in, 292
    illustrations in, 289
    influence of FRBR on,
        289,290,291, 292,293
    objectives for, 288
    proposals for second draft, 292-94
    reaction to first draft, 290-91
    and "rule of 3," 289
    and single-record approach,
        290,293
    and sources of information, 292
    structure of first draft, 289
    timeline for second draft, 291-92
    use outside library community,
        287,289,290-91,292

RDF Site Summary. *See* RSS
Really Simple Syndication. *See* RSS
recursive relationships (entity-
        relationship model), 85-86
    and serials in FRBR, 98-100
reflective relationships (entity-
        relationship model), 85-86
relationships (entity-relationship
        model), 85
*Report of the International Conference
        on Cataloguing Principals,*
        286
requests for proposals. *See* RFP
        process (Univ. of Memphis)
Research Support Libraries Program
        (UK), 132
Resource Description and Access. See
        RDA
return codes, 150
RFP process (Univ. of Memphis),
        320-23
    consortium libraries, 320
    sources of information for, 321
    timeline, 321
RightNow (CRM software), 214
Riva, Pat, 288
Rosenberg, Frieda, 8
Royal Society, 51
RSS
    auto-discovery tag, 309
    finding feeds, 307
    library applications for, 307-9
    reading feeds on mobile devices,
        307
    sources of information on, 306,310
    use by news media, 308
    use by publishers, 308
    versions, 305-6
RSS Compendium, 306
RSSReader (feedreader), 306
"rule of 3" and RDA, 289

Sadeh, Tamar, 127
Saudargas, Thom, 8

scholarly communication. *See*
 scholarly publishing
Scholarly Communications Newsletter,
 246
scholarly publishing
 as an industry, 52,143,144
 blog as tool for discussing, 245-47
 creating dialogue with faculty
  about, 244-45
 functions of, 51
 growth of, 51, 53,198
 history of, 50-52,53
 impact of e-journals on, 57-59,198
 Web sites on problems in, 246
Scholarly Publishing and Academic
  Resources Coalition,
  199,245-46
Scholars' Bank (Univ. of Oregon),
  201-3
 communities in, 203,207
 and copyright, 202
 harvesting HTML, 205-6
 license agreement, 202-3,204
 metadata, 203,206,207
 policy issues, 201
 review of submissions, 203
 searching in, 203-4
 serials in, 204-7
 structure of, 203-4
 submission of content, 201,
  204,205,207-8
 types of publications in, 207
Scholar's Portal (Ontario), 182
scientific publishing. *See* scholarly
  publishing
screen scraping, 127,133
scribe (meeting recorder), 23
selection criteria for journals, 138
self-describing resources, 294
September Project, 42
serials union catalogs, 328
serials vendors. *See* subscription
  agencies
SHERPA, 202

Shibboleth (access management tool),
  130
single-record approach, 290,293
SMDs, 292
social cataloging, 35
social networks. *See* community
SPARC, 199,245-46
speaking techniques, 315-17
specific material designations, 292
SQL database, 309
 See also Microsoft SQL database;
  MySQL database
SRW/U search protocols, 127,133
staff training for e-resources, 329
standards
 benefits of, 8
 for international cataloging,
  286-87
steady state collections, 261, 264
Stewart, Jon, 39,43
storage facilities. *See* off-site storage
Strategic Plan for AACR, 287
stress in serials librarians, 326-27
Suber, Peter, 246
subscription agencies
 assessing financial health of,
  140-41, 142-43
 changing, 327
 economic factors affecting, 13-15
 history of, 12-16
 impact of e-journals on, 15
 mergers and acquisitions of,
  13,14,15
 relations with libraries, 13,15-16,
  142
 relations with publishers, 15,16
 role in e-journal access, 236-42
 service by, 141-42
 services in Big Deals, 193,268-70
 and standing orders, 144
 use of multiple, 141
subscription cancellations. *See under*
  journals
SUNCAT (UK union catalog), 328
Syndic8.com, 307

Tao of Democracy, 42
Teets, Mike, 128
Tennant, Roy, 128
textual holdings fields (MARC), 9
ThermaBind, 231
Tillett, Barbara B., 88-89,102
Toronto Conference, 286
transcription in cataloging, 290
two-party system, 44

ubiquitous technology, 32-33
Ulrich's International Periodicals Directory, 198
Ulrich's Periodicals Directory Online, 256
usage statistics, 138,139-40,147
  causes of over reporting, 150-51, 159-61
  for e-books, 158-58
  full text requests in, 151, 152f
  integrity of data in, 163,171
  merging from various sources, 165-67
  and program planning, 301-2
  reasons for, 164-65
  resources for development of, 169
  showing preference for e-journals, 168
  standards for, 148
  tracking for government e-resources, 297-302
  traditional methods of tracking, 296
  treatment of multiple clicks in, 150,155
  using to determine value of e-journals, 313
use data. *See* usage statistics
username/password authentication, 130
users, obtaining information on, 302
Utne Magazine, 39-40
Utne Reader. See Utne Magazine

value analysis of e-journal packages, 312-14
values (entity-relationship model), 85
Vanuatu as business haven, 34
vendors. *See* subscription agencies
version control, 65
visual aids in presentations, 317

Walker, Jenny, 128
We the People Declaration, 41
weblogs. *See* blogs
Wellcome Trust, 66,202
Wooden Horse Publishing News Alert, 256
work (FRBR entity), 87,88
workflows for e-resources, 174, 280-83,329
  staffing issues, 282

You Can Negotiate Anything, 115-16

Z39.7, 148
Z39.88, 222
Z39.50 protocol, 126-27
ZeeRex metadata scheme, 132
ZING initiative, 127

BOOK ORDER FORM!

Order a copy of this book with this form or online at:
http://www.HaworthPress.com/store/product.asp?sku= 5860

Roaring Into Our 20's
NASIG 2005

___ in softbound at $29.95 ISBN-13: 978-0-7890-3288-1 / ISBN-10: 0-7890-3288-0.
___ in hardbound at $49.95 ISBN-13: 978-0-7890-3287-4 / ISBN-10: 0-7890-3287-2.

COST OF BOOKS ___

POSTAGE & HANDLING ___
US: $4.00 for first book & $1.50
for each additional book
Outside US: $5.00 for first book
& $2.00 for each additional book.

SUBTOTAL ___
In Canada: add 7% GST. ___

STATE TAX ___
CA, IL, IN, MN, NJ, NY, OH, PA & SD residents
please add appropriate local sales tax.

FINAL TOTAL ___
If paying in Canadian funds, convert
using the current exchange rate,
UNESCO coupons welcome.

❑ **BILL ME LATER:**
Bill-me option is good on US/Canada/
Mexico orders only; not good to jobbers,
wholesalers, or subscription agencies.

❑ **Signature** _____

❑ **Payment Enclosed: $**_____

❑ **PLEASE CHARGE TO MY CREDIT CARD:**
❑ Visa ❑ MasterCard ❑ AmEx ❑ Discover
❑ Diner's Club ❑ Eurocard ❑ JCB

Account #_____

Exp Date_____

Signature_____
(Prices in US dollars and subject to change without notice.)

PLEASE PRINT ALL INFORMATION OR ATTACH YOUR BUSINESS CARD

Name _____

Address _____

City _____ State/Province _____ Zip/Postal Code _____

Country _____ Tel _____

Fax _____ E-Mail _____

May we use your e-mail address for confirmations and other types of information? ❑Yes ❑No We appreciate receiving
your e-mail address. Haworth would like to e-mail special discount offers to you, as a preferred customer.
We will never share, rent, or exchange your e-mail address. We regard such actions as an invasion of your privacy.

Order from your **local bookstore** or directly from
The Haworth Press, Inc. 10 Alice Street, Binghamton, New York 13904-1580 • USA
Call our toll-free number (1-800-429-6784) / Outside US/Canada: (607) 722-5857
Fax: 1-800-895-0582 / Outside US/Canada: (607) 771-0012
E-mail your order to us: orders@HaworthPress.com

For orders outside US and Canada, you may wish to order through your local
sales representative, distributor, or bookseller.
For information, see http://HaworthPress.com/distributors

(Discounts are available for individual orders in US and Canada only, not booksellers/distributors.)

Please photocopy this form for your personal use.
www.HaworthPress.com